# MOTORCYCLE YEARBOOK
## 1998–99

© 1998, Chronosports Editeur, Jordils Park, Chemin des Jordils 40, CH-1025 St-Sulpice, Switzerland
This is a Dempsey Parr Book, Dempsey Parr, 13 Whiteladies Road, Clifton, Bristol BS8 1PB, United Kingdom
ISBN 1-84084-390-X
Printed in France

# MOTORCYCLE YEARBOOK
## 1998–99

**Pictures**
Maurice Büla
Roger Lohrer

**Text**
Jean-Claude Schertenleib
Eric Silbermann

DP
DEMPSEY
PARR

# Summary

# Editorial

## Towards 2000

*426 days before the start of the third millennium, came the final verdict on a racing season full of change and incident and turnarounds. It was 1st November 1998. At Cartagena, in the extreme south of Spain for the European championship and at Sugo in Japan, a country celebrating the important 50th birthday of Honda, for the national championships. 426 days before the year 2000 it was time to see what was left of a year which marked an important turning point in the structure of racing on a world scale. Feelings were mixed as there was, on the one hand, a sense that there was a more united front which made for a rosy future. On the other hand there was a sense that much had been left undone, as the importance of money in this business had taken away some of the essence of the sport it was being used to promote at its most basic level.*

*Up until 20th September, 1998 had been the year of reversals. The outright king of speed, Mick Doohan had done battle with a straightforward Roman, Max Biaggi, who was happy to put the cat among the pigeons and make life difficult on at least three occasions for the undisputed Number 1 of the nineties.*

*Then, in the space of a few minutes, everything tipped. The rules were interpreted to the letter. Two riders were penalised, Alexandre Barros totally unjustly as photos proved. Max Biaggi had a rush of blood to the head and the championship was all decided when it was least expected.*

*Events were played out not only on the track, but also in the courts as in the case of the Rio Grand Prix, cancelled just before its due date, which ended the suspense.*

*It is pointless to try and work out what the championship organisers did to their championship, just as it is pointless to forgive Max Biaggi for ignoring the order to come in for a stop-go penalty, an unforgivable act. In no way, should any of these events cast a shadow over Michael Doohan's fifth championship. All season long, the Australian was the best rider out there and but for a mechanical failure in Japan and an unintentional fall at the first corner in the Madrid GP, the title would have been in the bag long before that fateful 20th September. Our duty is to recall the facts and their consequences. That way those responsible on the organisational, sporting or commercial side of the sport can be reminded that the future of the sport is built on its past, when it comes to the level of competition. It is exactly the opposite of the situation that created the success that was Soichiro Honda. As we are told in the pages devoted to the Honda empire, post-war Japan could only be an ideal setting for turning dreams into reality: "As we no longer have a past, we can only have a future," said Honda san.*

Racing has its rules, its history and its giants and while on the subject, not to be missed is "Continental Circus 50," a book of almost 800 pages, dedicated to the 50 years of the world championship, available from the same publishers in the Spring of 1999. The important element to note is that the lessons of the recent past and further back, have to be kept in mind. Here are the main lessons of 1998:

1)The commercial side of the competition must essentially remain at the service of the sporting side and not the other way round. It is wrong to suggest increasing the number of races in the "exotic" locations if the necessary guarantees are not in place a long time ahead. This would have avoided the Rio GP debacle.

2)When the authorities have to decide between two parties, it has to be done in a strict manner, independently of any external pressure. Look at the way the entire issue was covered up when tests proved the rules had been broken in the instance of the fuel used by the Repsol riders in Malaysia, but in Catalunya five months later, measures were taken in accordance with the letter of the law.

3)The popularity of motorcycle racing in each country is dependent on fashion. As riders of one nation become successful, so the youth of that country are drawn to copy the achievements of their heros, thus providing a constant pool of competitors, as the current case in Italy. However, organisers should not assume the sport is in rude health. Rather, they should ask themselves, for example, why the major media in France and Germany completely ignore the sport which is so dear to us.

But the year that now comes to a close also gives us cause to be hopeful:

1)The promise of youth, as portrayed by Valentino Rossi's move to the 250cc class and the astonishing maturity of a 15 year old kid, Marco Melandri in the 125 class.

2)The popular success of the major meetings of the season, the sell outs at the three Spanish races, the incomparable atmosphere of the world superbike meeting at Brands Hatch.

3) The gamble taken to relocate the German GP paid off. It was moved to a centre of dense population where the passion of the crowd, in the Saxe area noted for its love of mechanical sports, was almost secular.

4)The new "training" role of the world superbike series and the ever increasing tendency to mix the categories at the top end of the sport. This will become a reality in 2001 with a possible GP1 class could run with different types of power unit.

This last point is the most important for a sport which wishes to have a place among the major events on the sporting calendar. Motorcycle racing must present a united front. It is the only way it can survive, which is why, since last year, the "Motorcycle Grand Prix Year" has not simply focussed on the grands prix, but has also covered other disciplines like supersport, sidecar, endurance, continental and national championships.

Because the future is built as much on the past as on what is to come with the champions of tomorrow.

Jean-Claude Schertenleib

# Lead shot!

*Kazuto Sakata was the champion, but only for a few days.*

**Tomomi Manako or Kazuto Sakata? Honda or Aprilia? For the first time in the fifty year history of the road racing world championship, the season finished with big question mark and the end of term photo did not feature a 125cc champion. What happened? After he came fourth in the penultimate race of the season, the Australian GP, fuel from Japan's Kazuto Sakata was checked and found not to conform to the regulations in several key areas, most especially in terms of its lead content. The result of all this was that, while Sakata's name was still at the top of the points table, after his team had appealed the decision, Honda's Tomomi Manako was pretty much guaranteed the world title!**

This verdict, arrived at in the courtroom, put an end to an enthralling season. At first, Aprilia and Sakata seemed to be operating at a clearly higher level than Honda, with four wins from eight grands prix, giving them a commanding early lead in the championship. The second part of the season belonged to the little Japanese machines. Thanks to Tomomi Manako, naturally, with his four wins, one second place and one retirement with a gear selector problem at Brno from the last six races. But other riders were also in on the action as the RS became the machine to beat. "At the start of the season, the Aprilia engine was the quickest, but the Hondas held the road better. Then, things went from bad to worse for us and I felt more and more on

my own," explained deposed champion Kazuto Sakato. "The other riders had semi-works Aprilias, apart from the Frenchman Arnaud Vincent, who was the revelation of the season and they had the upper hand. At every race, any number of riders was capable of winning and day by day, Manako got mentally stronger."

## The young and the old

In this quality Honda pack, apart from Tomomi Manako, this season also belonged to Marco Melandri, who became the youngest ever winner of a grand prix, at Assen and Brno, and he was still mathematically in with a chance of taking the title in Buenos Aires. Also worthy of note was the first win at this top level for Masao Azuma,

a former Japanese champion who had the heavy responsibility this year of successfully developing the Bridgestone tyres. Azuma was definitely the top man of the second half of the season, capable of amazing lap times in the race. Final word of praise for the old boy, Lucio Cecchinello. As team boss, his top rider Noboru Ueda sustained a very serious injury to his right hand at the French GP. Ueda made a comeback at the end of the season, thanks to Dr. Claudio Costa's latest invention; a jointed glove with strong elastic to compensate for the partial paralysis of the radial nerve. Meanwhile, Cecchinello proved he could ride as well as team manage, taking victory in Madrid, much to the delight of Carlo Ubbiali, the man with nine world titles to his name, called in as an adviser to the Italian team.

## Yamaha: a podium

With quantity and quality from Honda lined up against one man very alone at Aprilia, Yamaha, the third constructor entered, had to settle for a solitary podium this season, thanks to Youichi Ui's third place in England. He did manage to be part of the leading group on several occasions and he was even in with a chance of winning in Brno, but for yet another fall.

Developed up until now by Harald Bartol,

*Carlo Ubbiali working for Lucio Cecchinello: nine world titles for one, a first grand prix win for the other.* ◁

the little Yamaha TZ will be an orphan in 1999, as the Austrian engine tuner will be working for Spanish marque Derbi, who are planning a world championship comeback. Other promising aspects for the future, the German former racer, Andreas Leuthe, is actually working on an all-new project for Italjet, the creation of a new 125 which should be a regular part of the world championship before 2000.

*Family photo in Buenos Aires: the best "privateer," (Youichi Ui,) Lucio Cecchinello, world champion Tomomi Manako and the best rookie of the year, Marco Melandri.*
▽

# 125cc key points

**Outgoing champion:**
Valentino Rossi (Italy, Aprilia.) The man who dominated in 1997 does not defend his title, having moved on to the 250cc category, still with Aprilia.

**The major players:**
Aprilia: the Italian company is less directly involved in the category than last year as it is providing machines to several outside teams. Thus one finds Kazuto Sakata with UGT 3000, Masaki Tokudome at Docshop, Ivan Goi in a new team financed by the singer Vasco Rossi, Gino Borsoi at Motoracing, Emilio Alzamoro at Angel Nieto's, while the German Steve Jenkner also has an official RS. During the season, the European champion, France's Arnaud Vincent was directly supported by the factory, before being invited to take part in several development sessions.

Honda: The world's largest constructor has followed the same philosophy in the 125 class for several years now, with the availability of "A kits" for the major teams: Givi Honda LCR with Noboru Ueda and Lucio Cecchinello (Carlo Ubbiali and his nine world titles come along for the ride,) Polini Inoxmacel with Roberto Locatelli and Gianluigi Scalvini, UGT 3000 (Tomomi Manako and Jaroslav Hules,)

Liegeois Competition (Masao Azuma, the only works rider in the category on Bridgestone tyres at the start of the season,) Benetton Matteoni and OXS Matteoni (Marco Melandri and Mirko Giansanti,) RMS (Frederic Petit) and Pileri (Andrea Ballerini, who is rapidly replaced.)

Yamaha: two teams with two riders each line up to start the season. The Italian Semprucci team has Japan's Yoshiaki Katoh and a newcomer, Christian Manna; the German Kurz Aral team keep the faith with Youichi Ui and Spain's Juan-Enrique Maturana, while Austria's Harald Bartol is in charge of the engineering side of the team.

**The Winners:**
Tomomi Manako (5), Kazuto Sakata (4), Marco Melandri (2), Noboru Ueda (1), Lucio Cecchinello (1) and Masao Azuma (1).

**Pole Positions:**
Noboru Ueda (4), Kazuto Sakata (4), Marco Melandri (3) and Roberto Locatelli (3).

**Fastest Laps:**
Masao Azuma (5), Tomomi Manako (4), Kazuto Sakata (2), Lucio Cecchinello (1), Mirko Giansanti (1) and Marco Melandri (1).

**The Final Podium:**
1. Tomomi Manako (Japan, Honda, 217 points); 2. Kazuto Sakata (Japan, Aprilia, 216); 3. Marco Melandri (Italy. Honda, 202).

**Constructors Classification:**
1. Honda (330 points); 2. Aprilia (237); 3. Yamaha (113).

**Rookie of the Year:**
Marco Melandri (Italy, Honda, 3rd in world championship).

**Best Privateer of the Year:**
Youichi Ui (Japan, Yamaha, 11th in world championship).

# An ogre named Aprilia

Jan Witteveen and
his favourite "clown,"
Valentino Rossi. "I did not
think he would be so
competitive right from
the start of the season."

After being snubbed in the previous year, most especially by the "treachery" of Massimiliano Biaggi, who left the Italian marque after three world titles, Aprilia was determined to reassert itself as the boss of the 250cc pack. The switch to lead-free fuel and the complete reorganisation of the competitions department at Noale, involved the disappearance of Carlo Pernat, the hot tempered sporting director and the presence of three 100% works riders, integrated into different structures. A lot of ink was used up during the season on this subject and the championship finale reached new emotional heights. However, none of this stopped Jan Witteveen, the "father" of the RSV250R, from celebrating an almost complete sweep, spoilt only by Daijiro Kato's solitary victory in Japan. We spoke to him.....

13 pole positions, 13 wins and 13 fastest laps out of 14 grands prix; had Jan Witteveen expected such an easy season? "Quite the contrary. Last year we were beaten by Honda and with the switch to lead-free fuel, I was convinced the Japanese company, with its incredible technological strength, would have a clear advantage over a comparatively small competitions department like Aprilia's. Given these circumstances, our dominance was very surprising."

**"Rossi impressed me."**

**Were you also surprised at how things worked out within the team?**
"Yes. First of all, I had not expected Valentino Rossi to be so aggressive and so competitive right from his first 250 race. Then, I did not expect Tetsuya Harada to

suffer so many technical problems. He really suffered a terrible run of bad luck. For example, if the small repair to one of his carburettors had been done in front of his pit, Harada would have settled the matter before the final GP of the year. In fact, the only one who did not surprise me was Loris Capirossi; I expected him to have this sort of season."

**The RSV250R was totally dominant. Does this mean your bike has reached the end of its development?**
"No, I am not sure in what areas and to what extent, Honda got it wrong this year, but I know we still have a little in hand. The switch to a green fuel has made the engines a bit more delicate and especially more difficult to tune. We therefore need to improve the reliability of our engines and also improve the chassis."

**After working alongside Carlo Pernat for over ten years, going back to an association at the time of the African rallies for Cagiva, this year Jan Witteveen was without his "brother." How did that feel?**
"Of course, Carlo and I were very close, but his absence did not cause me any particular problems. During winter testing and at the start of the season, I had to get used to working with other people, but it all went well."

**Aprilia in 1999?**
"Every year, our competitions department gets bigger. At the moment I am in charge of 90 people and with the superbike project - the Mille" is in its final phase of homologation - we are not short of work. Not all the decisions as to our future have yet been taken, but as far as the 250 class is concerned, we will probably take on the

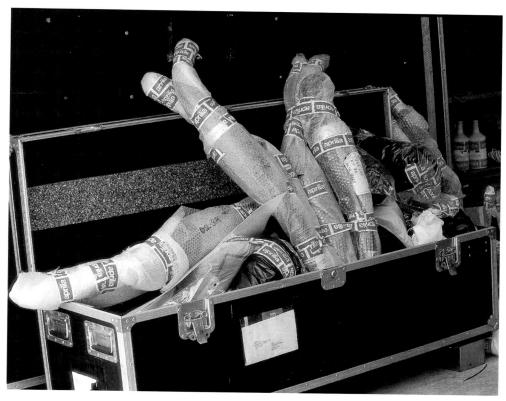

△
One of Aprilia's many treasures.

defence of our title with three or maybe four works riders, even though they might not all be officially entered by the factory."

## Waiting for Yamaha

Aprilia therefore dominated the season, head and shoulders above the opposition. Honda was beaten, well and truly beaten. To such an extent that at one point in the season, France's Olivier Jacque even asked his partners to put a premature end to his season so he could undergo surgery. Suzuki never managed to raise its game (Numata's sixth place in Buenos Aires was the company's best result of the season.) The very pleasant surprises came from the handling of the TSR-Honda (the Japanese chassis builder had set up its own structure in England) especially in the hands of Jeremy McWilliams, who finished ninth in the championship. A word finally about Yamaha, whose new YZR created a sensation at the Japanese GP with Nakano and Matsudo getting to the second and third rungs of the podium, before going on to dominate the All-Japan Championship with Nakano. This performance has convinced the company with the three tuning forks emblem to make a return to the world stage in 1999. That should provide a thrilling three way scrap between Aprilia, Honda and Yamaha. It should be tense, as it is hard to imagine the Honda giant sleeping after the lesson dished out by Aprilia in 1998.

## 250cc Key Points

**Outgoing champion:**
Massimiliano Biaggi (Italy, Honda.) The triple world champion stays faithful to Erv Kanemoto and Honda, but he changes category, moving up to the 500 class.

**The major players:**
Honda: Biaggi and his pretender Ralf Waldmann having chosen to move up a class, the Frenchman Olivier Jacque (Chesterfield Elf Tech 3) and Japan's Tohru Ukawa (Benetton Honda) are on paper the main weapons of the largest constructor in the world. Italy's Stefano Perugini (in the Dieter Stappert run team with Sepp Schlogl technical input) and Haruchika Aoki (FCC TSR) also have much modified NSRs compared to the 1997 championship winning bike (swing arm of traditional design again and a completely reworked engine.)
Aprilia: At Aprilia, the works riders now find themselves in more or less independently run teams: Tetsuya Harada run by Giovanni Sandi, Loris Capirossi with Mauro Noccioli and Valentino Rossi with Rossano Brazzi, who in recent years had been working on the 500 V2 project. Germany's Jurgen Fuchs (at Docshop) and Argentina's Sebastien Porto (at PR2) also had 1998 spec. RSV250R machines.
Suzuki: The second Japanese marque officially entered in this category, Suzuki still worked with Dutchman Arie Moelenaar, who kept his number one rider (Japan's Noriyasu Numata) and also took on a young Swede from the European championship - Johan Stigefelt.
Yamaha: Still no official entry for the YZR, despite their being very competitive, as

we saw in the Japanese GP. Yamaha entered the world championship with TZMs, the "M" standing for modified. Just like the previous year, these were entrusted to three teams: Luis D'Antin and Jose Luis Cardoso for the Spanish Antenna 3 outfit, Franco Battaini and Osamu Miyazaki upholding the Italian colours of Edo, with Takeshi Tsujimura entered by the Semprucci team.

**The winners:**
Testsuya Harada -5, Valentino Rossi -5, Loris Capirossi - 2, Marcellino Lucchi -1, Daijiro Kato -1.

**Pole positions:**
Loris Capirossi -8, Tetsuya Harada -4, Daijiro Kato -1 and Jurgen Fuchs -1.

**Fastest race laps:**
Testuya Harada -6, Loris Capirossi -3, Valentino Rossi -3, Naoki Matsudo -1 and Marcellino Lucchi -1.

**The final placings:**
1. Loris Capirossi  Italy Aprilia 224 points
2. Valentino Ross Italy Aprilia 201
3. Testuya Harada  Japan Aprilia 200

**Constructors' classification**
1. Aprilia 338 points
2. Honda 215
3. Yamaha 134
4. TSR-Honda 128
5. Suzuki 59
6. ERP Honda 14

**Rookie of the year:**
Valentino Rossi Italy, Aprilia- championship runner up.

**Best privateer of the year:**
Takeshi Tsujimura Japan, Yamaha-8th in the world championship.

# Honda, the ultimate weapon

The NSR500 Number 1 in the buff: it was still the tool to have in 1998!

A quick look through the 500cc results sheet and one is left with a clear feeling of deja vu. Michael Doohan is still there, so is Honda in the constructors' listing with 13 wins from 14 races. So what happened to all the mid-season promise of something different? In 1998, even more so than in the past, the lesson to be learnt from the championship is very simple: while there might well be more of a balance on the technical front, as long as the top riders are still all on the same Honda NSR, then the other competitors cannot yet perform at the same level. However, although there are several important rider changes in the offing, this balance of power could come into play in 1999.

"Today, there are a lot of good bikes and very good teams in the 500 and superbike world championships, but one has to ask where are the riders capable of winning the championships, especially in the United States." These were the words of Wayne Rainey, talking to the Americans on Saturday 11th July in the pokey little press office at Laguna Seca, two kilometres as the crow flies from his Monterey home. Just as he had done a few weeks earlier at Assen, he was explaining why he had decided to hang up his team manager's hat: "because I have to listen to my body. Because my son Rex is going to start school and I want to spend more time with my family." However, the triple world champion was soon back on the subject of racing:

"My dream? That America has a grand prix again and even more, that it produces some more 500 cc world champions. There is a lot of work to do in this area and I am interested in the challenge."

## What training?

This season's results prove that there is plenty of talent in the 500 GP field right now, with the performance of class newcomer Massimiliano Biaggi being the most obvious proof of this fact. Another marker is the performance of New Zealand's Simon Crafar, the only rider to break Honda's dominance, putting on a faultless performance with his Yamaha to win at Donington.

But in such a tough series, talent alone is not enough and years of experience are needed to minimise the errors over the course of the championship. That experience took Mick Doohan to victory once more. He is without equal when it comes to putting the hammer down when conditions are difficult. "It's surprising, but whenever the track is slippery, I seem to have a big advantage over my rivals," said the champion with a smile.

There can be no doubt he is an amazing talent. He is also undoubtedly experienced. Did he have the right training? Today, Michael Doohan is the last of a generation of riders who did not come up through the ranks of the lower classes in the world championship. Instead, they started off their careers, fighting heavy and powerful bikes. While there might be some pleasure in anticipating what the races will be like in the post-Doohan era, maybe in 2000, it still has to be said that the Australian will forever be the only reference point for the last decade of the century.

## Kocinski disappoints

Biaggi won his first ever 500 GP, before making a big mistake in Catalunya and eventually finishing the season in only average form. Alex Criville was the only Honda rider to break the Doohan dominance, with wins in Jerez and Le Castellet (Simon Crafar did it on a Yamaha at Donington.) Carlos Checa was going very well in the early part of the season until his huge Donington crash. Alexandre Barros went very well in the second half of the season. This left John Kocinski as the disappointment of the Honda camp. This year, the 1997 world superbike champion could do no better than a fourth place in France.

While Norifumi Abe was the most consistent of the Yamaha riders, it was Simon Crafar who came up with the marque's only win. France's Regis Laconi missed the first two grands prix after falling in qualifying for the Japanese GP and then settled for consistency.

In the Suzuki camp, all that winter optimism came to very little and the Kenny Roberts Modenas definitely benefited from the ideas of Ralf Waldman, even if best placed rider, Kenny Junior was only 13th. That leaves the MuZ-Swissauto team, who were without their main rider, Dario Romboni as from the second GP. The bike made progress as the reduction in the gap to pole proved, but like their colleagues at Yamaha and Suzuka, Urs Wenger and Serge Rosset, the two men in charge of the project came up against the usual problem; namely the lack of riders capable of running at the highest level.

*The Yamaha YZR (here with Regis Laconi,) is soon good enough for the title. The question is, with which rider?*
▽

# The key points of the 500 category

**Outgoing champion:**
Michael Doohan (Australia, Honda.) The four times world champion was in the title hunt once more, still with the same team, barring a few personnel changes, but always faithful to Honda. He was the only one to have the latest generation engine in the NSR500, although Criville got his hands on it for Argentina.

**The major players:**
Honda: in this the year of its fiftieth birthday, the largest constructor in the world wants the title. To this end and for the first time, there were three champions all with similar mounts; Michael Doohan, Massimiliano Biaggi with Erv Kanemoto and John Kocinski with Sito Pons. The other NSR 500s went to championship runner up Tadayuki Okada and Spain's Alex Criville alongside Doohan in the Repsol Honda outfit, to Carlos Checa (Movistar Honda Pons with Kocinski) and to Alexandre Barros (Honda Gresini.) The Honda works V2, which should have been ridden by Takuma Aoki was picked up by Sete Giberneau after the Japanese rider was injured in private testing.
Yamaha: two teams with two riders each, just like last year. Wayne Rainey still trusted in Norifume Abe and he also took on Jean-Michel Bayle, who was injured at the start of the season. At Red Bull WCM there were two new faces, those of New Zealander Simon Crafar, fifth in world superbikes last year with Kawasaki and the young Frenchman, Regis Lanconi, who had been the revelation of the 1997 season, when he made his 500 debut on a V2 Honda.
Suzuki: No longer sponsored by Lucky Strike, the Suzukis are now in 100% factory livery and with two new riders. Nobuatsu Aoki, the transfer of the year

and Katsuaki Fujiwara, who would only start racing very late in the season at Brno after an injury sustained in winter testing and before disappearing after a first corner accident at the Catalunya GP.
MuZ: The Elf-Swissauto is dead, long live the MuZ 500! Then ancient and mythical East German marque, bought out by the Malaysian group Hong Leong, returned to racing with Doriano Roboni. The name had change but not the men. MuZ took over the engine side (Swissauto) and the rider's salary. Serge Rosset brought in his organisation which produced a chassis that evolved a great deal during the winter, with the weight distribution completely sorted. With Romboni injured in practice for the second grand prix, the team called on Switzerland's Eskil Suter, the team's test rider to fill most of the duties, with the exception of Assen, where Jean-Philippe Ruggia stepped up to the mark and finally in Argentina, the first class substitute, Luca Cadalora.
Modenas: There had been doubts for a long time about the whether or not Kenny Roberts' bikes would show as the research budget was proving hard to find. However, two KR3s were at the start, one for the 250 championship runner-up, Germany's Ralf Waldman and his Philip Morris Germany cash and the other for Kenny Roberts Junior. A new engine, designed in Japan by a team built around the former Number One man at HRC, Oguma san, made its appearance at the Czech GP.
Aprilia: The Italian marque officially disappeared from the category, perhaps to rise again, stronger than before. The Noale based company actually bought the rights to use the Swissauto engine and developed a V4, while still using its V2 for comparison testing.

**The Winners:**
Michael Doohan (8), Massimiliano Biaggi (2), Alex Criville (2), Carlos Checa (1) and Simon Crafar (1).

**The Pole Positions:**
Michael Doohan (8), Massimiliano Biaggi (2), Carlos Checa (1), Simon Crafar (1), Jean-Michel Bayle (1) and Alex Criville (1).

**Fastest race laps:**
Michel Doohan (3), Alex Criville (3), Massimiliano Biaggi (2), Simon Crafar (2), Alexandre Barros (2), Carlos Checa (1) and Tadayuki Okada (1).

**The final podium:**
1. Michael Doohan (Australia, Honda, 260 points); 2. Massimiliano Biaggi (Italy, Honda, 208); 3. Alex Criville (Spain. Honda, 198).

**Constructors Classification:**
1. Honda (345 points); 2. Yamaha (198); 3. Suzuki (111); 4. Modenas KR3 (73); 5. MuZ-Swissauto (11).

**Rookie of the year:**
Massimiliano Biaggi (Italy, Honda, runner-up in world championship).

**Best Privateer of the year:**
Jurgen Van den Goorbergh (Holland, Honda V2, 15th in the world championship).

*The argumentative Max Biaggi.*
▽

# The swan song

The brothers Steenbergen fighting it out in front of a packed crowd: Assen was the last appearance of the Side Car World Cup.

On the world stage, the side-car category has survived all sorts of ups and downs, but it felt the shockwaves with the departure of Rolf Biland, the Swiss who had made this discipline his own over the past twenty years. The 1998 world cup, which was finally held over six rounds, went to the English pairing of Steve Webster and David James. That is about the only thing that will be remembered in the history books.

Over the winter, there were bravely held opinions that the world cup was just what was needed and that the departure of Biland would get other nations interested in the category. What is left now of all that enthusiasm? Nothing but the ashes of a series which still had a future a decade ago. Switzerland's Charly Wirth and his "Side Car Promotion" company who had wanted to take over the marketing of the category, disappeared off the face of the planet, leaving behind a nice brochure which sang the praises of three wheelers. Dutchman, Theo Van Kempen, general secretary of ISRA, the side-car riders association, was unable to enter more than the results of the first event on his group's Internet site.

### The only hope

On the track, life was hardly any better. Many of the crews devoted most of their energies to objecting to the efforts of Switzerland's Markus Bosiger, who had dared to come up with something different, with the rider sitting on his machine:

"It was never a case of creating a new formula for three-wheeled cars, but it was simply a case of trying to attract new riders by offering a more conventional riding position."

Bosiger entered the world cup purely for fun - he scored no points - but no one wanted to listen. It seemed that nobody wanted to buy a drink in the side car last chance saloon. Fitting side-cars with four stroke engines was also a failure. The ISRA and the FIM had authorised the formula, but failed to reach agreement with the race organisers at Assen and Donington in support of the grands prix. The side-cars also disappeared from another of their planned events at the Czech Republic GP.

### Webster out on his own

As far as the sport was concerned, Steve Webster and David James were out on their own and too dominant to be really worried by anyone. They were only beaten twice - the race at Most in strange weather conditions and the Rijeka final. Dominating the Oschersleben event on 9th August, Steve Webster claimed his sixth title, before the final Croatian round.

Not much else happened. England's Stuart Muldoon was a new winner, the supposedly modern Swissauto V4 engine of Switzerland's Markus Schlosser was beaten and the brothers Paul and Charly Gudel, so long in Biland's shadow were also ignored by the media in favour of Markus Schlosser, also in Swissauto colours. The fiftieth anniversary of the side-car world championship was definitely not a vintage year.

## Side-car key points

**Outgoing champions:**
Steve Webster/David James (Great Britain, LCR-Honda R4.) The Englishmen mounted a successful defence of their title, once again thanks to Markus Bosiger who provided them with an LCR fitted with a four cylinder in line Honda, prepared in Roggwil by Hanspeter Butzberger.

**The major players:**
LCR-Honda R4: the engine is an evolution of the 4 cylinder ADM and it is used by both reigning champion Steve Webster and his boss Markus Bosiger, who enters a side-car in which the rider sits up. Accepted by the FIM bosses on a one season trial basis, this new design which should encourage more people to enter the side-car category is allowed to enter but is not eligible for points. The V4 camp has lost its most illustrious ambassador with the retirement of Rolf Biland. On paper, the Swiss brothers Paul and Charly Guidel should be the new number ones at Swissauto, but right from race one they are blown away by the other Swiss team of Markus Schlosser and Daniel Hauser. There are other Swissauto entries for Dutchman Benny Janssen, the Swiss Kurt Liechti and the English duo of Roger Body and Ian Guy.

LCR-ADM R4: the majority of an ageing pack are kitted out with ADM engines, their best runner being third placed man Klaus Klaffenbock, who had originally announced his retirement but bounced back the enthusiasm of Swiss tuner Adolf Hanni, who had been Brindley's team-mate the previous season.

LCR-Suzuki: other technical innovations, the four stroke powered side-cars. In a late bid to bring the size of the field up to an acceptable level had opened the doors to four stroke engines (already used in the ISRA Cup,) although grand prix promoters refused to have them. The European champion, Walter Galbiati from Italy and German champion Jorg Steinhausen were therefore forced to scratch from Assen and Donington, with Galbiati soon pulling out of the other world cup races.

**The winners:**
Steve Webster/Dave James, 4 wins (Salzburgring, Assen, Donington and Oschersleben,) Stuart Muldoon/Chris Gusman, 1 win (Most,) and Klaus Klaffenbock/Adolf Hanni (Rijeka.)

△
*Stuart Muldoon/ Chris Gusman: a first win on the world stage.*

**Pole positions:**
Steve Webster/David James (5,) Markus Bosiger/Jurg Egli (1.)

**Fastest race laps:**
Steve Webster/David James (3,) Markus Bosiger/Jurg Egli (1,) Markus Schlosser/Daniel Hauser (1) and Paul Gudel/Charly Gudel (1.)

*The sidecar of tomorrow, conceived by Switzerland's Markus Bosiger. Sadly, his peers did not realise that maybe, the machine of their salvations was in front of them.*
▽

**The championship podium:**
1. Steve Webster/David James (GB, LCR-Honda R4,) 124 points; 2. Klaus Klaffenbock/Adolf Hanni (A/CH, LCR-ADM R4,) 90: 3. Markus Schlosser/Daniel Hauser (CH, LCR-BRM-Swissauto) 87.

**Constructors' classification:**
1. LCR-Honda R4 (124 points;) 2. LCR-ADM R4 (119;) 3. LCR-BRM-Swissauto (109;) 4. LCR-TRF R4 (22;) 5. LCR-Suzuki (11;) 6. LCR-Yamaha (10.)

# Foggy finally finishes first

When they unpacked in Sugo, that first weekend in October, the world superbike crowd were under extreme pressure. On the eve of the final race the atmosphere has enough suspense to make a film, what with Tory Corser heading Aaron Slight by only 0.5 of a point and Fogarty in third just sixth lengths behind the Australia. On top of all that, total war has broken out between the two Ducati teams, Carl Fogarty and Pierfrancesco Chili having come to blows at Assen, during the penultimate round of the season. When the chips were down it would all go the way of King Carl once again.

In qualifying, Noriyuki Haga was quickest, but Troy Corser won the first round of this showdown by taking second place ahead of Slight. He reinforced his position in the superpole shoot out, the Australian having become something of a specialist in this newly introduced element, brought in this year for the world superbike series. Corser in front, Slight only tenth on the start grid - it was all smiles in the "red" camp where intervention at the highest level had ensured the hatchet was buried.

## Corser: ouch!

Troy Corser had been on the royal road all season, having proved to be the most consistent rider throughout the year, returning to the fold after a difficult season in the 500 class of the world championship.

On that Sunday morning of the 4thOctober, everyone believed he would do it, as the riders in the world superbike championship came out on the track for their warm-up session. A few minutes later and it is all over. Troy Corser is a faller and has several broken ribs. The Australian will not be the world champion!

While Aaron Slight is struggling with his RC45 and the Suzukis offer themselves a one-two finish courtesy of its two Japanese championship riders, Kitagawa and Ryo, Foggy makes sure of third place on the podium: 338.5 to the Englishman, 337 for Slight, a Ducati rider is still leading the intermediate classification. The last leg of the year changes nothing: the Japanese are riding like crazy at home, Foggy controls Slight, all is said. One of the most fascina-

ting seasons in the recent history of the world superbike championship has just been decided.

## Haga, the big surprise

The season had been one of several distinctive and separate episodes. At first, the surprise came from Noriyuki Haga (Yamaha on Dunlop) who put in some sensational performances: three wins and a third place in the first four legs. For a while, Haga was, mathematically at least, a solid leader of the championship, but he was to start making some fairly major mistakes, thanks to his rather spectacular riding style which saw him struggle at times (a double zero at Misano.)

At this point in the season, the two Honda boys, Aaron Slight and Colin Edwards were dominant. In the Ducati camp, tension was brewing between the Virginio Ferrari and Davide Tardozzi teams; for Yamaha, Scott Russell is but a shadow of his former self, while the Suzuki RGV 750 is just a tad off the pace on the European circuits, before Kitagawa and Ryo prove at Sugo, that it has massive potential.

When Slight does the double in Austria, everyone reckons that the title is in the bag for Honda, but everyone is wrong. Fogarty is still the king of Assen, even he has to make recourse to tactics not at all appre-

Slight ahead of Edwards: At Monza, on Ducati's home turf, Honda dominated. But, five months later at Sugo, it was a "red" rider who made sure of the title.

ciated by Pierfrancesco Chili in the second leg. "He wanted to kill me," said Frankie a few moments after the race! The final hour is near and with it the end of Troy Corser's hopes.

## The future and towards 2001

While there is much talk of a gradual change for the 500cc grand prix class, from two stroke to prototype four stroke, the superbike category is also set to change quite considerably in the year 2001. "The superbike world championship must remain as the window to the world for production bikes, while the grands prix should be the canvas where engineers can express their imagination. But more than ever, both series need to exist in harmony." Thus spoke FIM president Francesco Zerbi at an evening meeting in Austria for all the constructors engaged in the superbike series. The Italian raised the subject of the image and the future of the superbike class as from 1st January 2001, when a new technical regulation will come into force. Amongst other changes, it will insist that manufacturers sell a minimum of 30 kits at with a fixed price limit (40,000 dollars for the four cylinder machines and 35,000 for the two cylinder bikes) in order to level out the field of the world championship and hopefully make it more of an international competition.

# Superbike key points

Outgoing champion: John Kocinski (USA, Honda.) The world champion quit the four strokes to return to the 500 GP class in the Movistar Honda Pons team.

**The major players:**
Honda: Colin Edwards took the place vacated by John Kocinski. He found himself teamed up with the New Zealander, Aaron Slight at the controls of a reworked RC45. During winter testing, the riders tried a single sided swing arm alongside a more conventional double sided unit.)
Ducati: With the return of Troy Corser, the Italian factory had to review the structure of its racing service. Virginio Ferrari's ADVF team took on Corser and Chili, now finally a 100% works rider. A new organisation (Ducati Performance) was set up to see to the needs of Carl Fogarty, run by Davide Tardozzi. Two other Italian teams entered 916s, Gattolone for Alessandro Gramigni and De Cecco for the Spaniard Gregorio Lavilla. After five years of 500cc grands prix, Lucio Pedercini made his four stroke debut, also on a Ducati.
Kawasaki: The official team is run by Harald Eckl as usual, who still has faith in Akira Yanagawa as well as taking on the Englishman Neil Hodgson. The Italian Bertocchi team also enters two riders, the faithful Piergiorgio Bontempi and the Slovenian Igor Jerman.
Yamaha: Mr. Daytona, a.k.a. Scott Russell gets a classy team mate in the shape of Japan's Noriyuki Haga, who will be the revelation of the early part of the season. A works Dunlop rider in Japan, Haga insisted on being able to work with the same company, while Russell stuck with Michelin. A works Yamaha is entrusted to Yamaha Motor France, for Jean-Marc Deletang.
Suzuki: reigning endurance champion, Australia's Peter Goddard, has joined British James Whitham.

**The winners:**
Noriyuki Haga, 5 wins (Australia II, Great Britain I & II, USA II and Japan II), Pierfrancesco Chili 5 wins (Spain I, Germany II, South Africa I & II, and Netherlands I), Aaron Slight, 5 wins (Germany 1, San Marino I & II, Austria I & II), Colin Edwards 3 wins (Italy I & II, Europe I), Carl Fogarty, 3 wins (Australia I, Spain II, Netherlands II), Troy Corser 2 wins (USA I and Europe II), Keiichi Kitagawa 1 win( Japan 1)

**Pole positions - superpole:**
Troy Corser 6, Aaron Slight 2, Pierfrancesco Chili 2 and Noriyuki Haga 1.
Only 11 superpoles were run as it had to be aborted in Donington because of a snow storm!

**Fastest laps in qualifying:**
Aaron Slight 4, Troy Corser 3, Peter Goddard 1, Gregorio Lavilla 1, Doug Chandler 1, Colin Edwards 1, and Noriyuki Haga 1.

**Fastest race laps:**
Aaron Slight 8, Pierfrancesco Chili 5, Noriyuki Haga 4, Carl Fogarty 2, Troy Corser 2, Akira Yanagawa 1, James Whitham 1.

**The final score:**
1 Carl Fogarty (Great Britain, Ducati, 351.5 points;) 2. Aaron Slight (New Zealand, Honda, 347;) 3. Troy Corser (Australia, Ducati, 328.5.)

**Constructors' Championship:**
1. Ducati 487.5 points; 2. Honda (416.5;) 3. Yamaha (307;) 4. Suzuki (251;) 5. Kawasaki (251.)

The main novelty of the season: the top places on the grid were decided with the superpole shoot out!

Andrew Stroud at Monza. Fire!

Troy Corser was beaten, unable to fight for it in Japan.

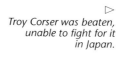

Superbike

# Suzuki: the triumph

*Almost total domination from Suzuki: Stephane Chambon ahead of Fabrizio Pirovano.*

▽

**Twelve months after his first engagement at the world summit of the category, Switzerland's Yves Briguet had last year developed the bike in the Suzuki - Italy team. The GSX-R 750 dominated the supersport world cup, taking six wins from ten starts. Fabrizio Pirovano gave the third largest Japanese company its first major title, apart from endurance racing, since Kevin Schwantz' 500 GP title in 1993.**

Surprise? Sensation? Not really, in as much as the GSX-R 750, first of the new generation of supersport machines until the new Honda CBR600 and the Yamaha arrive in 1999, followed an evolution in the most professional outfit in the series, the Coronas-Alstare team, run by the Belgian Francis Batta.

## Dunlop's progress

With a bike at the start of its development and an experienced team, Suzuki's triumph also belongs to Dunlop, who made a big effort to dominate a category which is known to have very close links to road bikes. The riders still had to be found, who were capable of getting the most out of this partnership. With the dependable Fabrizio Pirovano and Frenchman Stephane Chambon, Francis Batta was onto a winner. Both men made very few mistakes; two for "Piro" and just one for Chambon, when he was unable to avoid Yves Briguet's who dropped his Ducati right in front of him at Monza.

## Roll of honour

A triumph for Suzuki, regular performances from Yamaha and drama at Honda (see opposite,) Ducati is the big loser in a programme that had started well with a memorable double (Casoli-Briguet) at Donington. Unfortunately for the Italian company, Fabrizio Pirovano would take command of the plot from Monza onwards (Briguet a faller and Casoli only sixth) only to knock the nail in a bit more at Albacete, where Suzuki did the double and Briguet fell for the second time in a six run series, while Casoli was down in eighth.

The only flies in the ointment came from Guareschi, who upheld Yamaha honour in the Nurburgring downpour and Frenchman Sebastien Charpentier who gave Honda its only win of the season in terrible condi-tions. Pirovano then tightened his grip with another win at Misano after Briguet and Guareschi fell while fighting for the lead. He added a third at Kyalami where Chambon won. "Piro's" only setback was a fall at Laguna Seca, when he broke two bones in his left foot.

## False start

At Brands Hatch at the beginning of August, the transfer of power could happen, even if it was not yet a done thing, mathematically speaking. There was a false start from the outgoing champion Paolo Casoli and Stephane Chambon and his yellow Ducati, who started behind him on the second row was also penalised. Pirovano won and the championship was only hours away. They were difficult hours for the Italian, who had suffered the death of his father a few days after his Brands Hatch triumph. He clinched the world title in Austria, where Suzuki again finished first and second. Although Guareschi won at Assen, it changed nothing.

△
*Michael Paquay.*

## Ciao Michael

Sadly the supersport season was marred by the death of the Belgian, Michael Paquay during practice at Monza. The former double European champion in 1993 and 1995 and works rider for the Castrol-Honda team died on the second lap of Saturday morning's free practice. Antonio Calasso, Paquay, Sebastien Charpentier and Francesco Di Maso were chasing one another down the long pit straight at almost 230 km/h. Paquay clipped the back of Calasso's bike, falling in the middle of the track, his machine literally flying off to the left side. Charpentier and Di Maso were unable to avoid the body of the unfortunate Belgian rider, whose death was confirmed in the early afternoon of 9th May 1998.

## The supersport year

**Outgoing champion:**
Paolo Casoli (Italy, Ducati.) The Italian defends his title, still with Ducati, but in a different organisation because of the arrival of Carl Fogarty at Gio. Ca. Moto, which is now Ducati Performance.

**The major players**
Ducati: Paolo Casoli at Ducati Performance is not the only one to have works versions of the Italian bike, as Yves Briguet and Cristiano Migliorati, riding for Endoug) enjoy the same status, as does the Spaniard Pere Riba Cabana at Garella.
Yamaha: Italian importer Belgarda has kept the same two riders, Vittoriano Guareschi and Miassimi Meregalli. Yamaha Motor France start the season with Christophe Cogan, before giving up. In the Netherlands, Wilco Zeelenberg stays faithful to the three tuning forks.
Honda: With the supersport category becoming ever more important, the Castrol-Honda team, who also run the Superbike outfit, enter two riders, Michael Paquay and the young Englishman James Toseland. After Paquay's death, Australia's Kirk McCarthy steps into the breach.
Suzuki: The sensation of the season, as Francis Batta has dumped Ducati to run Suzuki's supersport programme. He runs Fabrizio Pirovano and Stephane Chambon. At Suzuki-Italy, who had developed the GSX-R last year, we find once again Giovanni Bussei and Giuseppe Fiorillo.
Kawasaki: The ZX6R is a touch off the pace, although Team Kawasaki Italia have the services of Marco Risitano. The "greens" also have national teams and the Kawasaki Junior team run by Harald Eckl with Stefan Nebel riding.
Bimota: Ambitious at the start of the season. Run by Stefano Caracchi, who was Casoli's team manager in 1997, France's

Jean-Philippe Ruggia and Serafino Foti are the riders. Ruggia will throw in the towel quite early, with Bimota only scoring points on three occasions.

**The winners**
Fabrizio Pirovano, 5 victoires (Monza, Albacete, Misano, Brands Hatch et A1-Ring), Paolo Casoli, 2 victoires (Donington et Laguna Seca), Sébastien Charpentier, 1 victoire (Nürburgring) et Vittoriano Guareschi, 1 victoire (Assen).

**The poles**
Vittoriano Guareschi (3), Paolo Casoli (2), Pere Riba Cabana (2), Cristiano Migliorati (1), Fabrizio Pirovano (1) et Stéphane Chambon (1).

**The fastest race laps**
Fabrizio Pirovano (3), Pere Riba Cabana (2), Cristiano Migliorati (2), Yves Briguet (1), Vittoriano Guareschi (1) et Stéphane Chambon (1).

**The final podium**
1. Fabrizio Pirovano (Italie, Suzuki), 171 points; 2. Vittoriano Guareschi (Italie, Yamaha), 149 points; 3. Stéphane Chambon (France, Suzuki), 137 points.

**The constructors championship**
1. Suzuki, 207 points; 2. Yamaha, 175; 3. Ducati, 174; 4. Honda, 65; 5. Kawasaki, 48; 6. Bimota, 15.

△
*Paolo Casoli:
The outgoing and beaten champion.*

◁ *Storm over the Ring: Honda takes its one and only win.*

# Honda - what suspense!

Williams Costes,
Christian Lavieille,
Doug Polen and
the Honda staff: victory!

**Honda had not won the world endurance championship since 1995. Then one week after they clinched the 500cc grand prix title to give them their first championship in this their fiftieth anniversary year, they picked up yet another title. This time it was in endurance racing, thanks to the efforts of France's Christian Lavieille and reigning champion Doug Polen from the States. It was an exciting finale which the main players will remember for many a long year.**

As has been the case for several years, the world endurance championship seems to have two separate speeds and faces. On the one hand one finds the 24 hour racing specialists, who are predominantly French. On the other, once a year, the big names from the world of grands prix and superbikes turn out for the Suzuka 8 Hours. Easy to understand why, when this race has a greater commercial impact than a world championship in a grand prix category in Japan.

### Say Hi to the journalist!

Title holders Suzuki found Kawasaki and Honda in their path, with Yamaha lacking an official presence in the championship, although Yamaha France made a big effort for the Bol d'Or, lining up an all-star team of Jean-Michel Bayle, Jean-Marc Deletang and Jean-Philippe Ruggia.
At Le Mans, the world championship kicks off with a few surprises. Suzuki is in trouble

with a lack of efficiency on a dry track after a very damp qualifying session and problems with fallers and brakes. This lets Kawasaki do the double, with the Moto Journal writer Bertrand Sebileau finding himself in the spotlight once more, along with Thierry Paillot and Igor Jerman. Better still (for him): second in the Liege 24 Hours at Spa-Francorchamps behind the Honda of Lavieille-Polen-Costes, Sebileau is out on his own at the head of the world endurance championship on arrival at the Le Castellet track for the Bol d'Or.

Honda's triumph at Suzuka and a triple for the RC45 has no influence on the championship, which means that the supreme title will be played out in the world's biggest endurance racing classic.

### Saturday 17h48

Less than three hours after the start, while the fight for the lead is going a storm

with the Suzuki of Goddard-Rymer-Morrison leading the Honda of Lavieille-Polen- Costes, the first drama unfolds. Kawasaki Number 10 comes into the pits and it does not take long for the verdict to come through. Dropped valves on one of the lower cylinders and the world championship leader is out of the running. But there is still hope for Bertrand Sebileau.

### Sunday 14h35

Because with fifteen minutes to go to the end of the world championship, Christian Lavieille, having just started his final stint, blows the engine on Honda Number 3, on the Mistral Straight. He limps back to the pits and goes out again for one slow lap, waiting before the finish line for the victorious Suzuki to take the chequered flag. The Honda is classified third and the Frenchman and his American team mate Doug Polen are world champions.

China comes to
the world championship:
a important premiere.
▽

△
Peter Goddard: a perfect
race at the Bol d'Or and
the double for Suzuki.

## Endurance - the key points

**Outgoing champions:**
Peter Goddard/Doug Polen (Australia/United States, Suzuki.) The two men became rivals. Peter Goddard, riding one of the two official Suzukis in world superbikes was to only take part in the Bol d'or, while Doug Polen switched to Honda.

**The major players:**
Honda RC45: the reigning superbike championship machine, the RC45, is still a serious tool for endurance racing. Entered officially by Honda-France in Europe and directly by HRC in Japan, it is the only machine to win two events in 1998 and the title of course!
Suzuki GSX-R 750: The reigning world champion bike was entered by Sert (Suzuki Endurance Racing team) run by France's Dominique Meliand.
Kawasaki ZX7RR: In 1997, Team Kawasaki France under the direction of Christian Bourgeois, produced a staggering performance to demolish the outright distance record for the Bol d'Or, with 692 laps at an average speed of over 168 km/h. At the controls of the ZX7RR, Bertrand Sebileau was the great revelation of the season.
Yamaha YZF: this bike provided Noriyuki Haga with the means to prove the revelation of the early part of the season in the world superbike series. In endurance racing, it made two appearances in the French races under the Yamaha Motor France banner as well as showing for the Suzuka 8 Hours.

**The Winners:**
Bertrand Sebileau/Thierry Paillot/Igor Jerman (Le Mans 24 hours), Christian Lavieille/Doug Polen/William Costes (24 hours of Spa-Francorchamps), Shinichi Itoh/Tohru Ukawa (Suzuka 8 hours) and Peter Goddard/Terry Rymer/Brian Morrison (Bol d'Or).

**Pole Positions:**
Sebastien Charpentier/Bertrand Stey/Nicholas Dussauge (1), Christian Lavieille/Doug Polen/William Costes (1), Shinichi Itoh/Tohru Ukawa (1) and Bertrand Sebileau/Igor Jerman/Ian MacPherson (1).

**The Final Podium:**
1. Christian Lavieille and Doug Polen (France/United States, Honda), 108 points; 3. Bertrand Sebileau (France, Kawasaki), 90.

**Constructors Classification:**
1. Honda, 133 points; 2. Kawasaki, 123; 3. Suzuki, 109; 4. Yamaha, 76; 5. Ducati, 4.

**500: From Leslie Graham
to Michael Doohan**

# Side-cars:
# from genesis to revolution!

# Michelin: from the earth to the moon

▷
*Michelin's racing service in 1976, with the boss, Claude Decottignies, leaning on te wheel balancing machine.*

**April 1898. On the Michelin stand at the Universal and Colonial exhibition at Lyon, two high piles of tyres of different sizes decorate the entrance and it gives Edouard Michelin an idea: "With arms and legs, it would look like a man!" he said to his brother Andre. And so Bibendum was born and today he is a world famous image of a tyre company, which made its name a few years earlier, inventing the first removable tyre, which allowed cyclists to affect a quick and easy repair.**

The history of Michelin is a family tale. At the end of the 19th century, Andre Michelin (born 1853) worked as a carto-grapher at the Ministry of the Interior, whi-le brother Edouard, six years his junior was in the paint business.

At Clermont-Ferrand, the parents of the two brothers ran a small factory producing agricultural implements. They also made toys as well as rubber belts and pipes. Around 1890, because of financial diffi-culties, Andre and Edouard took control of the business.

### The big idea

At this time, tyres were not in general use and the nearest one got to them was a flim-sy strip of rubber stuck to a wooden rim on a velocipede.

In 1891, Edouard Michelin had his big idea, imagining a removable tyre, before coming up with an "air wheel" for bicycles with an independent air chamber in a outer envelope, the ends of which are fitted to three bolted metal rims. A win in the Paris-Brest-Paris stage race gave Michelin great publicity. In 1895, the first car tyres appea-red and Michelin quickly developed a repu-tation for innovation which still holds good today all over the world for the Clermont-Ferrand based company.

The name Bibendum comes from a verse from Horace in Latin. "Nunc est biben-dum," or "now is the time to drink," whi-ch represents the idea that the Michelin tyre "drank" or "swallowed" obstacles on the road, an idea that holds good today.

### Long live the radial!

In 1904, Michelin produced its first bolted tyres and then the double wheels for trucks and buses in 1908. Steel rims with remo-vable centres appeared in 1914 and in 1919, came tyres made specifically to run on rails. The future beckoned and steel belted tyres appeared in 1937 and most importantly, the first radial was made in 1947. Michelin was soon to carve out a reputation on the race tracks of the world, on both two and four wheels and it was also the first make to leave this earth as its products were fit-ted to the space shuttle.

Present in grand prix racing since 1974, the French company has won, up to the end of 1998, over sixty riders' world cham-pionships, including superbikes, and a dozen or so world and endurance titles. Racing is still an ideal test bed for the deve-lopment of different materials used in tyre production.

*Bibendum:
the history of a character
in three pictures.*
◁

*Claude Decottignies
with Greg Hansford,
Imola 1976.*
▽

## Michelin today

As the world's number one tyre manu-facturer, Michelin tyres are fitted to one in five vehicles on the planet. 74 facto-ries are located in 17 different countries, in Africa, North and South America, Asia and Europe. There are 7 research centres in France, Japan, the United States and Spain. Michelin also produces natural rubber in six plantations in Brazil and Nigeria.

Every day the Michelin group produces:

-770,000 tyres

-95,000 inner tubes

-4 million kilometres of steel cable

-1,100 tonnes of steel

-46,500 wheels

-60,000 maps and guides.

# Manako in the courts

△
*Tomomi Manako and his ever present smile.*

**It is hard to remember ever having seen him without that huge grin on his face and Tomomi Manako, the 125cc world champion epitomises a new generation of Japanese riders. At Buenos Aires, for this rather strange final event, Manako rode faultlessly. Never mind that one week after the race there was still no official confirmation that the Honda rider was the champion. He just had to wait.**

Tomomi Manako, what do you remember most about the final race of the season?
-When I arrived in Argentina, I understood what I had to do. I had to win at all costs and Sakata had to finish no better than fourth. But that was just the theory and I had to put it into practice.
Exactly, the race was not easy. Quite the opposite in fact!
At the start, Sakata was moving around a lot on the track, trying to make us lose contact with Marco Melandri and Lucio Cecchinello who were out in the lead. In fact I was saved by Masao Azuma. When he managed to take the lead of the chasing group, I managed to hang on and he pulled me up to the leaders.

### "All the risks"

The leaders did not seem ready to give anything away to their similarly mounted colleagues?
-Oh no! The positions changed at every corner and on the last lap, I wonder if I didn't actually close my eyes. I said to myself, 'now you have to stop thinking and just gor it. It's win or bust.
And it worked?
-I won... but I still do not know if I am world champion. Now, I must wait. (A moment of silence.) Having said that, now that I have come so close, I think I will be very angry if I cannot hang onto this crown!
Tomomi Manako kicked off in the world championship right in the middle of the 1994 season (German GP at Hockenheim) when he was called to arms by the FCC Technical Sports team to replace Tomoko Igata, the Japanese girl who had injured herself two weeks earlier in Austria. He started off well, coming third in his first ever grand prix after a titanic struggle with, guess who... Kazuto Sakata, already with Aprilia and that year's 125cc champion!

△
*Tomomi's lucky charms at the Argentinian final were a passport to a first title.*

# CURRICULUM VITAE

Name: Manako
First Name: Tomomi
Date of Birth: 16th September 1972
At: Saga Prefecture/ Japan

**First Race:**
1993

**First GP:**
German GP 1994 (125)

**First GP win:**
Catalunya GP 1996 (125)

**Number of GP wins:**
6 (125)

**Number of world titles:**
1 (1998 125 cc)

# RACING CAREER

**1993:** a win at Suzuki and two wins at Mine in Japanese 125 national B championship
**1994:** 20th in world 125 championship, 7th in Japanese 125 championship and 115th in world endurance championship (Honda)
**1995:** 8th in world 125 championship, 134th in world endurance championship
**1996:** 3rd in world 125 championship, Rookie of the year (Honda)
**1997:** 3rd in world 125 championship (Honda)
**1998:** world 125 champion (Honda)

*The world champion in action.*
▽

# Capirossi, out on his own

△
*Loris Capirossi out on his own:
an image summed up
the end of the season.*

**Sunday evening, 25th October 1998. For the third time in his career, Loris Capirossi is a world champion. He has been chasing this 250 title for a long time and finally it is his. But the Italian, suddenly all alone in the world is more introverted than ever. His arrival in the press office was not met with the usual ovation. Everyone is just beginning to talk about that final corner of the 1998 250 cc world championship.**

Loris Capirossi, how do you explain the no holds barred move on Tetsuya Harada in this Argentinian GP?

-Those who think I deliberately brought Harada down are mistaken. At this point on the track, I was much quicker than him all through the race. I attacked and I got past! Tetsuya left a gap and I made the most of it. Even if he had not been there I am sure I would have got through the corner perfectly.

All the same, you do not seem particularly overjoyed with this world title. Feelings of remorse?

-No, even though I am not very happy that the title has been decided by a fall. Having said that, I have worked very hard all season to reach this goal and I think I have proved that given equal equipment I had the potential to be world champion.

### "The number 1"

Will this third title change anything in your life?

-Now I am 250 world champion I can say what I like! I am looking forward to racing next year with the Number One on my fairing. I am happy at Aprilia and I will simply ask the bosses to give me equal treatment with the others. One thing is for sure; in 1999 I will start with a completely different mentality, because this title has been my revenge on a lot of people. - He would not name them.

Your thoughts on the technical side of the season?

-Until the race at Barcelona, my bike was not as good as Harada's. As soon as I had competitive equipment like the others, you could see the difference on the track. I am world champion and I think I deserve the title, because I suffered a lot, last year when I came back to this category, as well as this year when there was a war with no quarter given within the same factory team.

## CURRICULUM VITAE

Name:      Capirossi
First Name:      Loris
Date of Birth:      4th April 1973
At:      Riolo Terme/ Italy

**First Race:**
1987

**First GP:**
Japanese GP 1990 (125)

**Number of GP wins:**
18 (125/8; 250/9; 500/1)

**First GP victory:**
British GP, 1990 (125)

**Number of world titles:**
3 ( 125 in 1990 and 1991; 250 in 1998))

## RACING CAREER

**1987:** 6th in Italian 125 production championships (Honda)

**1988:** 9th in European 125 championship (Mancini)

**1989:** 4th in European 125 championship (Honda)

**1990:** world 125 champion (Honda)

**1991:** world 125 champion (Honda)

**1992:** 12th in world 250 championship (Honda)

**1993:** runner-up in world 250 championship (Honda)

**1994:** 3rd in world 250 championship (Honda)

**1995:** 6th in world 500 championship (Honda)

**1996:** 10th in world 500 championship (Yamaha)

**1997:** 6th in world 250 championship (Aprilia)

**1998:** world 250 champion (Aprilia)

*He thought he was condemned to playing Number 2 to Valentino Rossi next season in the Aprilia team, but the title changed all that.*
▽

# Doohan, of course

△
*The same salute for the 54th time from Michael Doohan, the undisputed king of the 500s.*

This was his fifth title and they have all been consecutive. With the number of GP wins currently stopped at 54, only Giacomo Agostini has done better in the 500 class, with 68 successes to his name, Michael Doohan is still the absolute Number One of the world motorcycle racing scene, after a season that looked uncertain for quite a while, mainly because the Australian rider had his fair share of bad luck this year.

Michael Doohan, seen from the outside, the 1998 seemed very difficult for you. What was it like from the inside?
"I have to admit, that at the start of the sea-

son, I was struggling with my motivation. But once Max Biaggi had started to shoot his mouth off after his win in Suzuka, I got it all back again."

**The duel between the two of you soon became the centre of attention - too much attention?**
"Everyone spoke about Biaggi a lot. It is true that he has done a good job this year, but don't forget that, before him, both Luca Cadalora and John Kocinski won grands prix in their debut 500 season."

### "He's not talking any more"

**The relationship between the two of you really deteriorated during the season?**
"As I said earlier, Max did nothing really special this season. The big difference with the two riders I mentioned, Cadalora and Kocinski, is that he talked a lot! As the races went by, I gradually lost my respect for him."

**Up until the "explosion" at the Imola GP, when you spoke out?**
"I never wanted to play politics. It is not my style. But when I got to Imola, I had enough. Anyway, since then, I have not heard Biaggi say much. He is a good rider but he is too boastful. That is the big difference between us: personally, I got my education on the streets."

**Looking at the sporting and technical side, how do you sum up this season?**
"It was a bit of an up and down year for me, with highs and lows. I suffered with bad luck - a mechanical failure at Suzuka, crashed out at the first corner of the Madrid GP, without him being at fault - but a bit of luck also came my way in the end - the Barcelona affair and the cancellation of the race in Rio."

## IDENTITY CARD

Name:         Doohan
First name:    Michael
Date of birth:   4th June 1965
At:            Brisbane, Australia

**First race:** 1984

**First GP:**
Japan, 500cc 1989

**First GP win:**
Hungary 500cc, 1990

**Number of GP wins:**
54 - 500cc

**Number of world championships:**
5 - 1994, 1995, 1996, 1997, 1998 - 500cc

## CAREER SUMMARY

**1987:** 13th, TT Formula 1 World Championship - Yamaha
**1988:** 12th World Superbike Championship, winner of the Swann Series, Yamaha
**1989:** 9th 500 World Championship - Honda
**1990:** 3rd 500 World Championship - Honda
**1991:** runner up 500 World Championship, 38th in world endurance championship, winner of the Suzuki 8 Hours - Honda
**1992:** runner up 500 World Championship - Honda
**1993:** 4th 500 World Championship, 86th World Endurance Championship - Honda
**1994:** 500 World Champion-Honda
**1995:** 500 World Champion-Honda
**1996:** 500 World Champion-Honda
**1997:** 500 World Champion-Honda
**1998:** 500 World Champion-Honda

*Riding perfection.*
▽

# Webster, who else?

*The sidecar champions*

△
*Steve Webster/David James:
out on their own at Assen,
it summed up the whole season.*

**Last year, Steve Webster and David James's mission was to beat the Swissauto armada led by its king, Rolf Biland. This year, free of the man who had been their main rival for the past fifteen years, the Englishman rapidly eclipsed the opposition, if indeed it can be called that, on the way to his sixth world crown!**

"This world cup creates very little interest in the media, so the only thing that matters in these circumstances, is to win the title. As I know my rider Steve Webster will be in the running for a win at every race, I can afford to do the season for the fun of it, without picking up any points." Thus said Markus Bosiger, a German-Swiss tyre salesman, who became the key figure in the paddock, ever since he employed Webster, who had been forced to hang up

his helmet at the end of 1994, having run out of funds.

### "I am bored"

As a rider and team owner, Markus Bosiger's gamble paid off again in 1998. Steve Webster and David James were in a class of their own and the Englishman was rather bored all season long.

In order to have a better understanding of the state of this strange year for this championship, here is a tale of a little incident which took place at Assen in Holland, on the eve of the grand prix. Once again Steve Webster and David James dominated practice and it was obvious to all they would be unbeatable in the race. The world champion summoned the Swiss press, the only group of journalists still interested in this dying discipline. "Itîs time you gave me a real hand. Write in your papers that the sidecar category has never been healthier and that new riders like Markus Schlosser are just as good as Rolf Biland, who, if he tried to make a comeback, would not be guaranteed a win! If you all write that, then maybe Biland will consider a comeback, because I am really bored without him!" Steve Webster was joking. 900 kilometres away, watching on television, Biland saw the joke, but he did not come back. Webster stayed bored and kept winning.

## CURRICULUM VITAE

Name: Webster
First Name: Steve
Date of Birth: 7th January 1960
At: York/ Great Britain

**First Race:** 1979

**First GP:**
British GP, 1983

**First GP victory:**
Belgian GP, 1986

**Number of GP wins:**
23 (side-cars)

**Number of World Cup wins:**
10 (side-cars)

## RACING CAREER

**1982:** British Clubmans side-car champion

**1983:** 16th in world side-car championship

**1984:** 8th in world side-car championship

**1985:** 4th in world side-car championship, British side-car champion

**1986:** 3rd in world side-car championship

**1987:** world side-car champion
**1988:** world side-car champion
**1989:** world side-car champion
**1990:** 3rd in world side-car championship

**1991:** world side-car champion
**1992:** runner-up in world side-car championship
**1993:** runner-up in world side-car championship
**1994:** runner-up in world side-car championship
**1995:** 19th in world side-car championship
**1996:** 3rd in world side-car championship
**1997:** winner of side-car World Cup
**1998:** winner of side-car World Cup

*Sir Steve and his passenger and one more title, but not much fun.*
▽

# King Carl

△ "Foggy" was never going to settle for being Number 2 for long.

He had set the nerves of his fans jangling a few days before that vital Brands Hatch race, by announcing he might be hanging up his helmet at the end of the season. Two months later, the season was over and so were the hopes of his rivals. Aaron Slight and the Honda RC45 which had dominated the previous year's championship in the hands of John Kocinski, was beaten. So was Troy Corser, returning from the 500 grand prix category to dare challenge King Carl at Ducati. In 1998, Fogarty took his sixth major title, a staggering achievement for a poor lad from the suburbs of Blackburn.

World superbike champion for the third time, Carl Fogarty was received like the hero he is in England.
- I heard some amazing things. Apparently on Sunday morning of the final in Sugo, it was dawn in London and all the pubs in England had their televisions tuned to the race. When I returned to London, dozens of journalists and loads of television stations were waiting for me. But the most emotional moment was yet to come, when I was met at Manchester Airport by about 200 screaming fans. It gave me goose bumps. It was not until then, that I realised I had done something special.

### "I was down in the dumps"

After two humiliating defeats, especially last year at the hands of John Kocinski, Carl Fogarty renewed his acquaintance with the number one. But it was not without its troubles.
In June, after the Nurburgring race all he had to show for it was one thirteenth place; Fogarty's worst ever result in world superbikes.
-At one point in the season I had ruddy well decided to pack it in. I was down in the dumps. Then, in the middle of the season, Ducati gave me a great bike. The use of a new air intake completely changed the power curve and the 996 was balanced

△
*Carl Fogarty and his "don't mess with me" look.*

*Troy Corser and Pierfrancesco Chili (here ahead of Hodgson and Fogarty) were more like rivals than team-mates for the world champion.*
▽

## CURRICULUM VITAE

Name:          Fogarty
First Name:     Carl
Date of Birth:    1st July 1966
At:             Blackburn/ Great Britain

**First race:** 1983

**First GP:** British GP 1986 (250)

**Number of world superbike championship wins:** 48

**First world superbike championship win:** Donington Park, 1992

**Number of world titles:**
6 ( TT Formula One, 1988; TT Formula One, 1989; endurance, 1992; superbike 1994, 1995 and 1998)

## RACING CAREER

**1985:** winner of Manx 250 GP, three wins in English 250 championship (Yamaha)
**1986:** runner-up in British Formula Two, 12 wins (Yamaha)
**1987:** runner-up in British Super Two, 16 wins (Yamaha)
**1988:** world TT Formula One champion (Honda)
**1989:** 45th in world superbike championship, world TT Formula One champion, British superbike champion (Honda)
**1990:** 18th in world 500 championship, 19th in world superbike championship, winner of FIM TT Formula One cup, winner of Formula One and Senior at Isle of Man TT races (Honda)
**1991:** 7th in world superbike championship, 61st in world endurance championship, 3rd in 8 Hours at Suzuki, 4th in Transatlantic match (Honda)
**1992:** 9th in world superbike championship (Ducati), world endurance champion (Kawasaki)
**1993:** 23rd in world 500 championship (Cagiva), runner-up in world superbike championship (Ducati)
**1994:** world superbike champion (Ducati)
**1995:** world superbike champion (Ducati)
**1996:** 4th in world superbike championship, 60th in world endurance championship, 3rd in 8 Hours at Suzuki (Honda)
**1997:** runner-up in world superbike championship (Ducati)
**1998:** world superbike champion (Ducati)

again and the road holding that had been missing at the start of the season was back again. With such a great machine, I was back on top form again.
That return to form gave Fogarty the title that was rightfully his, that of the undisputed king of the superbike category. And what about next year?
-I am thinking a lot about my future. One thing is certain. You will never find Fogarty out on the track just to earn money. My career will go on for as long as I want to win!

# Piro: in the name of the father

**The supersport championship**

△
*Pirovano in front, ahead of his lieutenant, Chambon in his wheel tracks just about summed up the year.*

**The champagne did not flow on the A1-Ring podium. In the tears that did flow from Fabrizio Pirovano, winner of the second ever supersport world championship, were the mixed emotions of joy at having won and a deep sadness. His father Gianni was not there to see his son's triumph. Three weeks earlier "Piro" had gone through the saddest moment of his life.**

So this title became a complex mix of sentiments for this great champion, who had waited over twenty years for this moment, ever since he had first sat on a little motocross bike.

A born winner and an eclectic racer, Fabrizio Pirovano had often come within a whisker of taking a title, having made it to the top rung of the world superbike podium on ten occasions. He missed out on the title by just a few points in 1988, after a titanic race in New Zealand.

## Total complicity

Was he to remain a brilliant and reliable rider, who would never take a world title? Meeting up with Francis Batta was definitely a decisive moment and the two men hit it off immediately. "When I suggested he quit superbikes to do supersports, at first he thought I was mad. It was a gamble on the future and we won."

The gamble was won in style - five wins and three fastest race laps ó but above all it was a gamble won in true Pirovano fashion. He is a cool customer, who never gets carried away in the heat of battle, as did Briguet - Guareschi at Misano. He always knew when to wait and when to strike. Perfection.

He also had to deal with the death of his father in a road accident three weeks before being crowned champion. Fabrizio Pirovano, winner of the world supersport title at the A1-Ring, had opened his heart. Under his leathers, on that important day, he carried a photo of him and his father on a start line somewhere, a long time ago.

◁
*"Piro" and Francis Batta:
total complicity.*

*Fabrizio Pirovano:
finally a major title.* ▷

## IDENTITY CARD

Name:         Pirovano
First name:    Fabrizio
Date of birth:   1st February 1960
At:            Biassano, Italy

**First race:** 1986

**Number of world superbike wins:** 10

**Number of supersport world cup wins:** 6

## RACE RECORD

**1986:** 2nd Honda Italy trophy, 3rd Yamaha Italy
Supertrophy
**1987:** Italian superbike champion, 3rd Italian 250
championship
**1988:** runner up in world superbikes, runner up
Italian superbikes, runner up Italian Formula 1
(Yamaha)
**1989:** 4th world superbike, 4th Italian superbike
(Yamaha)
**1990:** runner up world superbike, champion Italian
superbike (Yamaha)
**1991:** 5th world superbike (Yamaha)
**1992:** 5th world superbike, Italian champion superbike (Yamaha)
**1993:** 4th world superbike, champion Italian superbike (Yamaha)
**1994:** 9th world superbike, champion Italian superbike (Ducati)
**1995:** 7th world superbike (Ducati)
**1996:** European supersport champion (Ducati)
**1997:** 8th world supersport cup (Ducati)
**1998:** winner of world supersport cup (Suzuki)

# Lavieille: what a final!

△
*Christian Lavieille and Honda
at Spa-Francorchamps: a win that threw open
the championship once again.*

**The world championship went down to the last fifteen minutes of the final race of the series. Christian Lavieille, Doug Polen and the entire Honda-France team must have lived through every emotion at the end of what was a very surprising Bol d'Or, proved by the fact that Christian Lavieille took his first world title.**

Psychologically, how did you live through that major mechanical problem, just 15 minutes away from a world title?
- My approach to endurance racing these days is very different to when I first started. In 1991, in the Le Mans 24 Hours, we had a 10 lap lead at 10 o'clock in the morning, when the bike broke. For me, it was a total disaster. Since then, I have gone through my fair share of disappointment and at the end of my twelfth Bol d'Or I knew better than to start dreaming about the title before the chequered flag.

"I will never make it...."
What really happened during that final stint?
-A generator broke while I was flat out in sixth going down the Mistral straight. At first I thought the engine had blown up or that a brake disc had shattered. There was a hole in the upper part of the sump. I cut the ignition. I managed to start it up again and struggle back to the pits. At that moment, I told myself, I really am plain unlucky and I will never make it.
What were you thinking about at that moment?
- Doing the right thing! First of all, I wondered if I should not stop at the Pont corner and wait for three o'clock. I decided to come into the pits. We took off the bodywork, patched up the holes as best we could and filled it up with oil. At 14h50, I got going again, running in the gravel, so as not to put oil on the track. Alex Viera, the team coordinator came and waited for me at Pont corner, where I waited for the winning Suzuki to cross the line, without having a clue how many laps we had lost and what the gap was to the others. It was only when I came into parc ferme that I knew I was world champion and I had not thought for a moment that I would also be stepping onto the Bol d'Or podium.

The endurance champions

△
*Christian Lavieille.*

## CURRICULUM VITAE

Name:         Lavieille
First Name:    Christian
Date of Birth:  16th December 1965
At:            Temon/ France

**First Race:** 1987

## RACING CAREER

**1988:** France Promosport 250 champion
**1989:** runner-up in French production championship
**1990:** 43rd in world superbike championship (Kawasaki), 11th in FIM endurance cup
**1991:** 74th in world superbike championship (Ducati), 9th in world endurance championship, winner of 24 Hours of Spa-Francorchamps (Suzuki)
**1993:** 38th in world superbike championship, 21st in European superbike championship (Ducati), 51st in world endurance championship (Suzuki)
**1994:** 26th in world endurance championship (Suzuki)
**1995:** 16th in world endurance championship (Suzuki)
**1996:** runner-up in world endurance championship, winner at Bol d'Or, 7th in French superbike championship (Honda)
**1997:** 30th in world superbike championship, 4th in world endurance championship, 6th in French superbike championship (Honda)
**1998:** world endurance champion (Honda)

*Doug Polen.*
▽

## CURRICULUM VITAE

Name:         Polen
First Name:    Doug
Date of Birth:  2nd September 1960
At:            Detroit/ United States

**First Race:** 1987

**Number of world superbike championship wins:** 27

## RACING CAREER

**1988:** 40th in world endurance championship (Suzuki)
**1989:** 20th in world superbike championship, 23rd in TT Formula One world championship, 95th in FIM endurance cup (Suzuki)
**1990:** 46th in world superbike championship, 60th in FIM endurance cup, 25th in FIM TT Formula One cup (Suzuki)
**1991:** world superbike champion (Ducati)
**1992:** world superbike champion (Ducati)
**1993:** United States superbike champion (Ducati)
**1994:** 4th in world superbike championship, 43rd in world endurance championship, winner of 8 Hours of Suzuki (Honda)
**1996:** 11th in world endurance championship (Suzuki)
**1997:** world endurance champion (Suzuki)
**1998:** world endurance champion (Honda)

# The *14* Grands Prix

 **JAPAN**

 **MALAYSIA**

**SPAIN**

**ITALY**

 **FRANCE**

 **MADRID**

 **NETHERLANDS**

 **GREAT BRITAIN**

 **GERMANY**

 **CZECH REPUBLIC**

 **IMOLA**

 **CATALUNYA**

 **AUSTRALIA**

 **ARGENTINA**

# Biaggi reinvents the 500 class

▷
*Massimiliano Biaggi: first 500 grand prix, first win!*

**With pole position, victory and lap record, Massimiliano Biaggi, the four times 250 cc world champion was setting new standards right from day one in 500 cc. Why and how? Welcome to the unveiling of the secrets.**

"From outside, everyone reckons I ride the 500 in the same style I used for the 250, but that is not the way it is at all. My only secret? I try to exit the corners as quickly as possible. Now, in order to do that" and at this point Massimiliano Biaggi, a man so willing to talk about himself in the third person, breaks into a huge grin. "Come on, you didn't think I would let you into my secret. That would make life far too easy for the opposition!"

Max has a hearty laugh and he has a lot to laugh about. "Whatever happens over the next few weeks, the damage is done," according to Alex Criville's chief mechanic Gilles Bigot. "He has put on a demonstration. He crushes any opposition as hard as he can and that will force all the others to rethink their approach. And I think in 500 it was about time too."

### Wrong answer?

Suddenly, all those theories put forward over the last few years, that tried to explain why 500 lap times had stagnated since the enforced retirement of Wayne Rainey and the voluntary one of Kevin Schwantz, began to look suspect. Perhaps the image of the too powerful and un-rideable 500 would have to be discarded. The unthinkable answer was that since the day of the dinosaurs that were the aforementioned

Rainey and Schwantz plus Spencer, Gardner and Lawson, the standard of riding was, at best mediocre. This would explain the endless series of wins for Michael Doohan, the only current rider to have rubbed racing shoulders with the dinosaurs.

There is an element of truth in this and Massimiliano Biaggi proved it that Sunday 1st April at Suzuka with his astounding performance. On Saturday night, after qualifying, the Emperor of Rome declared: "I have surprised myself, not just my position but also with my times." The next day Biaggi was all smiles. "As I ride in a different way to the others, in theory, what I had to do was very simple: I had to get in the lead as quickly as possible in order to be able to take the lines I like. Today it all went like a fairytale and by the time my back tyre started to go off I had already made the gap."

### "Warning - Danger"

It was an incredibly mature statement from the mouth of Massimiliano Biaggi, a 500 debutant who constantly reminds us that he still has a lot to learn at this new weight. "You know, of all the drivers in this category, I am the one who did the least running over the winter, as the deal to move up a class took some time to arrange. To

learn about the 500 I only had six days of testing on three different circuits. Even so, I did set a new track record every time!" It is hard to believe that such an easy looking dominance can simply be the result of a superior talent. Behind the "re-invention" of the 500 class, as engineered and displayed by Biaggi, there must surely be a technical explanation. Over to the reigning and four times champion and the big loser at this first grand prix, Mick Doohan: "If the lap times are coming down so much, even though the engines have less power since the switch to lead-free fuel, it is simply because they are easier to ride. Corner speed is definitely up, which is not a disadvantage for those coming in from the 250s. But look out!" The one thing that has been forgotten in all this is safety, because the laws of physics and dynamics are still the same. With higher corner speeds come higher risks and I am worried the 1998 season will see a lot of highsides, spectacular crashes and unfortunately, some serious injuries."

## The scratched and the sore

Regis Laconi forced to withdraw, Doriano Romboni starts with broken bones in both feet, Sete Gibernau sits out Friday afternoon after a serious knock in the morning, 14 of the 39 fallers this weekend come from the 500 class, supporting Doohan's theory. Only time would tell, if the alternative, put forward by the Max men would hold good: "There is a simple truth as to why Biaggi is dominant. He has a unique ability, which has possibly never been seen before in the history of grand prix racing. Bearing that in mind, it should come as no surprise to see him comfortably dominate the subject, even in the toughest category of motorcycle racing in the world."

◁
*The smile of a job well done.*

▷
*Doriano Romboni-Sebastien Gimbert: it's getting rough at the chicane.*

## 125 cc

Noboru Ueda was quickest in practice and starts as very hot favourite. Unfortunately, as several times in the past, most notably here at Suzuka 12 months ago, the man who became a father over the winter, makes a mess of his start and is ninth on the first lap. Sakata leads the pack away, ahead of Cecchinello, Locatelli, Giansanti and Ui.

Ueda fights back to take the lead on lap 8. Giansanti is no longer in the running thanks to a fall and Sakata and Ueda look like running away with it by lap 10. Further back, Masao Azuma and his Bridgestone tyres are working miracles and things come to a head at two thirds race distance: Locatelli is a faller, Ueda walks back to the

pits, his clutch gone, leaving three Japanese to fight it out for the win: Sakata, Manako and Azuma. The Aprilia rider has the last word, calling on the slightly greater power of the Italian machine on the final lap.

## 250 cc

Last year's winner, Daijiro Kato is quickest in qualifying, practice marked by the incredibly rude health of the Yamaha YZR 250 of Matsudo and Nakano. The only European to make it among the front runners is Olivier Jacque and he gets the best start when the time comes, leading Kato away with the rest of the Japanese pack in

hot pursuit. Ukawa leads for the first two laps, before handing over to Kato, who is followed by two wild card entries. From that point on there are two dramas to watch unfold. The first is the question of honour among the Samurai riders in front of their home crowd, who all want to win their home grand prix; the second battle is

the important one for world championship points. Harada has, like last year, some surprising reactions, Ukawa has to retire on lap 14 and Jacque takes home a nice load of points for fifth place. Kato takes his second grand prix win having finished "only" third in 1996!

## 500 cc

A rookie (Biaggi) on pole position, three Yamahas (Abe, Haga and Nanba) leading the first lap: a new wind is blowing through the blue riband category. On lap three, Biaggi makes his mark pulling out a 1.105 second lead, at the precise moment that Doohan takes a trip through the gravel. The demonstration put on by Biaggi smacks of insolence as the Italian was lapping a second quic-

ker than anyone else. John Kocinski is forced to stop more often than a courier, pitting once for having jumped the start and the second time for having done 113 km/h instead of the 93 allowed in the rules which allow for 85 + 10% margin of error, when he came in for his penalty. When Abe goes off into the gravel having made contact with Okada, the race is run. Biaggi lead grows to

10.216s on lap 15 of the 21; Doohan retires with a broken crankshaft on lap 16; Abe puts on a show once again as he crashes into a tyre barrier on lap 17, much to the amusement of team boss Wayne Rainey. Biaggi wins, Okada will catch Haga at the last chicane. The championship tally reads 25 to the Roman Emperor and zero for the King of the 500s!

… no Takuma Aoki. The second of the three Aoki brothers, who had broken the little finger of the left hand during practice at Sugo in November 1997. He suffered a terrible crash on 5th February 1998 when he first got back in the saddle on the works Honda V2 at Honda's new track at Motegi. Aoki, suffered a fracture of the spine between the seventh and eighth vertebrae and has lost the use of his legs. Hospitalised since the accident at Tsunomia, the Japanese man stayed in telephone contact with the goings on at Suzuka and especially with his old mate Valentino Rossi. At the beginning of April, Aoki was confined to a wheelchair, but his family and the directors of HRC were looking at the possibility of taking him to a specialised clinic in the USA.

….the compulsory use of lead-free fuel and the arrival of Nutec. The main change to the technical regulations for the 1998 season is that all the grands prix must be run on lead free fuel. It was the main talking point over the winter months, along with the arrival of a new supplier from the USA. The American company Nutec works in the aerospace industry and has been tasked with developing a fuel with the lowest possible pollution levels. Right from the start of winter testing, most of the teams did back to back fuel comparison tests and in the 500 cc class, both Yamaha and Suzuki opted for the new product. Frenchman Jean-Francois Balde played a key role as he was responsible for the distribution of Nutec products throughout the paddock, having previously held down the same job for Elf over the past few years. At Suzuka, it is estimated that around 40% of riders used the new fuel.

….the new start procedure for the 500s. Yet another change aimed at improving the image of grand prix motorcycle racing: the 500s would have to form up on the grid ten minutes earlier, to increase the time spent on the grid before the parade lap. During this extra time, the riders would

have to remove their crash helmets, so that the television cameras could show their faces to the world. However, this new rule was put back to Spain as many of the teams did not have sufficient portable generators to power the tyre blankets needed to keep the bikes on the grid this long!

….the new role for Carlo Pernat. The all powerful sporting director at Aprilia for the past few years has taken a step back in the world of bikes. Carlo Pernat is now in charge of marketing, communications and image for the Italian second division football club, Genoa. Pernat will still attend all the grands prix this season with the brief to "advise the president Ivano Beggio." "At the age of 50, it was time for a new challenge. I have no regrets as Genoa is the club I supported as a child," explained Pernat.

….the incredible record. Massimiliano Biaggi wins the first 500 GP which he enters. Only two men had achieved this feat before him: Harold Daniell (by virtue of winning the first 500cc GP ever held - on 17th June for the 1949 Tourist Trophy) and Jarno Saarinen (the French GP on 22nd April 1973.)

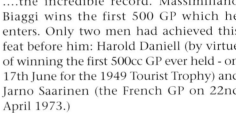

△
*Nutec:
the petrol war
is declared.*

*Springtime in Suzuka.*
▽

◁
*Takumi Aoki: the major
absentee of this meeting.*

◁ Wayne Rainey behind
Kevin Schwantz:
"That day, nothing
could happen to me."

Yamaha into slides that would have been the envy of any top line rally driver and remember, they have the advantage of four wheels. It was a bad start: "I rode like my old granny in the first few minutes of the race." But he fought back over the remaining laps, passing Barros, who made a great start, Schwantz and the Japanese rider Itoh, who was piling it on in front of 71,000 countrymen. Then he took control for the second half of the race running the pack like some malevolent boss. He never took his eyes off the opposition. Beattie tried to break away, so Rainey fought back. Schwantz goes for a do or die move at the famous last chicane and Wayne blocks his passage. It was a win for perfection and a tribute to a team who had got every last drop out of a machine that was not always the most powerful in the pack. Was it easy? Well it might be if you are a man called Wayne Rainey and you carry with you the ideal recipe for making this the year you go for a fourth consecutive world championship.

**18th April 1993: Wayne Rainey**

"It might be easy to say these things with hindsight, but right from the opening few laps of the Italian GP, that Sunday when I had my big accident, I was thinking I wished this was over! It was exactly the opposite feeling I experienced a few months earlier at Suzuka. It was my best win. The race could have gone for hours and that day I knew I was untouchable." We are in the last few days of January 1994 and in his Monterey home, Wayne Rainey is starting a new life, different but still full of hope. When he recalled the 1993 Japanese GP and that fantastic Sunday 18th April, his eyes lit up. He experienced a flashback that said it all.

Rainey's Japanese win, at the end of one of the great races in the sport's history, left its mark. In Rainey's mind after winning of course, and on the emotion-charged face of team boss Kenny Roberts. His triple world champion had joined him in the record books, thanks to this 22nd 500cc win. More than this, it left its mark on the opposition. Because Rainey, already rightly considered as the brains of motor cycle racing, a near perfect machine which makes no mistakes, had just shown the world the full range of his fantastic talents. He threw his

*Wayne Rainey.*
▽

# fallers

## Friday 3rd April 1998

125 cc:  Noboru Ueda (Japan, Honda) and Marco Melandri (Italy, Honda).

250 cc:  Jason Vincent (Great Britain, Honda), Tohru Ukawa (Japan, Honda), Yasumasa Hatakeyama (Japan, Honda), Shinya Nakano (Japan, Yamaha), Luis D'Antin (Spain, Yamaha), William Costes (France, Honda), Makoto Tamada (Japan, Honda) and Stefano Perugini (Italy, Honda).

500 cc:  Doriano Romboni (Italy, MuZ), Juan Bautista Borja (Spain, Honda V2, twice), Sete Gibernau (Spain, Honda V2) and Regis Laconi (France, Yamaha).

## Saturday 4th April 1998

125 cc:  Gino Borsoi (Italy, Aprilia) and Juan Enrique Maturana (Spain, Yamaha).

250cc:  Luis D'Antin (Spain, Yamaha), Haruchika Aoki (Japan, Honda), Sebastian Porto (Argentina, Aprilia), Takeshi Tsujimura (Japan, Yamaha), Roberto Rolfo (Italy, Honda) and Johan Stigefelt (Sweden, Suzuki).

500 cc:  Juan Bautista Borja (Spain, Honda V2) and Doriano Romboni (Italy, MuZ).

## Sunday 5th April 1998

125 cc:  Mirko Giansanti (Italy, Honda), Roberto Locatelli (Italy, Honda) and Youichi Ui (Japan, Yamaha).

250 cc:  Federico Gartner (Argentina, Aprilia), Sebastian Porto (Argentina, Aprilia), Johan Stigefelt (Sweden, Suzuki) and Franco Battaini (Italy, Yamaha).

500 cc:  Garry McCoy (Australia, Honda V2), Matt Wait (United States, Honda V2), Keiichi Kitagawa (Japan, Suzuki), Ralf Waldmann (Germany, Modenas KR3), Scott Smart (Great Britain , Honda V2), Sebastien Gimbert, (France, Honda V2) and Norifumi Abe (Japan, Yamaha, restart)

## Ouch!...

1.  Sete Gibernau (concussion, injured little finger - right hand).
2.  Tohru Ukawa (bruised right hand).
3.  Noboru Ueda (bruising to left shoulder and elbow, also to middle finger - left hand).
4.  Regis Laconi (fractured right ankle, open wound to left hip, dislocated little finger land fractured ring finger - left hand).
5.  William Costes (multiple bruising).
6.  Doriano Romboni (fractured 4th toe - right foot and big toe - left foot).
7.  Luis D'Antin (concussion and back injury).
8.  Gino Borsoi (bruising to right testicle).
9.  Roberto Rolfo (bruised right shoulder).
10. Scott Smart (suspected fractured clavicle).

## Non starters...

1.  Jean-Michel Bayle (fell during private practise at Shah Alam and fractured his right wrist. Suffering from concussion, he returned to his home in France where he stayed for several weeks. Relaced by Kyoji Nanba).
2.  Katsuaki Fujiwara (the second Suzuki driver also injured himself over the winter - a broken ankle - at Eastern Creek. He got back on his bike one week before the GP, at an IRTA test at Suzuka. After trying for the first day he had to give up. Replaced by Keiichi Kitagawa).
3.  Regis Laconi (result of fall in practise).
4.  Luis D'Antin (result of fall in practise).
5.  William Costes (result of fall in practise).

## Retirements...

125 cc:  Jaroslav Hules (Czech Republic ,Honda, disc), Christian Manna (Italy, Yamaha, ignition), Gino Borsoi (Italy, Aprilia, piston), Noboru Ueda (Japan, Honda, clutch)and Steve Jenkner (Germany, Aprilia, cylinder).

250 cc:  Roberto Rolfo (Italy, Honda, result of fall in practise), Valentino Rossi (Italy, Aprilia, crankshaft), Tohru Ukawa (Japan, Honda, engine) and Yasumasa Hatakeyama (Japan, Honda, ran out of fuel).

500 cc:  Jurgen Van den Goorbergh (Holland, Honda, seized) and Michael Doohan (Australia, Honda, crankshaft).

△
*Mirko Giansanti: ouch!*

◁
*Broken engine (Gimbert).*

# Soichiro Honda: the legend

△
A 50cc machine from 1947.

## The anniversary

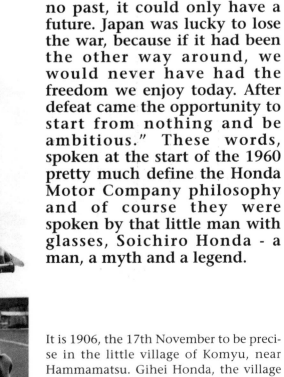

△
Soichiro Honda.

"Imagination and a fertile mind, new ideas and solid theories; these are the secrets of my success. If our company has grown to the point it has reached today, it is because Honda had no tradition. With no past, it could only have a future. Japan was lucky to lose the war, because if it had been the other way around, we would never have had the freedom we enjoy today. After defeat came the opportunity to start from nothing and be ambitious." These words, spoken at the start of the 1960 pretty much define the Honda Motor Company philosophy and of course they were spoken by that little man with glasses, Soichiro Honda - a man, a myth and a legend.

▷
"Imagination and a fertile spirit. That is the secret of my success!"

It is 1906, the 17th November to be precise in the little village of Komyu, near Hammamatsu. Gihei Honda, the village blacksmith comes home. His wife present him with their seventh child, Soichiro

Honda. They would have nine in total, but only four would get past childhood. As is the Japanese tradition, Soichiro worships his father and through him he gets a feeling for things mechanical, creating and shaping raw and base metals into a beautiful and useful object. Right from the start, the little lad stands out at school- for his complete lack of interest in the educational curriculum. However, he is obsessed with anything of a mechanical nature.

## A Model T Ford is losing oil

Legend has it that Soichiro Honda experienced his defining moment when just nine years old. The village of Komyo had hardly ever seen a stranger and there came a model T Ford which parked there for several days. When it moved on, it left a trail of oil in the dirt. Soichiro plunged his hands into the sticky mess, fascinated by this life fluid of the mechanised world. At the age of ten he became fascinated with the new fangled aviation, having spent whole days playing truant in the countryside. There, he would watch the smoke rise from the rice mill situated near his father's forge. When the aviator Niles Smith landed his airplane on the infantry regiment's airfield at Hammamatsu, he was there to watch it. He relived the event, terrorising the inhabitants of his village by rushing down the narrow streets on a bicycle-airplane he had builthimself. When he was twelve he developed a foot brake for his bicycle. A year later he left school to become an apprentice in a Hammamatsu garage. At sixteen, he lodged his first patent: a metallic spoked wheel. It was the spring of 1922.

## From the country to the city

Sochiro Honda then made his way to the capital city, Tokyo to become an apprentice mechanic in the Art Shokai garage. Here he worked on repairing the first cars to hit the streets of Japan. It was a frustrating time for this man who loved all things mechanical as he was the garage dogsbody and spent more time looking after the owner's baby than holding a spanner in his hands. In September 1923, Tokyo was rising from the rubble of the terrible earthquake which had claimed the lives of around 100,000 people and had buried the garage under the rubble. Soichiro Honda somehow unearthed a motorcycle sidecar combination in working order. He used it to branch out as a taxi driver! Once the garage was up and running again, he was finally allowed to work as a mechanic and he immediately gained a reputation as an excellent fettler.

## 1928: "Soichiro Number One"

In 1928 he went back home to Hamamatsu. There, he rented a wooden shed which he turned into a workshop. A friend knocked up a sign to put above the door, which read: "Here you can find a good mechanic, Soichiro Honda, who does a great job of fixing engines." Lower down he scrawled: "Soichiro Number One." After a year in business, he made a profit of 80 Yen. By the age of 25 he was employing 50 people and made a profit of 100 Yen per year. The wooden shack had a strong reputation and not just for its ability to fix engines. The main talking point was the geisha parties organised by the boss. The evenings always ended with gangs riding the night time streets waking the dead with the sound of unrestricted motorcycle exhausts, all the work of Soichiro Honda. As a young man, Honda became the local playboy. He learnt traditional music and the art of the love song. In a "tea house," a polite euphemism for a brothel, he once threw a young woman from a second floor window onto some power lines below. She owed her life to the heavy winter kimono she was wearing! In 1933 at the age of 27, Soichiro married Sachi, the daugher of a neiighbouring farmer and a chidldhood friend. She would present him with a daughter and two sons.

## The race and the accident

Soichiro Honda was now competing in boat races on Lake Haman. With hsi brother he starts building cars and motor bikes for racing. He has but one dream; to become the best driver in Japan. He starts in more than 50 races and is a frequent winner, thanks to the power of his home built engines. He is unbearable when he loses. It is said that at one race, he was found lying face down in the grass having a tantrum because he had only finished fourth, after running out of fuel 200 metres from the finish line. In July 1936, Soichiro Honda enters his supercharged Model A Ford with a modifed cylinder head in the "All Japan Speed Rally." Right from the start he establishes a new Japanese record of 170 km/h. A few kilometres later disaster strikes. His Ford tangles with another competitor, skids, takes off and barrel rolls several times. The wreck slides along the dirt track, while its driver, who was thrown out after the first roll lies motionless in the middle of the road. He is picked up with multiple fractures, mainly to his left arm and wrist. He has also taken a heavy blow to the head. His racing career is at an end. But starting from scratch is not something Soichiro Honda finds daunting. Indeed it will be a sort of theme which runs through his life. During an eighteen month long recuperation period, he spends his time scrawling over several school notebooks. He draws nothing but strange

motorcycles of his own design, powered by extremely complicated engines. He has made the transition and now, all the excess energy which drove him to race cars at the weekend is transformed into sustained mental effort. He enrols for classes at the Hamamatsu technical college to study metallurgy. In 1937 he produces his first standard piston and sets up his own company, Tokai Seiki Heavy Industry. At the time, his biggest client is Toyota. Each year he registers about ten new technical patents. Sadly, all this rush of new ideas was not translated into a thriving business and life was tough. To such an extent that, at one point, he has to resort to dressing in wife Sachi's clothes so that his Awata foundry, in the Shizuoka prefecture, would not be closed down.

## On the dawn of the 7th December 1941

Dawn, 7/12/1941 An aerial assault force takes off from the decks of Admiral Nagumo's fleet and heads from Pearl Harbour. At 10h30 local time in Washington, the Japanese Ambassador hands the American government the official declaration of war. Soichiro Honda is exempted from military service as he suffers with facial neuralgia as a result of his accident. He fights the war at home, stepping up production in his factories. He has contracts with the airforce and navy, producing pistons, aircraft propellers and even speed boats. On the 15th August 1945 Japan surrendurs. While the war might have made Soichiro's fortune , it also took it off him. Having transformed his profits into new production facilities, he saw them all reduced to a tangle of twisted metal buried under rubble. All that was spared was a tiny six metres by four work area and a few machine tools. Once more, Honda would start from nothing.

## A stroke of genius

His master stroke would come now in the immediate post-war period. He acquires a consignment of 500 engines; tiny two strokes which had been fitted to small items of military equipment. He dismantled them, studid their internals, modified them and a few weeks later appeared a strange bicycle with a little engine fitted to the rear wheel. The Motoback Type A was on the local market and the Honda Technical

## Research company was born.

Soichiro Honda had taken the first step which would lead to a true commercial enterprise. His people had no means of transport, they were poor yet motivated, dynamic and under constant pressure. Honda gave them a work tool which was both economical and efficient - the cyclomotor. Twelve mechanics fit the 500

engines to bicycle frames and within a few months every single one is sold. At the same time, Soichiro has already started producing his own engine; the first of many.

## 24th September 1948

Effectively, Soichiro Honda has a fifteen year head start on the economic theories of the Sixties: it is not so much a case of meeting the current market demand, but rather looking to the future by actually creating a demand and being able to meet it immediately. In Tokyo, on 24th September 1948, he creates the Honda Motor Corporation Ltd. with a capital of 2,777 dollars which was all he owned in the world. That was fifty years ago.

*Soichiro Honda and his right hand man Takeo Fujisawa.*

▽

## The Honda way

When establishing the first factory at Hamamatsu in 1947, Soichiro Honda also establishes a company creed, which is the basis for an astounding philosophy.
1) To act with the faith and enthusiasm of youth.
2) To base company activity on the principal of resarching and developing new ideas and to make maximum use of the time available.
3) To work in a happy environment and to make the workplace a happy place.
4) To fight constantly to guarantee harmony in work.
5) To be inculcated with the merits of research and effort.

*Tom Phillis (125, 1961), Ralph Bryans (50, 1965), Luigi Taveri (125, 1966), Jim Redman (250, 1966), Mike Hailwood (250, 1967), Freddie Spencer (500, 1983), Spencer again (250, 1985), Anton Mang (250, 1987), Wayne Gardner (500, 1987), Alfonso Pons (250, 1989),*

# From 1948 to 1998

**24th September 1948:** Honda Motor Corporation Ltd. founded.

**End of 1949:** Honda Motor launches his first motorbike: The Honda Dream Type C.

**March 1950:** Soichiro Honda finds his super salesman, Takeo Fujisawa, who takes control of administration and finance. "Without him, I would have been nothing but an ingenious tramp," said the master.

**September 1950:** Production unit knocking out 300 motorcycles per month is set up in Kami Jojo, to the north of Tokyo. The number of distributors increases from 200 to 18,000.

**May 1954:** New production line set up at Hamamastsu. First low key entry in the TT ends in failure. Soichiro returns from Europe claiming: "My heart is tight."

**1957:** In Japan, the period of incredible growth reaches a plateau as the country's rate of inflation spirals. It is vital for Honda to go in search of foreign markets.

**1st August 1958:** The Cub 50 is unveiled in Tokyo, a cyclo-scooter capable of 75 km/h, which would lead to Honda's world domination. Soichiro's master plan to was to replace 10% of the world's bicycle market with Honda scooters and motorcycles. The company would sell 26.5 million Super Cub 100s.

**1959:** Creation of the American Motor Company Inc.

**3rd June 1959:** By coming sixth in the 125cc Tourist Trophy, Naomi Taniguchi scores Honda's first world championship point, while the company also takes the 125 team prize.

**1961:** European Honda Trading is established in Hamburg. Honda is already producing 100,000 two wheelers per month.

**23rd April 1961:** Tom Phillis wins the 125 cc Spanish Grand Prix at Montjuich Park. It is Honda's first grand prix victory, soon to be followed by its first triumph in the Isle of Man. Tom Phillis (125cc) and Mike Hailwood (250cc) offer Honda its first world titles.

**1962:** Honda Motor SA is established in Belgium and Asian Honda Motor Co. Is founded in Thailand to coordinate exports to South East Asia. The first Honda car is built. Luigi Taveri (125cc) and Jim Redman (250 and 350cc) are crowned world champions.

**1963:** Jim Redman does the double again in 250 and 350cc. Honda becomes the world's number one motorcycle manufacturer. In the United States, sales reach 150,000 units per year.

**1964:** Honda tackles F1. In August, Ronnie Bucknum takes part in the German GP at the Nurburgring. Soichiro Honda had dictated that the debut takes place at this famous track. Luigi Taveri is 125cc world champion and Jim Redman keeps his 350 cc title.

**1965:** First F1 victory comes courtesy of Ritchie Ginther in Mexico. Ralf Bryans is 50cc world champion, while Jim Redman takes his fourth and final 350 title.

**1966:** Three more championships: Luigi Taveri in 125, Mike Hailwood in 250 and 350.

**1967:** The previous season's Formula 2 champion, John Surtees takes Honda's second F1 win at Monza. Mike Hailwood does the 250/350cc double.

**1968:** Sensationally, Honda pulls out of the motorcycle grands prix just weeks before the start of the season, unhappy with rules restricting the number of cylinders in the various categories. Weary at the end of a difficult season which claimed the life of Jo Schlesser in the French GP, the company also turns its back on car racing. Commercially, the company passes the significant milestone of ten million units.

**1973:** Soichiro Honda and Takeo Fujisawa retire from the day to day running of Honda Motor Corporation. Kiyochi Kawashima becomes the head man.

**1976:** Jean-Claude Chemarin and Christian Leon win the European endurance racing championship.

**1977:** Chemarin and Leon do it again. Honda wins its first 500cc motocross grand prix in England.

**1978:** Yet again the endurance title goes to Chemarin/Leon. Honda wins the first bike 24 Hours of Le Mans race. Honda America, which will go on to build the Honda Gold Wing, is established in Marysville, Ohio.

**1979:** Soichiro Honda publishes his memoirs. In them he writes: "My father lived to see my success and I am glad I was able to offer him this satisfaction. He knew how much I owed to the precepts he taught me, the dignity of his life and his calm example, his will and above all I learnt to love and appreciate others." Honda makes its GP comeback while Chemarin/Leon are still endurance champions in Europe. Graham Noyce takes Honda's first world motocross championship.

**1980:** Another endurance title, this time a world one for Honda, with Marc Fontan and Herve Moineau. Andre Malherbe is the 500cc world motocross champion.

**1981:** Malherbe keeps his title.

**1982:** The CX 500TB is launched as the first production motorcycle to be built with a tur-

bocharger. Eddy Lejeune takes the world trials championship. First official entry and first win for Honda and Cyril Neveu in the Paris-Dakar rally.

**1983:** Tadashi Kume is made president. Freddie Spencer is world 500cc champion. Lejeune repeats his trial championship win. Honda returns to F1 with a V6 Turbo fitted to the Spirit car, evolved from Formula 2 and driven by the Swede Stefan Johansson.

**1984:** Gerard Coudray and Patrick Igoa perpetuate the Honda tradition in endurance racing. Malherbe picks up another 500 cross title, while Lejeune wins his third and last trials championship. In F1, Honda supplies the Williams team and they kick off with victory for Keke Rosberg in the United States.

**1985:** Historic double in the 250 and 500cc for Freddie Spencer. Coudray/Igoa win in endurance, Dave Thorpe wins the 500cc in motocross.

**1986:** Patrick Igoa wins the world endurance title on his own, thanks to the permutation of the team riders. Thorpe is crowned in the 500 cross yet again. Neveu is the king of the Dakar with his new NXR750R. Honda takes its first F1 constructors' title with Williams.

**1987:** Anton Mang (250) and Wayne Gardner (500) are GP world champions. Eric Geboers (250) and Georges Jobe (500) do the same in motocross. Neveu makes it three in the Dakar. Nelson Piquet takes the drivers' title and Williams the constructors' in F1.

**1988:** First 250 world championship for Sito Pons. Fred Merkel is the first world superbike champion. A certain Jean-Michel Bayle wins the 125 cross title, while Eric Geboers dominates in 500s. Edi Oriolo wins the Paris-Dakar. Another driver- constructor double in F1 with courtesy of Ayrton Senna and McLaren.

**1989:** Thanks to Sito Pons in 250 and Eddie Lawson in 500, the world's grand prix number one takes two more titles. Fred Merkel successfully defends his superbike title. Alex Vieira wins what has become the FIM endurance championship. In motocross, Bayle takes the 250 crown this time, Thorpe wins the 500. Paris-Dakar victory goes to the late Gilles Lalay. Yet another double championship in F1, this time thanks to Alain Prost and McLaren-Honda. The company sets up Honda Motor Europe Ltd. in Rome to look after activities in Europe, the Middle East and Africa.

**1990:** Nobuhiko Kawamoto, who retired from the post this year, is appointed President in Tokyo. Only one GP title, thanks to Capirossi in 125cc. Vieira wins his second FIM endurance title and Eric Geboers is 500cc cross champion. Ayrton Senna and McLaren-Honda are F1 world champions.

**1991:** At 10h43, Japan time on 5th August, Soichiro Honda dies. He had been working right up until the last moment on the Honda Foundation, an organisation dedicated to harmonising technology and the environment. "The older I get the more I dream. When man stops dreaming, life stops making sense. That is why I will continue to set myself new targets until I die and one of those is to continue dreaming," said Soichiro Honda just days before his death. Honda and Italy win with Loris Capirossi (125) and Luca Cadalora (250.) Trampas Parker (250) and Georges Jobe (500) are world motocross champions. Ayrton Senna and McLaren-Honda dominate in F1.

**1992:** Luca Cadalora (250) successfully defends his title. Greg Albertjin (125) and Georges Jobe (500) offer Honda two more world motocross championships.

**1994:** It is the start of the Michael Doohan era (500.) In cross it is still Albertjin (250) and Marcus Hanson in 500.

**1995:** Still Doohan, as well as Haruchika Aoki (125.) Jean-Michel Mattioli and Stephane Mertens are world endurance champions, a triumph for a private team running a Honda RVF/RC45. In cross Alex Puzar is the 125 champion.

**1996:** Same people, same story: Aoki (125) and Doohan (500.) In cross 250 it is Stefan Everts' turn. In trials, Marc Colomer dominates with a Montesa-Honda built in Spain.

**1997:** Massimiliano Biaggi, who has turned his back on the Aprilia factory is 250 world champion on a Honda, while Mick Doohan takes his fourth 500 title. After an eight year gap, Honda is once again dominant in Superbikes, thanks to John Kocinski. Belgium's Stefan Everts keeps his 250 cc cross title. Thirty years after the creation fo Suzuka, Honda opens a new sports complex in March, "Twin Ring Motegi" to the north of Tokyo. The facility has both a normal road circuit and an oval and also offers training facilities.

**1998:** Honda celebrates its fiftieth anniversary. Today Honda has over 90,000 employees and 69 factories in 36 countries and produces 5 million machines per year! There are over 100 million Honda motorcycles in the world. In economic terms, Honda is the 22nd largest company in the world with a consolidated value of over 40 billion dollars. World leader on two wheels, Honda is also the third largest car manufacturer in Japan. On 27th April, Hiroyuki Yoshino becomes the fifth president in the history of Honda Motor Co.

▷
*Eddie Lawson (500, 1989), Loris Capirossi (125, 1990), Wayne Gardner (500, 1990), Luca Cadalora (250, 1992), Dirk Raudies (125, 1993), Michael Doohan (500, 1994), Haruchika Aoki (125, 1995), Michael Doohan (500, 1996), Massimiliano Biaggi (250, 1997) and Michael Doohan (500, 1997): Honda wins!*

# A unique collection

In the four corners of the earth, old motorcycle enthusiasts covet their treasures with love. In a small Swiss valley, between Berne and Lucerne, Hansruedi Zihlmann has gathered the biggest collection of Honda's in the world, made up today of 72 different models. Interview with an extraordinary man.

▷ Hanruedi Zihlmann: Did you say dedicated?

Behind every collection, there lies a story. What is the story of Hansruedi Zihlmann? "It started a bit by accident, which is quite common among collectors I think. I had the opportunity to buy a CB 92 SS made the year I was born and that was started it all. The twin cylinder 125cc four stroke was about on a par with the racing Maico. At that time, the beginning of the sixties, Honda already had a production engine which developed 120 hp per litre. But to go from that, to starting a complete collection, we have to go on a step or two.
At the time I found the machine in 1984, I was finding it very difficult to get any documentation on the origins of my Honda. It was while researching this that my desire to start collecting grew. The more progress I made, the more I discovered about this company's fantastic history, especially its innovative nature as Honda was the inventor of, among other things, the five valve engine and the turbo charged motorcycle engine."

## "They laughed at me"

What was the reaction of other collectors whom you met on your travels?
"In Switzerland, as in many European countries, a lot of enthusiasts are interested in English machinery: Velocette, AJS, and also Italian bikes. When I spoke of my desire to collect Hondas, many of them laughed, in as much as the distance between Japan and Europe seemed too big a handicap to make this a serious enterprise."
Where did you find some of these treasures, like this surprising Juno?
"For the first five years, I worked day and night and as soon as I had earned some money, I would scour Europe in search of that rare pearl. I must have seen thousands of different motorcycles on these trips. Once, I came back with a lot made up of over thirty different marques. The collection became a game and I was buying lots because they contained one or two items which interested me. Then I would try and sell or exchange the other makes to other collectors. That is how, one day, I came across the Juno, a rarity on the Continent, because as far as I know, there are only three of them in Europe."

## A private collection

Today, Hansruedi Zihlmann's collection is carefully maintained at the family home. "For several years, the public could come and visit, but I soon noticed traces of jealousy. Today, I do not want to keep them

*Honda Juno: three known examples in Europe.*

*Jim Redman autographs one of the parts
from the amazing collection.*

to myself, but anyone wanting to see the collection must prove they have a genuine interest."

### In motorcycles or in Hondas?

"It's true I haven't just collected bikes. I keep everything with a Honda logo on it, from T-shirts to outboard motors, from the Gold Wing to the mini-bike, via puzzles, Honda pens and who knows what else. When I did not have enough money to buy a real bike, I came back from my trip with models."

Today, in this collector's treasure chest, one can find some original items, from an electronic game, to a portable generator, just powerful enough to run a razor; all of it Honda of course.

"A lot of these parts are not for sale, but they are exchanged between collectors. The goal is to always find the right thing and sometimes that involves going to the country of origin to find what is not avai-

lable over here. So I imported a CBR 250 RR Super Four 16v model from 1991, which makes an incredible noise as it revs to 20,000 rpm. It reminds me of Luigi Taveri's six cylinder racer."

Today, Hansruedi Zihlmann continues his research. His dream? To one day own a works Honda racer. "I am still young. I have time to dream and to keep looking." As this is the company's fiftieth anniversary, his collection has taken on a new sentimental value and Jim Redman came to put his name to one of the rare machines when on a recent visit to Switzerland. One more episode in the life of this man and his passion.

*"When I have not got
enough money,
I buy scale models."*

# 2. Johor Bahru

# Aprilia: the war between the teams

▷
*Valentino Rossi: sulking in Malaysia!*

**The previous year's loss of the 250 world title to Massimiliano Biaggi and Honda was a big shock for Aprilia. For 1998, it changed its approach and supplied three riders with 100% works bikes, each run by their own team. It only took until the second grand prix of the season for the inevitable to happen!**

"If the race comes down to the last corner, it's going to be spectacular," said Valentino Rossi, who had already worked out the race could all come down to the final few metres. "The final corner on the track is very wide and so it is impossible for the leader to shut the door. The trick might be to brake much harder than before, forcing the others to do the same and end up off line. Whoever is on the outside will be in the best position to accelerate out of the corner." These were Rossi's thoughts on the eve of the Malaysian Grand Prix on the Johor Bahru circuit, which was a new experienced for everyone. What he could not have known however was that he would be the victim of his own plan, thus offering victory to his team-mate Tetsuya Harada and inevitably it led to a scandal within the heart of the Aprilia team.

### Three riders, three teams

Aprilia had made a better job of adapting to the move to lead-free fuel than Honda had done. The Italian firm benefited from the experience gained in the previous year's European championship and this helped chief engineer Jan Witteveen. Thus they dominated the early part of the season, taking five of the top six places in qualifying. There were the three factory bikes for Rossi, Capirossi and Harada, plus the two leased machines leased to Jurgen Fuchs, who took the first pole of his career and for the Argentinian Sebastian Porto. The only one to spoil the party was Honda mounted Olivier Jacque.

Given that this very evident technical advantage is not limited to just one rider as in the days of Massimiliano Biaggi, the fight was going to be close, to say the least. Back at the factory, which has recently moved its racing department to San Marino, each rider has his own team structure: Giovanni Sandi is still looking after Testuya Harada, Rossano Brazzi has quit the Aprilia 500 V2 project to work with Valentino Rossi, while Rossi's chief engineer from last year, Mauro Noccioli who looked after him in the 125 class, now works with Loris Capirossi.

### Run by committee

There were also changes at the head of the race department as the ebullient Carlo Pernat had left the role of sporting director. He was not actually replaced and a

committee was set up to run the racing department, made up of president Ivano Beggio, the engineer Jan Witteveen, Matilde Tomagnini who worked for Chesterfield at the time that Biaggi rattled off his three consecutive titles was appointed to look after the media over the winter and of course the faithful Fabrizio Guidotti. A long time servant of Aprilia customers, he was appointed as team liaison man for this year.

So that is the new organigam, the one that did not work in Malaysia, in as much as it seems that Rossi's fall was avoidable. Carlo Pernat, in Malaysia on a "private" visit was keen to point this out and stir things even more. "If I was still the sporting director I would have instructed the riders not to overtake," he affirmed. "Now the situation can only get worse as Valentino Rossi will be out for revenge."

This statement would cost the good Carlo his role as special adviser to the president, even though it did not stop it from being confirmed when the season moved to Europe. But that is another story.

### A good sport, but...

The Malaysian 250 cc race produced reams of copy but above all it belonged to Valentino Rossi. From his second place in the category the reigning 125 world champion surprised everyone with his mastery of the subject.

First he tried to clear off into the distance and built up a 1.244s lead by lap 6. Then he fought a duel with Harada, before letting his first his team-mate and then Tohru Ukawa pass, in order to study their strengths and weaknesses in preparation for the final showdown. It was indeed a royal final. Rossi set a new lap record on the penultimate lap but he ran a bit wide into the last corner. The door is open, Harada slips through, the two Aprilias touch, Rossi accelerates on part of the track where there is less grip and down he goes. "I did exactly what I shouldn't have. First I gave Tetsuya too much room. Then I opened the throttle too quickly. Of course I should have just settled for crossing the line, but after a race like that, I could not settle for second place."

He's a good sport, Valentino Rossi. Even if a few weeks later, the tension would step up a notch in the Aprilia camp!

*Tetsuya Harada:*
*no pushover for the Italians.*
▽

▷ Biaggi, Doohan, Checa: fighting in the 500.

◁ Michael Doohan can smile again.

## 125 cc

The day did not get off to a good start for Youichi Ui, who had set fourth fastest time in qualifying, but fell and broke his left ankle. Roberto Locatelli made the best start, ahead of a surprising Mirko Giansanti, who would turn out to be the revelation of the weekend. Taking the lead on lap 3, the Italian would lead for most of the race, although Azuma would take the lead on the eleventh of twenty six laps on a very quick Honda, prepared by the Belgian Olivier Liegeois. From then on it was a case of who was eliminated -the lead group of Giansanti, Azuma, Ueda, Manako and Sakata would soon be reduced as Sakata had electrical problems and Azuma fell at the last corner. Ueda wins ahead of Giansanti and Manako, the latter now leading the world championship.

## 250 cc

The Aprilias dominated the weekend, with five of the top six qualifiers. Surprisingly it was Jurgen Fuchs who did the quickest lap in qualifying while the Argentinian Sebastian Porto dominated the warm-up. So who would be the main man in the 1998 Malaysian Grand Prix? In the lead right from the start, Valentino Rossi pulls out a lead of 1.244s by lap six. Tetsuya Harada comes back at him by lap nine and the two men are joined by Tohru Ukawa, who shakes off Olivier Jacque, the Frenchman suffering with suspension and tyre problems. At half distance, Rossi lets Harada and Ukawa slip by so he can watch what they are doing, with everyone keeping close tabs on everyone else. With two laps to go, the leading trio are separated by only 613 thousandths of a second. Rossi takes the lead by going round the outside of Ukawa, before making his only mistake of the race at the last corner. The result is that Harada wins and takes the lead in the championship. Ukawa is second and Jacque, although a long way back, finds himself third.

## 500 cc

It was Michael Doohan's turn to play mind games with the opposition and specifically with Massimiliano Biaggi. Fastest time in qualifying, while the Italian fell twice without injury, the quadruple world champion is the man to beat on the Johor Bahru track. The race is not without its exciting moments. Okada, Barros and Crafar are all out after but one lap, Namba falls on the straight and Mick Doohan only just misses him by a matter of millimetres. Biaggi grabs the lead, but is soon caught by the Number One. The two men do battle at a pace only they can maintain but then they are joined by Carlos Checa on lap 15. Doohan takes the lead on lap 22 of the 30 lap race. He would not be troubled again. Checa takes the second place ahead of Max Biaggi, who will land in Europe leading the world championship. It is a great performance by this first class rookie who is forcing the reigning champion to step up his game. That effort is written all over Doohan's face on the podium and a few moments later in the press conference.

Gino Borsoi's Cobra. We are in the final moments of Saturday morning's 125 free practice. A very dangerous type of black Cobra, which lives nearby, preferably in piles of stones and rubbish, crosses the Johor Bahru track. Lucio Cecchinello cannot avoid it and runs over the tail of the deadly reptile, which rises majestically to confront its strange assailant. At this precise moment, Gino Borsoi arrives on the scene, his right knee sticking out from the fairing of his Aprilia. Knee meets Cobra, knee wins and the Italian's leathers bear the scars to prove it. The red flag had to be brought out so that the dead snake could be removed. The snake charmers spent the rest of the weekend looking for its mate, while the photographers were very careful when it came to choosing their spot.

....Michael Doohan's haste in getting his plane home on Sunday night. Flight SQ322/BA12 from Singapore had a VIP guest on 19th April 1998; none other than Michael Doohan. The four times world champion was in a hurry because he had a seat fitting appointment the next day at the Williams F1 factory. The following Wednesday, Doohan got behind the wheel of Jacques Villeneuve's F1 car at the Catalunya circuit, outside Barcelona. He only got as far as the second corner before stuffing it into the wall.

....Valentino Rossi's lost bet. The 125 world champion loves to fool around and dare people to do things. Sitting by the pool of the Johor Bahru Holiday Inn he gave teammate Loris Capirossi the hard star. "I'll give you a million Lire (about US$600) if you jump in the pool from your bedroom bal-cony." No sooner said than done. Capirossi shot up to the third floor and dived in. Luckily for Rossi's wallet, "Capi" forgot to claim his winnings for weeks after the event!

....the physical condition of the top 500 stars at the end of the race. Doohan was flexing his hands and forearms before climbing onto the podium, his face clearly showing signs of the effort he had just expended. "When the team hung out the "7 laps" board, I was asking myself how I would hang on ëtil the end," admitted the Number 1 rider.

....the new injury to Doriano Romboni's right wrist. The MuZ-Swissauto rider suffered a fall, having had to brake hard while cranked over to avoid Carlos Checa, who had looked as though he was heading for the pits. While he was trying to pick his bike up, the scaphoid bone of his "Rambo's" right wrist broke again, forcing him to withdraw from the race and take a long break. "The" grand prix for the MuZ team, the former East German company having been taken over by the Malaysian group Hong Leong, was thus over before it had even begun.

△
The Cobra and Gino Borsoi:
image of the year!

# Welcome to Johor Bahru!

*A gas station in the early morning.*

**The new Sepang circuit is actually built at the centre of a huge complex which also houses the biggest airport in South East Asia. On the outskirts of Kuala Lumpur, the track was not actually completed in time to welcome the 1998 Malaysian GP. 1500 workmen worked 24 hours a day on the century's biggest building society. As Shah Alam had been abandoned, the Continental Circus set its sights on the southern end of the Peninsula and its frontier with Singapore.**

The Johur Bahru circuit is situated in the Pasir Gudang region, a thirty minute drive for the country's capital city. Built in 1986, it was approved by the FIM in 1990, it staged two rounds of the world endurance championship in 1991 and 1992, as well as two World Superbike rounds in 1992 and 1993. It is 3,860 metres long, boasts twelve corners on a demanding layout which makes intelligent use of its different contours.

To host the 1998 Malaysian Grand Prix, major work was undertaken to reach the required safety standards. The work did not come cheap, but it was good enough to give the track the possibility of hosting an international event every year, possibly alternating road racing and world superbikes.

### 20,000 square kilometres

The state of Johor is, in terms of size, the second largest in Malaysia with a surface area of 19,984 square kilometres. It is bordered on the west by the most important waterway in the world, the Malacca canal and on the east by the South China Sea. Johor is made up of eight districts and is linked to Singapore by a 1200 metre long bridge. A second viaduct is under construction to cope with the daily flow of Malaysians into and out of Singapore.

Johor Bahru attracts millions of tourists every year with its huge Duty Free shopping area. Visitors can also enjoy several beautiful white sand beaches, numerous islands and the odd historical site. The architecture is a mixture of British colonial and American modernism and most areas feature a bizarre mix of futuristic high rises and wooden huts.

*And a big smile from Johor Barhru.*

### Friday 17th April 1998

125 cc: Masao Azuma (Japan, Honda) and Yoshiaki Katoh (Japan, Yamaha).
250 cc: Shahrol Yuzi (Malaysia, Honda), Davide Bulega (Italy, Honda), Loris Capirossi (Italy, Aprilia, twice) Olivier Jacque (France, Honda) and Stefano Perugini (Italy, Honda).
500 cc: Carlos Checa (Spain, Honda), Katsuaki Fujiwara (Japan, Suzuki) and Kyoji Nanba (Japan, Yamaha).

### Saturday 18th April 1998

125 cc: Jaroslav Hules (Czech Republic, Honda).
250 cc: Johan Stigefelt (Sweden, Suzuki).
500 cc: Sebastien Gimbert (France ,Honda), Massimiliano Biaggi (Italy, Honda, twice), Simon Crafar (New Zealand, Yamaha), Doriano Romboni (Italy, MuZ), Sete Gibernau (Spain, Honda), Fabio Carpani (Italy, Honda)and Kenny Roberts Junior (United States , Modenas KR3).

### Sunday 19th April 1998

125 cc: Youichi Ui (Japan, Yamaha), Gino Borsoi (Italy, Aprilia), Marco Melandri (Italy, Honda), Gianliugi Scalvini (Italy, Honda, restart) and Masao Azuma (Japan , Honda, restart).
250 cc: Franco Battaini (Italy, Yamaha), Yasumasa Hatakeyama (Japan, Honda) and Valentino Rossi (Italy, Aprilia).
500 cc: Alexandre Barros (Brazil, Honda), Tadayuki Okada (Japan, Honda), Simon Crafar (New Zealand, Yamaha), Sete Gibernau (Spain, Honda), Kyoji Nanba (Japan, Yamaha), Russel Wood (South Africa, Honda), Nobuatsu Aoki (Japan, Suzuki), Norifumi Abe (Japan, Yamaha), Juan Bautista Borja (Spain, Honda) and Matt Wait (United States , Honda, restart).

### Ouch!...

1. Loris Capirossi (concussion, bruised right hand).
2. Stefano Perugini (bruising to left leg and arm).
3. Sebastien Gimbert (abrasion to big toe - left foot).
4. Jaroslav Hules (cut on right foot).
5. Doriano Romboni (fractured right wrist).
6. Fabio Carpani (slight concussion, bruising to right shoulder).
7. Youichi Ui (fractured left ankle).
8. Gino Borsoi (Multiple abrasions).
9. Marco Melandri (multiple abrasions).
10. Yasumasa Hatakeyama (abrasions).
11. Valentino Rossi (cracked left kneecap).

### Non - Starters...

1. Jean-Michel Bayle (result of fall in pre-season practise. Replaced by Kyoji Nanba).
2. Katsuaki Fujiwara (result of fall in pre-season practise. Replaced by Yukio Kagayama).
3. Regis Laconi (result of fall in practise for Japanese GP. Not replaced).
4. Scott Smart (result of fall in Japanese GP. Not replaced).
5. Youichi Ui (result of fall in warm-up).
6. Doriano Romboni (result of fall in practise).

### Retirements...

125 cc: Jose Ramon Ramirez (Spain, Aprilia, loss of confidence).
Christian Manna (Italy, Yamaha, front brake)
and Juan Enrique Maturana (Spain, Yamaha, piston).
250 cc: William Costes (France, Honda, dehydration),
Luca Boscoscuro (Italy, TSR-Honda, seized).
Luis D'Antin (Spain, Yamaha, result of fall in practise for Japanese GP).
Davide Beluga (Italy, Honda, front forks).
and Johan Stigefelt (Sweden, Suzuki, cramps).
500 cc: Fabio Carpani (Italy, Honda, result of fall in practise).

*Doriano Roboni has just got up, but no one knows his season is already over.*
▽

◁
*Nobuatsu Aoki: Suzuki in flames.*

# Criville: In the Name of the Father!

## 3. Jerez de la Frontera

▷ Alex Criville's first glory day of the season…

Just like last year, the Catalan Alex Creville won a fantastic race at Jerez in front of 120,000 spectators. It was an emotional moment when Alex dedicated his triumph to his father, who had died that winter. There were a few tears at the end of a weekend which had come up with a strange situation. One where there were question marks asked about the use of fuel that did not comply with the rules.

He had a lump in his throat. You could see from his eyes that for a moment he was elsewhere, that he had left the cauldron that was Jerez de la Frontera. For a few seconds Alex Criville was somewhere else entirely. "I would like to dedicate this victory to my father, Jose. I think he would have been happy today". Jose Criville had departed this earth one dark day last February, with an incurable illness. At that time, Alex was landing in Australia for a series of tests.

### Open to Doubt

"Of course I dreamt of winning the Spanish Grand Prix, but as I was not on top form since the start of the season, I had doubted my ability to do it. Over the last few laps, with Doohan right behind me and Biaggi not far away also, I was very nervous. I could only think about one thing and that was to get to the finish line as soon as possible." So Alex Criville had won, just as he had done twelve months earlier. And the 120,000 spectators at Jerez de la Frontera -and that was only the Sunday figure as the total over the three days had hit a record 170,000- did not stop chanting " Cri-vi-lle, Cri-vi-lle, Cri-vi-lle."

The Race? It was just over 47 minutes of pure madness between Criville, Doohan, and Biaggi. There was a contagious madness in this unique atmosphere. But Alex Criville still held it all together even though he too might have succumbed to the mood of that day on the third of May 1998. When you start a difficult day like this by falling off in the morning warm-up, the tension increases by a tangible amount. As I started the race with a bike which had been rebuilt after the accident, I started by making a few little checks on it before really going at it. And apart from a few worries with the clutch, everything worked perfectly. After the problems I've had in the last few races, my bike is now definately

better in all areas." It seemed that Alex Criville was also in far better shape than he had been twelve months earlier. He had returned to Europe and gone on a training programme on Kenny Robert's ranch, right next to the Catalunya track and he had built himself up both physically and mentally and was ready to fight for the supreme title.

## An Unforgettable Day

With the pressure and emotion behind him, Alex Criville was able to start savouring the first moments of what would be an incredible day for him. By his side Michael Doohan: "I thought Alex would be the man to beat at Jerez and my front tyre was not too good towards the end of the race, I chose to make sure of second place." Also there was Max Biaggi: "For a learning year, three podiums from three races isn't bad." However, these two could do nothing but admire Barros that day.

However, the 500cc Spanish GP also pro-vided the sequel to the petrol war. At Jerez de la Frontera, it reached a level of intensity and suspicion that would not have been out of place in a James Bond film. At Elf, the company who had reigned supreme up until last year in the paddock, four chemists lost their jobs, including Jean-Claude Fayard, the former head of the company's Research and Development department. The official reason was that they: "Had made private use of the company's resources." Behind this polite formula, lay the very deep suspicion of industrial espionage, or even collaboration with the enemy.

## Nutec: From America With Love

The enemy? Since the winter the enemy had been Nutec, the American aerospace fuel company, whose arrival in Grand Prix racing also marked the return of former French racer, Jean-Francois Balde, who until last year occupied the same role for Elf. Elf against Nutec and another bomb was about to go off in the Spanish paddock with the publication of a press release put out by the President of the Technical Commission and the President of the FIM Road Racing Commission. It said: "In order to put an end to the rumours, we state officially that the fuel samples taken at the Malaysian GP on 19th April 1998 at Johor Bahru are still being examined. The results will be made known very soon."

Just rumours? Much more, as Elf drums were there for all to see in the HRC-Repsol pit, home to world champion Mick Doohan, Tadayuki Okada and Alex Criville. It was a cheeky situation that had all the same been accepted by the team's principal sponsor, a rival fuel company. What is the truth behind all these goings on? We would find out a few days later, that the fuel taken from the bikes of Okada and Kocinski did not conform to the current rules introduced this year. Verdict? Read on.

◁
*... at the end of a Sunday which had got off on the wrong foot.*

▷ Kazuto Sakata and the Aprilia 125 were unbeatable at Jerez.

### 125 cc

Roberto Locatelli set the fastest time in qualifying, but he is suffering from the effects of a serious fall and a badly bruised left ankle. Only sixth on the grid, Kazuto Sakata surprises everyone at the start, takes the lead at the first corner and disappears into the distance. He leads by over a second after two laps, almost three after eight and the Aprilia rider, rare in the 125 category, is about to make a successful one man break. Second place is therefore the point of interest and a fine fight is on between Ueda, plus championship leader Manako, Cecchinello and Locatelli. These last two collide on lap four and Locatelli falls in spectacular fashion, followed by Cecchinello who crashes on lap eleven and it is left to Masao Azuma who comes from behind to join the chasing group. Sakata wins and leads the championship, while Mirko Giansanti celebrates his second consecutive podium.

△ Rossi and President Ivan Beggio look to the future.

### 250 cc

With five Aprilias in the first five places on the grid, the Italian bikes are still in a world of their own, according to Honda rider Olivier Jacque. This domination promises high drama, given that the tension has risen to unbearable levels at Noale after the chaotic finish to the Malaysian GP. We are not to be disappointed. Harada makes the best getaway ahead of Jose Luis Cardoso, who confirms his excellent start to the season and the progress made with the Yamaha TZM. After one lap, Harada leads the dance ahead of Olivier Jacque and Stefano Perugini, but before crossing the line for a second time, the championship leader slows with a carburation problem. Valentino Rossi makes the most of it to take the lead and he is soon joined by Loris Capirossi on lap 5. The two Italians can forget about the rest. Harada rejoins the race, but is black flagged for having ignored article 7 of the regulations, which forbids the bike to be worked on inside the pit, although he would have been okay if his mechanics had worked on the machine in the pit lane, just outside the garage. Capirossi-Rossi slog it out for the lead and Ukawa-Jacque do likewise for third place. Loris makes the break two laps from home with a 1.327s advantage over Rossi and Olivier surprises Ukawa on the final lap. The championship has seen everyone close up: Capirossi leads Jacque by two points and deep in the Aprilia factory all one can hear is the noise of grinding teeth.

### 500 cc

Having falling in the morning warm-up, Alex Criville would go on to run the perfect race in front of delirious fans. Third at the end of lap one, behind the Brazilian, Alex Barros, who made a great start and Mick Doohan, on lap 6, Criville mixed it with the two strong men of the early part of the season, Doohan and Biaggi. The three Honda riders pulled away until by lap 16, they had a 1.713s lead over Carlos Checa who was trying in vain to catch up. The end of the race was fabulous and as the atmosphere at the track reached boiling point, Criville took the lead with 10 of the 27 laps remaining. The Spaniard would have the last word, despite the constant pressure from Doohan who this nibbled away at Biaggi's points advantage.

Aprilia: a new hospitality, but no longer under the shadow of Carlo Pernat.

The disappearance of Carlo Pernat. Aprilia management would confirm the news a few days later, but for the first time in a long time, Carlo Pernat was not at the Spanish GP. Appointed "consultant to president Beggio" this winter, specifically in the company's dealings with IRTA (the team association) and Dorna (the Spanish company which promotes the grands prix,) Pernat will now be able to concentrate on his great love of soccer. After the Malaysian GP he declared: "If I was still the sporting director, I would have demanded they maintain station on the last lap." This did not go down well with the top brass and the president, Ivan Beggio stressed that: "Carlo Pernat went to Johor Bahru entirely on a private visit." And so we say goodbye to someone who had been one of the key figures in the paddock over the past ten years.

Max and Mick, flying friends. As they both live in Monte Carlo and that away from the track they are friends, at the moment, Massimiliano Biaggi and Michael Doohan shared a private plane from the Principality to Andalusia. The comment from the reigning 500 champ: "It was very tiring, because Max never stopped talking." Once they had landed the two men went their separate ways, Doohan and fiancÈ Selina heading for the hire carsm while His Majesty Max was met by his motorhome driver.

The petrol war and the ticking off. Those riders who had used the Repsol fuel in Malaysia - Doohan, Criville and Checa had not been checked - were having the finger of doubt pointed at them by almost everyone. The petrol war, which could have direct consequences on the way the 500 title went, was completely unnoticed by the Spanish press, who normally are so quick to pick up scandal and gossip. As a colleague who wished to remain nameless for obvious reasons said: "If I mention this business in my paper, Repsol will immediately withdraw all its advertising."

Article 7 of the grand prix regulations. At least the people at Aprilia will have learnt a new rule this weekend; the one which prohibits any work to be carried out inside a team's garage during the race. Worse, how to explain the behaviour of Tetsuya Harada, who was running between Capirossi and Rossi, even though he was four laps down. He then jumped for joy at the finish because Loris had beaten Valentino. It's a team sport you know!

Graziano Rossi's new hotel. It is possible to be the father and personal manager of a very well paid rider and still not have illusions of grandeur. Graziano Rossi drove down to Jerez in his own car - an estate - which he proceeded to turn into a bed. "Now that Valentino has a new motorhome, faster but smaller, there is no room for me. Sleeping in the paddock saves me money and gives me peace of mind." An example to others.

Graziano Rossi: a champion's dad with simple tastes.

▷
*Marco Gentile on the grid in 1987: "Claude Fior? If someone trusted him…"*

### 26th April 1987: Marco Gentile

Three years after his grand prix debut, the 1985 European Champion Marco Gentile, arrives at Jerez de la Frontera for the first time with a brand new motorcycle - the Fior-Honda, built by Claude Fior at Nogaro. He has already put behind him the dismal Japanese grand prix where he had stopped for no apparent reason after just a few laps. Here in 40 degree heat, the Swiss will offer himself a surprising twelfth place in the 500 race. It is surprising given that his bike was only completed four days before the first GP in the history of the Jerez de la Frontera circuit. "It's encouraging. Last year it took me four races to get the hang of my bike and here we are without any testing under our belt and I am already twelfth." Over to the press cuttings library again....

"European 500 champion in 1985, Marco Gentile from Geneva did a complete season of the Continental Circus last year, without scoring any points, even though he got very close in Sweden. But at least he has made progress with every outing. Technically, he has not gone for the easy option as he has chosen to work with a small constructor, in this case Claude Fior from Toulouse, a motorcycle genius or just a genius plain and simple, given his work from single seater planes to lawn mowers with four wheel drive. He has arrived in the motorcycle world and attracted a great deal of interest. The two men understand one another, as if life long friends had shared a common dream of taking part in one of the most difficult race series of all, the 500 grand prix class. Financially, they cannot compete with the other teams, relying on a few small sponsors and a lot of goodwill. Marco Gentile still has a regular job between the races. "Claude Fior? Yes of course I believe in him. If someone trusted him and gave him the means to develop some of his ideas, he could go much further." Gentile's face lights up. "I still love motorcycling and I know I can still make progress. The day I see I have reached my level, then I won't hesitate to pack it all in. But for the moment, I know you cannot be a front runner from one day to the next."

### Friday 1st May 1998

125 cc: Alfonso Gonzales-Nieto (Spain, Aprilia), Christian Manna (Italy, Yamaha), Yoshiaki Katoh (Japan, Yamaha) and Vicente Esparragoso (Spain, Yamaha).
250 cc: Valentino Rossi (Italy, Aprilia), Jurgen Fuchs (Germany, Aprilia) and Olivier Jacque (France, Honda).
500 cc: Norifumi Abe (Japan, Yamaha) and Fabio Carpani (Italy, Honda).

### Saturday 2nd May 1998

125 cc: Noboru Ueda (Japan, Honda), Lucio Cecchinello (Italy, Honda), Roberto Locatelli (Italy, Honda), Kazuto Sakata (Japan, Aprilia), Alvaro Molina (Spain, Honda) and Steve Jenkner (Germany, Aprilia).
250 cc: Noriyasu Numata (Japan, Suzuki), Yasumasa Hatakeyama (Japan, Honda), Luca Boscoscuro (Italy, Honda), Tohru Ukawa (Japan, Honda) and Stefano Perugini (Italy, Honda).
500 cc: Regis Laconi (France, Yamaha), Garry McCoy (Australia, Honda), Norifumi Abe (Japan, Yamaha) and Sete Gibernau (Spain, Honda).

### Sunday 3rd may 1998

125 cc: Yoshiaki Katoh (Japan, Yamaha), Ivan Goi (Italy, Aprilia), Roberto Locatelli (Italy, Honda), Emilio Alzamora (Spain, Aprilia) Lucio Cecchinello (Italy, Honda), Juan Enrique Maturana (Spain, Yamaha), Andrea Ballerini (Italy, Honda) and Paolo Tessari (Italy, Honda, restart).
250 cc: Jeremy McWilliams (Great Britain, TSR-Honda), Johan Stigefelt (Sweden, Suzuki), Jason Vincent (Great Britain, Honda, twice).
500 cc: Yukio Kagayama (Japan, Suzuki, restart).

### Ouch!...

1. Roberto Locatelli (bruising to ankle and left thigh from a fall in practise; bruising and cuts to right shoulder, from fall during the race).
2. Juan Enrique Maturana (slight concussion).
3. Andrea Ballerini (bruising to wrist and right foot).
4. Jeremy McWilliams (cut to right hand).

### Non Starters...

1. Jean-Michel Bayle (result of fall in winter practise. Jean-Michel Bayle, who had participated in an Albacete test between the Malaysian and Spanish GPs, turned back on arrival in Barcelona, still in trouble with balance problems. Replaced by Kyoji Nanba).
2. Katsuaki Fujiwara (result of fall in winter practise. Replaced by Yukio Kagayama).
3. Doriano Romboni (result of fall in practise for Malaysian GP. Not replaced).

### Retirements...

125 cc: Christian Manna (Italy, Yamaha, rear tyre)
250 cc: Davide Bulega (Italy, Honda, battery), Tetsuya Harada (Japan, Aprilia, retired in pits with a carburettor problem. Starts again but is black flagged for having effected repairs in his pit,) Jose Luis Cardoso (Spain, Yamaha, bad tyre choice) Sebastian Porto (Argentina, Aprilia, broken seat after collision with another rider.) and Jurgen Fuchs (Germany, Aprilia, ignition.)
500 cc: Juan Bautista Borja (Spain, Honda V2, result of going off the track and damaging rear tyre) and Fabio Carpani (Italy, Honda V2, handling problems.)

▷ *Valentino Rossi a mere 250 class apprentice!*

# The old man and the child

## 4. Mugello

*Marcellino Lucchi: "The best day of my life."*

**At the age of 41, Marcellino Lucchi takes his first world championship win. Right behind him is Valentino Rossi who came up with yet another of his tricks. Aprilia's domination in the 250 class was stronger than ever.**

He stopped at a precise point on the track, where he was engulfed by an army of his fans. You could see there were items of clothing flying around. Then, as the crowd backed away, Valentino Rossi appeared as a beach boy wearing T-shirt, shorts and a towel round his neck. Plastic flip flops had replaced his leather boots. At the same moment, on another part of the track, Marcellion Lucchi was living the dream, with a tear running down his ravaged features and clutching an Italian flag which floated in the breeze.

### The Aprilia podium

Then they climbed onto the podium. On the left, Testusya Harada, the austere Japanese. On the right, Rossi, cap on back to front, sun glasses on the top of his head. In the middle, Marcellino Lucchi, overcome with emotion. He was happy to have finally achieved his childhood dream of winning a grand prix. Even better he had won "his" grand prix on the Tuscan track where he knows every metre from all the testing he has done here, as the Aprilia RS250V became a machine which would crush its opponents. Aprilia boss, Ivan Beggio joined his riders to accept the manufacturers' trophy. It was as though this 250 Italian GP podium had been transformed into a promotional event for this young company,

which had taken just over ten years of existence to win its 75th grand prix.

A few moments later and everyone was facing a barrage of questions. It was time to forget the tension of the weekend, the promised internal war, the nervousness caused by the race being interrupted by a sudden shower. Marcellion Lucchi was greeted with a standing ovation. "It still hasn't sunk in yet. When I think I made the wrong tyre choice for the first start! Without the rain and the re-start I might not have won." Second in both legs and winner when both times were added together, Lucchi still had more thank yous to deliver. "To Aprilia who have always had faith in me. And above all, to my technical team who richly deserve this win. Finally a big thank you to the doctor, Claudio Costa who made sure I was in fine shape physically. It's not easy looking after an old man of 41, I can tell you!"

### Rossi's laughter

Alongside him and young enough to be his son, Valentino Rossi is still laughing at the trick he had played on his fans: "I won the first leg, but I was not happy with myself because my times were no good. On the other hand, I am quite pleased with the second race after I made a complete mess of the start."

For his part, Harada had little to say. Loris Capirossi, even less, although the fourth placed Aprilia man had just extended his lead in the championship from 2 to 4 points. But there you go, he knows his understudy is no longer Olivier Jacque (brave until his retirement, but is now Tetsuya Harada who, like him, has an Aprilia, which should be unbeatable for many weeks to come. And that changes everything.

## Olivier Jacque injured

Aprilia's domination in the 250 has changed the class into a demonstration. Trying to salvage something, the Honda riders have had to take too many risks (Perugini twice a faller, Ukawa one and one with more serious consequences for Olivier Jacque during practice. The race was sim-

ply a reflection of what had happened in qualifying. "Right from the start, I tried to calm things down by reminding Olivier the important thing was to be the best of the HRC riders. We all expected Honda to react quickly, but every time we asked for something we were told to wait. The last time, we were even told not to expect miracles as all industry in Japan had ground to a halt because of a one week compulsory holiday," explained Herve Poncharal, the boss of Olivier Jacque's Team Tech 3. He was the only one, up to this Italian GP who had managed to hang onto the Aprilia armada. "I can't hold it against Olivier. At first he lost control of the front end, but he recovered the situation before an engine misfire caused the back to step out of line."

"The most annoying aspect is that teams who have the NSR have spent a fortune to lease them and their riders are fighting the TSR-Hondas and the Yamaha TZM, machines which cost one tenth of the price," added Dieter Stappert, Stefano Perugini's boss. It was all the more of a bitter pill for Honda to swallow as the battle raging between the Aprilia boys might leave room for a regular outsider to sneak in and run off with the prize.

◁
*A fine tuner and a winner!*

△
Michael Doohan wins
his sixth consecutive
Italian Grand Prix.

△
Tomomi Manako leads
the 125 championship.

## 125 cc

The Japanese dominated practice and were going to win a very spectacular race. Sakata is first out of the blocks. On the second lap, a group of four is in the lead (Ueda, Sakata, Manako and the very young Milandri.) The group will grow with the passing of time with the addition of Cecchinello, Giansanti and Sclavini. We now have seven at the front. A handkerchief would cover all of them, separated by just 729 thousandths of a second on lap 12. With three laps to go, Ueda tries to make the break, using all the track and more as he goes through the dirt on two occasions. It is in vain. So it will all come down to the last corner of the last lap: in the lead, Mirko Giansanti has a terrible fall and it is a miracle that none of the others hit him. Ueda has to ride through the gravel trap, Sakata collides with the Italian's bike but keeps going, unlike Cecchinello. At the line, Manako has a lead of just 44 thousandths over Marco Melandri, who makes it to his first podium at only 16 years of age. Manako now has an 8 point lead over Sakata in the championship.

## 250 cc

At the start, Testusya Harada has clutch problems, while Lucchi, Rossi and Capirossi make the running. Harada begins a fantastic recovery which takes him from 22nd place on the first lap to fourth on lap 7, when a heavy shower forces the organisers to red flag the race. A short while later and they are off again for fifteen laps and Harada leads this time, while Lucchi tucks in behind, ensuring the overall lead when the two times are added together. Harada and Lucchi in front, Rossi and Capirossi behind, the NSR riders are a long way, a very long way back, fighting with some high class privateers like McWilliams, before he retired, D'Antin, and Cardoso. Harada crosses the line first, Lucchi wins on added times, Rossi has fun with his fans and Capirossi keeps his lead in the championship.

## 500 cc

Michael Doohan is particularly keen on the Tuscan track and right from the start of practice he wastes no time in reminding the rest of the paddock that he is king of this particular category. During Saturday morning's free practice he actually sets a new outright track record and it is obvious that the four times world champion is planning to take a sixth consecutive win here at Mugello, where he rediscovered the taste of victory in 1993 after his terrible practice accident in practice for the 1992 Dutch GP. As Okada is out after practice and Biaggi has some problems, there are fears the race will be a one man show. It will not, thanks at first to Alex Barros, followed by Max Biaggi, who takes the lead on lap two and even pulls out a lead of 1.491s, before being caught by Doohan on lap nine. The roles are thus reversed and Doohan goes from hunter to hunted. From lap 18 to 22, the gap is never more than half a second and then the Australian puts the hammer down. The race is won, it is another Honda triumph and Biaggi hangs on to his title lead.

▷
*Repsol was using a strange fuel in Malaysia, but the samples were not taken according to the rule book.*

The Italian 125 grand prix has written itself into the history books as it is in fact the 500th 125 cc world championship grand prix, an anniversary celebrated in style by Tomomi Manako. The 500th 250 grand prix was run at Mugello in 1996 and was won by Max Biaggi, while the 500th 500 was held against the backdrop of Imola in 1997, when the race was shortened by torrential rain and was won by Michael Doohan.

The first divorce of the season - The first contract broken between team and rider was recorded in Italy. The Pileri S.r.l. team and Andrea Ballerini had decided "in a joint agreement that because of the disappointing results of the first three races of the season," that they would put an end to their collaboration.

Epilogue to the fuel scandal...Follow up and finale to the 500 Malaysian GP fuel scandal. The samples taken from the mounts of Tadayuki Okada, a faller, and John Kocinski, fifth, were analysed in the EMPA labs in Switerzerland. Apparently they "needed further examination," as some figures were out. But as "there was nothing litigious about the lead content, the octane rating or the oxygen level, the decision was taken to submit the case to an independent specialist chosen by the international federation. This expert, Englishman Jim Laxton, pointed out that: "certain parameters such as the very high temperatures when the fuel samples were taken can alter the results of the distillation test." He reckoned that: "Nothing in the EMPA figures would lead one to think the riders used any fuel other than the one approved by the FIM rules and that the method of taking and analysing samples needed to be improved."

The fall of Garriga. Everyone remembers Juan Garriga and his epic duels with Sito Pons for the 250 world title in 1988 and a few good 500 races. On the Italian GP weekend came news, confirmed by police on 15th May, that the Spanish rider had been jailed in Barcelona, accused principally of drug trafficking (25 grammes of cocaine were found at the home of the former champion, plus another 500 in the air conditioning of the bar where he was found with two accomplices.) The police also found six firearms, counterfeit money, stolen cash and jewellery. Garriga was let out after three days.

Rossi meets the president. 125 cc champion, Valentino Rossi was presented on Wednesday 20th June with the "Collare d'oro," the highest sporting honour bestowed by the Italian Olympic Committee. Max Biaggi who had received this the previous year was honoured this time with an honours diploma. The awards were presented by the president of the Italian National Olympic Committee (CONI) Mario Pescante. 33 athletes from various disciplines were honoured and after the ceremony they were introduced to the President of the country, Oscar Luigi Scalfaro.

*Andrea Ballerini.*
▽

*Juan Garriga.*
▽

### 16th May 1976: Ago and Suzuki

Five Suzukis in the top five places on the grid, nine Suzukis in the nine first rows. When Tuscany hosted a world championship grand prix for the first time, all eyes were on Giacomo Agostini, who for the first time that season, lined up on the 500 grid with a machine from Japan's third marque. It was to be a black day as the pages of issue number 2269 of Moto Revue revealed. "I have never seen so many fallers in my life," said Patrick Pons at the end of the Italian GP. There had been over 60 fallers over the weekend, two of which proved fatal for Otello Buscherini and Paolo Tordi. The Mugello circuit was a series of rapid corners which rise and fall, where the quickest machines were averaging over 150. The medical support is excellent, but the ever-present guardrails and the lack of escape roads, make it one of the most dangerous tracks. The technically demanding nature of the track also makes it very tiring for the riders. Therefore, the slightest loss of concentration can have dramatic consequences, as can mechanical failures. It would be the machinery which would be Giacomo Agostini's downfall that day. The 100,000 spectators present at Mugello wanted only to see their idol win yet again in the pinnacle of the sport. Their enthusiasm was unbridled right from the start as Ago charged into the lead, ahead of Sheene. Read had been slightly left behind, but he put in an incredible ride to close up again by lap seven and a trio of kings led the race. Sheene got the jump on Ago on lap ten, then Read took second when the Italian rider began to slow and headed for his pits. His rear brake was locking up and was causing the engine to overheat. The spectators finally sat down but not for long as the Sheene-Read fight was a beauty. On the last lap, Read and Sheene keep passing one another around every inch of the five kilometre track. At the final corner, Read dives down the inside and passes Barry, who then gets better acceleration out of the corner and wins by half a wheel. What excitement! What champions!

▷

*Giacomo Agostini and the Suzuki.*
*Their first meeting at Mugello ended in failure.*

◁
*Tohru Ukawa:*
*"this time I've a bit*
*a too much of a lean on."*

### Friday 15th May 1998

125 cc: none.
250 cc: Stefano Perugini (Italy, Honda, twice), Johan Stigefelt (Sweden, Suzuki) and Jurgen Fuchs (Germany, Aprilia).
500 cc: Juan Bautista Borja (Spain, Honda) and Tadayuki Okada (Japan, Honda).

### Saturday 16th May 1998

125 cc: Roberto Locatelli (Italy, Honda), Masao Azuma (Japan, Honda), Kazuto Sakata (Japan, Aprilia) and Yoshiaki Katoh (Japan, Yamaha).
250 cc: Tohru Ukawa (Japan, Honda) and Olivier Jacque (France, Honda).
500 cc: Eskil Suter (Switzerland, MuZ) and Kyoji Nanba (Japan, Yamaha).

### Sunday 17th May 1998

125 cc: Christian Manna (Italy, Yamaha), Mirko Giansanti (Italy, Honda) and Lucio Cecchinello (Italy, Honda).
250 cc: Johan Stigefelt (Sweden, Suzuki), Federico Gartner (Argentina, Aprilia), Roberto Rolfo (Italy, TSR-Honda), Sebastian Porto (Argentina, Aprilia) and Osamu Miyazaki (Japan, Yamaha).
500 cc: Matt Wait (United States, Honda).

### Ouch!...

1. Tadayuki Okada (fractured left wrist).
2. Stefano Perugini (slight concussion).
3. Olivier Jacque (fractured right calcaneum.)

4. Kazuto Sakata (bruised left hand).
5. Kyoji Nanba (wounded little finger - left hand).
6. Johan Stigefelt (concussion).
7. Mirko Giansanti (fractures to 3rd and 4th toes - right foot).
8. Lucio Cecchinello (abdominal bruising).

### Non Starters...

1. Jose Ramon Ramirez (the Spaniard has suffered tendonitis in his right arm for some time and it needed surgery . Replaced by Jeronimo Vidal).
2. Andrea Ballerini (the Italian and the Pileri team decided jointly to end their collaboration, because of disappointing results in the first three races . Replaced by Andrea Iommi).
3. Doriano Romboni (result of fall in practise for Malaysian GP. Replaced by Eskil Suter).
4. Jean-Michel Bayle (result of fall in winter practise. JMB had taken part in IRTA tests at Jarama, one week before the Italian GP, where he did about thirty laps in two days. "The problem" explained his boss Wayne Rainey, "is that Jean-Michel gets bad headaches when he gets off his bike." More testing is planned for the Monday after the Italian GP, at Mugello. Replaced by Kyoji Nanba).
5. Katsuaki Fujiwara (result of fall in winter practise. Still replaced by Yukio Kagayama).

6. Tadayuki Okada (result of fall in practise).
7. Johan Stigefelt (result of fall in warm-up).

### Retirements...

125 cc: Jaroslav Hules (Czech Republic, Honda, piston ring), Roberto Locatelli (Italy, Honda, engine) and Angel Nieto Junior (Spain, Aprilia, seized).
250 cc: Jeremy McWilliams (Great Britain, TSR-Honda, fuel supply), Noriyasu Numata (Japan, Suzuki, broken chain), Olivier Jacque (France, Honda, ignition), Jason Vincent (Great Britain, TSR-Honda, clutch) and Jurgen Fuchs (Germany, Aprilia, seized).
500 cc: Juan Bautista Borja (Spain, Honda V2, broken gear selector) and Kenny Roberts Junior (United States, Modenas KR3, engine).

# Criville does the double

## 5. Le Castellet

**The French Grand Prix was the race where the leadership of the 500 cc championship changed hands. The king of Rome, Massimiliano Biaggi was injured and he handed over his seat to Alex Criville, the prince of Spain. It led to a surprising return to form for the winner of the Spanish Grand Prix.**

At the Castellet, a Spaniard would take the lead in the blue riband championship and what is more he did it two weeks before the second of three grands prix to be held on Iberian soil, at Jarama outside Madrid. Alex Criville won the race in great style, like the mature rider he has become, like a man who knows he is now capable of beating anyone in the world, and not just on his home turf at Jerez de la Frontera. "For me, this win is particularly pleasing, as I had a lot of problems on this track over the past two years. This time, thanks to the special tyres developed by Michelin, everything went marvellously."

### The secret of Bibendum

The French tyre company came up with a revolutionary tyre. It was designed to reduce the possibility of crashing on this particularly strange Le Castellet track where it is all too easy to be caught out by the sudden and marked changes in grip levels. One year earlier it was still a jealously guarded secret. But in the Le Castellet paddock, Michelin competition boss, Jacques Morelli opened his heart. "Yes we are using tyres made with two different compounds, one of which is softer on the left side, so that it warms up quicker to a working tempe-

rature to ensure good handling in the only two left hand corners of this circuit." This solution is supposed to get over the problem of having done almost half a lap where only the right side of the tyre is made to work. "The first time this type of tyre was used it was at Daytona in Florida with its high speed oval which runs left handed. In GP racing, apart from Le Castellet, some riders have already used this specification in Malaysia and a few years ago at Hockenheim." The calculation of temperature difference carried out by Michelin engineers at Le Castellet came up with some surprising results. "Of course it is impossible to come up with exact figures," said Jacques Morelli, "As they are travelling flat out when they get to the first left hander. But we reckon that on the first lap, if the right hand side of the tyre is already at 120 degrees, the left hand side must be around the 80 or 90 mark."

Two different compounds on the same construction. "At Michelin, the construction method, which is of course highly confidential, has now been perfectly mastered. In theory, combining two compounds on the same carcass is not so easy, but modern technology has made it possible. However, even though it was avai-

▷ *Honda is as dominant as ever and this time it is Criville's turn to lead the dance.*

lable to all of them, not all our riders chose to use this tyre."

We are still left with some surprising figures: 15 fallers on Friday, ten on Saturday and ten on Sunday and 60% of them were at these famous left hand corners. "When they come to Le Castellet, all the riders know the track and the risks it entails in two key areas. However, it does not stop the mistakes, which is completely understandable, as even if there is less grip, lap by lap every rider gets more confident and pushes that little bit harder. When they lose grip, it is too late to do anything about it."

## Concentrate: danger!

For his part, Alex Criville did not make a mistake, but his day was not exactly a party. "It is always difficult to maintain concentration here, because of the length of the Mistral straight (1100 metres.) I also knew there were a lot of Catalan spectators who had made the trip. I know the next race is at home and that I will not be alone there, as Carlos Checa is more on form than ever. That was a lot of reasons to be motivated."

Despite being beaten, Doohan had at least taken back the lead from Biaggi in the championship. However, he knew that the man who had been his main rival last season, until his bad crash at Assen, was now back and on top form. The four times world champion was careful with his words and

began by paraphrasing Massimiliano Biaggi: "Today my standard bike was not working properly. In these conditions it is impossible to fight off opponents with work bikes and special bits?" before taking on a far more serious tone: "My carburation was not perfect and I soon realised that I had no chance of winning."

Jacques Morelli: "it is possible to have two different compounds on the same carcass."
▽

## 125 cc

Practice was dominated by Noburu Ueda, despite a spectacular crash. At the start, his team-mate Lucio Cecchinello took the lead, while the young German Steve Jenkner never left the grid. Cecchinello leads the pack ahead of Ueda, Manako and "baby" Melandri. Pumped up in front of his home crowd, Frenchman Frederic Petit leads "his" grand prix on the fourth lap, the first time he had led a race, until Kazuto Sakata simply flies by the rest of the field on the Mistral straight, without any apparent need for a tow! The Japanese's Aprilia was evidently the quickest bike on the grid and his opponents had been warned. On lap seven, Ueda and Sclavini hit the deck. Now there are only five ahead as the race reaches half distance: Manako, Sakata, Azuma, Giansanti and Melandri. One lap later and they are down to four as Giansanti is a faller and on lap 17, Tomomi Manako, the championship leader, slows on the straight with gear selection problems. Three men will fight it out and as expected, Sakata made the most of his technical advantage.

*Frederic Petit in the lead of "his" grand prix and the day of glory has arrived!*
▽

▷
*Olivier Jacque: injured and heroic.*

## 250 cc

Once again the Aprilias straight aced qualifying, while the injured Olivier Jacque was heroic. Harada makes the best start and he is joined on lap two by Valentino Rossi. Loris Capirossi meanwhile has messed up his start and is down in fifteenth slot at the end of lap one. The race will now be played out on three levels. Firstly, Harada and Rossi leave everyone else for dead with a 6.446s lead after seven laps. Secondly, Jacque, Aoki, Ukawa and Perugini fight out the Honda Cup and thirdly, Loris Capirossi is climbing through the field. Ukawa falls on lap eight. On lap 17 of 29, braking for the Raccordement, Harada moves over to let Rossi through, but the Italian refuses to take the lead. Way ahead of the pack, these two have come to a virtual standstill, allowing Capirossi to sail past into the lead. But Loris soon loses ground as his tyres go off and Rossi pulls wheelies seven laps from the end. Harada is back in the lead and he will not let go.

## 500 cc

Hondas dominated practice, which was the cue for a surprising and stunning return from Luca Cadalora. Doohan took off in the lead, which does not happen too often, but he was unable to break away. In his wheel tracks were Alex Criville, Carlos Checa, Alex Barros and Max Biaggi, the world championship leader suffering from his fall the previous day and by John Kocinski. So by lap nine, there are nine of them covered by only 2.227s and this hard charging group was about to explode. To start with, Criville, who leads Doohan, Checa, Biaggi and Kocinski start to pull away. Then on lap 13 and 16, Biaggi and Kocinski touch on the pit straight and lose touch with the group. Now, only three are in the chase. It was plain to see that the NSR V4 No. 1 was by no means the quickest bike on the track and Alex Criville manages to fight off his two chasers, while Doohan passes Checa on a very heated last lap.

The return of Luca Cadalora to grand prix racing and in fine style at that. Fifth in qualifying, sixth in the race, best non-Honda rider on both counts, the Italian had fun at Le Castellet, where he replaced Jean-Michel Bayle who was still convalescing: "Wayne told me to go out there and have fun and I did. On Friday morning, I asked myself some questions after a seventh month complete break and as anyone who knows me will have guessed, an intensive training programme. I was most worried about travelling at high speed on this track where you go through the magic 300 km/h barrier. But after a few laps it was as though I had never been away."

The yellow card for Rossi. It is not the done thing to turn up on the podium dressed like a beach bum. Francesco Zerbi, the president of the International Motorcycle Federation (FIM) and Carmelo Ezpeleta, the boss of Dorna, the company which organises the grands prix, asked Aprilia to hand Valentino Rossi a warning letter, following his lap of honour minus leathers after the Italian Grand Prix. The warning read that: "Valentino Rossi must no longer behave in a manner which does not comply to the safety regulations!"

Noburu Ueda's injury. "Doctor Costa is pessimistic and as everyone here knows him well we can understand what that means." The world championship press officer, Roberto Nosetto did not need to say any more. With the radial nerve almost completely destroyed, Noburu Ueda was in serious trouble. This nerve allows the radius, the outermost of the two bones in the forearm to rotate around the wrist.

Clay Regazzoni pays a visit. The former F1 driver, Clay Regazzoni made a flying visit to the French GP paddock. He had come to the Castellet to study the hand operated braking system fitted to Mick Doohan's Honda, since the Australian's 1992 accident. The Swiss racer would love to adapt this system to the karts he is developing for the handicapped. He enjoyed the atmosphere in the paddock: "It is like Formula 1 used to be 30 years ago. I went up to Doohan whom I had never met before and

he explained it all to me. If I had wanted to do that sort of thing in the current F1 paddock, I would almost certainly have been told that the man I wanted was in a meeting."

The rise to power of Alex Criville. Thorn in the side of Michael Doohan over the past two years, Alex Criville finally leads the 500 championship classification. Even more significantly, it is the first time a Spaniard has ever been in this position and the first time since 1979 that a European has taken the lead off another European. Then it was Virginio Ferrari who came second in Venezuela and Austria to take the lead off Barry Sheene who had won in South America. This time it was Biaggi who was overhauled in the points.

### 22nd April 1973: Saarinen

By winning his first ever 500 grand prix at Suzuka, Massimiliano Biaggi took his place in the history books alongside the late Jarno Saarinen, the Finn who achieved the same master stroke on 22nd April 1973 at the first French GP to be held on the Paul Ricard circuit at Le Castellet. With the help of Moto Revue Number 2122, we glance back at that day.

For a trial run, it was a master stroke. The brand new liquid cooled Yamaha TZ4 was ridden by Jarno Saarinen to its first and crushing victory. What a race! It was years since we had witnessed such a fight in this category. "I had never seen riders looked so strained," commented Jean-Claude Olivier, the Yamaha importer.

### Eye to eye

Already in the last few seconds before the start, tension reigned on the track. On the front row, starinf at one another were the two heavies, Agostini and Saarinen, waiting for the ogf. The crowd was completely silent with anticipation. As the lights went off Ago tore off into the lead, but it would only last a few hundred metres, before the works Yamaha with Saarinen on board shot past to initiate a fantastic duel. Right from the opening lap, the best qualifying time, set by Kanaya on the other

TZ4 is beaten by Saarinen. Stuck to his rear wheel is Agostini, who chose to stick with the old three cylinder. Giacomo is visibly on the ragged edge and his style is rougher than usual as he literally drives the thing off its tyres and yet, he is gradually dropping back. By lap 8, Saarinen has a seven second lead and the drama unfolds. Agostini exceeds his own limits, as they say, or did it jump out of gear? Whatever, he falls at almost 150 km/h at the chicane after the Verrerie corner. Luckily hee comes out of it with two stitches to a thumb and badly wounded pride. From then it all went Saarinen's way. He even backed off a little and the 25 second lead he had over Read and Kanaya in the first part of the race would get smaller right down to the final lap.

It was the 22nd April 1973. One month later at Monza, Jarno's blue eyes and those of Renzo Pasolini would close for ever…

▷
*The unforgettable Jarno Saarinen.*

**Friday 29th May 1998**

125 cc: Lucio Cecchinello (Italy, Honda), Mirko Giansanti (Italy, Honda), Juan-Enrique Maturana (Spain, Yamaha), Noboru Ueda (Japan, Honda) and Gino Borsoi (Italy, Aprilia).

250 cc: Noriyasu Numata (Japan, Suzuki), Tohru Ukawa (Japan, Honda), Osamu Miyazaki (Japan, Yamaha) and Jeremy McWilliams (Great Britain, TSR-Honda).

500 cc: John Kocinski (United States, Honda), Nobuatsu Aoki (Japan, Suzuki), Regis Laconi (France, Yamaha), Matt Wait (United States, Honda), Fabio Carpani (Italy, Honda) and Sebastien Gimbert (France, Honda).

**Saturday 30th May 1998**

125 cc: Noboru Ueda (Japan, Honda), Kazuto Sakata (Japan, Aprilia) and Youichi Ui (Japan, Yamaha).

250 cc: Matthieu Lagrive (France, Honda, twice), Vincent Philipe (France, Honda).

500 cc: Sebastien Gimbert (France, Honda), Kenny Roberts Junior (United States, Modenas), Yukio Kagayama (Japan, Suzuki) and Massimiliano Biaggi (Italy, Honda).

**Sunday 31st May 1998**

125 cc: Gino Borsoi (Italy, Aprilia), Gianluigi Scalvini (Italy, Honda), Noboru Ueda (Japan, Honda) and Mirko Giansanti (Italy, Honda).

250 cc: Yasumasa Hatakeyama (Japan, ERP-Honda), Osamu Miyazaki (Japan, Yamaha), Tohru Ukawa (Japan, Honda), William Costes (France, Honda) and Noriyasu Numata (Japan, Suzuki).

500 cc: Eskil Suter (Switzerland, MuZ-Swissauto).

## Ouch!...

1. Noboru Ueda (bruising to and abrasions to little finger right hand, during practise. Fractured upper right arm with damaged radial nerve which was nearly completely destroyed. Operated on Sunday afternoon by Professor Prost in Marseille hospital where an attempt was made to rebuild it.
2. Regis Laconi (Bruising to right shoulder and elbow).
3. Fabio Carpani (slight arm injury).
4. Yukio Kagayama (Fractured left scaphoid, right wrist, bruising to right shoulder and wounded right hand).
5. Massimiliano Biaggi (injury to middle finger right hand, nail torn out and small fracture, bruising to left hip).
6. Matthieu Lagrive (injured little finger, right hand).
7. Gino Borsoi (bruised right hand, bruised little finger left hand, slight concussion).
8. Mirko Giansanti (small fracture to left foot).
9. Yasumasa Hatakeyama (injured right foot).
10. Osamu Miyazaki (badly fractured little finger of right hand, operated on Sunday afternoon at a hospital in Toulon).

## Non Starters...

1. Jose Ramon Ramirez (the Spaniard had a tendon operation. Replaced by Jeronimo Vidal).
2. Tadayuki Okada (result of fall in practise for Italian GP. Not replaced).
3. Doriano Romboni (result of fall in practise for Malaysian GP. Replaced by Eskil Suter).
4. Jean-Michel Bayle (result of fall in winter practise. JMB had again tried testing the day after the Italian GP (27 laps of Mugello) before giving up at the Grands Prix of France and Madrid. Replaced by Luca Cadalora).
5. Katsuaki Fujiwara (result of fall in winter practise. Replaced by Yukio Kagayama).
6. Yukio Kagayama (result of fall in practise).

## Retirements...

125 cc: Jaroslav Hules (Czech Republic, Honda, engine), Christian Manna (Italy, Yamaha, engine), Angel Nieto Junior (Spain, Aprilia, exhaust), Tomomi Manako (Japan, Honda, gear selector) and Emilio Alzamoro (Spain, Aprilia, seized).

250 cc: Johan Stigefelt (Sweden, Suzuki, blocked carburettor), Sebastian Porto (Argentina, Aprilia, spark plug), Luca Boscoscuro (Italy, TSR-Honda, seized) and Federico Gartner (Argentina, Aprilia, piston ring).

500 cc: Scott Smart (Great Britain, Honda V2, spark plug cap) and Alexandre Barros (Brazil, Honda V4, personal decision, after realizing he couldn't keep up a good enough pace, after a dozen laps).

△
*Mattieu Lagrive: the Castellet gravel is hard, very hard.*

◁
*Noboru Ueda: a bad fall and a pessimistic doctor. 100 days later...*

# Cadalora, the trump card

## 6. Jarama

▷
*Luca Cadalora within a gnats whisker of victory.*

**The return of Luca Cadalora after seven months of enforced rest was one of the big events of the French GP. Two weeks later on the Jarama track which was made to measure for the Yamaha, the Italian literally set fire to the 500 pack. This was what the ace of the pack had to say.**

"Saturday afternoon, after qualifying, I walked over to Doohan, I looked him in the eye and I said, we are too old to do this sort of thing. Can you imagine? At our age we should be sitting in a comfortable armchair, sucking on a pipe!" What type of thing was he talking about? Simply, fighting down to the last one hundredth of a second on a bumpy, slippery track which is also very demanding physically. During the fight, the pole went from Michael Doohan to Luca Cadalora and then back to Doohand.

### He plays with words

Back in business, Luca of Modena was happy to play with words and his answers to questions. Asked if, following his own recent experience, he would advise his fellow riders to do the same as him and take a long holiday, he replied with a straight face: "Why not? They have enough talent to come back at a pretty good level." At this point in the weekend, the two Spaniards, Alex Criville and Carlos Checa are still filled with wonder at the performance and domination of the two dinosaurs in the category. "After the French GP, I gave a lot of thought to what I had just been through," explained Cadalora. I tried to understand how and why I had come to feel so comfortable and competitive so quickly. Now I have the answer. The Yamaha is a very good bike, the team run by Wayne Rainey is excellent and these two elements when put together mean a good rider can win with this package." That was on Saturday, the day before the

race. The next day, with just four laps to go, Yamaha number 20, stopped with a broken engine. Luca Cadalora, who had temporarily been on top of it all was now walking back to his pit, frustrated that all the promise of this adventure had ended in a red herring.

## A simple tale

It was an achievement nevertheless, this return to form of the lad who had not sat on a racing bike for over 200 days. "The 1997 season was a terrible year for me and I think this long lay off did me the world of good, both physically and mentally. I had several offers this winter, but the only one I was keen on was the one from Wayne Rainey and Yamaha. Here, I joined up with Mike Sinclair again, the engineer with whom I had already worked back in the Kenny Roberts day. In fact I felt I was coming home."

For his part, Wayne Rainey was in sparkling form at this point in the season. At the French Grand Prix, one only had to see the way the two men looked at one another to see that, having been team-mates in 1993, when the three times world champion lost the use of his legs after his Misano accident, the boss of the official Yamaha team had just rediscovered the joy of racing again. "From the moment we got together again, Wayne told me to ride for fun, to think of myself and that is what I did. Of course, I had some doubts before getting back on the bike again, but everything came back to me quite quickly and my reflexes seem as good as ever."

## And afterwards?

Brilliant in the French Grand Prix and heroic at Jarama, where he felt victory was within his grasp, Luca Cadalora really lit up the pack, a bit like Massimiliano Biaggi a few months earlier, when he had dominated his first 500 GP in Japan. "I know the rules of the game and everything between me and my partners was very clear when I signed the contract. I know this Madrid Grand Prix might be my last of the season. After that? I will go home as the grass probably needs cutting. I might get back on the Yamaha in a few months, for some testing, maybe at Brno or elsewhere."

But maybe the Yamaha factory realised it could not get by without such a talent, such huge experience and knowledge. "If that's what you think, it makes me happy. You can rest assured that Wayne Rainey and the Yamaha bosses know where to find me when they need me."

It was Sunday evening in Madrid. Luca Cadalora, a cigarette between his lips ("I am making a big effort with my training and my smokes are less strong!") had just had an unforgettable weekend. The following Tuesday, the Italian was testing at Barcelona with "his" Yamaha, before getting on the Suzuki XR-88 on the Wednesday, a case of trying a new machine, setting on the way the quickest time of the test, equal with Carlos Checa, the Madrid GP winner. It was yet another chapter in the long career of Luca Cadalora.

The sequel, with some surprises in store? Just turn a few more pages for the answer.

*Party time in Madrid.*
◁

### 125 cc

Kazuto Sakata had dominated practice and there were fears of another Aprilia one man show from the Japanese rider. Luckily, for the spectators, it would not be the case and right from the start, the Hondas dictated the pace, with Azuma. Locatelli, Cecchinello and Giansanti. On the third lap, Gainsanti and Cecchinello had a 859 thousandths lead over their pursuers. Things were about to get busy: Azuma fell on lap 14, Alzamora's engine let go on 18, Locatelli retired on lap 20 after a fall. Three men were now fighting for victory and a handkerchief covered all of them. As they crossed the line for the 24th time, there is only 110 thousandths separating Giansanti, Manako and Cecchinello. It will not last. At the last corner of the 25th and penultimate lap, Manako falls as his engine siezes, Giansanti cannot miss him and Lucio Cecchinello is all alone at the front. The Italian, so unlucky at times, celebrates his first win at the age of 29 and it is also his first podium finish!

### 250 cc

Honda brought along some new parts for its riders, but Aprilia or to be specific, Loris Capirossi, still dominated practice. At the start, Harada is the first away, taking with him, Rossi, McWilliams, Ukawa, Jacque and Capirossi. Rossi crosses the line in the lead at the end of the second lap and it starts to get exciting. Capirossi gets McWilliams at the first braking point and he hits the back of Olivier Jacque's bike, knocking him over. The Italian meanwhile keeps going through the sand trap. A few yards further on, it is Numata who is the faller and at the same moment, Rossi loses control of his front wheel. It is only the start of lap 3, but the race seems run already. By lap 9, Harada and Ukawa have a 5.507s lead over the pack and the main point of interest is the progress of Loris Capirossi, who had started last and is already seventh. The Italian catches the mid-grid pack, Harada pulls away from Ukawa and the the podium is sorted.

A first podium finish and a win at that: Lucio Cecchinello richly deserved a lap of honour alongside team mate Kikuchi.

### 500 cc

On Saturday evening after qualifying, everyone is hoping that for the sake of the race and the championship, that Michael Doohan will not be too dominant. He had done in practice along with Luca Cadalora and he had scored important psychological points over his two Spanish rivals, Carlos Checa and Alex Criville. It had an even greater effect on Massimiliano Biaggi who is desperately trying to find the right gear ratios for his NSR. Is the race won before it starts? Right from the first corner, the opposite was true. Biaggi leans on Doohan who falls after being hit by Crafar, while a few yards later, Barros eliminates Kocinski. The rest of the race would be a treat, thanks to the pressure applied by Luca Cadalora, acrobatics from Alex Criville, who rides across the gravel trap having missed his braking point, Nobuatsu's performance on the Suzuki and finally, the duel between Carlos Checa and Norifume Abe. It was an infernal sight full of strong emotions. The Madrid GP certainly marked a turning point in a championship which was becoming ever more exciting.

Checa ahead of Criville and Spain wins.

△
*Angel Nieto now has "his" corner at Jarama.*

and we must treat them as such. We were too easy going and obviously this has not worked. The time has therefore come to change. Our president, Ivano Beggio and chief engineer Jan Witteveen have explained to our three riders how we expect them to behave in future." Thus spoke Aprilia's press officer, Matilde Tomagnini after the French GP. This was the reaction of Graziano Rossi, father and manager of Valentino world champion. "I don't think Vale can change and even less that he is willing to do so. Harada took him for a clown, which he is not. Everything about him is spontaneous and I hope he will stay that way for a long time to come."

New parts from Honda. New heads, crankshaft and bodywork. Honda finally reacted in the 250 class, bringing in a host of new parts for the works teams.

A corner for Nieto. The "Farina" corner (the right hairpin before the climb) on the Jarama track now carries the name "12 + 1" in honour of the thirteen world titles held by Angel Nieto. RACE (Royal Automobile Club d'Espagna) the owners of the Madrid track chose to honour Angel the Great. The Madrid City Council had plans for Jarama which included building a brand new track complex, but maybe not on the same site.

Jarama was a sell-out. 55,000 tickets were on sale and they were all sold, making the second of the three Spanish grands prix a great success. On Sunday morning, the motorway from the centre of Madrid to the Jarama circuit was under the control of officers of the law and if you did not have a ticket, a U-turn was the order of the day.

Biaggi in the Nino Jesus hospital. On Thursday afternoon, Massimiliano Biaggi and a few of the top Spanish riders (Alex Criville, Carlos Checa, Luis D'Antin, Emilio Azamora and Angel Nieto Junior) visited the Nino Jesus children's hospital in Madrid. By the time Biaggi made it to the paddock at Jarama, it was already half-time in the Italy v Chile game in the World Cup. "You can always record a match and watch it later, but children who are suffering are worth a live visit!"

Repsol renews contract for three years. HRC's main sponsor in the 500 cc class, the Spanish oil company Repsol, extended its contract with Honda for a further three years: "with a minimum of two and maximum of four riders next year."

Aprilia riders get a talking to. "We made a big mistake in the past, treating our boys like normal people. In fact, they are racers

▷
*Graziano Rossi: "I hope Vale will always be as spontaneous…"*

△
*Alexandre Barros in 1993,
Adu Celso-Santos
twenty years earlier. Brazil wins
at the gates of Madrid.*

### 1973 and 1993: Long live Brazil!

Incredible but historically true: a Brazilian has only twice been on the top rung of the podium in world championship races. Nothing special about that you might say, but by winning the FIM 500 GP on 26th September 1993 at the Jarama track, Alex Barros joined Adu Celso-Santos, winner of the Spanish 350 GP here at this track twenty years earlier.

Flashback. 23rd September 1973, the motorcycle world championship ends with Phil Read taking the 500 cc honours. On the Madrid track of Jarama, where four years earlier RACE had organised the first Spanish GP, for the first time ever a Brazilian rider, Adu Celso-Santos wins a grand prix with his TZ Yamaha.

A few pages further on in the photo album, we come to the Spanish GP of 4th May 1986, again at Jarama. A young lad, not yet 17, has falsified his identity papers to get an interational license and take part in his first 80 cc grand prix. He is called Barros, Alexandre Barros. He was born in Sao Paulo and carries the passion of his countrymen in his eyes.

26th September 1993, 20 years after Celso-Santos' historic first and a few yards from the track, on the topmost step of the podium, a young man of 24 tries to hold back the tears. Alex Barros has finally won his first grand prix. The mistakes of Jerez and Assen, where he looked set to win, are forgotten. This time Barros' performance has been faultless. "I soon realised I would have to look after my tyres. Cadalora, then Itoh and Kocinski fell because of this. I tried to concentrate on not making the same mistake." Little Alex was having difficulty finding the right words. On the tallest flag pole flies the green, yellow and blue flag. A few Brazilians are crying, all say thank you. Obrigado, as they say. End of flashback.

Organised as a replacement for the Yugoslav GP, the 1993 FIM GP had been the last race held at Jarama until this 1998 Madrid GP, put on the calendar when the Portuguese race fell through. On this 14th June, Barros would finish a lowly ninth, after making a bad tyre choice.

## Friday 12th June 1998

125 cc: Federico Cerroni (Italy, Aprilia), Sebastian Perello (Spain, Honda), Lucio Cecchinello (Italy, Honda) and Angel Nieto Junior (Spain, Aprilia).

250 cc: Ismael Bonilla (Spain, Honda), Ivan Clementi (Italy, Yamaha), William Costes (France, Honda), Yasumasa Hatakeyama (Japan, ERP-Honda), Alex Debon (Spain, Aprilia) and Takeshi Tsujimura (Japan, Yamaha).

500 cc: Kenny Roberts Junior (United States, Modenas KR3), Sebastien Gimbert (France, Honda) and Matt Wait (United States, Honda).

## Saturday 14th June 1998

125 cc: Lucio Cecchinello (Italy, Honda), Masao Azuma (Japan, Honda), Youichi Ui (Japan, Yamaha) and Gino Borsoi (Italy, Aprilia).

250 cc: Sebastian Porto (Argentina, Aprilia), Haruchika Aoki (Japan, Honda), Takeshi Tsujimura (Japan, Yamaha) and Franco Battaini (Italy, Yamaha).

500 cc: none.

## Sunday 15th June 1998

125 cc: Lucio Cecchinello (Italy, Honda, warm-up), Arnaud Vincent (France, Aprilia), Masao Azuma (Japan, Honda), Federico Cerroni (Italy, Aprilia), Gino Borsoi (Italy, Aprilia, restart), Jeronimo Vidal (Spain, Aprilia), Roberto Locatelli (Italy, Honda, restart), Tomomi Manako (Japan, Honda) and Mirko Giansanti (Italy, Honda).

250 cc: Alex Debon (Spain, Aprilia), Luca Boscoscuro (Italy, TSR-Honda), Olivier Jacque (France, Honda), Noriyasu Numata (Japan, Suzuki, restart), Valentino Rossi (Italy, Aprilia), Haruchika Aoki (Japan, Honda) and Jeremy McWilliams (Great Britain, TSR-Honda, restart).

500 cc: Michael Doohan (Australia, Honda), John Kocinski (United States, Honda) and Matt Wait (United States, Honda, restart).

## Ouch!...

1. Kenny Roberts Junior (fractured fifth metatarsal of left foot with injured cuboid bone).

2. Sebastian Perello (dislocated left clavicle).

3. Sebastien Gimbert (fractures to third, fourth and fifth metatarsals of left foot, fractured right hand).

4. Franco Battaini (fractured right radius).

5. Federico Cerroni (bruising and abrasions).

6. Jeronimo Vidal (bruising and abrasions).

7. Alex Debon (bruising and abrasions).

8. Olivier Jacque (bruising and abrasions).

9. Michael Doohan (partial fracture to radius of left fore-arm).

10. John Kocinski (serious wound to little finger of left hand. Wounded left foot).

## Non Starters...

1. Noboru Ueda (result of fall in French GP. Ubi underwent an operation in Marseille before going back to Japan. He spoke to team-mate Lucio Cecchinello by phone on the eve of Madrid GP practice. Ueda had not lost hope of coming back before the end of the season. Replaced by Hiroyuki Kikuchi.)

2. Jose Ramon Ramirez (result of operation to arms. Replaced by Jeronimo Vidal).

3. Osamu Miyazaki (result of fall in French GP. Replaced by Ivan Clementi).

4. Tadayuki Okada (result of fall in Italian GP. Not replaced).

5. Katsuaki Fujiwara (result of fall during winter practise. His replacement, Keiichi Kitagawa had to scratch after falling in practise for French GP. Not replaced).

6. Doriano Romboni (result of fall in practise for Malaysian GP. Replaced by Eskil Suter. The Spaniard Gregorio Lavilla tested the MuZ-Swissauto after the French GP, but he did not get permission from his superbike boss - the Flammini group, which promotes the championship, finances the De Cecco team and enters Lavilla! - to take part in the Madrid GP.)

7. Jean-Michel Bayle (result of fall during winter testing. JMB did some more tests at Le Castellet after the French GP. The former motocrosser did 87 laps with a best time of 1.23.00, which would have placed him 15th on the grid of the French GP.) Replaced by Luca Cadalora.

8. Kenny Roberts Junior (result of fall in practise).

9. Sebastien Gimbert (result of fall in practise).

10. Franco Battaini (result of fall in practise).

## Retirements...

125 cc: Christian Manna (Italy, Yamaha, gearbox problem), Ivan Goi (Italy, Aprilia, front tyre) and Emilio Alzamora (Italy, Aprilia, fuel supply).

250 cc: William Costes (France, Honda, went off the track), Stefano Perugini (Italy, Honda, comes into pits complaining about his Honda engine) and Sebastian Porto (Argentina, Aprilia, electrical problem).

500 cc: Juan Bautista Borja (Spain, Honda, result of a coming together), Jurgen Van den Goorbergh (Holland, Honda, gearbox) and Luca Cadalora (Italy, Yamaha, crankshaft).

*Sebastien Gimbert: "Where am I?"* ▽

# Melandri, only 15 and already a winner!

▷
*Marco Melandri and Kazuto Sakata: the "baby champion" is going to beat the more experienced man.*

**By winning the Dutch Grand Prix at Assen on 27th June 1998 at the age of 15 years, ten months and 20 days, Marco Melandri became the youngest ever winner in the history of the world championship. The Italian works Honda rider is the Benetton figurehead and without doubt a motorcycle racing phenomenon.**

Like the gnarled veteran he is not, Marco Melandri had the last word in his incredible last lap tussle with Kazuto Sakata. How can a 16 year old be so mature? How to explain the Melandri phenomenon? Simply by meeting him and letting him talk. "From the age of four, I was racing mountain bikes. In 1988, I won the Italian championship and the next year I was runner up in the European series. I also did some world cup races before moving up to mini-bikes in 1990."

### With Reggiani's number 13

Then, one day in 1994, Marco Melandri threw his leg over a "real" racingmotorbike. "A few years ago, my father had competed in the Aspes trophy, a promotional championship running at that time in Italy. He was racing against Loris Reggiani and we stayed in touch. In 1994, Loris was helping a young rider in the Italian production-sports category and we went to see a test session at the Magione circuit. I tried to get on the bike, but I could not reach the pedals. So we had to raise the brake and gear levers and that's how I went on a proper track for the first time. That day, Melandri lapped as quickly as Reggiani's nominated driver.

The experienced Loris realised this was an unusual talent. From then on the two men would work together and Marco Melandri was more than happy to adopt the lucky number 13, so dear to his mentor. "Thanks to him, I got into motorcycle racing and thanks to him, I have got to where I am today. Loris organised the link with Benetton and Matteoni and he still advises me on what to do to this day."

### At Benetton

He certainly needed a cool head, when at the age of 15 he found himself outside the door leading to the office of the larger than life personality of Alessandro Benetton. "I could not believe it when I was shown into Mr. Benetton's office. You know, in Italy he is a big man, a real name!"

Today, Marco Melandri is a winner and what surprises observers the most is his maturity and his race craft. Has he got a secret? To be honest I don't know. I certainly don't go though any special psychological preparation," says Melandri with a laugh. Everything I do comes naturally. Then, I do try and ignore all the attention that is focussed on me. Of course, it is nice to be famous, but I am not so keen on it when people come up to me just as I am going out on the track. Having said, I think it is always good to be recognised in this game." A winner after just one year in grands, prix, Marco Melandri is already a

star. "Compared to last year in the European championship, I am far more aggressive on the track. I have also improved in terms of my technical knowledge and my riding. Tactically, I can comfortably analyse what is going on and what I can do in the last few laps, as well as trying to work out what the opposition will do. In fact, I have developed a good idea of how it all comes together."

## Marco and school

He might be a brilliant rider, but Melandri did not shine at school, at least when it came to his studies. "I have just had to repeat my second year at the professional institute of industrial studies. The problem is simple; I never have time to catch up with my studies in between the races. I do not have time to get up to date with the work, hence I am always rowing with the head. But some of my teachers are very nice, especially if I give them a T-shirt or poster."

Marco is always smiling, but during the conversation he suddenly got more serious when talking about his parents. "Since I started racing, my father has done nothing but drive the motorhome around and complain each time he has to wash it in the paddock. My mother died of an incurable disease when I was only four years old and I don't remember her very well. At the time, my father was racing in the Italian 250 championship."

Marco Melandri evidently does not want to say much more about this part of his life he regards as private. "When I crossed the finish line, I saw my life flash before my eyes in a just a few seconds. But already, I can no longer remember these images and everything is unclear in my mind." Over there, Massimo Matteoni sheds tears of joy: the name of Ivan Goi has just been removed from the record books!"

*Massimo Matteoni and Melandri: the moment of triumph.* ▽

◁
*Rossi: first 250 win.*

## 125 cc

Kazuto Sakata once again dominated practice and Mirko Giansanti makes the best start. But Marco Melandri took only three laps to catch the leader, lock onto his rear wheel as the two men cleared off into the distance. Behind them, the group of six - Tokudome, Giansanti, Locatelli, Sclavini, Cecchinello and Petit. Manako is a long way back having messed up his start as well as suffering with a slipping clutch. Scalvini is a faller on lap nine when Sakata-Melandri have a 5.644s lead. It will therefore all come down to the last lap. "Baby Melandri" attacks first, Sakata passes him before being caught out for a second time under braking for the chicane. History has been made as Melandri, 15 years, 10 months and 20 days had just experienced the sweet taste of success.

## 250 cc

Aprilia wins, Aprilia loses as the Italian machines are the talk of the paddock right from the start of practice, just 464 thousandths of a second covering the top three factory riders with Capirossi in the lead. Olivier Jacque is first away, with Stefano Perugini and Jeremy McWilliams, who has come from the fourth row of the grid, right behind. The Englishman was about to be penalised with a stop-go for having jumped the start. Capirossi and Rossi make the most of the Aprilia's power advantage to leave the Hondas for dust. By the time Tetsuya Harada pulls away from the pack on lap 3 and the three black arrows are out ahead, separated by 812 thousandths. On lpa five, Perugini crashes heavily into Jacque, who is injured once again. After a catastrophic start because of an ignition failure, Fuchs starts coming up through the ranks when Aprilia sees its first sign of trouble when Harada's engine seizes. Six kilometres later, Loris Capirossi suffered a similar fate, leaving Rossi alone out in front with a 22 second lead. Fuchs is back up there and finishes second with just one lap to go, giving Aprilia the double.

▷
*Michael Doohan does not like Assen, but he wins all the same.*

## 500 cc

Michael Doohan does not like the Assen track, but in order to master it better, he always grabs the bull by the horns, ever since his serious accident here in the 1992 GP. So on Saturday, in the final qualifying session, the four times world champion pulled off an incredible feat. The session had been red flagged after Ralf Waldmann crashed, his machine caught fire and several airfences were damaged. Once running again there was only 2m 12. left. Taking around 2.06 to do a flying lap, Doohan, followed by Abe, Barros, Biaggi and Checa have only just enough time to get across the line before the chequered flag. Doohan somehow managed to set a sort of superpole which had not been expected. In the race, the Aussie made the perfect getaway, leading Abe, Barros, Biaggi and Crafar. Cadalora drops his Suzuki on lap 10 and the end of the race is kept buzzing by Max' constant attacking runs and the resistance put up by Doohan the master. What this means for the championship is that Biaggi is back in the lead ahead of Doohan, Criville and Checa.

Valentino Rossi:
orange hair and
good reading.

Randy Mamola:
"Any teams looking
for old riders?"

The record set by Marco Melandri. By winning a grand prix at the age of 15 years, 10 months and 20 days, he becomes the youngest ever winner in the history of the world championship. The previous record had stood since the 4th August 1996 and was held by his compatriot Ivan Goi, who won the Austrian GP at the age of 16 years, 5 months and 6 days.

Wayne Rainey says farewell. "I want to go back home to Monterey. I have to think of my son Rex, who is going to start school. I have to think of my wife, Shae. I also have to think of my body, which is taking a pounding with all this travelling. At the end of the season I will retire from the role of team manager." On the eve of first practice for the Dutch GP, Wayne Rainey officially said goodbye to racing, even though he will continue as a consultant to Yamaha for the foreseeable future.

Luca Cadalora's new colours. Following his brilliant qualifying in Barcelona, Luca Cadalora signs a two race contract (Assen and Donington) with Suzuki. A faller in the very first session and knocked out of the race, Luca was not very successful. "The bike was handling very well at Barcelona, but here at Assen, it is impossible to ride it normally and it goes straight on at all the corners." Following this sorry tale, Cadalora decided not to bother with pursuing the Suzuki experience.

The return of Jean-Philippe Ruggia. Seven years after his last 500 GP and 18 months after his very last GP of any kind. France's Jean-Philippe Ruggia was back in the saddle, at the controls of a the MuZ-Swissauto. "Once I had got out of my Bimota contract and then the Suzuka deal fell through

because of Cadalora, I was able to get used to riding a bike again with fifty odd laps at Barcelona." There as well, things did not go to plan, Ruggia forced to stop after a few laps, complaining of vibrations from the front end. His temporary employers were of the opinion he simply was not fit enough to race a GP bike.

Valentino Rossi's orange hair. "Tino" certainly does not miss an opportunity and as the Dutch GP was taking place during the World Cup, he turned up at Assen with stunning bright orange hair. "Firstly because I like it and then because it's cool!" Carlos Checa, on the other hand, went blonde in the Netherlands.

Randy Mamola's joke. The scene is the Wayne Rainey garage on Thursday morning. Randy Mamola turns up in leathers, puts his lid on the bike which should be ridden by Jean-Michel Bayle and slips onto the Yamaha, much to excitement of the photographers present. A few minutes later, after Luca Cadalora had fallen, Mamola, still in leathers, rushed to the Suzuki pit to offer his services to Gary Taylor. "I hear you are keen on hiring the old boys, well here I am!"

Another set of leathers
in the Luca Cadalora collection.

## 30th July 1955 - The strike

It was the fiftieth 500 Grand Prix and for this its twenty fifth running, the Dutch Grand Prix was being held on a brand new circuit. It should have been a fantastic event. Instead, it was a time of tension as the privateers had gone on strike. They were complaining, quite rightly, that they were not being paid enough. The result of this action was that at the end of the season, thirteen riders were given a six month ban and four others received a four month penalty.

Six months suspension for the Australians Jack Ahearn, Robert Brown, Keith Campbell and Tony McAlpine, the Irishmen, Reginald "Ray" Armstrong, and Bob Matthews, the Englishmen, Peter Davey, Geoff Duke, Rob Fitton, Paul Heath and Eric Houseley, as well as New Zealanders John Hempleman and Chris Stormont. Four months was the ban for Italy's Giuseppe Colnago, Umberto Masetti, Alfredo Milani and Federico Flahaut. You did not mess about with the sporting authority back in the fifties. How had it come to this? Take a trip down memory lane thanks to issue 1,251 of Moto Revue.

"Bringing together all the categories, this Dutch Grand Prix was affected by some incidents in the 250 class and even more so the 350 cc. In the quarter litre race, Lomas was first across the line, was demoted to second, having failed to stop his engine when he pitted to take on fuel. He is the victim of an incomprehensible ruling which is not to be found in the International Sporting Code, which carries at the top of the list of punishments: a reprimand (private or public,) a fine, exclusion, suspension and disqualification. Nowhere does it mention losing one place. Lorenzetti and H-P Muller appealed against this irregular decision to the International Jury, but on hearing the evidence, the appeal was thrown out.

At the end of the first lap in the 350 race, 12 riders came back into the paddock as a protest to the organisers who they felt had offered insufficient start money. A similar protest, which included riders like Duke and Armstrong, nearly took place in the 500 class, but the organisers agreed to the competitors' demands and the race started as planned."

In a strange twist of fate, it was at Assen, thirty years later that IRTA, the GP teams' organisation, was created to defend the interests of the actors on the Continental Circus.

▷ Geoffrey Duke: the most famous of those "punished" at Assen.

▷ *Cadalora and Suzuki: the end of a love story which ended in hate.*

### Thursday 25th June 1998

125 cc: Wilhelm Van Leeuwen (Holland, Honda) and Andrea Iommi (Italy, Honda).
250 cc: Federico Gartner (Argentina, Aprilia), Johan Stigefelt (Sweden, Suzuki) and Jeremy McWilliams (Great Britain, TSR-Honda).
500 cc: Luca Cadalora (Italy, Suzuki), Matt Wait (United States, Honda) and John Kocinski (United States, Honda).

### Friday 26th June 1998

125 cc: Roberto Locatelli (Italy, Honda) and Harald De Haan (Holland, Honda).
250 cc: Jurgen Fuchs (Germany, Aprilia) and Osamu Miyazaki (Japan, Yamaha).
500 cc: Tadayuki Okada (Japan, Honda), Scott Smart (Great Britain, Honda), Nobuatsu Aoki (Japan, Suzuki) and Ralf Waldmann (Germany, Modenas KR3).

### Saturday 27th June 1998

125 cc: Gianluigi Scalvini (Italy, Honda).
250 cc: Olivier Jacque (France, Honda), Stefano Perugini (Italy, Honda) and Jose Luis Cardoso (Spain, Yamaha).
500 cc: Luca Cadalora (Italy, Suzuki) and Juan Bautista Borja (Spain, Honda).

### Ouch!...

1. Federico Gartner (fractures to 2nd and 3rd metacarpals).
2. Matt Wait (injured left knee).
3. Johan Stigefelt (bruised right shoulder).
4. Jeremy McWilliams (Injury to third finger, left hand).
5. Tadayuki Okada (injured right ankle, bruised left knee).
6. Jurgen Fuchs (bruised right knee).
7. Nobuatsu Aoki (bruising to buttocks and left hip).
8. Ralf Waldmann (bruising to left side, fractured right wrist).
9. Osamu Miyazaki (fracture to radius of right wrist).
10. Olivier Jacque (re-opened wound sustained at Mugello to heel of right foot, fractures of 2nd, 3rd, 4th and 5th metatarsals of right foot).

### Non Starters...

1. Noboru Ueda (result of fall in French GP. Replaced by Hiroyuki Kikuchi).
2. Franco Battaini (result of fall in practise for Madrid GP, replaced by Ivan Clementi.)
3. Doriano Romboni (result of fall in practise for Malaysian GP. Replaced by Jean-Philippe Ruggia, who, at Barcelona, tried the MuZ-Swissauto for the first time on the Monday before the Dutch GP, doing 52 laps - about 200 kilometres).
4. Sebastien Gimbert (result of fall in practise for Madrid GP. Replaced by Bernard Garcia).
5. Katsuaki Fujiwara (result of fall during winter practise. Replaced by Luca Cadalora).
6. Jean-Michel Bayle (result of fall during winter practise. JMB, who had taken part in new tests in Barcelona after the Madrid GP, still suffers from headaches. Wayne Rainey advised him to do more training, on a cross bike, before making a decision. Bayle thus delayed his return once again. He was not replaced.
7. Federico Gartner (result of fall in practise).
8. Ralf Waldmann (result of fall in practise).
9. Osamu Miyazaki (result of fall in practise).

### Retirements...

125 cc: Emilio Alzamora (Spain, Aprilia, fuel supply), Christian Manna (Italy, Yamaha, loss of power) and Yoshiaki Katoh (Japan, Yamaha, piston).
250 cc: Tetsuya Harada (Japan, Aprilia, engine) and Loris Capirossi (Italy, Aprilia, engine).
500 cc: Jean-Philippe Ruggia (France, MuZ-Swissauto, vibration problems at the front end according to the rider, rider problems according to Swissauto boss Urs Wenger,) Sete Gibernau (Spain Honda, rear tyre) and Norifumi Abe (Japan, Yamaha, engine).

# Crafar springs a surprise

▷
*Simon Crafar was unbeatable at Donington.*

**Question: Which 500 rider from the Pacific area can dominate practice at a GP and be head and shoulders above the rest, before dominating the race and being the boss of the pack, regularly taking half a second a lap off the opposition? The usual answer this last decade has been Michael Doohan. But at the 1998 British GP at Donington, the correct answer turned out to be Simon Crafar from New Zealand.**

Dunlop's Grand Prix chief, Jeremy Ferguson was beside himself. Less than 100 kms from Fort Dunlop, where the race tyres are developed and built, here was Simon Crafar securing the company's first 500 win in a long time. Better still, the Kiwi has just ridden the perfect race, giving Yamaha its first win of the season.

### "Thank you everyone"

This is not the usual post-race conference full of platitudes. Like a groom who does not know which aunt he is supposed to thank first at a wedding, he is almost lost for words. "Thank you everyone. Thanks to those who opened the door for me once again to get into grands prix after my stint in superbikes. Thank you Yamaha, thank

you Dunlop. A bit later, like all winners of major events that demand respect, he also thanked his mother and father who ensured he saw the light of day on 15th January 1969, in Waiouru, New Zealand.

What is the new winner really like as a person? Quite simply, he is a straightforward lad who came to Europe in 1992 having stood on virtually every podium in the southern hemisphere. First off, he was a privateer in 500. He impressed everyone when he switched to the 250 class with Suzuki, after the Japanese company fell out with John Kocinski when he deliberately blew the engine on his RGV on the slowing down lap of the Dutch GP.

After this first stint of grand prix racing, Simon Crafar turned his hand to the world superbike championship, where this time he was a works rider, first with Rumi, with Honda then at Kawasaki for the past two years.

### "In a state of shock"

"After my win at Donington, it might have looked as though I was calm, but it wasn't true at all. I was very excited, almost mad, but I could do nothing. It was as though I was in a state of shock." Once over the emotion, Simon Crafar regained the power of speech. Quiet in real life and not very

chatty in the paddock, here he was explaining his progress and his first impressions of riding the 500s with a factory team. "The important thing is to work very hard, to do a lot of training and to only have one idea in your head - to win. The modern 500s are very light and very powerful. In superbikes, a lot of riders can get 100% out of their machines, but in 500s not one of us can say we manage it every time during the course of a season. That is where the main difference lies between these two types of bike." On that day at Donington, he, Simon Crafar was the only one to get the maximum out of his bike, the Yamaha YZR500, which was back on top again. "Compared to last year, most of the work has been done in the area of suspension and the tyres. In England, the Dunlops worked perfectly. But to be really honest, I think I could have won on other brands of tyre. Today, the YZR is a very good machine, that does not need

much doing to it. We must therefore continue to work on all areas, the most important being the cycle parts and the tyres."

## The winning example

The main point is that where Scott Russell and Anthony Gobert failed in switching from superbikes to 500s and at a time when John Kocinski is struggling, although in his case it is different as he has already succeeded in grands prix and at a high level, Simon Crafar is today, the symbol of success. He is the bridge head between the superbike championship and the grands prix. Of course the New Zealander took his first steps in the world championship riding two strokes. "Today, it is hard to say which superbike rider could rapidly make the switch to 500s. Personally I rate Noriyuki Hagi very highly and I think he could be a serious player. But as I have said before, the bikes are too different to risk making predictions. A star without a

world superbike win and a star now that he had won a grand prix, is Simon Crafar the star of tomorrow? Is he ideal for the new four stroke formula, which is set to replace the current 500s? "Of course the move to another format would not upset me, but with one condition: that the power to weight ratio of the current 500 is retained, because that is what makes the category so great and the 500s so fantastic to ride. They are totally different to anything else and they must absolutely retain their exclusive character."

*All the determination of a single minded man.*
▽

△
*Simon, the surprise.*

Donington Park
THE GRAND PRIX CIRCUIT

△
*Loris Capirossi was the best
of the Aprilia bunch in England.*

## 125 cc

Having battled with Melandri at Assen, this time Sakata found Giansanti in his way. Having set fastest time in qualifying the man from Japan made a complete mess of his start. Melandri gets it all wrong braking for the hairpin and so the race was set to be played out at different levels. At first Manako and Ui had it all their own way with a 1.821s lead over the pack by lap six. Next up, Sakata starts racking up the fastest laps to get up to third on lap 7. Then the shape of the race changed as Manako was a faller, leaving Giansanti out in front ahead of Sakata. They led Ui, who miraculously missed Manako, by 3.389s. Finally, the chasing pack catches up, especially the German Steve Jenkner, who is about to pay for his enthusiasm. Victory is now a two way struggle between Giansanti and Sakata and on the last lap, the Italian puts it beyond doubt.

## 250 cc

Nothing new on the 250 front; the Aprilias are still on a different planet with their three works riders monopolising the first three places on the grid, ensuring the race is an Aprilian affair. Harada gets the best start ahead of Rossi, Perugini and Aoki, although these last two are not going to last long, and Capirossi. Harada and Rossi have a small lead of 964 thousandths by lap two, but the Assen winner is not to finish as he crashes in spectacular fashion. Harada is out in front on his own, but Capirossi will catch up on lap 6 and one lap later, the Italian flies past. The two black arrows have a 19.224s lead over the three riders fighting it out for honours in the "Honda Cup" - Aoki, Ukawa and Perugini. Capirossi leads his team mate by 804 thousandths on lap 18 but Harada takes the lead with three laps remaining. On the penultimate lap, both men set their quickest laps and then, incredibly, as they start the downhill section, Harada makes a sign, Capirossi goes round the outside, the Japanese tries to hang on but something is not as it should be on the championship leader's machine. One recalcitrant spark plug and Harada struggles home as best he can and saves second place.

△
*Steve Jenkner:
a crazy charge
through the field
which would end badly.*

## 500 cc

Practice was marred by several falls and it ended with a first ever pole position for Simon Crafar, who was going really well since Dunlop came up with a brand new tyre. Would Doohan be able to take his revenge in the race? Right from the start, the Yamahas were running the show, with Abe doing a Wayne Rainey style opening lap and pulling out a 791 thousandth of a second lead. Crafar and Doohan caught the Japanese rider on lap three and at this point Crafar proved to be the boss, taking the lead on lap 5 of the 30 lap race before giving himself an impressive lead, pulling out seven or eight tenths per lap. Everything seems settled. Alex Criville closes on Max Biaggi, who had made a bad tyre choice and passes him on lap ten. Doohan has shaken off Abe and all eyes are on the fight for the minor places, between Barros, Biaggi and Criville. Crafar wins and Doohan is back in front in the championship, while Criville has made the best of a bad job.

▷
*Smile*

**Simon Crafar's first win.** After Massimiliano Biaggi in Japan, a new name appears on the list of 500 grand prix winners, that of New Zealand's Simon Crafar. He is the first rider from the world superbike series to make his mark in the 500 GP in recent years, but not the first ever as Michael Doohan had won the two Australian legs of the SBK world championship in 1988 at Oran Park, before switching to 500s.

**Carlos Checa's accident.** The winner of the Madrid GP had a serious fall in free practice on Friday morning. He got up unaided and got back to his motor home, before making the trip to the mobile medical centre where Doctor Claudio Costa immediately diagnosed an internal haemorrhage. Transported to the Queen's Hospital in Nottingham, Checa was apparently out of danger on Sunday morning, when a blood clot formed at the back of the brain. In the space of a few hours, Checa lost his sight and use of his right hand. The worst fears were calmed however, when the clot was reabsorbed in the night of Sunday to Monday.

**Presentation of the South African GP.** It's official; for the next five years, a South African GP will be part of the world championship on the new Welkom circuit in the Free State province in the middle of the country. The track, 4,200 metres in length will be part of an ambitious complex which will notably include an Indy-style oval. Present at Donington, the Free State Minister for Sport, Mr. Webster Mfabe, that the democratically elected government led by Nelson Mandela had set itself various challenges: "Around 20,000 jobs, most of them for blacks were lost when the gold mines were closed. It is therefore the duty of the government to bring in some dynamic policies for this region. We are not looking for a direct profit but we need to create an economic impact."

**Luca Cadalora's job hunt.** Luca Cadalora's freelancing at Suzuki did not last and on the eve of the Dutch GP, the Italian decided to give up. Luca sped off to make a new offer to Yamaha. He was met with the usual politeness, but the company with the three tuning forks for a logo were less than happy with his treachery after the Madrid GP. The result was that Cadalora watched the British GP on television, at home in Modena.

**Biaggi's victory over Doohan.** On Thursday before the British GP, Max Biaggi beat Mick Doohan at the traditional "Day of the Champions" organised for Riders for Health. Max' leathers were auctioned for the incredible sum of 3,900 pounds, while Mick's suit of lights went for a hundred pounds less. An English banker had bought both sets on a day when total sales netted a record 20,000 pounds and total profit for the event, including admission tickets, topped the 50,000 mark.

*Biaggi: Is he really more popular than Doohan?*
▽

Donington Park
THE GRAND PRIX CIRCUIT

### 31st July 1992: Wayne Gardner

The Donington park circuit has been on the championship calendar since 1987 and it has seen several great premieres, such as Wayne Rainey's first 500 GP win in 1988 and Loris Capirossi's first 125 win in 1990. It has also been the scene of some emotional farewells, none more so than that of Wayne Gardner just before the 1992 British GP.

Two chairs set behind a table, Wayne Gardner has just got time to sit down and take his sunglasses off. His wife Donna steps out of the team bus and collapses in tears in the arms of her husband. The 1987 world champion is also crying, his face streaming with tears. He fiddles with his glasses, sits down and tries to explain; "It's very difficult," he says as his voice cracks with emotion. "I think Donna will speak for me," says Gardner. The blonde by his side is shaking all over. Her nerves have suffered enough over the past five years, those years when "Crocodile" Gardner racked up the falls and the injuries. "When I broke my leg yet again in Japan, I really asked myself what I was doing there. Too much, it was too much. I want to stop while I am still in one piece, even though I know nothing in the world can beat the 500 grands prix." The muscles in Gardner's face twitch. Donna throws him a look of tenderness, admiration and thanks. She knows it is for her sake he has taken this decision. He still wants to race but he knows what he has to do. At Donington tomorrow, and in Brazil and South Africa a month from now, Wayne Gardner will try and add to his total of grand prix wins, 17 of them in the 500 class. Right to the bitter end, "Crocodile" will use all his teeth to help savour the sweet taste of motorcycle racing at its highest level. He wants to bite hard into the apple, even though he knows the worm is always there somewhere. A great career, a major career will end in a month.

That was the 31st July 1992. Two days later on the 2nd August, Wayne Gardner would make it to the top rung of the podium for the very last time, after a strange race where a patch of oil would catch out Schwantz, Chandler and Fogarty.

*Wayne Gardner and Erv Kanemoto: the last win.*
▽

# fallers

◁
Tomomi Manako trips up, Kazuto Sakata slips by: has the 125 title just been decided?

## Friday 3rd July 1998

125 cc: Ivan Goi (Italy, Aprilia), Masao Azuma (Japan, Honda, twice), Youichi Ui (Japan, Yamaha), Juan Enrique Maturana (Spain, Yamaha), Federico Cerroni (Italy, Aprilia), Marco Melandri (Italy, Honda), Arnaud Vincent (France, Aprilia) and Leon Haslam (Great Britain, Honda).

250 cc: Jurgen Fuchs (Germany, Aprilia), Paul Jones (Great Britain, Aprilia), Julien Allemand (France, Honda), Yasumasa Hatakeyama (Japan, ERP Honda) and Jose Luis Cardoso (Spain, Yamaha).

500 cc: Carlos Checa (Spain, Honda), Fabio Carpani (Italy, Honda), Alex Criville (Spain, Honda), Fernando Cristobal (Spain, Honda) and Eskil Suter (Switzerland, MuZ-Swissauto).

## Saturday 4th July 1998

125 cc: Leon Haslam (Great Britain, Honda), Jeronimo Vidal (Spain, Aprilia), Marco Melandri (Italy, Honda), Lucio Cecchinello (Italy, Honda) and Masao Azuma (Japan, Honda).

250 cc: Luca Boscoscuro (Italy, TSR-Honda), Noriyasu Numata (Japan, Suzuki), Davide Bulega (Italy, ERP Honda), William Costes (France, Honda), Gary May (Great Britain, Aprilia) and Ivan Clementi (Italy, Yamaha).

500 cc: Fernando Cristobal (Spain, Honda) and Juan Bautista Borja (Spain, Honda).

## Sunday 5th July 1998

125 cc: Roberto Locatelli (Italy, Honda), Christian Manna (Italy, Yamaha), Jeronimo Vidal (Spain, Aprilia), Tomomi Manako (Japan, Honda) and Steve Jenkner (Germany, Aprilia).

250 cc: Paul Jones (Great Britain, Aprilia, twice/warm-up & race), Luca Boscoscuro (Italy, TSR-Honda), Noriyasu Numata (Japan, Suzuki, restart), Valentino Rossi (Italy, Aprilia), Ivan Clementi (Italy, Yamaha), Jurgen Fuchs (Germany, Aprilia), Gary May (Great Britain, Aprilia).

500 cc: Matt Wait (United States, Honda), Sete Gibernau (Spain, Honda) and Garry McCoy (Australia, Honda, restart).

## Ouch!...

1. Carlo Checa (internal bleeding which required urgent surgery at the Queen Mary Hospital in Nottingham, where his spleen was removed).
2. Jurgen Fuchs (concussion and bruising to both hands).
3. Masao Azuma (multiple bruises from two falls on Friday, bruising to little finger of left hand from Saturday's fall).
4. Marco Melandri (bruising to right hip on Friday, bruising to left foot on Saturday).
5. Arnaud Vincent (bruised left heel).
6. Leon Haslam (bruising to both heels).
7. Alex Criville (bruised right knee).
8. Eskil Suter (small fracture to left wrist).
9. Yasumasa Hatakeyama (bruising to right foot).
10. Jose Luis Cardoso (left shoulder injury)
11. Luca Boscoscuro (bruised right buttock during practise, fractured left wrist and fractures to 2nd, 3rd and 4th metatarsals of left foot in warm-up).
12. Noriyasu Numata (bruising to little finger of left hand).
13. Davide Bulega (bruising and lacerations to left shoulder).
14. Juan Bautista Borja (dislocated left shoulder, dislocated ring finger of left hand).
15. Tomomi Manako (cut to little finger of left hand).

## Non Starters...

1. Noboru Ueda (result of fall in French GP. Replaced by Hiroyuki Kikuchi).
2. Osamu Miyazaki (result of fall in practise for Dutch GP. Replaced by Jamie Robinson).
3. Olivier Jacque (result of fall in Dutch GP. Replaced by Julien Allemand. In the Tech 3 team, William Coste is back on Jacque's NSR.)
4. Franco Battaini (result of fall in practise for Madrid GP. Replaced by Ivan Clementi).
5. Federico Gartner (result of fall in practise for Dutch GP. Replaced by Gary May).
6. Tadayuki Okada (fractured both wrists at Mugello and a badly sprained right ankle at Assen, he decided on Friday morning to give up on the British and German GPs to save himself for the Suzuka 8 Hours. Not replaced.)
7. Doriano Romboni (result of fall in practise for Malaysian GP. Replaced by Eskil Suter. After just one GP (five laps) Jean-Philippe Ruggia threw in the towel. Just hours before the start of the Dutch GP, he asked for double his retainer from the MuZ-Swissauto team, if he was to continue.)
8. John Kocinski (result of fall in Madrid GP, or to be more precise, because he dashed off to the States just before the Dutch GP. Kocinski is replaced by Juan-Bautista Borja in the Sito Pons team. The Spaniard's place with Shell Advance Racing is picked up by Fernando Cristobal, who was already entered in the Madrid GP on a wild card.)
9. Ralf Waldmann (Result of fall in practise for Dutch GP. Not replaced.)
10. Sebastien Gimbert (result of fall in practise for Madrid GP. Replaced by Bernard Garcia.)
11. Jean-Michel Bayle (result of fall during winter practise. Not replaced....Yamaha refused to employ Luca Cadalora.)
12. Katsuaki Fujiwara (result of fall during winter practise. Not replaced because Yukio Kagayama was also injured while Luca Cadalora threw in the towel after the Dutch GP.)
13. Carlos Checa (result of fall in practise).
14. Juan Bautista Borja (result of fall in practise).
15. Davide Bulega (result of fall in practise).
16. Luca Boscoscuro (result of fall during warm-up).

## Retirements...

125 cc: Masao Azuma (Japan, Honda, bad tyre choice), Yoshiaki Katoh (Japan, Yamaha, water pipe) and Jaroslav Hules (Czech Republic, Honda, clutch).

250 cc: Sebastian Porto (Argentina, Aprilia, chain stretched on the parade lap, then he had a broken sprocket in the warm-up lap).

500 cc: Eskil Suter (Switzerland, MuZ-Swissauto, broken valves on the first lap, then he gave up because he was in pain after his practise fall) and Kenny Roberts (United States, Modenas KR3, engine).

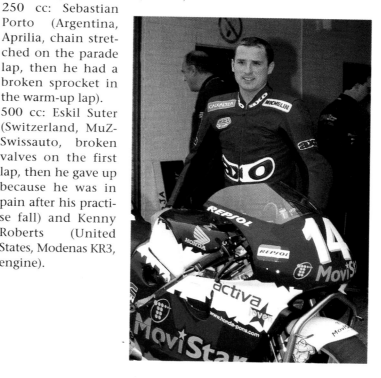

△
*Juan Borja: a golden opportunity which came to an end on Saturday evening.*

Donington Park
THE GRAND PRIX CIRCUIT

# Love and kisses from Sax!

△
*Ralf Waldman,
the people's hero.*

**With 140,000 spectators in three days it was a real show of enthusiasm. The first GP to be held on the new Sachsenring was a total success, even if not all the 500 riders appreciated the layout of the German track.**

Ever since Bernie Ecclestone had got interested in motorcycle grands prix, at the time when it looked as though it could pose a threat to his F1 empire in some countries, Germany had reacted with a show of force. The last grands prix at Hockenheim had been boycotted and there was a complete lack of interest in going to the Nurburgring set in the remote Eifel mountains and the promoters all had the same worries.

### The big idea.

So, an idea was born. There were hundreds of thousands of people who loved machinery and were racing fans in the former East Germany, a country with a fine engineering tradition, which had been stamped on by the soviet authorities.

While there was a big pool of spectators, the problems arose as those East German Trabant drivers, once they had made the long journey and stayed in modest accommodation, could no longer afford the cost of the admission ticket.

Therefore if the spectator could not afford to go to the big event, the big event would come to the spectator. The rebuilding of the Sachsenring made this possible and over two months before the German GP, available tickets for the Sunday had been sold.

### Contrasts

As the world championship returned to the former East Germany, it was a journey of discovery for everyone, filled with contrasts. Purpose build modern factories sat uneasily next to gigantic old production plants, which looked in danger of collapsing at any moment.

This time warp can be seen in this meeting between two race fans at the paddock entrance of the new Sachsenring. "An original 1939 MZ, " recounts one of them proudly and convincingly, while standing next to a large bike, obviously built some time after 1950, which has aged as badly as its owner. "I've got one of Luca Cadalora's wet suits," says his neighbour, his watery eyes and sickly breath reminding one that since the collapse of the wall and the job market, many spend their unemployed hours drinking alcohol of less than convincing provenance.

"Everyone has worked"

The two men are delighted to have got an audience prepared to listen and thus continue: "Have you seen what we have managed to do? Everyone has worked, even at weekends, just so you can have this circuit," said one, before turning bitter. "We have not got any passes to get in and we won't see any of the action all weekend." Then they are on their way; one leaning on his MZ, the other on his wife. For the whole weekend, watching the racing as they try and pick out riders they recognise, they would have dug out that old cardboard box, full of all the old programmes, passes and photos of the good old days, when the Sachsenring could draw crowds of a quarter of a million spectators.

### Striking contrasts

For today's visitor it is time to pass through the entrance to the paddock. Time to forget the DDR and the communist regime and to be back in a unified Germany which dreams of reviving the people of the East. The Sachsenring offers a tortuous

track with climbs and descents, surrounded by hills and giant grandstands which, on the day of the race, accommodated 64,000 spectators.

A miracle? The Saxe Land government had invested 10 million D Marks in November 1997, which gave life to the project which took just a month to come to fruition in the shape of a circuit as modern as any other.

## The Mayor is a Green!

There is one estonishing aspect of the Sachsenring revival. The Mayor of Hohenstein-Ernstthal, a community of 15,500 souls which borders the track, is a Green. He insisted that all activities taking place on the track have some educational impact in terms of improving road safety in the area.

According the agreement between the authorities and the ADAC Sachsen, who have the sporting authority in the area, they can organise three sporting events per year; the motorcycle GP, a German national motorcycle meeting and a round of the German touring car championship. Three meetings, three popular successes. The place definitely deserves another GP and it is not too unpopular with most of the riders of the apparently too powerful 500 V4s! As the final result was Doohan ahead of Biaggi, Criville and Barros, the twisty track can hardly be said to have upset the equilibrium of the sport.

*A fabulous atmosphere at the new Sachsenring.*
▽

### 125 cc

Marco Melandri was head and shoulders above the rest, taking the first pole of his career. The track reminded him of his mini-bike days and the young Italian was going to prove his intelligence, up to the final lap that is! To start with, he tried to get away on his own with a 1.807s lead by lap four. Sakata, the championship leader is way down in seventh spot. Then, he lets Manako and Sakata catch up and the three men play cat and mouse for a while with only 191 thousandths separating them on lap 22 of 29. On lap 25, Melandri feels the game has gone far enough. He takes the lead and steps up the pace to leave everyone for dead. Sakata tries too hard and falls two laps from home when eighth. But then pushing hard, the unbelievable happens and Melandri highsides it out of the race in spectacular fashion. Manako is back in the lead, with European champion, Arnaud Vincent picking up second place and with it his first podium.

▷
Doohan also
has fans
in Germany.

◁
Arnaud Vincent:
a surprise podium.
What talent!

### 250 cc

As he leaves the paddock on Saturday evening, Aprilia's chief engineer Jan Witteveen is in a good mood. "The track is not as big a disaster as some German newspapers would have had us believe." The three works Aprilia riders plus Sebastian Porto have just given the Italian company another complete front row. Harada makes the best start to the race, ahead of Rossi and Perugini. Very soon, HRC is to lose two of its pieces when Ukawa touches Perugini, sending both of them crashing out. Three Aprilias are already out in front, Porto falls, Aoki retires, while Costes is fighting it out at the back of the pack. One third distance and Honda has no works runners left. However, at the commands of his standard TSR, its Jeremy McWilliams whos catches the Rossi-Capirossi duo, before taking second place in two acts by passing Rossi on lap 19 and Capirossi one lap later.

### 500 cc

At the end of practice, it seemed that the four times world 500 champion was suffering a bad case of nerves. Three mistakes in qualifying and unable to make the right tyre choice, Michael Doohan was sulking at this point in the weekend, criticising the track: "Which has no place on the world championship calendar." Max Biaggi on the other hand was having a rare old time. "It will be a very tough race physically and I am ready for it." There were reasons to feel the world championship could be thrown open again. It was not to be, for the simple reason that Mick Doohan is too strong. Best start, a perfect first lap with a 708 thousandths lead over Max Biaggi, the Australian did not get rattled when Alex Barros took the lead on lap 5. On lap 10, the order was Doohan ahead of Barros, Crafar, Biaggi and Roberts Junior, who were all scrapping behind the leader. It was all too easy. Crafar was a faller on lap 12 and Doohan's lead was 2.587s. Criville passes Roberts for fourth place on lap 16, while Doohan extends his lead to 3.458s. Criville disposes of Barros on lap 23 and Biaggi understood the master was unbeatable that day and was too strong. The Number One now has a twelve point lead in the title race.

The return to the former East Germany. 140,000 spectators over the three days, or over four times as many as at the last few German GPs at the Nurburgring. Going East had been a total success.

Marco Melandri's first pole position. After his first GP win, the Dutch, the young Italian scored his first pole position at the Sachsenring. "I felt as though I was back on one of those mini-bike tracks where I had spent the last few years."

Ralf Waldman's gift. Against the advice of the directorate of his national party, the Green mayor of Hohenstein-Ernstthal, Erich Homilius authorised the reconstruction of the Sachsenring training centre, turning it into a GP circuit. Son of a former racer, Mister Mayor only wanted one thing: "That our community be worthy of hosting such an event." He succeeded and German hero Ralf Waldman made the most of it by offering the man his race suit, which was to have pride of place in the fine Sachsenring museum.

Carlos Checa goes home. A faller in the first free practice session for the British GP and post-operative complications when a blood clot formed on the brain, Carlos Checa was back home in Spain. A wall of over 1000 fans was there to greet him. "I have just fought a no holds barred fight with death. I had reached the limits of my life and I did not have the experience to fight it. Faith, illusions, hope and and the will to live helped me get rid of that damned clot," declared the Madrid GP winner.

Kocinski's ultimatum. John Kocinski was not in Germany. Movistar team boss Sito Pons even put out an ultimatum. "Our next test is on 15th and 16th August on the Catalunya circuit and if John does not show up, he can go back to California and stay there." We all know how it ended.

Valentino's license. Reigning 125 champion and winner at Assen of his first 250 grand prix, Valentino Rossi made the most of the four week gap between the German and Czech races to finally pass the test and get his motorcycle license!

A visit from Ueda. Seriously injured at the French GP, there were fears he would permanently lose the use of his right arm, the Japanese rider Noboru Ueda made a return to the paddock at Sachsenring. Smiling as usual "Nobby" with his right arm still immobile, made the most of his visit to see Dr. Claudio Costa. "Looking at the situation as it stands, I am convinced that Noboru will regain all his movement, even if it is too early to talk about a return to competition."

◁ Noboru Ueda is back in the paddock and is all smiles.

△ Waldmann: a gift for Mr. Mayor.

Jack Findlay was a racer in the Seventies. Now is the GP technical director.

### 1971: The anthem of Dieter Braun

"We had so many worries with the machinery that we had no time to take any interest in what was going on in the other categories." Jack Findlay, the permanent technical directort at the grands prix was reminiscing. "I only remember one thing about that day in 1971: the wind of change had blown across the Sachsenring."

What was it all about? Having just won the 250 cc GP, the West German, Dieter Braun had just posed a serious problem of protocol for the East German organisers. A privileged observer at the time was the photographer Frank Bischoff. The Party had ordered the race director, Hans Zacharias, to find some reason to disqualify Braun for having ridden over a white line at the side of the track. Zacharias had refused and the "federal" anthem had to be played. To avoid a riot, only the loud speakers on the start-finish line had been left on while the military and the police with dogs formed a cordon to maintain order. Tomatoes and stones rained down and out in the surrounding forest, heavily armed soldiers were ready to join in!

### "One of my favourites"

Today, a few hundred metres of this legendary track are still used; a track where Bill Ivy and James Guthrie were killed. "After Francorchamps, the Sachsenring was my favourite track," recalls Jack Findlay. "It's a bit surprising as nothing about the place was like anything I had seen in my native Australia. Of course, when you walk round the old track today, you get the impression that danger was ever present, but all the tracks were dangerous in those days if you look at them with today's standards in mind. The most remarkable thing about this place is how friendly the locals are and their passion for racing."

A moment of silence and the look in Findlay's eyes show he is lost somewhere in the Saxe forests, in that descent where a plaque commemorates James Guthrie. "It was my favourite section, flat out between two rows of trees. You came out of the forest and attacked the long uphill left hander which led to the finish line."

### Friday 17th July 1998

125 cc: Masaki Tokudome (Japan, Aprilia), Maik Stief (Germany, Yamaha), Lucio Cecchinello (Italy, Honda) and Federico Cerroni (Italy, Aprilia).

250 cc : Julien Allemand (France, Honda), Adrian Schmidt (Germany, Honda), Stefano Perugini (Italy, Honda, restart) and Yasumasa Hatakeyama (Japan, ERP-Honda).

500 cc: Nobuatsu Aoki (Japan, Suzuki), Gregorio Lavilla (Spain, Honda), Ralf Waldmann (Germany, Modenas KR3, restart) and Bernard Garcia (France, Honda).

### Saturday 18th July 1998

125 cc: Maik Stief (Germany, Yamaha) and Youichi Ui (Japan, Yamaha, restart).

250 cc: Ivan Clementi (Italy, Yamaha, restart), Tohru Ukawa (Japan, Honda), Roberto Rolfo (Italy, TSR-Honda), Mike Bellinger (Germany, Honda), Jurgen Fuchs (Germany,

Aprilia), Haruchika Aoki (Japan, Honda), Sebastian Porto (Argentina, Aprilia) and Yasumasa Hatakeyama (Japan, ERP Honda).

500 cc: Sets Gibernau (Spain, Honda, restart), Norifumi Abe (Japan, Yamaha, twice, gets back on second time), Gregorio Lavilla (Spain, Honda), Michael Doohan (Australia, Honda) and Scott Smart (Great Britain, Honda).

### Sunday 19th July 1998

125 cc: Frederic Petit (France, Honda), Ivan Goi (Italy, Aprilia, restart), Gianluigi Scalvini (Italy, Honda), Jaroslav Hules (Czech Republic, Honda), Jeronimo Vidal (Spain, Aprilia), Youichi Ui (Japan, Yamaha), Gino Borsoi (Italy, Aprilia), Mirko Giansanti (Italy, Honda), Kazuto Sakata (Japan, Aprilia, restart) and Marco Melandri (Italy, Honda, restart).

250 cc: Haruchika Aoki (Japan, Honda), Federico Gartner (Argentina, Aprilia, twice, warm-up and race), Adrian Schmidt (Germany, Honda), Stefano Perugini (Italy, Honda), Tohru Ukawa (Japan, Honda), Sebastian Porto (Argentina, Aprilia), Johan Stigefelt (Sweden, Suzuki), Ivan Clementi (Italy, Yamaha), Mathias Neukirchen (Germany, Aprilia) and Markus Ober (Germany, Honda).

500 cc: Sets Gibernau (Spain, Honda), Norifumi Abe (Japan, Yamaha) and Simon Crafar (New Zealand, Yamaha).

### Ouch!...

1. Julien Allemand (fracture of right clavicle and of radius at right wrist).
2. Lucio Cecchinello (twisted right clavicle, cut to cervical spine).
3. Jurgen Fuchs (broken left ankle).
4. Yasumasa Hatakeyama (fractures to 4th and 5th metatarsals of right foot, injured left arm).
5. Frederic Petit (Fracture to 5th Dorsal vertebrae).
6. Jaroslav Hules (general bruising).
7. Jeronimo Vidal (general bruising).
8. Kazuto Sakata (injured right kneecap).
9. Marco Melandri (slight fracture to right ankle, injured scaphoid at right wrist, torn muscles).
10. Federico Gartner (new fracture of left hand).
11. Stefano Perugini (cut to cervical spine).

### Non Starters...

1. Noboru Ueda (result of fall in French GP. Replaced by Hiroyuki Kikuchi).
2. Osamu Miyazaki (result of fall in practise for Dutch GP. Replaced by Jamie Robinson).
3. Olivier Jacque (result of fall in Dutch GP. Replaced by Julien Allemand,

4. Franco Battaini (result of fall in practise for Madrid GP. Replaced by Ivan Clementi).
5. Tadayuki Okada (having broken both wrists at Mugello and badly twisted his right ankle at Assen, the Japanese
6. Doriano Romboni (result of fall in practise for Malaysian GP. Replaced by Eskil Suter).
7. Carlos Checa (result of fall in practise for British GP.
8. Jean-Michel Bayle (result of fall during winter practise. Replaced by Kyoji Nanba).
9. Juan Bautista Borja (result of fall in practise for British GP. Replaced by Fernando Cristobal).
10. John Kocinski (result of fall in Madrid GP.
11. Katsuaki Fujiwara (result of fall during winter practise. Not replaced because Yukio Kagayama was also injured and Luca Cadalora threw in the towel after the Dutch GP).
12. Sebastien Gimbert (result of fall in practise for Madrid GP. Replaced by Bernard Garcia).
13. Lucio Cecchinello (result of fall in practise).
14. Julien Allemand (result of fall in practise).
15. Jurgen Fuchs (result of fall in practise).
16. Yasumasa Hatakeyama (result of fall in practise).
17. Frederic Petit (result of fall in warm-up).

### Retirements...

125 cc: Masao Azuma (Japan, Honda, conrod)

250 cc: Haruchika Aoki (Japan, Honda, broken rear brake caliper) and William Costes (France, Honda, gave up).

500 cc: Scott Smart (Great Britain, Honda, broken rear wheel nut), Sete Gibernau (Spain, Honda, rear suspension) and Garry McCoy (Australia, Honda, rear tyre).

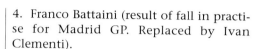

△
*Stefano Perugini (4) and Tohru Ukawa go for a high speed waltz which is not quite under control.*

# Biaggi back with a bang

Four Sundays off in a row, right in the middle of the season. Such a long break was unheard of. How would everyone have coped with the time off? Would the return to work bring with it some surprises? These were the questions on everyone's lips on arrival in Brno. Four days later, on a wet Monday morning, everyone knew the answer; Massimiliano Biaggi had just done it to the Max!

"No way was I going to have a real holiday. I kept my mind firmly on the job, as I know that if I am to worry Doohan, now is the time to strike." Rather than heading for the beach, Biaggi got on with his job. Two days at Brno, immediately after the German GP and two more days at Barcelona. "We learnt a lot in testing without being hurried along by a lack of time," said Biaggi as he arrived in Brno. Michael Doohan knows that his position at the head of the championship is quite comfortable with a 12 point lead. However, he also knows that one slip up and he will have to start all over again. Worse for him was that the previous week, he was stung by a wasp while out training on his mountain bike. An apparently innocent incident, but it had some physical consequences.

### The stage is set

The stage is set for a duel royal. On Friday, right from the start of free practice, the two kings and adversaries begin their fight for the top. In the first act, Massimiliano Biaggi ruled. He took pole position very early in the session and as the time ticked by and his opponents or more accurately his opponent caught up, Max would go out to improve his time. The first result of

this sequence of events is that the Brno lap record took a pasting. On Saturday, the two men continued to rule the roost but the balance of power had changed as Mick Doohan had not appreciated the way things had gone until then, even though he showed no sign of nerves.

Biaggi played with him on the track and now it was Doohan's turn as a new act began. The morning's free practice session was held on a cold track, which still showed the odd sign of the previous night's storm. In these conditions, the majority measured the risks and backed off. The majority, but not all, as Doohan was determined to take on the King of Rome. He was the only one to get near the 2m 02s barrier and it was a warning of things to come.

What followed was superb stuff. The sun came out and so did both men at the same time. Doohan sends his NSR into an incredible slide and leaves a rubber "comma" mark on the track. Biaggi can only watch

▷
*Massimiliano Biaggi:
his second 500 win.*

Flowers and champagne
and the championship
comes to life.
◁

# GRAND PRIX

# Brno 1998

## The Number One's mistake

and lose his concentration and fall, although no damage is done. Qualifying has just been decided and at eight minutes and forty seconds past three o'clock, Michael Doohan becomes the first man to dip under the 2m 02s barrier at the Czech track.

### The Number One's mistake

On 22nd August 1998, there is a feeling in the air that history is in the making, after Michael Doohan taught Massimiliano Biaggi, who had dominated the first day, a lesson in qualifying. "Do you realise," said someone in the paddock, "that even with two no-scores (broken crankshaft in Japan and a fall at Jarama) it is impossible to beat Doohan over the length of a season as he is just too strong."

But one should not forget that the season is not over until after the last race and that a race is never won until the chequered flag. That even the best, the biggest can get it wrong when taking the turns at an average speed of over 160km/h.

Errors are costly and Doohan makes one right at the very first corner of the race, going into the long tortuous climb at this superb track. Biaggi leads with Barros behind him and the four times world champion has realised he must not let his rival get away. Barros is dealt with but the front wheel of Honda number 1 starts to slide and slide and slide too much. Doohan hits the deck in the gravel trap on his back. He gets up, jumps on the bike and gets going again. He is a long way behind Biaggi who is getting messages about his rival's progress.

### To the bitter end

It is like the start of another race with Biaggi in front and Doohan behind in 22nd place. Then he is 20th and 19th, like a diligent student who has worked out that points, any points might be worth their weight in gold later in the year. How far can he go? Not very is the answer. On lap 13 of the 22, he parks his bike in the pits. When he fell, one of the exhaust pipes was twisted and had burnt the carbon fibre seat. It's over. It is his third race with no points and Massimiliano Biaggi is back in the lead of the world championship.

Winning look
▽

Marco Melandri
knows how to party.

## 125 cc

The very small gaps in qualifying promise a very exciting race and so it turns out with at least half a dozen different leaders, including France's Arnaud Vincent, who had been the revelation of the German GP. While Sakata takes the lead at the start, a gaggle of 14 riders is all covered by just 2.765s on lap 4. The lead changes and there are retirements at the back. Youichi Ui takes the lead with his Yamaha on lap 12 and the Japanese rider tries to make a break for it. Two laps later he has a 1.788s lead and the race looks run. However, Ui makes a mistake. Manako retires with gear selection problems, Azuma leads and sets an amazing record, before he too is a faller. This leaves Marco Melandri out in front, the youngest winner in the history of the sport, fighting off the demented attentions of Sakata.

Tetsuya Harada
and Marcellino
Lucchi. Aprilia still
as dominant
as ever.

## 250 cc

With Fuchs still injured after his fall in practice for the German GP, the Aprilia factory calls on the veteran 41 year old Lucchi to stand in for him. He rides a 1999 evolution model painted in Docshop colours. With four works Aprilias attacking practice it looks like the Italian machines are going to have the front row to themselves, even though Honda has reacted with some technical changes, including moving the side radiators forward and a new steering arm. Aprilia is going to win, but will it be with Capirossi who seems on great form at Brno, or maybe Rossi, who is upset that the Italians seem to have forgotten about him, or maybe Lucchi? Wrong on all counts, as it is Testsuya Harada who gets the job done. It was soon decided. Perugini and Rossi touched on the first lap and the winner of Assen was eliminated. By lap 6, the three remaining Aprilias have a lead of 6.859s over the best of the Hondas, but Harada steps up the pace. Lucchi is the first to give up the chase before Capirossi is also forced to admit he is beaten.

## 500 cc

Biaggi got straight down to business, dominating Friday practice. On Saturday, the paddock wakes up to find the results of an overnight storm and Doohan scores the equaliser, with best time in free practice and pole position and a new lap record in the afternoon, changing the position of dominance. It will be an exciting race. Biaggi and Barros make the best starts, Doohan passes the Brazilian in the long climb of the Czech track on tyres which had not yet reached their full operating temperature. He tries to surprise Biaggi, but the result is a fall and although Doohan rejoins, he is forced to pull out before the end of the race as his seat has melted through contact with a bent exhaust pipe, as a result of the accident. Biaggi only needs to get to the flag without making any mistakes. He fights off Alex Barros, then the attentions of Tadayuki Okada and a determined Alex Criville. The Italian's performance is faultless even if he gives everyone a terrible fright, putting his Honda into a vertical wheelie that is almost his undoing. Doohan is now only third in the championship.

Max Biaggi seizes the initiative. A third no-score for Michael Doohan and a second win for Massimiliano Biaggi: the 500 championship is wide open again, with five races to go to the end of the season.

Aprilia's all too evident domination is beginning to get on Jacque's wick. It is making the racing a trifle dull, but it is a tremenous tribute to the work of Jan Witteveen and his team at Noale. Jacque is fed up with Aprilia's clear superiority in the 250 class and he even asked if he could pack up before the end of the season, in order to have an operation on his foot, which is still giving him problems, but this request is refused by the Tech 3 team's principal sponsor.

Almost full house in the 500s. Apart from Doriano Romboni, the 500 class has finally shown its true face at Brno, with Jean-Michel Bayle's first GP of the season and also the first appearance of the named driver for the second works Suzuki, Katsuaki Fujiwara. Absent in Germany, Checa, Kocinski and Okada were also back in action.

Michael Doohan's sting. It happened in the Principality of Monaco, ten days before the GP. While out training on his mountain bike, Doohan was stung on the throat by a wasp. He had a serious allergic reaction and the whole of his upper body and his left arm swelled up alarmingly. He was rushed to the Princesse Grace hospital to be checked over. Doohan lost consciousness for a moment when he was asked to breathe deeply for an X-ray and the poor man cracked open his left eyebrow when he suddenly collapsed. The end result was three stitches and Doohan quickly signed himself out of the place.

The new Modenas KR3. With a balance shaft to reduce vibrations, new ignition, a completely revised engine design, the two rear cylinders face upwards with a double exhaust under the seat, the front cylinder points downwards - the second generation Modenas KR3, made its debut at Brno. Ralf Waldman tried it at Donington before this ordeal by fire, other tests having been carried out in the States on the Thunder Hill and Willow Springs circuit. After a few tentative laps on Friday, the new Modenas had to be kept home on Saturday suffering from problems of adolescence in the crankshaft area.

A new look paddock. 27 pits to the very highest standards, improved access for the team transporters; the Brno circuit is being modernised, even if not quite all of it is finished. So the upper level of the new building will not be ready until 1999. It will house a new media centre as well as around twenty hospitality units for VIP guests.

△
The new Modenas makes its debut. After Friday's practice it was put back in the truck.

△
Jean-Michel Bayle is back in business.

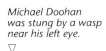

Michael Doohan was stung by a wasp near his left eye.
▽

◁ New look paddock.

# looking back

### 26th August 1989: Herreros

The 80cc category had replaced the 50cc class, which had run since 1962, at the start of 1984. It was stopped at the end of the 1989 season, one year after a new technical regulation was introduced, featuring 125cc single cylinder engines. Ths sports governing body felt that two "tiddler" classes was one too many and so the "coffee cup" class was dispensed with, taking with it a few tuning geniuses. On 26th August 1989, at Brno, the Spaniard Manuel Herreros would thus enter the history books, winning the last ever title in that category.

"I was following with my arms crossed. I was watching and waiting. But I was no longer in control of my own destiny." The Swiss Stefan Dorflinger with four world championships and all the experience that entails, got off his red and white Krauser while a smile played across his lips.

Mathematically, he could still be the 80cc world champion, the last one in the history of the small category. However, there would be no miracles at Brno.

No miracles, but a fantastic race with plenty of emotion and the crowning of Manuel Herreros or "Champi" as he was known to the Spaniards. Herreros was actually beaten to the chequered flag by his compatriot, Torrontegui, but all eyes were on the batt-le for second place, which would decide the world championship. The race brought together all the elements necessary to make it a classic: emotion, team orders with Martinez riding for his team-mate Manuel Herreros and finally, the drama of Peter Ottle, the young baby-faced German, who saw all his hopes disappear just two kilometres from the end of the 1989 world championship. The front wheel of his Krauser suddenly slipped away and he had a long slide, luckily getting up uninjured, apart from the more serious damage of a broken heart. It had been his crazy dream and he had almost become world champion.

Torrontegui had been quickest off the line ahead of Martinez and Herreros. On lap five of thirteen, Ottl caught the two Spanish Derbis, taking Herreros on several occasions, leaving him with just Martinez to deal with. A battle royal ensued during which the reigning world champion gave his heart and soul to the battle of helping his number two, Manuel Herreros, who was to succeed him.

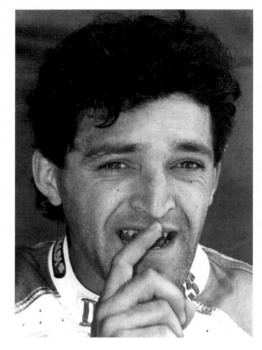

△
*Manuel Herreros, "Champi" was the last ever 80cc class world champion.*

◁
*Youichi Ui: it looked as if victory was his.*

## Friday 21st August 1998

125 cc: Mirko Giansanti (Italy, Honda), Masao Azuma (Japan, Honda), Bohuslav Seifert (Czech Republic, Honda), Roberto Locatelli (Italy, Honda), Youichi Ui (Japan, Yamaha) and Yoshiaki Katoh (Japan, Yamaha).
250 cc: Johan Stigefelt (Sweden, Suzuki) and Luca Boscoscuro (Italy, TSR-Honda).
500 cc: Jurgen Van den Goorbergh (Holland, Honda) and Kenny Roberts Junior (United States, Modenas KR3).

## Saturday 22nd August 1998

125 cc: Jaroslav Hules (Czech Republic, Honda), Andrea Iommi (Italy, Honda), Gino Borsoi (Italy, Aprilia) and Hiroyuki Kikuchi (Japan, Honda).
250 cc: Yasumasa Hatakeyama (Japan, Honda, twice), Jose Luis Cardoso (Spain, Yamaha) and Radomil Rous (Czech Republic, Yamaha).
500 cc: Massimiliano Biaggi (Italy, Honda), Juan Bautista Borja (Spain, Honda) and Carlos Checa (Spain, Honda).

## Sunday 23rd August 1998

125 cc: Jakub Smrz (Czech Republic, Honda, twice, warm-up and race), Federico Cerroni (Italy, Aprilia), Jeronimo Vidal (Spain, Aprilia), Emilio Alzamora (Spain, Aprilia), Masaki Tokudome (Japan, Aprilia), Youichi Ui (Japan, Yamaha) and Masao Azuma (Japan, Honda).
250 cc: Jason Vincent (Great Britain, TSR-Honda), Noriyasu Numata (Japan, Suzuki) and Valentino Rossi (Italy, Aprilia).
500 cc: Garry McCoy (Australia, Honda) , Fabio Carpani (Italy, Honda) and Michael Doohan (Australia, Honda).

## Ouch...

1. Carlos Checa (bruised left buttock).
2. Garry McCoy (fractured right ankle).

## Non Starters...

1. Noboru Ueda (result of fall in French GP. Replaced by Hiroyuki Kikuchi).
2. Jurgen Fuchs (result of fall in practise for German GP. Replaced by Marcellino Lucchi).
3. William Costes (the Frenchman and his team agreed to a divorce after a disastrous early part of the season. Replaced for the rest of the season by Matthieu Lagrive).
4. Doriano Romboni (Result of fall in practise for Malaysian GP. Replaced by Eskil Suter. Luca Cadalora has finally tried the MuZ-Swissauto at the Castellet circuit and the plan is to tackle the Catalunia GP).
5. Garry McCoy (result of fall in warm-up).

## Retirements...

125 cc: Jaroslav Hules (Czech republic, Honda, gearbox) and Tomomi Manako (Japan, Honda, broken gear selector).
250 cc: Federico Gartner (Argentina, Aprilia, exhaust valves), Sebastian Porto (Argentina, Aprilia, bad tyre choice) and Olivier Jacque (France, Honda, rear tyre).
500 cc: none.

# Doohan attacks Biaggi

*11. Imola*

**Michael Doohan is now within four points of Massimiliano Biaggi, using his Italian opponent's favourite weapon. At Imola, it was Doohan who played with the opposition, hence the surprising story of an exclusive interview.**

▷ *When Michael Doohan resumes control of the situation.*

Sunday 6th September. Diane Michiels, the Repsol-Honda team press officer is looking for someone to give her a rough translation of an interview published that morning in the Italian paper, "Corriere dello Sport." The war of nerves between Doohan and Biaggi is now fiercer than ever and the title holder has just used Max' favourite trick of playing with the media.

### "Max is wrong"

It did not take long for Doohan's attack to spread through the paddock. One television commentator even got the translation of the story completely wrong with disastrous consequences. He mistook "Max e finto" (Max is wrong) for "Max e finito" (Max is finished.) A few hours before the start, this really set off a bomb.

Corriere dello Sport: You have won the last four world championships. Who was your strongest opposition?

Doohan: Each season I had to beat a strong rival. The first year it was Kevin Schwantz, then Daryl Beattie, Alexi Criville and Tadayuki Okada.

Corriere: Where would you place Biaggi in this group?

Doohan: He is not yet at the same level as the other four. Up until now, he has never beaten me. He might have won two races, but my engine broke in the first one and I had an accident the second time. He is inferior to the four guys I mentioned before. I have already lost 75 points this year and if he was as good as he says he is, then he would have a very clear lead in the championship at this point in the year.

### "Like a child"

Corriere: Max says your engine is more powerful than his. What do you have to say about that?

Doohan: That Biaggi is looking for excuses! We have the same machine and he is lying to appear braver than he really is. Actually, you only have to look at the races on television to see who is right. I have lost a lot of respect for him since he has started saying this sort of thing. He makes me

◁
*A light show
in the rain at Imola.*

laugh. He is acting like a child.

Corriere: Why?

Doohan: Because he is not sure of himself and he tries to make out he is tougher than he is in front of his fans.

Corriere: You do not seem to rate him very highly?

Doohan: He is a product, not a real person. He thinks too much about his appearance. He does not amaze me. There are a lot of guys like him. He is a strange individual, who always wants to make out he is a hero. I think he loves himself a bit too much.

Corriere: How do you rate Max Biaggi, the rider?

Doohan: Brave, quick and very talented. He knows how to get the most out of his bike.

Corriere: And as a man?

Doohan: He's not real. He's plastic.

Corriere: Not that long ago you were friends. You even travelled to some of the races together. Isn't that true?

Doohan: I had organised the flights and he offered to split the costs with me. But during those journeys, we did not say much. The plane was big enough.

There then followed some questions on the Doohan career until the interview returned to the thorny subject of Biaggi.

Corriere: After what you have said, it is unlikely that the two of you stay friends.

Doohan: I am no one's enemy, or at least not until I get on the track. But then, excuse me but it was Max who started throwing lies into the game, not me.

## Second lesson

Lesson 1 over, Michael Doohan had destabilised his opponent in psychological terms.

Lesson 2, pour salt on the open wound. Over to Doohan once again: "A race is 90% in your head. The 10% left over is a mixture of elements that have to be brought together. With my experience, I can deal with any form of attack."

Lesson 3, take charge of the race as soon as possible, then step up the pace and wait for disaster to strike. On lap nine of the Imola GP, Doohan has a lead of almost two seconds and Biaggi makes a mistake in the final chicane, somehow managing to stay on his bucking bronco of a bike.

## "A good afternoon"

Lesson 4, control the situation, look back a few times and then play the part of someone out for a Sunday afternoon drive. "My bike was perfect, which was perhaps not the case for everyone today. I could easily maintain a good pace and it was really good."

He said all this, while glancing in triumph at his neighbour at the table, Massimiliano Biaggi, who had suddenly become very small and humble. Michael Doohan was smiling broadly. Max less so.

### 125 cc

Marco Melandri dominated practice but he was to butt up against an on-form Tomomi Manako in the race. In the lead at the start, the Japanese rider tried for a solo run, pulling out a lead of 1.086s by the end of the second lap. But the young Italian fought back and from then on the two men were inseperable. The last lap is a cliffhanger and at the final chicane, Melandri slips through a mouse hole on the inside, but then finds he has overdone it. Manako has the better line and get the power down earlier. At the line, only 87 thousandths separate the two men. On a circuit where the Aprilia arrow was not quite at its best, Sakata made the best of a bad job as he still had a forty point lead over his closest rival in the championship.

▷ New colours and another win for Valentino Rossi.

▷ The 125 race at the first chicane.

▷ Loris Capirossi closes on Tetsuya Harada for the championship.

### 250 cc

In the middle of Friday afternoon, the skies darken over the town of Imola. The first few drops of rain start to fall and the 250 riders are bumping and boring to get out on the track as soon as possible. Testuya Harada was the most "cunning" at this art, to borrow the word from Valentino Rossi and he sets the fastest time after four laps and before the rain. On Saturday, the track is still wet and the championship leader gets it all wrong and breaks his left ankle. Will he be forced to scratch? While some are already doing their sums - Capirossi is "only" 26 points down in the classification - Doctor Costa goes to work. And on Sunday, sensational news - Harada is riding! Olivier Jacque is quickest away but he is only third at the end of the opening lap, behind Perugini and Ukawa. Harada gets it all wrong and is down in twelfth place, while Capirossi has not done much better; he is tenth. On lap two, order is reestablished with Rossi leading. Perugini tries to hang on for a while and Harada fights back and is up to second on lap 9. Would it be the miracle comeback? Sadly know, because he had a fall. Getting up in the gravel trap, he forgot he had a fracture, climbed back on and finished tenth. Out in front, Capirossi pushed hard to get back to second and Rossi wins his second 250 GP. Making sure the podium is an all Italian affair, Stefano Perugini is third.

### 500 cc

Jean-Michel Bayle is on pole for only the third time in his career. The former motocross rider had lost none of his talent, even if he faced a hard task in fighting for victory over the length of the race. Biaggi was first away and has a 0.636s lead over Bayle, Doohan and Criville by lap two, but the reigning champion took the lead on lap four, never to be seen again as Doohan puts in a series of eight race fastest laps to pull out a two second advantage. Alex Criville was back in second by lap 16, while Barros closed on Biaggi for third spot on the podium. But the Italian fights back in response to the attack from the Brazilian. In the championship, there is now only seven points separating the top three: 189 for Biaggi, 185 for Doohan and 182 for Criville.

◁ Takuma Aoki surrounded
by his brothers,
Haruchika and Nobuatsu:
he would like to believe it!

the saving of the Imola GP. Its future in doubt for some time, through reasons of ill health for the race promoter Maurizio Carrano, the Imola GP is saved thanks to the intervention of the town council and the arrival of a new sponsor, the food company Cirio. The Mayor of Imola, Raffaelo De Brasil stated the desire "to build a motorcycling tradition in the city." Federico Bendinelli, the president of Sagis, the company that runs the Enzo and Dino Ferrari circuit went even further. "If, as has happened over the past two years, the crowd is less than 20,000, it will be a dramatic signal that Italy does not want a second grand prix and that Imola does not want a major motorcycle meeting." On Sunday, there were 30,000 souls who had payed for their tickets and the paddock was heaving.

▷ Manuel Poggiali:
Massimo Matteoni's
latest find.

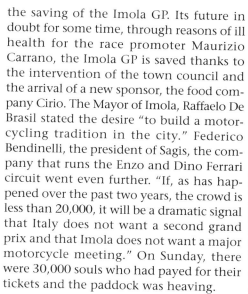

◁ Marco Melandri and
Valentino Rossi have
the same idea!

**Marco Melandri's and Valentino Rossi's hair** Valentino Rossi strolled into the paddock with tricolour hair; green, white and red. Very pleased with himself and this new stunt, the 125 world champion had the wind taken out of his sails, when he bumped into a potential successor, Marco Melandri, who had had exactly the same idea!

**The presence of Manuel Poggiali.** After Goi, Rossi and Melandri we now have Manuel Poggiali. The latest of Massimo Matteoni's proteges is barely 15 years old, born in San Marino on 14th February 1983. Poggiali set tenth fastest time in qualifying, despite falling three times, braking his right shoulder blade at the final attempt and he had to scratch from the race.

**The visit of Marco Pantini.** "Il Elefanto," Marco Pantini, winner of the cycling Tour of Italy and Tour de France was a major attraction when he visited the paddock, where he arrived on his Harley-Davidson. He was a guest of the Aprilia team and more specifically of Marcellino Lucchi, with whom he trains during the winter. Pantini showed an excellent grasp of paddock life. "You can feel the latent tension and the omnipresent threat of danger," he said.

▷ Marco Pantini
is the host of choice
at Aprilia.

**The visit of Takuma Aoki.** Victim of a bad fall in private testing at the Motegi circuit on 5th February, the third of the Aoki brothers, Takuma, returned to the paddock in a wheelchair. Unable to move his lower limbs, the Japanese had not lost hope. "I feel very well and I am very happy to be here with you. Since I came out of hospital, nothing much has changed, although I do feel a few more things. Today, I am concentrating on getting well again, but I am following what is going on at the races. It is true that I hope to come back one day."

**The transfer rumours.** Kenny Roberts Junior (and the engineer Warren Willing) to Suzuki, Carlos Checa who rightly feels he is badly underpaid at the Sito Pons teams, has a very lucrative offer to switch to Yamaha. It is that time of the season for rumours and indiscretion and only time will tell if they are true.

◁
*1969 Italian 250
Grand Prix:
Laslo Szabo (12,)
Santiago Herrero (7,)
Karl Bojer (21,) and
Cliff Carr (27.)*

*Phil Read was
the star of the day.*
▽

### 1969: Count me out

On 7th September 1969, for the first time since the world championship began, exactly twenty years earlier, the Grand Prix of Nations would not be held at the mythical Monza circuit. It was in fact run a little bit further south in the Italian peninsula, at Imola, on a track which ran alongside the Santerno, a quiet little river which runs through a huge park and all the best riders in the world were there. Or not quite, as this surprising story taking from volume 1946 of the French magazine Moto Revue reveals, as we look back the first recorded incident of a constructor boycotting a race.

*Francesco Villa:
more frightened than
hurt, but what style!*
▽

The walls of tradition are breached in Italy: this year, Monza gave up its grand prix to Imola, the other temple of Italian motor-cycle sport. The transition did not exactly go smoothly and the most turbulence was caused by Giacomo Agostini being a non-starter after Count Agusta did not want to leave his home turf of Monza. The count figured the championships were already in his pocket and he did not need to bother. Pasolini and Bergamonti were also absentees through injury. It seemed this edition of the Italian GP might be a sad affair. Nothing of the sort. Staged with impeccable organisation, worthy of the prestige and value of a grand prix, we lived through an intense day, with rich in surprise with races that were exciting to the very end. This was due, it has to be said, in great part to the return at Imola of a big star, Phil Read. He had been rather forgotten that year, but the English champion put himself back in the public eye in the most spectacular of fashions, by winning both races in which he was entered. On his Yamahas, he beat Carruthers and the Benelli 4 on the one hand and Grassetti and the Jawa 4 on the other. Well done!

### Linto: a first

Read was therefore the big star of the day, making a major contribution to the success of the Imola meeting. But one should not forget the panache of Lodewijk, winner of the 50cc race after a remarkable climb to catch Smith in the last lap, who must be regretting the start of his season. There were two other winners: Simmonds, (definitely untouchable in the 125cc) and Pagani, who thus gave Linto its first win in a grand prix. All in all, it was a great world championship event, despite the absence of the Italian superstars. It was also an undoubted success for Imola and its perfect organisation.

### Friday 21st August 1998

125 cc: Mirko Giansanti (Italy, Honda), Masao Azuma (Japan, Honda), Bohuslav Seifert (Czech Republic, Honda), Roberto Locatelli (Italy, Honda), Youichi Ui (Japan, Yamaha) and Yoshiaki Katoh (Japan, Yamaha).

250 cc: Johan Stigefelt (Sweden, Suzuki) and Luca Boscoscuro (Italy, TSR-Honda).

500 cc: Jurgen Van den Goorbergh (Holland, Honda) and Kenny Roberts Junior (United States, Modenas KR3).

### Saturday 22nd August 1998

125 cc: Jaroslav Hules (Czech Republic, Honda), Andrea Iommi (Italy, Honda), Gino Borsoi (Italy, Aprilia) and Hiroyuki Kikuchi (Japan, Honda).

250 cc: Yasumasa Hatakeyama (Japan, Honda, twice), Jose Luis Cardoso (Spain, Yamaha) and Radomil Rous (Czech Republic, Yamaha).

500 cc: Massimiliano Biaggi (Italy, Honda), Juan Bautista Borja (Spain, Honda) and Carlos Checa (Spain, Honda).

### Sunday 23rd August 1998

125 cc: Jakub Smrz (Czech Republic, Honda, twice, warm-up and race), Federico Cerroni (Italy, Aprilia), Jeronimo Vidal (Spain, Aprilia), Emilio Alzamora (Spain, Aprilia), Masaki Tokudome (Japan, Aprilia), Youichi Ui (Japan, Yamaha) and Masao Azuma (Japan, Honda).

250 cc: Jason Vincent (Great Britain, TSR-Honda), Noriyasu Numata (Japan, Suzuki) and Valentino Rossi (Italy, Aprilia).

500 cc: Garry McCoy (Australia, Honda), Fabio Carpani (Italy, Honda) and Michael Doohan (Australia, Honda).

### Ouch...

1. Carlos Checa (bruised left buttock).
2. Garry McCoy (fractured right ankle).

### Non Starters...

1. Noboru Ueda (result of fall in French GP. Replaced by Hiroyuki Kikuchi).
2. Jurgen Fuchs (result of fall in practise for German GP. Replaced by Marcellino Lucchi).
3. William Costes (the Frenchman and his team agreed to a divorce after a disastrous early part of the season. Replaced for the rest of the season by Matthieu Lagrive).
4. Doriano Romboni (Result of fall in practise for Malaysian GP. Replaced by Eskil Suter. Luca Cadalora has finally tried the MuZ-Swissauto at the Castellet circuit and the plan is to tackle the Catalunia GP).
5. Garry McCoy (result of fall in warm-up).

### Retirements...

125 cc: Jaroslav Hules (Czech republic, Honda, gearbox) and Tomomi Manako (Japan, Honda, broken gear selector).

250 cc: Federico Gartner (Argentina, Aprilia, exhaust valves), Sebastian Porto (Argentina, Aprilia, bad tyre choice) and Olivier Jacque (France, Honda, rear tyre).

500 cc: none.

*The Aprilia of Tetsuya Harada wears the scars of another fall. But the Japanese rider got back on and gritted his teeth to the flag.*

▽

# Biaggi sees red

## 12. Catalunya

▷ *Max Biaggi does a lap of honour... for nothing!*

Everyone had a presentiment about it: the final European round of the season would have important repercussions on the fate on the 500 world title. For one thing, Criville, third in the rankings, was on home turf, in front of a crowd entirely devoted to cheering him home and on Sunday alone there were 83,000 of them!

Then, we had Biaggi, turning up on the track where he had done the most 500cc testing and where he held the absolute lap record. Finally there was Michael Doohan, who brought all his rich experience to Montmelo, but also the knowledge he had a fight on his hands - something he was not used to.

### Promising pole

All the ingredients are therefore in place for the Catalunya GP to be a "must see" event. The Iberians have turned up en masse to support Alex Criville and the shy and quiet man was not about to disappoint them, throwing off his timidity and reserve in practice, responding to every attack in order to keep posting the quickest time.

At two o'clock on the afternoon of this Sunday 20th September, a dead silence hung over the giant grandstands of the Circuito de Catalunya.

Barros gets away perfectly, Criville much less so and the bikes become a blur. Fujiwara brings chaos to the first lap, hitting the first corner far too fast. He clips Bayle, who brings down Criville. The race continues with Barros and Biaggi leading. After one lap the excitement continues as Criville picks his bike up. He keeps going but slowly and retires in his pit. Catalunya is crying. In the gravel trap, everyone fusses around Bayle in a disorganised manner. He gets up but lies down immediately with pains in his lower back. Barros' head pops up from behind the bubble screen as he spots the yellow flags and senses that Biaggi has just taken him down the inside. The Italian runs a bit wide and Barros is back in front. No one has yet realised that the 1998 world championship has just been decided in that simple move that is such an everyday occurrence.

### The yellow flags

That was it: the overtaking move had taken place when the yellow flags were out and that is in contravention of article 1.20.2 of the GP regulations. On lap 16 of the 25 laps, the penalty for this offence, a ten second stop-go, has to be put in writing to the teams involved, which then have three laps to call in their rider. The penalty is first shown to Max Biaggi and then two laps later to Alex Barros. While the ,

**The most exciting 500 championship in a long time could well have been decided at the first corner of the Catalunya GP. By ignoring a penalty, had Biaggi kissed his dreams of glory goodbye? While the paddock tried to get some sleep for the night in an edgy atmosphere, the questions bounced round and around. It would be a day that would go down in history.**

Brazilian acquiesces, the Italian ignores it and is then shown the black flag.

It is not on, not right. Biaggi refuses to stop and is playing with Mick Doohan. He tries to intimidate him until the Australian errs on the side of caution, certain of his 25 points and aware that now is not the time to take unnecessary risks. Biaggi is up on his pegs for his victory lap, only to find he is denied access to the podium. It's official, he has been disqualified.

There then follows the official statement from the permanent race director, Roberto Nosetto: "At the first corner, on the first lap there was an accident, involving riders number 4 (Criville,) 12 (Bayle) and 27 (Fujiwara.) The yellow flags were waved immediately to allow the rescue crews to work as rider number 12 was on the ground. Arriving at that corner at the end of the first lap, while Bayle was still on the ground, rider number 6 (Biaggi) passed the number 9 (Barros) before the latter retook, at the exact spot where the flags were; the left side of the track, 200 metres from the accident and on both sides of the straight, 80 metres earlier, in the riders' line of vision. The first flag was stationary, the others waved, in accordance with the GP regulations."

Next act in the drama was the statement of Alex Barros: "At the exact moment when I braked and put my head above the screen, I saw the yellow flags. Max was on the inside, my bike was at its maximum angle of lean and if I had slowed at that point, I would definitely have fallen. It would have been very serious for me and almost certainly for Biaggi also. Then, Max ran very wide, I was on the inside and that is why I ended up ahead of him."

Massimiliano Biaggi, for his part, chose to remain perfectly silent, as was his right. "I have no comment to make on the penalty, as we have appealed against it," he said having just charged into the race director's office, made with rage: "If I am not awarded the 25 points for the win, then I will not take part in the remaining three grands prix!"

It was Sunday 20th September 1998 and it was very hot in Catalunya.

The crash that started it all: Fujiwara (blue bike,) takes out Bayle (12) and Criville (rear view,) Barros, Biaggi, Abe and the others ride by.

## 125 cc

40 points separate the world championship leader, Kazuto Sakata and his young pretender Marco Melandri as we head for the Catalunya GP. On the grid, the two men can see one another in the distance, Kazuto from his vantage point on the front row and Melandri from the third. At the front, it is Locatelli who has the honour of pole position, ahead of Tomomi Manako, who will be the star of the day, winning the race and regaining second place in the championship, 33 points down on Sakata. However, it is hard to find the words to explain the intensity of the battle: nine different leaders, including Noboru Ueda and his magic glove and the gaps will be tiny right to the end. At the halfway point, the top eight were split by just 1.105s and with everyone bumping and boring, it allowed the rest of the gang, led by Alzamora to catch up. The figures make interesting reading with 15 riders covered by just 2.443s on lap 14. The race will all come down to the final few metres with Manako keeping a 79 thousandths of a second lead over Giansanti as they cross the line.

## 250 cc

Three works Aprilias on the front row, but Tetsuya Harada could do no better than fifth. It was obvious that the race would, once again, be a procession to glorify Italian technology from the town of Noale. However, at the end of the first lap, it is unbelievable but true: with Ukawa, Perugini and Jacque, Honda is holding down the top three places ahead of Capirossi on the first of the Aprilias. Having made a complete mess of his start, Valentino Rossi is only thirteenth. On the second lap, everything is back to normal: Harada leads, Rossi is lapping quicker than anyone and by lap five he is in the wake of the championship leader. Capirossi is beginning to have problems as the engine cuts out for a moment, locking the Aprilia rear wheel and he drops to tenth place on lap seven, when Rossi snatches the lead. It is the start of act two. Rossi goes off on his own, Capirossi has climbed back up to third, while on lap 19, Jeremy Williams picks himself up, unhurt after a very high speed crash on the straight, when he collided with the fiery young Italian hope, Roberto Rolfo. On his lap of honour, Rossi has come up with yet another demonstration of his talent to amuse, by taking a giant chicken with him as a sop to one of his personal sponsors who runs a chicken farm!

## 500 cc

The first corner of the Catalunya 500 GP will have repercussions which will be talked about for much of the winter in acrimonious terms. Criville makes an average start, Fujiwara (Suzuki) surges forward from the fourth row and arrives far too fast, locks his rear wheel, before clipping Jean-Michel Bayle. The Frenchman went down, taking Alex Criville with him. One of the candidates for the title was already out. Another is about to follow, when on the second lap, Biaggi and Barros pass and re-pass one another under the yellow flags, both of them being hit with stop-go penalties. The rest is history and the race has two endings: on the track, Biaggi is first across the line but is disqualified with the black flag, while Doohan is second across the line, but declared the winner ahead of Okada and Abe.

*Chop and change in the 125s. Azuma (20) ahead of Manako and Giansanti. The order would be quite different at the finish.* ▽

◁
*Biaggi has perfect style, but his behaviour is somewhat strange!*

**Biaggi excluded.** Biaggi was black flagged for failing to pit for a stop-go penalty imposed after he passed another competitor, (Barros) while the yellow flags were being waved. The Italian chose to ignore the black flag as well.

**The return of Noboru Ueda.** "I feel I've been turned into Robocop." Noboru Ueda was back in action in Catalunya. Having crashed on 31st May at the French GP, the Japanese rider had suffered serious damage to the radial nerve of the right arm, which had partially paralysed some movement of his wrist and hand. After a few weeks, some movement returned, especially the ability to close the fingers of his right hand. However, Ueda was unable to spread them again and for this he resorted to the latest invention of Doctor Costa; a glove fitted with special strong elastic which, once the fingers had closed naturally, would open his right hand again.

**The first of the 1999 moves confirmed.** While they might not be first on the track, the Suzuki 500 team had the honour of being first to kick off the transfer market. The team confirmed what had been rumoured for several weeks, that Kenny Roberts Junior and his chief engineer, Warren Willing had signed a two year deal with Suzuki. This was very good news for team boss Gary Taylor: "Kenny is a very promising rider and Warren Willing will bring his vast experience to our team."

**Max Biaggi's reply.** After the incendiary declarations of Michael Doohan at Imola, everyone waited with baited breath for Biaggi's reply. It was not long in coming: "I could only forgive Doohan on one condition- if I opened his passport and discovered he was only fifteen years old! But that is not the case. He is 33 years old and at that age, if he has a problem with me, then he should come and speak to me about it. He has done the opposite and is trying to use the press to make me feel nervous. So that's the end of it. I don't want to say anymore."

**Graziano Rossi's little joke.** It is a well known fact that Valentino Rossi is not a morning sort of person. Quite the contrary and every morning for free practice, he gets to his pit just as proceedings are about to get underway. To make him understand that his ride might go to someone else if he does not shape up, his father Graziano and his team organised a little stunt on Saturday morning. Graziano got kitted out in his son's leathers and replica helmet and sat warming the bike up outside the Aprilia pit. The real rider looked very surprised when he finally put in an appearance. "Valentino does not arrive at the last moment, he arrives after the last moment and his team wanted him to understand the virtues of timekeeping," explained Rossi senior. Dad abstained from riding off onto the track, even though he was sorely tempted. "Luckily my engineers did not let Graziano do a few laps, as he is very dangerous near any form of motorised vehicle," quipped Rossi.

▷
*A glove worthy of Robocop: Noboru Ueda was to be the hero of the weekend.*

## Farewell to the paddock

As the last European round of the championship, the Catalunya GP was also time to say farewell to the paddock. It was time to cast a fond eye over the travelling village and also to say thank you to the Elf motorhome, which gets the richly deserved award for best restaurant in town. Our taste buds are already looking forward to the first European race of the 1999 season, at Jerez de la Frontera.

1998 ROAD RACING
WORLD CHAMPIONSHIP

**elf**

◁
*Jorge Martinez preferred his homonym Ivan, to his regular rider Jeronimo Vidal.*

## Friday 18th September 1998

125 cc: none
250 cc: Tohru Ukawa (Japan, Honda) and Stefano Perugini (Italy, Honda).
500 cc: Ralf Waldmann (Germany, Modenas KR3) and Eskil Suter (Switzerland, MuZ-Swissauto).

## Saturday 19th September 1998

125 cc: Youichi Ui (Japan, Yamaha) and Federico Cerroni (Italy, Aprilia).
250 cc: Federico Gartner (Argentina, Aprilia), Sebastian Porto (Argentina, Aprilia) and David Ortego (Spain, Honda).
500 cc: none

## Sunday 20th September 1998

125 cc: Adrian Araujo (Spain, Honda) and Youichi Ui (Japan, Yamaha).
250 cc: Ivan Silva (Spain, Honda, restart), Federico Gartner (Argentina, Aprilia) and Jeremy McWilliams (Great Britain, TSR-Honda).
500 cc: Alex Criville (Spain, Honda restart), Jean-Michel Bayle (France, Yamaha), Katsuaki Fujiwara (Japan, Suzuki), Juan-Bautista Borja (Spain, Honda), Eskil Suter (Switzerland, MuZ-Swissauto) and Craig Connell (Australia Honda).

## Ouch!...

1. Federico Cerroni (fractured left clavicle).
2. Youichi Ui (injured right radius).
3. Jeremy McWilliams (multiple bruising).
4. Jean-Michel Bayle (serious lumbar injury).

5. Katsuaki Fujiwara (bruising and laceration to shoulder and left foot).

## Non Starters...

1. Christian Manna (result of fall in Imola GP. Replaced by Andrea Ballerini).
2. Jeronimo Vidal (Jorge Martinez, team manager, wanted to give Ivan Martinez a chance).
3. Jurgen Fuchs (result of fall during practise for German GP. Replaced by Diego Giugovaz).
4. Doriano Romboni (result of fall during practise for Malaysian GP. Replaced by Eskil Suter. Luca Cadalora, the rider who was supposed to ride the MuZ-Swissauto at this GP, decided not to.)
5. Garry McCoy (result of fall during warm-up for the Czech Republic GP. Replaced by Craig Connell).
6. Federico Cerroni (result of fall in practise).

## Retirements...

125 cc: Ivan Martinez (Spain, Aprilia, electrical problems) and Juan Enrique Maturana (Spain, Yamaha, loss of power).
250 cc: Davide Bulega (Italy, ERP Honda, loss of revs.)
Sebastian Porto (Argentina, Aprilia, engine) , Marcellino Lucchi (Italy, Aprilia, bad choice of tyres) and Jose Luis Cardoso (Spain, Yamaha, front tyre).
500 cc: Massimiliano Biaggi (Italy, Honda, disqualified for failing to observe a stop-go penalty), Fabio Carpani (Italy, Honda, loss of power) and Sebastien Gimbert (France, Honda, rear tyre).

# Doohan: that makes five!

△
*A triumphant image of Michael Doohan out alone on the track under a blue sky at Phillip Island.*

The suspense is over. Two weeks after the Catalunya affair and a few days after the cancellation of the Rio GP, Mick Doohan claimed his fifth 500cc world championship. At Phillip Island, the Australian proved he was, is and promises to be for a while yet, the best rider of the modern era. It was the crowing glory to a close fought season which saw the title swing several ways.

Phillip Island, Sunday evening 4th October 1998. John is happy but at the same time anxious to be back home. His mates are reliving the race over and over, talking about the win and the title. "Mick's the best! He won with his head. What a demonstration! Did you see Biaggi? The Italian did not know where he was." And so it goes, but as the steaks cook on the grill, John, who left Italy as a young man, to make a new life for himself in Australia, has not forgotten his roots. But he has to admit that the "kangaroo" did it. Michael Doohan is the hero of the entire nation, named as sportsman of the year on several occasions, he is the emblem of a country that has succeeded; just like its airline Quantas, for which he is a roving ambassador around the world.

## A big softie

Jeanne-Claude Strong, the Swiss-born wife of the Quantas MD, met Mick Doohan a few years ago, when the Australian GP was still held at Eastern Creek. "In everyday life, Michael is full of humour, which people in the sport do not see. His reserved nature can be explained by the fact he is basically very shy. Doohan is also faithful to his friends and despite his worldwide fame, he is still the same with his friends from childhood."

With the Quantas bosses, Doohan shares his passion for a wide range of sports from scuba-diving, where he is meticulous in every detail and likes to remind us that "to come second is to be the first loser" to flying. "The first time he flew with me," explained Mrs. Strong, I let him fly the plane. He had never flown, but he was certainly the best beginner I have seen. He practically landed the plane at his first attempt."

Is this unknown Michael so different to the Doohan who has dominated the 500 class for well nigh a decade? If it had not been for his serious practice accident in the 1992 Dutch GP, he would almost certainly be on his seventh title by now and he never misses an opportunity to confirm his dominance. Who knows?

## A lesson for Biaggi

Michael Doohan certainly needed to be on the case that first weekend of October 1998: "Of course, my position in the championship looked very interesting again after the Rio GP was cancelled. But all the same, to become world champion despite three no scores!" In just a few words, the Australian had swept aside what had been a simple arithmetic problem since his retirement in that first race, the Japanese GP. Then there was one mistake at Brno, a

The Australian people honour their hero and for Doohan, this fifth title had special meaning.
▷

mechanical problem when the crankshaft let go in Suzuka and a fall that was not his fault at the first corner of the Madrid GP. Apart from that, Doohan overwhelmed Biaggi, his opponent who had moved up from the 250 class, intending to turn the sport on its head. The Italian was beaten, well and truly in fact, even at Phillip Island, where he fell, while Doohan piled in the fastest laps, before going on to have a very mediocre race on a bad Australian Sunday afternoon. "It was a strange feeling for me," continues Doohan. "A mixture of enjoyment and worry. I was in front of my home crowd, I could clinch this title, but I was under total pressure from the start of the week, with everyone telling me not to take too many risks and to avoid falling at any cost. Then when I looked back and I could see no one behind me, I remembered that last year I had lost the Australian GP on lap 17, while I was cruising out in front. I got through the eighteenth lap and at that point, I told myself I was going to bring the bike home!"

What followed was a joyous display. Doohan, alone out in front is cheered all the way by tens of thousands of shouting fans. He knows, even though he is finding it harder to read his pit signals, that the next man, who is closing slightly, Simon Crafar, who his not a championship contender. As the skies darken with menace over Phillip Island, the white gulls follow Hond number one for the final time. The emotions could not be running higher and the moment of glory is at hand. "To take the world title by winning your home grand prix is a unique moment; intense, rich in emotion. I think that every sportsman in the world should have at least one chance to experience that."

### A human swarm

For John and almost 60,000 of his countrymen, the party was only just starting and while others might have puffed up their chests with pride, Doohan stayed the same, a perfectionist, thinking of all the details. "The image of the track swarming with people like ants is great television, but to be completely honest, in future something will have to be done to control this type of demonstration, because we must not forget that while it was going on, we were still travelling at between 80 and 140 km/h. And while everyone saw the scenes on the start-finish line, it was actually just the same all round the track."

Doohan had spoken. At the foot of the Phillip Island grandstand, at the foot of the podium where he had dragged up the doctor, Claudio Costa who had saved him in June 1992 after his Dutch accident. They stood and waited several hours for their hero to reappear.

John, well he was already back home getting the evening meal ready. And when everyone was at the billiard table for a match between the Aussies and the Europeans, he settled for being the referee. To rule that here again, Australia ruled the roost.

*Poetry in motion as Mick attacks!*
▽

◁
*Yet another world champion's jersey and it is time for the thank yous.*

Green hair for Rossi, "Because there is a lot of grass on this island!"

In the second half of the season, Kazuto Sakata had his work cut out fending off the Honda riders (here Melandri and Azuma.) Illegal fuel saw him kicked out.

## 125 cc

Marco Melandri dominated practice on a track which was new to him - "really fantastic," but once again he is up against a Japanese coalition which is not about to roll over for him. It has to be said that Tomomi Manako has not entirely lost hope of beating Kazuto Sakata for the title. Masoa Azuma is certainly ripe for a win. Riding for the team led by Olivier Liegeois, he has been on the up and up as Bridgestone has pushed the development of its tyres. The race is run in several acts. At first, Manako tries to go it alone (0.972s lead on the first lap) before being caught by Sakata on lap three. Going for it, but caught out with brake problems, the Frenchman Arnaud Vincent falls on lap four, before remounting and moving through the field up to the half way point of the race. At this point, there is a four way battle for the lead: Azuma, Manako, Melandri and Sakata. This quartet swop places at every corner and the calculating Sakata eases off for the last two laps but at the line 44 thousandths of a second separate the top three, with Masao Azuma giving Bridgestone their first win for many years. Kazuto Sakata in fourth place thinks his second world championship is in the bag, but he is in for a rude shock: his fuel did not conform to the rules (0.4gr/l of lead, as opposed to the 0.013 permitted) and the Japanese rider was disqualified.

Clearly beaten, Biaggi also had to give best to Regis Laconi.

## 250 cc

Arriving on the island, there was a feeling that the duel between Tetsuya Harada and Loris Capirossi for the world 250 title could take a decisive turn here. Right from the start of practice, the Aprilia riders reminded everyone they had the best machinery, snatching three of the four front row positions on the grid, the other place going to the surprising Shinya Nakano, the new Japanese champion and his equally surprising Yamaha YZR. Capirossi had the break of four tenths of a second, while Valentino Rossi preferred to work on his tyre choice. As for Harada, the limping leader of the championship, he was still suffering in the left ankle, fractured during practice for the Imola GP and did not have much to say. Nakano made the best start, ahead of Perugini and Harada. Rossi was only average off the line and was sixth, but he worked his way to the front by lap four, with Olivier Jacque, who was going to amaze everyone in this race, in his wheel tracks. The Aprilias are still in a league of their won, but OJ is the king of the late brakers. It is a stunning spectacle and far more intense than previous races in this category, but the show is only just beginning. On lap 15 of the 25 lap race, Harada's engine tightens, his rear wheel locks and down he goes, getting up with bad bruising to his already injured ankle. The championship has just tilted. Rossi leads by a few metres while Jacque tries all he knows to stay with Capirossi, attempting the impossible on the last lap, before being passed again on the straight. In the championship, the two Aprilia boys have swopped places and now it is Loris Capirossi who has the upper hand as they head for the final showdown.

## 500 cc

Right from the start of practice, Michael Doohan shows who is boss. However, he has a few worrying moments as he takes to the track. The Australian noticed that the engine in his NSR has an intermittent misfire, running on only three cylinders. Then, as his mechanics change the spark plugs, a few drops of rain start to fall on Phillip Island. The day of drama is here and Doohan will emerge as hero. He makes an incredible start - "I still don't understand what I did" - and pulls out 1.578s over Biaggi on the first lap. Four laps later he is 3.028s ahead of the pack led by Norifume Abe as this time it looks as though Biaggi is well and truly beaten. Doohan is unbeatable and he goes on to fulfil the role of national hero with his fifth consecutive 500 title. His near neighbour, New Zealand's Simon Crafar puts in a series of race fastest laps to take second on lap 20 of 27. Doohan is world champion, Alex Criville makes sure of third place on the podium and passes Biaggi, the big loser of the Australian GP, in the championship. It is party time on the island.

Two of the three titles are decided. By winning his 53rd grand prix in the 500 class, Michael Doohan has completed his fourth successful defence of his title, making a total of five crowns. After his triumph, he confirmed he would be racing for yet another year, although he did not make a big issue of going for Giacomo Agostini's record of 68 wins in the 500cc races. The other title decided at Phillip Island was the 125 category. Kazuto Sakato took the crown, having already been champion back in 1994.

The cancellation of the Rio GP. Twenty one days before its due date of 18thOctober, the penultimate GP of the season had to be cancelled. The FIM did not grant homologation to the Nelson Piquet circuit at Jacarepagua, Rio de Janeiro after a final visit just one week before the Australian race and the world championship promoters were forced to scrap the event. Explanation from the man who took the decision, the Belgian Claude Danis, president of the FIM road racing commission. "When we made our first visit back in January, we suggested different track building methods, but the Brazilians wanted to do it their own way. When an FIM consultant returned in July, it became clear that the tarmac that seals the gravel that makes up the track surface was not of a high enough standard. The Brazilians were then approached by Tilke, the German company which built Sentul (Indonesia,) the A1- Ring (Austria) and is actually working on the Sepang site (Malaysia.) They were unable to give any guarantees that the work could be completed in time, because of practical problems as most of their construction team is working on Sepang. As they could take complete control of the work, Tilke did not want to take on the financial risk. The Brazilians therefore went their own way with the result we know. On the last weekend of September, during the Brazilian championship races, the track began to fall apart within minutes, even though many of the bikes (125, super-sport and superbike and production 500 class,) were not fitted with slicks. So on Saturday at midday, I understood that the situation was irreversible, as there was no question of taking any risks with the riders' safety."

The rejection of the appeals from Biaggi and Barros. It is hard to see how the outcome could be any different. The appeals lodged by Massimiliano Biaggi and Alex Barros were against the FIM stewards' decision at the Catalunya GP to award them a stop-go penalty for overtaking under the yellow flag and in the case of Biaggi, for also ignoring a black flag put out as he had refused to come into the pits for his penalty. The appeals were rejected by the International Disciplinary Court which met on 30th September at the FIM headquarters at Mies in Switzerland.

More transfer news. Sito Pons feels "betrayed" while Carlos Checa admits that: "tensions were beginning to grow within the team, but no way am I leaving the team over a question of money." The first big transfer is done and dusted, with the Spaniard moving to Yamaha. Other certainties: Michael Doohan and Alex Criville will stay put with the Repsol-Honda team for one more year. Germany's Ralf Waldman will be moving back to the 250 class after one season in 500, to race a factory Aprilia in Marlboro colours for the Docshop team, which will now be run by Dieter Stappert, with technical wizard Sepp Schlogl. The Dutchman, Jurgen van den Goorbergh has signed with MuZ-Swissauto and the team will now be run by former multiple sidecar world champion, the Swiss Rolf Biland and will be based at Burgdorf in Switzerland rather than Serge Rosset's French base in Annemasse.

...Kazuto Sakata's lost opportunity. Already champion in 1994, Japan's Kazuto Sakata was also hailed as a world champion in Phillip Island, before his 13 points for fourth place were taken off him in accordance with article 2.10.2 of the GP regulations: 0.4g/l instead of 0.013 of lead content, MON of 98.5 as against the permitted 90 and a RON reading of over 110 instead of 102.

*Michael Doohan triumphs.*
▽

◁
*Alexandre Barros was wrongly penalised in Catalunya and the Brazilian also failed to achieve the dream of winning his home GP in Rio.*

◁ A one-two finish for Gardner and Doohan in the 500 class. Cue the Australian track invasion!

## 1990: Move over for the youngsters!

For the second ever Australian GP on 16th September 1990, the crowds turned out en masse at Phillip Island, were two world titles were going down to the wire. Capirossi was up against Prein and Spaan in the 125 class, while Kocinski was battling Cardus in the 250s. It would be a day of new beginnings. "It was a noisy party in the Isola di Capri pizzeria, over there on the point of Phillip Island. They had all turned up; all the Italian branch of the Continental Circus were there to celebrate with Loris Capirossi, the new 125 world champion. They did juast about everything, including wheeling him around in a pram, before giving him a baby bottle and getting him to suck his thumb. Capirossi, like a young lad thrown too quickly into the company of adults, was the same as ever. At eleven o'clock he wanted to go to bed, noticing that his tired blue suit was stained with champagne. He even had a go at cleaning it, unaware that as the youngest world champion in history, he could wear new suits everyday as befits the emperor of his sport.

The Australian GP had brought the 1990 season to a close and it was time to take a quick look back. In 125cc, little Capirossi's big smile will long be remembered as will Dunlop's first solo championship for many a year. Above all the year will be remembered for the great success of the new technical regulations, which imposed a single cylinder limit on this category of the world championship. It meant that private teams were as competitive as the factory ones. It was a bad year however for Derbi and Ezio Gianola who, after a terrible start in Japan, decided to give up from the Spanish GP onwards as the Iberians did not want to be a laughing stock in front of their own people.

In the 250 class, we witnessed a fantastic demonstration from the likeable John Kocinski, who put an end to Honda's domination and also confirmed the arrival of a new European force in the shape of Aprilia. We also saw the first win for Wilco Zeelenberg. Sadder moments were there too and no one in Australia could forget that in a German clinic, Reinhold Roth was still in a coma after his terrible accident in Rijeka. Finally, in the 500 class, a big smile for Wayne Rainey, an impressive world champion and a smaller smile for Michael Doohan who had shown promise towards the end of the season."

▷ Loris Capirossi (65) fights for the title with Hans Spaan (2,) while the Italian guard of Gresini (5,) Romboni (20,) and Casanova wait and watch.

# fallers

**Friday 2nd October 1998**

1 25 cc: Kazuto Sakata (Japan, Aprilia.)

250 cc: Franco Battaini (Italy, Yamaha, restart,) Tohru Ukawa (Japan, Honda,) Martin Craggill (Australia, Aprilia,) Takeshi Tsujimura (Japan, Yamaha,) Osamu Miyazaki (Japan, Yamaha) and William Strugnell (Australia, Yamaha.)

500 cc: Sete Gibernau (Spain, Honda V2,) Carlos Checa (Spain, Honda V4) and Sebastien Gimbert (France, Honda V2.)

**Saturday 3rd October 1998**

125 cc: Noboru Ueda (Japan, Honda) and Jay Taylor (Australia, Honda.)

250 cc: Jose Luis Cardoso (Spain, Yamaha,) Jason Vincent (Great Britain, TSR- Honda) and Shaun Geronimi (Australia, Yamaha.)

500 cc: Massimiliano Biaggi (Italy, Honda) and Regis Laconi (France Yamaha.)

**Sunday 4th October 1998**

125 cc: Chedryian Bresland (Australia, Yamaha,) Arnaud Vincent (France, Aprilia, restart,) Yoshiaki Katoh (Japan, Yamaha,) Anthony West (Australia, Honda) and Jeronimo Vidal (Spain, Aprilia.)

250 cc: Tetsuya Harada (Japan, Aprilia,) Jeremy McWilliams (Great Britain, TSR-Honda,) Franco Battaini (Italy, Yamaha) and Jason Vincent (Great Britain, TSR-Honda.)

500 cc: Sete Gibernau (Spain, Honda V2) and Ralf Waldmann (Germany, Modenas KR3.)

## Ouch!...

1. Sete Gibernau (bruising to left side of chest during Friday's fall; light concussion and injured little finger on left hand during race.)
2. Kazuto Sakata (bruising to arms and right hand.)
3. Martin Craggill (triple fracture to hip.)
4. Noboru Ueda (slight facial injury, chin abrasions.)
5. Jose Luis Cardoso (new fracture to right ankle.)
6. Massimiliano Biaggi (bruising to left side of chest.)
7. Chedryian Bresland (severe concussion.)
8. Yoshiaki Katoh (fractured right clavicle.)
9. Anthony West ( fractured right tibia.)
10. Jeronimo Vidal (slight concussion.)
11. Tetsuya Harada (bruised left ankle.)
12. Jason Vincent (dislocated left shoulder.)

## Non Starters

1. Federico Cerroni (result of fall at Barcelona, replaced by Alessandro Romagnoli.)
2. Christian manna (result of fall during Imola, replaced by Andrea Ballerini.)
3. Jurgen Fuchs (result of fall during practise for German GP. Replaced by Martin Craggill.)
4. Doriano Romboni (result of fall during practise for Malaysian GP. Not replaced, Eskil Suter was officially said to be suffering from his fall in the Catalunya GP. Really, he had rowed with Serge Rosset, who was acting as Team Manager and his German (MuZ) and Swiss (Swissauto) partners.
5. Jean-Michel Bayle (result of fall in Catalunya GP. Not Replaced.)
6. Katsuaki Fujiwara (result of fall in Catalunya GP. Replaced by the Australian Mark Willis.)
7. Martin Craggill (result of fall in practise.)
8. Chedryian Bresland (result of fall in warm-up.)
9. Carlos Checa (result of fall in practise, but more especially because of the bad atmosphere in the Sito Pons team since announcing that Checa was to move to Yamaha.)

## Retirements....

125 cc: Alessandro Romagnoli (Italy, Aprilia, engine) and Arnaud Vincent (France, Aprilia, problems with front brakes during race.)

250 cc: Davide Bulega (rear tyre,) Jose Luis Cardoso (result of fall in practise) and Sebastian Porto (engine.)

500 cc: Garry McCoy (result of fall in warm-up for Czech Republic GP,) Fabio Carpani (gearbox) and Sebastien Gimbert ( nycasil unstuck in one of the cylinders.)

*Hope runs out in two acts for Arnaud Vincent, the reigning European champion. Melandri (13) had a very lucky escape.*
◁

*Another Vincent, but an English one this time: Jason and his TSR-Honda put on the style.*
▽

# Capirossi: angel or demon?

▷ *Loris Capirossi and father: pulling a face on the eve of a championship which would be talked about for a long time.*

**For several years now, even more so since his return to the 250 class with Aprilia, where he is the best paid rider in the category, Loris Capirossi is tagged with the reputation of being a loser, who is often incapable of standing up and being counted at the critical moments. Too calculating, not "mad" enough to mix it with the pack, this label, the Italian conclusively tore up in the last corner of the 1998 250cc world championship. In Buenos Aires, he became world champion, but he did not make many friends.**

Flash back to Jarama, GP FIM, 26th September 1993. Loris Capirossi (Honda) has a ten point lead over Tetsuya Harada (Yamaha) at the start of the final round of the world championship. Better still, the young Italian, already a double world champion in 125cc, has dominated practice and he will start from the best place on the grid. He makes a perfect start to the race. He leaves everyone for dust, he improves on the Madrid circuit's lap record, before noticing

that Harada is beginning to close. The Japanese rider moves ahead and pulls away. Loris Capirossi has been knocked out while still in the saddle. Did he push his tyres too hard in those first frantic laps? Is he the victim of a problem with the tyre compound? At the finish, the little Italian is in tears. He does not know what happened. It is as though the sky fell on his head. Tetsuya Harada, who did not speak a single word of Italian or English back then has just given Yamaha its last 250 title.

### "I have changed"

Back to the present day. Buenos Aires, 22nd October 1998. Twenty days after the Australian GP - Harada a faller because of a broken engine - Loris Capirossi arrives on Argentinian soil as championship leader. He is still not the 250 champion, he spent two years in the 500 class, winning just one race and now, since last year, he is back in the category which suits him so well and he is paid millions of lire by Aprilia, so they can forget about Massimiliano Biaggi. Tetsuya Harada is still there and like Capirossi, he has one of these Aprilia RSV250Rs that has dominated the championship. Four points is a little and a lot. It can be the difference between heaven and hell. Loris Capirossi made the journey on his own, one day before the rest of the team (Harada and Rossi.) He is calm and appears relaxed. "Psychologically I have never

felt so well as I do now. I have proved over the last few races that I can get the job done when my equipment is the same as my opponents' and I know I can be world champion on Sunday." The battle can begin, with all that Italian pressure in the paddock where everyone is reminding him of 1993 and his lost duel with Harada. "I am ready. I fear no one. Everything is possible for Sunday. Maybe I will lose the title, but I will be happy, because I will have given it my all and I have proved I am a competitive rider."

More so than in 1993? Less than in 1993? Since his arrival in Buenos Aires, Loris Capirossi is constantly pursued by the past: "I have changed! At the time, I was a daring rider, I took a lot of risks and sometimes I would fall. This year, apart from my mechanical failure in Assen, I have scored points in every race. I knew how to settle for less than a win when conditions did not allow me to go for victory. I am more mature, more relaxed. I am ready." Ready to trace his race on that of his last opponent? "I had acted that way in 1993 and I lost. I will not make the same mistake again. If he is in front, then I will see him and I will know what to do. If he is behind, I will not worry and I will run my own race."

### Cunning Tetsuya

At this point in the weekend, Loris Capirossi's

speech is in marked contrast to Tetsuya Harada's silent demeanour. He is still complaining about the ankle he broke in Imola and hurt again in Australia. He also complains about not having yet found the right tyre choice for the race. He complains further that his machine seems to break too often compared with those of his Italian team mates. In short, in the space of a weekend, the roles have been reversed. Capirossi is once again the conqueror, while it is Harada who is the loser. The spectacle would be unique, a mixture of drama and grandeur, of desperate acts and vengeful looks.

## "Why?"

First came a gesture of fury from Tetsuya Harada. Then a haggard look with eyes that appeared to be out on stalks. And that question: "Why? Why me? Why now? Why like this? The final corner of the 1998 250cc world championship has produced the ultimate verdict in the war that has raged since the start of the season, between the Aprilia riders. It was a bitter verdict for the Japanese rider and almost total victory for Loris Capirossi, who had been seen as a shadow of the rider who had burst on the world scene in 1990 when he was just a post-adolescent teenager and became the 125 world champion.

In this final, where the rules were so simple between Capirossi and Harada, whichever one of them crossed the line first, as long as they were both in the top three, would be the new world champion, the Italian pulled out all the stops and emerged victorious. But then, he had exceeded all the limits in the final corner and was excluded from the results by the race stewards. They did not however, take away the world title, his third. Capirossi's race that 25th October 1998 got off to a bad start. Then he climbed through the field at an incredible pace, taking the lead on lap nine. There were a few suicidal moves and then a titanic tussle with Harada. They swopped places at almost every corner, getting closer and closer to the kerbs and to each other, even touching fairings.

This was only the start of it though. Valentino Rossi was closing on them, like a wolf in a sheep pen, more determined than ever to demonstrate he was top dog in this second half of the season. He took the lead when Capirossi made a slight mistake - "I had a slight gearbox problem," - and he ignores the rest - "that way I was not stuck between the two men fighting for the title,"- and they get to that last corner. Capirossi is caught out much sooner than Harada, the two men touch and the Japanese rider hits the deck. Loris is champion. "That's racing. I do not take any great pleasure in having won my title in these circumstances, but it does not change anything. On this part of the track, I was much quicker than Tetsuya and he was in a bad position on the track so I got past. Now way did I deliberately try and make him fall."

A few hours later, Capirossi was disqualified. It was meagre consolation for Tetsuya Harada, who would later say: "Even Massimiliano Biaggi has never behaved like this!" Then, two weeks after the event, on Friday 6th November 1998, Loris Capirossi was reinstated by the International Disciplinary Court of the FIM, who sat in judgement of the appeal lodged by the world champion. "The behaviour of Loris Capirossi, which until then, had been irreproachable throughout his career as a GP rider, had indeed been dangerous. However, it is not possible to say that there was deliberate intent to cause an accident."

△
*We will never know what Master Mick said to the new world champion.*

▷
*Capirossi and Harada capture the intensity of battle in a single frame.*

### 125 cc

As a result of the fuel checks carried out in Phillip Island, the 125 championship is once again wide open and all the possible permutations have been worked out before making the journey to South America. Tomomi Manako knows as well as anyone what is required: if he wins and Sakata does no better than fourth, then he is world champion, as long as the appeal lodged by Aprilia is unsuccessful. Marco Melandri for his part, only has a slim mathematical chance - he has to win with Sakata not scoring any points. In practice, after what amounted to a demonstration from Sakata on Friday, it was the Honda mounted Italians who seized power on the Saturday, with another pole for Roberto Locatelli, who will fall and fail to finish the race. While Sakata made the best start, he did not have time to cruise around in front. Quite the contrary in fact. On lap six, Melandri and Cecchinello pull away. Two laps later, the veteran and the baby champ have 4.753s advance over Azuma, who is closing at a great rate of knots, bringing Manako with him. Soon, the four Hondas will be out on their own. Sakata battles with Ui who falls and Giansanti and everyone is asking if there are such things as team orders among the various HRC teams. The riders give the answer on the track by taking every possible risk over the final two laps of madness. Manako takes the lead just two kilometres from the end of the championship. It was just the right moment. However, with the Aprilia appeal still outstanding, this turnaround still left everyone in the dark on the night of the Argentinian Grand Prix. Who was the 125cc world champion, Kazuto Sakata or Tomomi Manako?

△
*Tomomi Manako:
champion, or not?*

### 250 cc

Pole position? Loris Capirossi is well used to it. And the title? And that as well, even though he was excluded for dangerous riding. Loris Capirossi was the man in Buenos Aires, in the middle of the final world championship podium and at the heart of many arguments that Sunday night, before he was disqualified. But he was still world champion! The only Honda rider capable of overcoming his machinery's shortcomings faced with the Aprilias was Frenchman Olivier Jacque. He made the best start and led the first few laps, before being passed by Harada. Capirossi got it wrong and was only eighth at the end of the opening lap, with Rossi even further back. All was in place for a three way war between the men from Noale. On lap 7 of the 25 lap race, Capirossi sticks the nose of his Aprilia into second place before closing on Harada at an astonishing pace, taking him on lap 9. The Japanese rider digs in and the gap stays at around the four tenths mark. Harada retakes the lead on lap 16 before having to give best yet again on lap 17, just when Olivier Jacque takes a trip through the gravel trap as his engine seizes. The end of the race is mind blowing with a comeback from Rossi and a fourth consecutive win and above all, the final attack from Capirossi at the last corner of the 1998 world championship. The title has just been decided and the Aprilia camp is on fire yet again.

### 500 cc

While Michael Doohan may have begun the weekend by commenting on the state of the very slippery Buenos Aires circuit, he still dominated practice and would go on to dominate the race. Best start, a fight for a few laps with Alexandre Barros, before making the break from lap 10 by putting in several record lap times, the world champion enjoyed himself and let the others fight it out behind. At first it was Barros who led the vain chase, happy to be in his native South America, then came Okada. Further back there was a battle going on between Biaggi and Criville for the runner up position in the championship - the Spaniard fell - then the confrontation between the Italian and some Yamaha riders really going for it (Abe, Laconi and Bayle.) Much further back came John Kocinski in a modest tenth place for whom this was probably the last GP of his career, as he could be heading home to the American dirt tracks for 1999.

△
*Max Biaggi and Luca
Cadalora together again.*

Smile...

### The pleasant surprise
### Eskil Suter

There was the worrying prospect of a "historic" year. At the beginning of the championship, not a single Swiss rider was entered for the GPs, something that had not happened since it all began back in 1949. A development rider for MuZ-Swissauto, Eskil Suter came back from a year's retirement in time for the Italian GP and after the short Jean-Philippe Ruggia (Assen) episode, he completed the European season, until the team ran into serious internal difficulties and scratched from the Australian GP, before finally getting Luca Cadalora in the saddle for Argentina. Suter's numbers: 26th in the final score sheet of the 500cc class, with a thirteenth place at the Sachsenring as his best result.

◁ *Eskil Suter.*

*Yves Briguet.* ▷

### The black sheep
### Yves Briguet

Six falls in a row and a seventh which could have had terrible consequences on the start line at the penultimate round of the supersport world cup. He was one of the favourites for the title, but only finished twelfth in the final standings. However, at every meeting, he was one of the best in qualifying.

Marco Tresoldi. ▷

## The revelation
## Marco Tresoldi

It is hard to be a revelation when one had already celebrated one's 28th birthday. But the Swiss, who this year competed in his first two 125 GP, thanks to wild cards at Mugello and Imola, shone above all in Italy, as he finished the very hotly contested Honda 125 Trophy in second place. He fought all season with the new discovery of Italian motorcycling, Manuel Poggiali.

◁ Markus Schlosser/
Daniel Hauser.

Oliver Petrucciani. ▽

## Cry from the heart
## Markus Schlosser

In a sidecar category which this year lost what little credit it still had, the young Schlosser came third in the world cup in his second full season on the world stage. Ahead of him were the unbeatable Steve Webster and Klaus Klaffenböck. Better still, after the retirement of Rolf Biland, Schlosser became the top Swissauto V4 user, stealing the limelight from the brothers Gudel, Paul and Charly.

## The confirmation          WET-Motos and the endurance

Robi Schlaefl and Urs Meier, both senior managers in a major Honda dealership had put up some of their best performances as endurance racers. After tackling the German superbike series, then the European and finally the world series, they came back to their first love, running a team made up of Andreas Hofmann, Marcel Kellenberger and Oliver Petrucciani, who for a while were in the lead of the Spa- Francorchamps 24 Hours.

## The high point

## Arnaud Vincent

The reigning European 125 champion, Arnaud Vincent surprised observers with the ease with which he brought himself up to world level. He scored his first points in only his second grand prix (tenth place in Malaysia,) his first podium in Germany. Arnaud was soon given a helping hand from the Aprilia factory as Jan Witteveen asked him to take part in several development sessions in Italy. At the end of the year he emerged with twelfth place in the 125 world championship and a contract with Jorge Martinez for 1999.

◁

*Arnaud Vincent.*

### The revelation     Bertrand Sebileau

It had never happened before, but on the eve of the final race, a journalist was leading a world championship. Bertrand Sebileau, also runner up in the French superbike series, came very close to taking the world endurance crown, having won the Le Mans 24 Hours.

*Bertrand Sebileau.* ▽

△ *Olivier Jacque.*

### The black sheep     Olivier Jacque

One of the main irritants in the Massimiliano Biaggi - Ralf Waldmann duel these past few years, "OJ" was reckoned to be a big favourite on paper for the 250 title and the logical Number One for HRC in the class. Sadly, the 1998 version of the NSR soon proved not to be up to the job and Jacque paid the price: he fell in practice at Mugello, trying to make the best of a bad job; a faller in Madrid, hit by Capirossi, then at Assen it was Perugini's turn to have him off, Jacque would have liked to stop before the end of the season in order to have his seriously damaged right foot treated. He was not allowed to and finished fifth in the championship after two hard fought battles in Australia and Argentina.

### The pleasant surprise     Christian Lavieille

With two races taking place in France, most of the factories are represented by their French companies and a Tricolore team took the world endurance championship. At the age of 33, Christian Lavieille also showed he had nerves of steel, as he proved in the finish to the Bol d'Or.

▽ *Christian Lavieille.*

*Stéphane Chambon.* ◁

### The confirmation     Stephane Chambon

A win at Kyalami and a constant presence at the head of the supersport field at Brands Hatch, he was the quickest man on the track and he would no doubt have won, but for a penalty for jumping the start. Stephane Chambon finished third in the world cup, proving to be the perfect team mate for Fabrizio Pirovano.

### The revelation
### Alexander Hofmann-Hammad

German champion, European 250 champion and a surprising tenth in the German GP at the Sachsenring, Hoffmann was without a doubt the revelation of the German racing scene. A well balanced young man with a good education, he speaks six languages fluently and the German hope has all that is needed to build a great career.

◁ *Alexander Hofmann.*

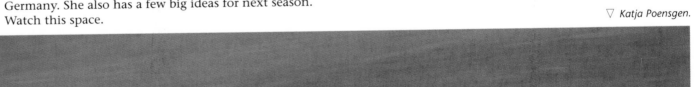

### The high point     Katja Poensgen

She is pretty and seems mischievous and she is also a winner! Katja Poensgen dominated the Supermono Cup, organised as part of the world superbike series and she did it with style. She also tried her hand at the supersport class in the European and German championships and at superbikes in Germany. She also has a few big ideas for next season.
Watch this space.

▽ *Katja Poensgen.*

### The confirmation
### Ralf Waldmann

A successful transition to 500cc for Ralf Waldmann, even if his actual results were nothing to write home about. His best result was seventh place in the German GP. Ralf was very much involved in the development of the Modenas KR3, working the settings on the basis of a "big" 250 rather than treating it like a "little" 500.

◁ *Ralf Waldmann.*

### The pleasant surprise     Reinhard Stolz

German Champion and third in the European 125 championship in the midst of a very strong Italian pack. Reinhard Stolz reaped the benefit of all the good work done a few years back in Germany and which now allowed a new generation of riders to follow in the footsteps of the Waldmanns and Fuchs.

*Reinhard Stolz.* ▷

◁ *Jürgen Fuchs.*

### The black sheep     Jurgen Fuchs

He had emerged from a dreadful 500 season with Elf-Swissauto and he hoped to bounce back with the 250 cc works Aprilia. In Malaysia, Jurgen Fuchs claimed the first pole position of his career, but he made a complete mess of the start. At Donington, he fell both in practice and the race, before having a serious accident in qualifying for the German GP. With a mangled left foot, Jurgen Fuchs had to sit out the rest of the season with a final tally of 17th place in the championship.

### The high point    Carl Fogarty

In 1998, "King" Carl resumed the role he has occupied for a half decade, that of the world superbike Number One. Having packed out Brands Hatch, where the race had been billed as possibly "Foggy's" final appearance on British soil, Fogarty made it clear he had no plans to retire just yet! He just had to, literally as well has metaphorically, tidy up the Ducati camp a bit, in order to take his sixth world title at Sugo.

◁ Carl Fogarty.

### The pleasant surprise
### Jason Vincent

This was the first full season in the 250cc GP class for the son of Chris Vincent, who was one of the best side car men in the Sixties. Nurtured by the Padgett clan, to whom so many British riders owe their successful careers, Jason Vincent finished 13th overall in the world championship and fifth in the IRTA rankings for privateers. His best result was fifth place in Germany.

◁ Jason Vincent.

### The revelation    Leon Haslam

The apple rarely falls far from the tree: aged 15, Leon Haslam took part in his first grand prix, at Donington. Son of "Rocket Ron," he finished seventh in the British 125cc championship, having claimed his first win at Knockhill on 9th August. A solid gold talent has blossomed in England.

◁  *Leon Haslam.*

### The black sheep    James Toseland

Honda having decided to enter a 100% official team in the supersport world cup, the young Englishman was offered the chance of his life with a ride in the official works Castrol team. Young and talented, Toseland nevertheless lived through a cruel season. He was outpaced throughout winter testing by his team-mate the sadly departed Belgian, Michael Paquay and Toseland found himself in the medical centre more often than in a good position at the end of the races.

*James Toseland.*  ▷

### The confirmation  Jeremy McWilliams

His past performances, both in 500 and 250cc had been enough to show the world championship regulars that Jeremy McWilliams had great potential. In 1998, in the saddle of a Team QUB (Queens University Belfast) TSR-Honda. In great form, Jeremy transformed himself into a hero, claiming ninth place in the final classification of the world championship, having allowed himself the luxury of stepping onto the second rung of the podium of the German GP, in between two Aprilia riders.

◁  *Jeremy McWilliams.*

Statistics...

## 125cc

### 5th April - Japanese GP - Suzuka

Pole position: N. Ueda (J, Honda), 2'15"162 (156.185 km/h).
1. K. Sakata (J, Aprilia), 18 laps in 41'23"963 (152.976 km/h); 2. T. Manako (J, Honda), at 0"156; 3. M. Azuma (J, Honda), at 0"201; 4. L. Cecchinello (I, Honda), at 2"783; 5. N. Osaki (J, Yamaha), at 26"381; 6. G. Scalvini (I, Honda), at 26"468; 7. H. Kikuchi (J, Honda), at 33"198; 8. M. Tokudome (J, Aprilia), at 34"422; 9. T. Akita (J, Yamaha), at 33"552; 10. M. Melandri (I, Honda), at 33"834; 11. F. Petit (F, Honda), at 34"215; 12. Y. Katoh (J, Yamaha), at 46"152; 13. A. Nieto Junior (E, Aprilia), at 46"574; 14. K. Takao (J, Honda), at 48"281; 15. I. Goi (I, Aprilia), at 59"684. 21 classified.
Fastest lap: M. Azuma (J, Honda), 2'16"128 (155.077 km/h). New record. Old: K. Sakata (J, Aprilia, 2'17"055/1996).

### 19th April - Malaysian GP - Johor Baru

Pole position: N. Ueda (J, Honda), 1'34"516 (147.022 km/h).
1. N. Ueda (J, Honda), 26 laps in 41'34"332 (144.846 km/h); 2. M. Giansanti (I, Honda), at 0"277; 3. T. Manako (J, Honda), at 1"902; 4. M. Tokudome (J, Aprilia), at 12"991; 5. R. Locatelli (I, Honda), at 14"086; 6. K. Sakata (J, Aprilia), at 31"874; 7. F. Petit (F, Honda), at 36"955; 8. A. Nieto Junior (E, Aprilia), at 37"508; 9. M. Azuma (J, Honda), at 39"492; 10. A. Vincent (F, Aprilia), at 42"748; 11. S. Jenkner (D, Aprilia), at 44"743; 12. L. Cecchinello (I, Honda), at 44"950; 13. G. Scalvini (I, Honda), at 56"948; 14. J. Hules (CZ, Honda), at 58"446; 15. I. Goi (I, Aprilia), at 1'01"914. 18 classified.
Fastest lap: M. Azuma (J, Honda), 1'34"782 (146.610 km/h). New record (new track).

### 3rd May - Spanish GP - Jerez de la Frontera

Pole position: R. Locatelli (I, Honda), 1'49"281 (145.705 km/h).
1. K. Sakata (J, Aprilia), 23 laps in 42'19"751 (144.196 km/h); 2. T. Manako (J, Honda), at 2"101; 3. M. Giansanti (I, Honda), at 2"229; 4. M. Azuma (J, Honda), at 2"731; 5. N. Ueda (J, Honda), at 8"516; 6. J. Hules (CZ, Honda), at 17"476; 7. Y. Ui (J, Yamaha), at 28"751; 8. G. Scalvini (I, Honda), at 28"950; 9. G. Borsoi (I, Aprilia), at 29"204; 10. M. Melandri (I, Honda), at 29"213; 11. F. Petit (F, Honda), at 35"679; 12. M. Tokudome (J, Aprilia), at 42"314; 13. A. Nieto Junior (E, Aprilia), at 42"872; 14. A. Vincent (F, Aprilia), at 49"952; 15. A. Gonzalez (E, Aprilia), at 52"822. 19 classified.
Fastest lap: T. Manako (J, Honda), 1'49"360 (145.599 km/h). New record. Old: K. Sakata (J, Aprilia, 1'49"400/1996).

### 17th May - Italy GP - Mugello

Pole position: N. Ueda (J, Honda), 2'00"419 (156.419 km/h).
1. T. Manako (J, Honda), 20 laps in 40'53"607 (153.912 km/h); 2. M. Melandri (I, Honda), at 0"044; 3. G. Scalvini (I, Honda), at 0"201; 4. K. Sakata (J, Aprilia), at 3"152; 5. Y. Ui (J, Yamaha), at 8"162; 6. G. Borsoi (I, Aprilia), at 8"195; 7. N. Ueda (J, Honda), at 10"097; 8. F. Petit (F, Honda), at 12"745; 9. M. Azuma (J, Honda), at 12"757; 10. M. Tokudome (J, Aprilia), at 24"284; 11. A. Vincent (F, Aprilia), at 24"388; 12. P. Tessari (I, Aprilia), at 24"415; 13. I. Goi (I, Aprilia), at 25"393; 14. S. Jenkner (D, Aprilia), at 31"066; 15. C. Cipriani (I, Aprilia), at 49"419. 20 classified.
Fastest lap: L. Cecchinello (I, Honda), 2'00"966 (156.093 km/h). Record: N. Ueda (J, Honda, 2'00"555/1997).

### 31th May - French GP - Le Castellet

Pole position: N. Ueda (J, Honda), 1'29"002 (153.704 km/h).
1. K. Sakata (J, Aprilia), 27 laps in 40'57"583 (150.294 km/h); 2. M. Melandri (I, Honda), at 0"292; 3. M. Azuma (J, Honda), at 0"393; 4. R. Locatelli (I, Honda), at 3"314; 5. L. Cecchinello (I, Honda), at 4"057; 6. F. Petit (F, Honda), at 4"824; 7. S. Jenkner (D, Aprilia), at 10"041; 8. M. Tokudome (J, Aprilia), at 14"660; 9. I. Goi (I, Aprilia), at 28"373; 10. Y. Katoh (J, Yamaha), at 32"660; 11. Y. Ui (J, Yamaha), at 35"533; 12. A. Vincent (F, Aprilia), at 35"617; 13. J. Vidal (E, Aprilia), at 48"609; 14. J.-E. Maturana (E, Yamaha), at 51"162; 15. P. Tessari (I, Aprilia), at 57"049. 18 classified.
Fastest lap: M. Azuma (J, Honda), 1'29"519 (152.816 km/h). Record: T. Manako (J, Honda, 1'28"383/1997).

### 14th June - Madrid GP - Jarama

Pole position: K. Sakata (J, Aprilia), 1'38"952 (140.067 km/h).
1. L. Cecchinello (I, Honda), 26 laps in 43'28"423 (138.152 km/h); 2. M. Melandri (I, Honda), at 9"173; 3. H. Kikuchi (J, Honda), at 9"317; 4. K. Sakata (J, Aprilia), at 17"268; 5. G. Scalvini (I, Honda), at 19"417; 6. A. Nieto Junior (E, Aprilia), at 19"511;

7. Y. Ui (J, Yamaha), at 21"010; 8. F. Petit (F, Honda), at 23"034; 9. M. Tokudome (J, Aprilia), at 23"066; 10. S. Jenkner (D, Aprilia), at 23"552; 11. Y. Katoh (J, Yamaha), at 26"762; 12. J. Hules (CZ, Honda), at 31"484; 13. A. Molina (I, Honda), at 41"584; 14. A. Gonzalez (E, Aprilia), at 42"512; 15. J.-E. Maturana (E, Yamaha), at 50"521. 19 classified.
Fastest lap: K. Sakata (J, Aprilia), 1'39"330 (139.534 km/h). New record. Old: N. Ueda (J, Honda, 1'41"113/1993).

### 27th June - Dutch GP - Assen

Pole position: K. Sakata (J, Aprilia), 2'13"411 (163.227 km/h).
1. M. Melandri (I, Honda), 17 laps in 38'27"391 (160.440 km/h); 2. K. Sakata (J, Aprilia), at 0"028; 3. T. Manako (J, Honda), at 9"626; 4. L. Cecchinello (I, Honda), at 10"331; 5. M. Tokudome (J, Aprilia), at 10"410; 6. M. Giansanti (I, Honda), at 10"425; 7. R. Locatelli (I, Honda), at 10"700; 8. F. Petit (F, Honda), at 11"417; 9. S. Jenkner (D, Aprilia), at 14"678; 10. M. Azuma (J, Honda), at 24"158; 11. G. Borsoi (I, Aprilia), at 25"011; 12. Y. Ui (J, Yamaha), at 30"265; 13. H. Kikuchi (J, Honda), at 30"369; 14. I. Goi (I, Aprilia), at 33"345; 15. J. Hules (CZ, Honda), at 33"527. 24 classified.
Fastest lap: T. Manako (J, Honda), 2'14"378 (162.053 km/h). New record. Old: T. Manako (J, Honda, 2'15"049/1997).

### 5th July - British GP - Donington

Pole position: K. Sakata (J, Aprilia), 1'39"294 (145.857 km/h).
1. K. Sakata (J, Aprilia), 26 laps in 43'48"777 (143.242 km/h); 2. M. Giansanti (I, Honda), at 0"431; 3. Y. Ui (J, Yamaha), at 4"600; 4. M. Melandri (I, Honda), at 5"197; 5. M. Tokudome (J, Aprilia), at 5"598; 6. L. Cecchinello (I, Honda), at 6"517; 7. G. Borsoi (I, Aprilia), at 20"153; 8. F. Petit (F, Honda), at 22"334; 9. G. Scalvini (I, Honda), at 31"971; 10. I. Goi (I, Aprilia), at 37"432; 11. A. Vincent (F, Aprilia), at 39"361; 12. A. Nieto Junior (E, Aprilia), at 39"559; 13. F. Cerroni (I, Aprilia), at 43"031; 14. E. Alzamora (E, Aprilia), at 43"714; 15. H. Kikuchi (J, Honda), at 44"370. 18 classified.
Fastest lap: K. Sakata (J, Aprilia), 1'39"465 (145.606 km/h). Record: V. Rossi (I, Aprilia, 1'39"236/1997).

### 19th July - German GP - Sachsenring

Pole position: M. Melandri (I, Honda), 1'30"793 (139.094 km/h).
1. T. Manako (J, Honda), 29 laps in

44'37"947 (136.759 km/h); 2. A. Vincent (F, Aprilia), at 16"513; 3. R. Locatelli (I, Honda), at 24"754; 4. H. Kikuchi (J, Honda), at 24"771; 5. E. Alzamora (E, Aprilia), at 25"778; 6. Y. Katoh (J, Yamaha), at 28"862; 7. K. Sakata (J, Aprilia), at 37"703; 8. S. Jenkner (D, Aprilia), at 39"681; 9. M. Tokudome (J, Aprilia), at 41"147; 10. A. Nieto Junior (E, Aprilia), at 49"449; 11. I. Goi (I, Aprilia), at 54"783; 12. J.-E. Maturana (E, Yamaha), at 54"868; 13. M. Melandri (I, Honda), at 55"292; 14. A. Iommi (I, Honda), at 55"350; 15. C. Manna (I, Yamaha), at 58"319. 20 classified.

Fastest lap: T. Manako (J, Honda), 1'30"838 (139.025 km/h). New record (new track).

### 23rd August - Czech Republic GP - Brno
Pole position: K. Sakata (J, Aprilia), 2'11"302 (148.137 km/h).
1. M. Melandri (I, Honda), 19 laps in 42'05"161 (146.353 km/h); 2. K. Sakata (J, Aprilia), at 0"038; 3. L. Cecchinello (I, Honda), at 0"364; 4. M. Giansanti (I, Honda), at 3"745; 5. G. Scalvini (I, Honda), at 3"794; 6. A. Vincent (F, Aprilia), at 7"082; 7. H. Kikuchi (J, Honda), at 7"144; 8. R. Locatelli (I, Honda), at 7"260; 9. I. Goi (I, Aprilia), at 9"179; 10. F. Petit (F, Honda), at 12"170; 11. S. Jenkner (D, Aprilia), at 15"272; 12. A. Nieto Junior (E, Aprilia), at 33"909; 13. J.-E. Maturana (E, Yamaha), at 35"083; 14. G. Borsoi (I, Aprilia), at 35"333; 15. Y. Katoh (J, Yamaha), at 54"524. 20 classified.

Fastest lap: M. Azuma (J, Honda), 2'10"899 (148.593 km/h). New record. Old: K. Sakata (J, Aprilia, 2'11"305/1995).

### 6th September - San Marino GP - Imola
Pole position: M. Melandri (I, Honda), 1'59"795 (148.153 km/h).
1. T. Manako (J, Honda), 21 laps in 42'05"831 (147.558 km/h); 2. M. Melandri (I, Honda), at 0"087; 3. M. Azuma (J, Honda), at 10"394; 4. K. Sakata (J, Aprilia), at 10"466; 5. M. Tokudome (J, Aprilia), at 22"699; 6. Y. Ui (J, Yamaha), at 26"133; 7. R. Locatelli (I, Honda), at 26"546; 8. Y. Katoh (J, Yamaha), at 28"161; 9. A. Vincent (F, Aprilia), at 30"584; 10. I. Goi (I, Aprilia), at 48"516; 11. F. Petit (F, Honda), at 48"656; 12. G. Scalvini (I, Honda), at 1'02"010; 13. E. Alzamora (E, Aprilia), at 1'12"085; 14. S. Jenkner (D, Aprilia), at 1'12"337; 15. A. Zappa (I, Honda), at 1'12"408.

19 classified.
Fastest lap: T. Manako (J, Honda), 1'58"880 (149.293 km/h). Record: V. Rossi (I, Aprilia, 1'58"490/1997).

### 20th September - Catalunya GP - Catalunya
Pole position: R. Locatelli (I, Honda), 1'52"641 (151.074 km/h).
1. T. Manako (J, Honda), 22 laps in 42'10"704 (147.934 km/h); 2. M. Giansanti (I, Honda), at 0"079; 3. M. Azuma (J, Honda), at 0"096; 4. L. Cecchinello (I, Honda), at 0"172; 5. R. Locatelli (I, Honda), at 0"336; 6. N. Ueda (J, Honda), at 0"724; 7. Y. Katoh (J, Yamaha), at 0"942; 8. M. Melandri (I, Honda), at 1"027; 9. K. Sakata (J, Aprilia), at 1"062; 10. G. Scalvini (I, Honda), at 1"540; 11. I. Goi (I, Aprilia), at 1"737; 12. A. Vincent (F, Aprilia), at 2"063; 13. M. Tokudome (J, Aprilia), at 2"607; 14. E. Alzamora (E, Aprilia), at 3"046; 15. F. Petit (F, Honda), at 5"025. 25 classified.

Fastest lap: M. Giansanti (I, Honda), 1'53"142 (150.405 km/h). New record. Old: K. Sakata (J, Aprilia, 1'53"773/1997).

### 4th October - Australian GP - Phillip Island
Pole position: M. Melandri (I, Honda), 1'40"490 (159.347 km/h).
1. M. Azuma (J, Honda), 23 laps in 38'56"336 (157.637 km/h); 2. T. Manako (J, Honda), at 0"025; 3. M. Melandri (I, Honda), at 0"044; 4. Y. Ui (J, Yamaha), at 2"847; 5. R. Locatelli (I, Honda), at 4"683; 6. L. Cecchinello (I, Honda), at 5"204; 7. J. Hules (CZ, Honda), at 12"758; 8. G. Scalvini (I, Honda), at 15"711; 9. G. Borsoi (I, Aprilia), at 22"620; 10. I. Goi (I, Aprilia), at 24"381; 11. M. Giansanti (I, Honda), at 24"415; 12. A. Nieto Junior (E, Aprilia), at 24"795; 13. F. Petit (F, Honda), at 25"156; 14. S. Jenkner (D, Aprilia), at 25"254; 15. M. Tokudome (J, Aprilia), at 28"938. 22 classified.
Fastest lap: M. Melandri (I,

Honda), 1'40"296 (159.655 km/h). New record. Old: K. Sakata (J, Aprilia, 1'40"348/1997).
Kazuto Sakata (J, Aprilia) a passé la ligne en quatrième position, at 2"403 du vainqueur, Masao Azuma. L'essence du Japonais a été contrôlée et, ne répondant pas aux normes en vigueur, Sakata a été déclassé, la contre-analyse effectuée à la demande du team ne changeant rien à l'affaire.

### 25th October - Argentinian GP - Buenos Aires
Pole position: R. Locatelli (I, Honda), 1'50"550 (141.655 km/h).
1. T. Manako (J, Honda), 23 laps in 42'43"976 (140.477 km/h); 2. M. Melandri (I, Honda), at 0"566; 3. L. Cecchinello (I, Honda), at 1"137; 4. M. Azuma (J, Honda), at 1"191; 5. K. Sakata (J, Aprilia), at 16"111; 6. M. Giansanti (I, Honda), at 16"314; 7. A. Vincent (F, Aprilia), at 21"921; 8. M. Tokudome (J, Aprilia), at 22"833; 9. N. Ueda (J, Honda), at 23"597; 10. G. Scalvini (I, Honda), at 23"922; 11. I. Goi (I, Aprilia), at 23"958; 12. G. Borsoi (I, Aprilia), at 27"543; 13. F. Petit (F, Honda), at 27"720; 14. Y. Katoh (J, Yamaha), at 27"822; 15. Y. Ui (J, Yamaha), at 42"461. 20 classified.
Fastest lap: M. Azuma (J, Honda), 1'49"917 (142.471 km/h). New record. Old: T. Yamamoto (J, Honda, 1'51"217/1995).

## Final classification

| | | | |
|---|---|---|---|
| 1. Tomomi Manako | Japan | Honda | 217 |
| 2. Kazuto Sakata | Japan | Aprilia | 216 |
| 3. Marco Melandri | Italy | Honda | 202 |
| 4. Masao Azuma | Japan | Honda | 135 |
| 5. Lucio Cecchinello | Italy | Honda | 131 |
| 6. Mirko Giansanti | Italy | Honda | 114 |
| 7. Masaki Tokudome | Japan | Aprilia | 98 |
| 8. Gianluigi Scalvini | Italy | Honda | 90 |
| 9. Roberto Locatelli | Italy | Honda | 88 |
| 10. Frédéric Petit | France | Honda | 79 |

11. Y. Ui (J, Yamaha), 78; 12. A. Vincent (F, Aprilia), 72; 13. N. Ueda (J, Honda), 62; 14. I. Goi (I, Aprilia), 54; 15. H. Kikuchi (J, Honda), 51; 16. Y. Katoh (J, Yamaha), 45; 17. S. Jenkner (D, Aprilia), 46; 18. G. Borsoi (I, Aprilia), 44; 19. A. Nieto Junior (E, Aprilia), 42; 20. J. Hules (CZ, Honda), 26; 21. E. Alzamora (E, Aprilia), 18; 22. N. Osaki (J, Yamaha), 11; 23. J.-E. Maturana (E, Yamaha), 10; 24. T. Akita (J, Yamaha), 7; 25. P. Tessari (I, Aprilia), 5; 26. J. Vidal (E, Aprilia), 3; 27. A. Molina (E, Honda), 3; 28. F. Cerroni (I, Aprilia), 3; 29. A. Gonzalez Nieto (E, Aprilia), 3; 30. K. Takao (J, Honda), 2; 31. A. Iommi (I, Honda), 2; 32. C. Cipriani (I, Aprilia), 1; 33. C. Manna (I, Yamaha), 1; 34. A. Zappa (I, Honda), 1. 34 classified.

**250cc**

## 5th April - Japanese GP - Suzuka

Pole position: D. Kato (J, Honda), 2'08"430 (164.372 km/h).

1. D. Kato (J, Honda), 19 laps in 41'17"096 (161.922 km/h); 2. S. Nakano (J, Yamaha), at 0"896; 3. N. Matsudo (J, Yamaha), at 0"962; 4. T. Harada (J, Aprilia), at 1"094; 5. O. Jacque (F, Honda), at 34"301; 6. Y. Kagayama (J, Suzuki), at 37"035; 7. L. Capirossi (I, Aprilia), at 37"104; 8. J.-L. Cardoso (E, Yamaha), at 43"094; 9. N. Numata (J, Suzuki), at 43"105; 10. J. McWilliams (GB, TSR-Honda), at 43"909; 11. H. Aoki (J, Honda), at 44"000; 12. S. Perugini (I, Honda), at 44"067; 13. C. Kameya (J, Suzuki), at 44"168; 14. O. Miyazaki (J, Yamaha), at 44"637; 15. T. Tsujimura (J, Yamaha), at 44"727. 20 classified.

Fastest lap: N. Matsudo (J, Yamaha), 2'09"284 (163.287 km/h). New record. Old: T. Harada (J, Aprilia, 2'10"253/1997).

## 19th April - Malaysian GP - Johor Bahru

Pole position: J. Fuchs (D, Aprilia), 1'30"395 (153.725 km/h).

1. T. Harada (J, Aprilia), 28 laps in 42'55"302 (151.084 km/h); 2. T. Ukawa (J, Honda), at 1"259; 3. O. Jacque (F, Honda), at 12"166; 4. H. Aoki (J, Honda), at 15"887; 5. L. Capirossi (I, Aprilia), at 18"934; 6. S. Perugini (I, Honda), at 19"162; 7. J. McWilliams (GB, TSR-Honda), at 21"821; 8. J. Fuchs (D, Aprilia), at 24"109; 9. S. Porto (ARG, Aprilia), at 26"216; 10. J.-L. Cardoso (E, Yamaha), at 34"541; 11. T. Tsujimura (J, Yamaha), at 40"510; 12. R. Rolfo (I, TSR-Honda), at 45"201; 13. N. Numata (J, Suzuki), at 45"397; 14. J. Vincent (GB, TSR-Honda), at 47"662; 15. O. Miyazaki (J, Yamaha), at 1'13"383. 17 classified.

Fastest lap: V. Rossi (I, Aprilia), 1'30"897 (152.876 km/h). New record (new track).

## 3 mai - Spanish GP - Jerez

Pole position: L. Capirossi (I, Aprilia), 1'44"431 (152.471 km/h).

1. L. Capirossi (I, Aprilia), 26 laps in 46'00"131 (149.990 km/h); 2. V. Rossi (I, Aprilia), at 3"415; 3. O. Jacque (F, Honda), at 7"576; 4. T. Ukawa (J, Honda), at 8"186; 5. M. Lucchi (I, Aprilia), at 14"337; 6. H. Aoki (J, Honda), at 24"939; 7. S. Perugini (I, Honda), at 28"435; 8. T. Tsujimura (J, Yamaha), at 31"492; 9. L. D'Antin (E, Yamaha), at 45"003; 10. O. Miyazaki (J, Yamaha), at 45"558; 11. L. Boscoscuro (I, TSR-Honda), at 45"999; 12. F. Battaini (I, Yamaha), at 49"032; 13.

R. Rolfo (I, TSR-Honda), at 1'04"043; 14. N. Numata (J, Suzuki), at 1'07"866; 15. W. Costes (F, Honda), at 1'37"376. 18 classified.

Fastest lap: L. Capirossi (I, Aprilia), 1'45"250 (151.285 km/h). New record. Old: M. Biaggi (I, Aprilia, 1'45"270/1996).

## 17th May - Italian GP - Mugello

Pole position: T. Harada (J, Aprilia), 1'54"683 (164.645 km/h).

1. M. Lucchi (I, Aprilia), 21 laps in 40'59"049 (161.250 km/h); 2. V. Rossi (I, Aprilia), at 5"701; 3. T. Harada (J, Aprilia), at 7"625; 4. L. Capirossi (I, Aprilia), at 10"029; 5. S. Perugini (I, Honda), at 47"830; 6. H. Aoki (J, Honda), at 48"205; 7. T. Ukawa (J, Honda), at 49"376; 8. J.-L. Cardoso (E, Yamaha), at 50"080; 9. L. D'Antin (E, Yamaha), at 50"161; 10. L. Boscoscuro (I, TSR-Honda), at 52"738; 11. F. Battaini (I, Yamaha), at 54"241; 12. T. Tsujimura (J, Yamaha), at 54"306; 13. Y. Hatakeyama (J, ERP Honda), at 1'50"752; 14. D. Bulega (I, Honda), at 1'53"990; 15. F. Gartner (ARG, Aprilia), at 2'22'611. 16 classified.

Fastest lap: M. Lucchi (I, Aprilia), 1'55"467 (163.527 km/h). Record: M. Biaggi (I, Aprilia, 1'54"925/1996).

## 31th May - French GP - Le Castellet

Pole position: T. Harada (J, Aprilia), 1'23"417 (163.995 km/h).

1. T. Harada (J, Aprilia), 29 laps in 40'59"018 (161.332 km/h); 2. V. Rossi (I, Aprilia), at 0"631; 3. L. Capirossi (I, Aprilia), at 14"406; 4. O. Jacque (F, Honda), at 27"017; 5. S. Perugini (I, Honda), at 28"024; 6. H. Aoki (J, Honda), at 28"045; 7. J. McWilliams (GB, TSR-Honda), at 36"228; 8. L. D'Antin (E, Yamaha), at 49"849; 9. T. Tsujimura (J, Yamaha), at 50"216; 10. J. Vincent (GB, TSR-Honda), at 51"672; 11. F. Battaini (I, Yamaha), at 53"376; 12. J. Fuchs (D, Aprilia), at 1'01"689; 13. J.-L. Cardoso (E, Yamaha), at 1'14"169; 14. R. Rolfo (I, TSR-Honda), at 1'18"169; 15. J. Allemand (F, Honda), at one lap. 18 classified.

Fastest lap: T. Harada (J, Aprilia), 1'23"688 (163.464 km/h). Record: L. Capirossi (I, Aprilia, 1'23"559/1997).

## 14th June - Madrid GP - Jarama

Pole position: L. Capirossi (I, Aprilia), 1'34"382 (146.850 km/h).

1. T. Harada (J, Aprilia), 28 laps in 44'44"553 (144.560 km/h); 2. T. Ukawa (J, Honda), at 8"738; 3. L. Capirossi (I, Aprilia), at 15"978; 4. J. Fuchs (D, Aprilia), at 22"545; 5. J.-L. Cardoso (E, Yamaha), at 24"444; 6. L. D'Antin (E,

Yamaha), at 33"716; 7. T. Tsujimura (J, Yamaha), at 33"791; 8. J. Vincent (GB, TSR-Honda), at 46"342; 9. J. McWilliams (GB, TSR-Honda), at 50"206; 10. R. Rolfo (I, TSR-Honda), at 51"016; 11. I. Clementi (I, Yamaha), at 1'04"474; 12. J. Stigefelt (S, Suzuki), at 1'11"969; 13. Y. Hatakeyama (J, ERP Honda), at 1'30"205; 14. D. Bulega (I, ERP Honda), at one lap; 15. I. Bonilla (E, Honda). 16 classified.

Fastest lap: T. Harada (J, Aprilia), 1'35"012 (145.876 km/h). Record: L. Capirossi (I, Honda, 1'34"941/1993).

## 27th June - Dutch GP - Assen

Pole position: L. Capirossi (I, Aprilia), 2'05"567 (173.424 km/h).

1. V. Rossi (I, Aprilia), 18 laps in 38'31"905 (169.546 km/h); 2. J. Fuchs (D, Aprilia), at 19"184; 3. H. Aoki (J, Honda), at 19"516; 4. L. D'Antin (E, Yamaha), at 21"682; 5. T. Ukawa (J, Honda), at 21"721; 6. S. Porto (ARG, Aprilia), at 21"927; 7. T. Tsujimura (J, Yamaha), at 22"084; 8. J. Vincent (GB, TSR-Honda), at 27"290; 9. L. Boscoscuro (I, TSR-Honda), at 33"444; 10. R. Rolfo (I, TSR-Honda), at 37"467; 11. N. Numata (J, Suzuki), at 42"228; 12. J. McWilliams (GB, TSR-Honda), at 42"659; 13. W. Costes (F, Honda), at 50"841; 14. I. Clementi (I, Yamaha), at 52"029; 15. J. Stigefelt (S, Suzuki), at 53"759. 21 classified.

Fastest lap: T. Harada (J, Aprilia), 2'06"452 (172.210 km/h). Record: O. Jacque (F, Honda, 2'06"047/1997).

## 5th July - British GP - Donington

Pole position: L. Capirossi (I, Aprilia), 1'34"085 (153.933 km/h).

1. L. Capirossi (I, Aprilia), 27 laps in 42'55"085 (151.853 km/h); 2. T. Harada (J, Aprilia), at 5"682; 3. S. Perugini (I, Honda), at 38"003; 4. T. Ukawa (J, Honda), at 38"349; 5. H. Aoki (J, Honda), at 38"461; 6. J. Vincent (GB, TSR-Honda), at 39"084; 7. J. McWilliams (GB, TSR-Honda), at 51"804; 8. T. Tsujimura (J, Yamaha), at 58"946; 9. L. D'Antin (E, Yamaha), at 1'18"487; 10. J.-L. Cardoso (E, Yamaha), at 1'19"532; 11. N. Numata (J, Suzuki), at 1'24"101; 12. R. Rolfo (I, TSR-Honda), at 1'25"956; 13. J. Stigefelt (S, Suzuki), at 1'26"887; 14. W. Costes (F, Honda), at 1'29"510; 15. Y. Hatakeyama (J, ERP Honda), at 1'35"487. 18 classified.

Fastest lap: L. Capirossi (I, Aprilia), 1'34"188 (153.764 km/h). Record: T. Harada (J, Aprilia, 1'34"137/1997).

## 19th July - German GP - Sachsenring

Pole position: T. Harada (J, Aprilia), 1'28"684 (142.402 km/h).

1. T. Harada (J, Aprilia), 30 laps in 44'43"421 (141.186 km/h); 2. J. McWilliams (GB, TSR-Honda), at 9"033; 3. V. Rossi (I, Aprilia), at 9"267; 4. L. Capirossi (I, Aprilia), at 10"611; 5. J. Vincent (GB, TSR-Honda), at 38"261; 6. T. Tsujimura (J, Yamaha), at 43"611; 7. J.-L. Cardoso (E, Yamaha), at 45"243; 8. L. Boscoscuro (I, TSR-Honda), at 45"702; 9. N. Numata (J, Suzuki), at 49"915; 10. A. Hofmann (D, Honda), at 51"523; 11. R. Rolfo (I, TSR-Honda), at 54"914; 12. L. D'Antin (E, Yamaha), at 1'20"499; 13. D. Bulega (I, ERP-Honda), at 1'23"418; 14. J. Robinson (GB, Yamaha), at 1'23"915; 15. M. Baldinger (D, Honda), at one lap. 15 classified.
Fastest lap: T. Harada (J, Aprilia), 1'28"625 (142.497 km/h). New record (new track).

## 23rd August - Czech Republic GP - Brno
Pole position: L. Capirossi (I, Aprilia), 2'03"974 (156.894 km/h).
1. T. Harada (J, Aprilia), 20 laps in 41'52"318 (154.843 km/h); 2. L. Capirossi (I, Aprilia), at 5"207; 3. M. Lucchi (I, Aprilia), at 28"254; 4. J. McWilliams (GB, TSR-Honda), at 30"432; 5. T. Ukawa (J, Honda), at 30"703; 6. H. Aoki (J, Honda), at 31"090; 7. J. Vincent (GB, TSR-Honda), at 49"163; 8. T. Tsujimura (J, Yamaha), at 49"284; 9. L. Boscoscuro (I, TSR-Honda), at 49"398; 10. J.-L. Cardoso (E, Yamaha), at 50"301; 11. S. Perugini (I, Honda), at 57"812; 12. L. D'Antin (E, Yamaha), at 57"996; 13. F. Battaini (I, Yamaha), at 1'01"297; 14. N. Numata (J, Suzuki), at 1'10"103; 15. R. Rolfo (I, TSR-Honda), at 1'15"633. 22 classified.
Fastest lap: L. Capirossi (I, Aprilia), 2'04"614 (156.088 km/h). New record. Old: T. Harada (J, Yamaha, 2'04"684/1995).

## 6th September - San Marino GP - Imola
Pole position: T. Harada (J, Aprilia), 1'53"560 (156.287 km/h).
1. V. Rossi (I, Aprilia), 23 laps in 43'43"815 (155.576 km/h); 2. L. Capirossi (I, Aprilia), at 2"687; 3. S. Perugini (I, Honda), at 4"175; 4. T. Ukawa (J, Honda), at 6"524; 5. O. Jacque (F, Honda), at 29"180; 6. H. Aoki (J, Honda), at 31"615; 7. L. Boscoscuro (I, TSR-Honda), at 32"948; 8. R. Rolfo (I, TSR-Honda), at 33"614; 9. T. Tsujimura (J, Yamaha), at 35"892; 10. T. Harada (J, Aprilia), at 39"595; 11. L. D'Antin (E, Yamaha), at 53"590; 12. J.-L. Cardoso (E, Yamaha), at 53"988; 13. F. Battaini (I, Yamaha), at 54"686; 14. N. Numata (J, Suzuki), at 56"383; 15. J.

Vincent (GB, TSR-Honda), at 1'00"924. 24 classified.
Fastest lap: T. Harada (J, Aprilia), 1'52"533 (157.713 km/h). Record: T. Harada (J, Aprilia, 1'51"872/1997).

## 20th September - Catalunya GP - Catalunya
Pole position: L. Capirossi (I, Aprilia), 1'47"457 (158.362 km/h).
1. V. Rossi (I, Aprilia), 23 laps in 41'48"737 (156.013 km/h); 2. T. Harada (J, Aprilia), at 3"922; 3. L. Capirossi (I, Aprilia), at 14"048; 4. O. Jacque (F, Honda), at 17"698; 5. T. Ukawa (J, Honda), at 29"855; 6. S. Perugini (I, Honda), at 38"668; 7. H. Aoki (J, Honda), at 38"701; 8. R. Rolfo (I, TSR-Honda), at 38"926; 9. F. Battaini (I, Yamaha), at 39"048; 10. T. Tsujimura (J, Yamaha), at 46"392; 11. J. Vincent (GB, TSR-Honda), at 46"431; 12. L. Boscoscuro (I, TSR-Honda), at 46"953; 13. N. Numata (J, Suzuki), at 49"845; 14. O. Miyazaki (J, Yamaha), at 51"142; 15. J. Stigefelt (S, Suzuki), at 1'09"499. 22 classified.
Fastest lap: V. Rossi (I, Aprilia), 1'47"585 (158.174 km/h). New record. Old: M. Biaggi (I, Aprilia, 1'48"490/1996).

## 4th October - Australian GP - Phillip Island
Pole position: L. Capirossi (I, Aprilia), 1'35"025 (168.511 km/h).
1. V. Rossi (I, Aprilia), 25 laps in 40'06"135 (166.374 km/h); 2. L. Capirossi (I, Aprilia), at 1"339; 3. O. Jacque (F, Honda), at 1"421; 4. S. Nakano (J, Yamaha), at 8"461; 5. T. Ukawa (J, Honda), at 30"795; 6. S. Perugini (I, Honda), at 31"875; 7. L. D'Antin (E, Yamaha), at 42"304; 8. H.

Aoki (J, Honda), at 42"740; 9. N. Numata (J, Suzuki), at 42"773; 10. L. Boscoscuro (I, TSR-Honda), at 45"696; 11. J. Stigefelt (S, Suzuki), at 47"850; 12. T. Tsujimura (J, Yamaha), at 48"121; 13. R. Rolfo (I, TSR-Honda), at 1'16"123; 14. Y. Hatakeyama (J, Honda), at 1'16"438; 15. O. Miyazaki (J, Yamaha), at 1'16"524. 20 classified.
Fastest lap: T. Harada (J, Aprilia), 1'35"253 (168.108 km/h). New record. Old: R. Waldmann (D, Honda, 1'35"409/1997).

## 25 octobre - GP d'Argentine - Buenos Aires
Pole position: L. Capirossi (I, Aprilia), 1'45"568 (148.340 km/h).
1. V. Rossi (I, Aprilia), 25 laps in 44'26"581 (146.817 km/h); 2. L. Capirossi (I, Aprilia), at 5"360; 3. O. Jacque (F, Honda), at 27"096; 4. T. Ukawa (J, Honda), at 27"451; 5. R. Rolfo (I, TSR-Honda), at 30"820; 6. J. McWilliams (GB, TSR-Honda), at 41"816; 7. N. Numata (J, Suzuki), at 42"555; 8. J. Stigefelt (S, Suzuki), at 42"708; 9. F. Battaini (I, Yamaha), at 43"148; 10. L. Boscoscuro (I, TSR-Honda), at 52"505; 11. T. Tsujimura (I, Yamaha), at 54"131; 12. D. Bulega (I, ERP Honda), at 1'07"509; 13. D. Giugovaz (I, Aprilia), at 1'12"506; 14. O. Miyazaki (I, Yamaha), at 1'35"028; 15. W. Coulter (GB, Honda), at 1'37"371. 20 classified.
Fastest lap: V. Rossi (I, Aprilia), 1'45"473 (148.474 km/h). New record. Old: M. Biaggi (I, Aprilia, 1'46"214/1995).

## Final classification

| | | | |
|---|---|---|---|
| 1. Loris Capirossi | Italy | Aprilia | 224 |
| 2. Valentino Rossi | Italy | Aprilia | 201 |
| 3. Tetsuya Harada | Japan | Aprilia | 200 |
| 4. Tohru Ukawa | Japan | Honda | 145 |
| 5. Olivier Jacque | France | Honda | 112 |
| 6. Haruchika Aoki | Japan | Honda | 112 |
| 7. Stefano Perugini | Italy | Honda | 102 |
| 8. Takeshi Tsujimura | Japan | Yamaha | 91 |
| 9. Jeremy McWilliams | Great Britain | TSR-Honda | 87 |
| 10. Luis D'Antin | Spain | Yamaha | 74 |

11. R. Rolfo (I, TSR-Honda), 61; 12. J.-L. Cardoso (E, Yamaha), 61; 13. J. Vincent (GB, TSR-Honda), 60; 14. L. Boscoscuro (I, TSR-Honda), 58; 15. N. Numata (J, Suzuki), 52; 16. M. Lucchi (I, Aprilia), 52; 17. J. Fuchs (D, Aprilia), 45; 18. F. Battaini (I, Yamaha), 34; 19. S. Nakano (J, Yamaha), 33; 20. D. Kato (J, Honda), 25; 21. J. Stigefelt (S, Suzuki), 22; 22. S. Porto (ARG, Aprilia), 17; 23. N. Matsudo (J, Yamaha), 16; 24. O. Miyazaki (J, Yamaha), 14; 25. D. Bulega (I, ERP Honda), 11; 26. Y. Kagayama (J, Suzuki), 10; 27. Y. Hatakeyama (J, ERP Honda), 9; 28. I. Clementi (I, Yamaha), 7; 29. A. Hofmann (D, Honda), 6; 30. W. Costes (F, Honda), 6; 31. D. Giugovaz (I, Aprilia), 3; 32. C. Kameya (J, Suzuki), 3; 33. J. Robinson (GB, Yamaha), 2; 34. W. Coulter (GB, Honda), 1; 35. F. Gartner (ARG, Aprilia), 1; 36. J. Allemand (F, Honda), 1; 37. I. Bonilla (E, Honda); 38. M. Baldinger (D, Honda), 1. 38 classified.

**500cc**

### 5th Avril - Japanese GP - Suzuka
Pole position: M. Biaggi (I, Honda V4), 2'05''772 (167.846 km/h).
1. M. Biaggi (I, Honda V4), 21 laps in 44'59''478 (164.223 km/h); 2. T. Okada (J, Honda V4), at 5''416; 3. N. Haga (J, Yamaha), at 5''502; 4. A. Crivillé (E, Honda V4), at 10''532; 5. K. Nanba (J, Yamaha), at 10''879; 6. N. Aoki (J, Suzuki), at 13''479; 7. A. Barros (BR, Honda V4), at 20''266; 8. C. Checa (E, Honda V4), at 20''439; 9. S. Crafar (NZ, Yamaha), at 20''773; 10. S. Gibernau (E, Honda V2), at 47''101; 11. K. Roberts Junior (USA, Modenas KR3), at 1'13''558; 12. D. Romboni (I, MuZ-Swissauto), at 1'22''856; 13. J. Kocinski (USA, Honda V4), at 1'24''964; 14. N. Abé (J, Yamaha), at 1'25''293; 15. J.-B. Borja (E, Honda V2), at 1'59''992. 16 classified.
Fastest lap: M. Biaggi (I, Honda V4), 2'06''746 (166.556 km/h). New record. Old: M. Doohan (AUS, Honda V4, 2'07''782/1997).

### 19th April - Malaysian GP - Johor Bahru
Pole position: M. Doohan (AUS, Honda V4), 1'28''225 (157.506 km/h).
1. M. Doohan (AUS, Honda V4), 30 laps in 45'15''533 (153.516 km/h); 2. C. Checa (E, Honda V4), at 2''634; 3. M. Biaggi (I, Honda), at 4''410; 4. A. Crivillé (E, Honda V4), at 10''619; 5. J. Kocinski (USA, Honda V4), at 13''079; 6. Y. Kagayama (J, Suzuki), at 19''382; 7. N. Fujiwara (J, Yamaha), at 41''494; 8. J. Van den Goorbergh (NL, Honda V2), at 48''970; 9. R. Waldmann (D, Modenas KR3), at 52''131; 10. G. McCoy (AUS, Honda V2), at 1'00''294; 11. K. Roberts Junior (USA, Modenas KR3), at 1'20''245; 12. M. Wait (USA, Honda V2), at 1'23''599; 13. S. Gimbert (F, Honda V2), at 1'34''532. 13 classified.
Fastest lap: M. Doohan (AUS, Honda V4), 1'29''636 (155.026 km/h). New record (new track).

### 3rd May - Spanish GP - Jerez
Pole position: C. Checa (E, Honda V4), 1'43''467 (153.892 km/h).
1. Alex Crivillé (E, Honda V4), 27 laps in 47'21''522 (151.297 km/h); 2. M. Doohan (AUS, Honda V4), at 0''393; 3. M. Biaggi (I, Honda V4), at 0''870; 4. C. Checa (E, Honda V4), at 2''368; 5. A. Barros (BR, Honda V4), at 13''311; 6. N. Abé (J, Yamaha), at 13''933; 7. T. Okada (J, Honda V4), at 14''471; 8. N. Aoki (J, Suzuki), at 24''127; 9. K. Roberts Junior (USA, Modenas KR3), at 26''700; 10. R. Waldmann (D, Modenas KR3), at 29''597; 11. J. Kocinski (USA, Honda V4), at 31''561; 12. S. Gibernau (E, Honda V2), at 36''141; 13. S. Crafar (NZ, Yamaha), at 41''486; 14. R. Laconi (F, Yamaha), at 54''947; 15. G. McCoy (AUS, Honda V2), at 55''158. 22 classified.
Fastest lap: A. Crivillé (E, Honda V4), 1'44''448 (152.447 km/h). Record: K. Schwantz (USA, Suzuki, 1'44''168/1994).

### 17th May - Italian GP - Mugello
Pole position: M. Doohan (AUS, Honda V4), 1'53''282 (166.681 km/h).
1. M. Doohan (AUS, Honda V4), 23 laps in 43'55''307 (164.795 km/h); 2. M. Biaggi (I, Honda V4), at 5''395; 3. A. Crivillé (E, Honda V4), at 13''141; 4. C. Checa (E, Honda V4), at 19''647; 5. J. Kocinski (USA, Honda V4), at 19''826; 6. N. Abé (J, Yamaha), at 21''881; 7. S. Crafar (NZ, Yamaha), at 22''626; 8. N. Aoki (J, Suzuki), at 24''235; 9. A. Barros (BR, Honda V4), at 27''943; 10. R. Laconi (F, Yamaha), at 40''767; 11. R. Waldmann (D, Modenas KR3), at 47''331; 12. K. Nanba (J, Yamaha), at 59''623; 13. G. McCoy (AUS, Honda V2), at 1'04''004; 14. S. Gibernau (E, Honda V2), at 1'09''319; 15. F. Gimbert (F, Honda V2), at 1'14''294. 20 classified.
Fastest lap: M. Doohan (AUS, Honda V4), 1'53''342 (166.593 km/h). New record. Old: M. Doohan (AUS, Honda V4, 1'53''829/1993).

### 31th May - French GP - Le Castellet
Pole position: M. Doohan (AUS, Honda V4), 1'21''188 (168.497 km/h).
1. A. Crivillé (E, Honda V4), 31 laps in 42'41''128 (165.583 km/h); 2. M. Doohan (AUS, Honda V4), at 0''283; 3. C. Checa (E, Honda V4), at 0''498; 4. J. Kocinski (USA, Honda V4), at 6''888; 5. M. Biaggi (I, Honda V4), at 10''447; 6. L. Cadalora (I, Yamaha), at 16''305; 7. N. Abé (J, Yamaha), at 16''791; 8. N. Aoki (J, Suzuki), at 17''041; 9. S. Crafar (NZ, Yamaha), at 20''553; 10. S. Gibernau (E, Honda V2), at 23''754; 11. R. Laconi (F, Yamaha), at 37''553; 12. R. Waldmann (D, Modenas KR3), at 43''819; 13. K. Roberts Junior (USA, Modenas KR3), at 48''079; 14. J.-B. Borja (E, Honda V2), at 51''451; 15. J. Van den Goorbergh (NL, Honda V2), at 1'03''343. 19 classified.
Fastest lap: A. Crivillé (E, Honda V4), 1'21''736 (167.368 km/h). Record: M. Doohan (AUS, Honda V4, 1'21''674/1997).

### 14th June - Madrid GP - Jarama
Pole position: M. Doohan (AUS, Honda V4), 1'32''493 (149.849 km/h).
1. C. Checa (E, Honda V4), 30 laps in 47'21''513 (146.330 km/h); 2. N. Abé (J, Yamaha), at 0''220; 3. S. Gibernau (E, Honda V2), at 1''886; 4. N. Aoki (J, Suzuki), at 5''206; 5. A. Crivillé (E, Honda V4), at 11''165; 6. M. Biaggi (I, Honda V4), at 11''579; 7. R. Laconi (F, Yamaha), at 11''711; 8. S. Crafar (NZ, Yamaha), at 32''658; 9. A. Barros (BR, Honda V4), at 36''226; 10. R. Waldmann (D, Modenas KR3), at 55''342; 11. G. McCoy (AUS, Honda V2), at 56''938; 12. S. Smart (GB, Honda V2), at 1'22''806; 13. M. Wait (USA, Honda V2), at 1'26''677; 14. E. Suter (CH, MuZ-Swissauto), at one lap; 15. F. Cristobal (E, Honda V2). 16 classified.
Fastest lap: C. Checa (E, Honda V4), 1'33''617 (148.050 km/h). New record. Old: J. Kocinski (USA, Cagiva, 1'34''090/1993).

### 27th June - Dutch GP - Assen
Pole position: M. Doohan (AUS, Honda V4), 2'02''092 (178.360 km/h).
1. M. Doohan (AUS, Honda V4), 20 laps in 41'17''788 (175.772 km/h); 2. M. Biaggi (I, Honda V4), at 0''560; 3. S. Crafar (NZ, Yamaha), at 1''151; 4. A. Barros (BR, Honda V4), at 5''151; 5. C. Checa (E, Honda V4), at 13''827; 6. A. Crivillé (E, Honda V4), at 21''256; 7. N. Aoki (J, Suzuki), at 28''877; 8. T. Okada (J, Honda V4), at 33''544; 9. R. Laconi (F, Yamaha), at 44''870; 10. J. Van den Goorbergh (NL, Honda V2), at 48''118; 11. G. McCoy (AUS, Honda V2), at 1'11''257; 12. K. Roberts Junior (USA, Modenas KR3), at 1'30''137; 13. M. Wait (USA, Honda V2), at 1'39''885; 14. S. Smart (GB, Honda V2), at one lap; 15. B. Garcia (F, Honda V2). 15 classified.
Fastest lap: M. Doohan (AUS, Honda V4), 2'02''941 (177.128 km/h). Record: K. Schwantz (USA, Suzuki, 2'02''443/1991).

### 5th July - British GP - Donington
Pole position: S. Crafar (NZ, Yamaha), 1'32''128 (157.203 km/h).
1. S. Crafar (NZ, Yamaha), 30 laps in 46'45''662 (154.859 km/h); 2. M. Doohan (AUS, Honda V4), at 11''530; 3. N. Abé (J, Yamaha), at 17''924; 4. A. Crivillé (E, Honda V4), at 22''933; 5. A. Barros (BR, Honda V4), at 23''430; 6. M. Biaggi (I, Honda V4), at 35''214; 7. N. Aoki (J, Suzuki), at 53''997; 8. R. Laconi (F, Yamaha), at 1'08''211; 9. J. Van den Goorbergh (NL, Honda V2), at 1'39''256; 10. S. Smart (GB, Honda V2), at one lap; 11. B. Garcia (F, Honda V2); 12. J. McGuiness (GB, Honda V2); 13. G. McCoy (AUS, Honda V2); 14. F. Cristobal (E, Honda V2); 15. F. Carpani (I, Honda V2), at two laps. 15 classified.
Fastest lap: S. Crafar (NZ, Yamaha), 1'32''661 (156.298 km/h). New record. Old: M. Doohan (AUS, Honda V4, 1'32''856/1997).

### 19th July - German GP - Sachsenring
Pole position: M. Biaggi (I, Honda V4), 1'27''894 (143.682 km/h).
1. M. Doohan (AUS, Honda V4), 31 laps in 46'00''876 (141.800 km/h); 2. M. Biaggi (I, Honda V4), at 2''873; 3. A. Crivillé (E, Honda V4), at 11''379; 4. A. Barros (BR, Honda V4), at 11''533; 5. R. Laconi (F, Yamaha), at 19''093; 6. K. Roberts Junior (USA, Modenas KR3), at 30''087; 7. R. Waldmann (D, Modenas KR3), at 34''881; 8. J. Van den Goorbergh (NL, Honda V2), at 35''033; 9. K. Nanba (J, Yamaha), at 46''078; 10. N. Aoki (J, Suzuki), at 48''684; 11. G. Lavilla (E, Honda V4), at 58''019; 12. B. Garcia (F, Honda V2), at 1'03''165; 13. E. Suter (CH, MuZ-Swissauto), at 1'10''827; 14. M. Wait (USA, Honda V2), at 1'10''941; 15. F. Cristobal (E, Honda V2), at 1'31''896. 16 classified.
Fastest lap: A. Barros (BR, Honda V4), 1'28''381 (142.890 km/h). New record (new track).

### 23rd August - Czech Republic GP - Brno

Pole position: M. Doohan (AUS, Honda V4), 2'01"585 (159.976 km/h).

1. M. Biaggi (I, Honda V4), 22 laps in 45'12"043 (157.784 km/h); 2. A. Crivillé (E, Honda V4), at 0"768; 3. A. Barros (BR, Honda V4), at 1"546; 4. T. Okada (J, Honda V4), at 2"235; 5. N. Abé (J, Yamaha), at 11"817; 6. S. Gibernau (E, Honda V2), at 11"946; 7. C. Checa (E, Honda V4), at 16"317; 8. J.-M. Bayle (F, Yamaha), at 18"526; 9. R. Laconi (F, Yamaha), at 24"157; 10. K. Roberts Junior (USA, Modenas KR3), at 30"549; 11. S. Crafar (NZ, Yamaha), at 34"563; 12. N. Aoki (J, Suzuki), at 38"113; 13. R. Waldmann (D, Modenas KR3), at 38"525; 14. E. Suter (CH, MuZ-Swissauto), at 53"129; 15. J. Kocinski (USA, Honda V4), at 53"129. 21 classified.
Fastest lap: A. Crivillé (E, Honda V4), 2'02"335 (158.996 km/h). New record. Old: M. Doohan (AUS, Honda V4, 2'02"560/1997).

### 6th September - San Marino GP - Imola

Pole position: J.-M. Bayle (F, Yamaha), 1'49"345 (162.311 km/h).

1. M. Doohan (AUS, Honda V4), 25 laps in 46'00"092 (160.755 km/h); 2. A. Crivillé (E, Honda V4), at 6"563; 3. M. Biaggi (I, Honda V4), at 8"721; 4. A. Barros (BR, Honda V4), at 11"244; 5. J.-M. Bayle (F, Yamaha), at 21"672; 6. N. Abé (J, Yamaha), at 28"407; 7. T. Okada (J, Honda V4), at 36"627; 8. S. Gibernau (E, Honda V2), at 36"876; 9. N. Aoki (J, Suzuki), at 37"332; 10. C. Checa (E, Honda V4), at 47"677; 11. S. Crafar (NZ, Yamaha), at 55"890; 12. R. Laconi (F, Yamaha), at 57"040; 13. J.

Kocinski (USA, Honda V4), at 58"878; 14. K. Roberts Junior (USA, Modenas KR3), at 1'06"104; 15. R. Waldmann (D, Modenas KR3), at 1'18"308. 19 classified.
Fastest lap: M. Biaggi (I, Honda V4), 1'49"556 (161.999 km/h). Record: M. Doohan (AUS, Honda V4, 1'49"436/1997).

### 20th September - Catalunya GP - Catalunya

Pole position: A. Crivillé (E, Honda V4), 1'45"583 (161.173 km/h).

1. M. Doohan (AUS, Honda V4), 25 laps in 44'53"264 (157.960 km/h); 2. T. Okada (J, Honda V4), at 1"974; 3. N. Abé (J, Yamaha), at 8"260; 4. S. Gibernau (E, Honda V2), at 20"865; 5. S. Crafar (NZ, Yamaha), at 22"967; 6. C. Checa (E, Honda V4), at 24"933; 7. A. Barros (BR, Honda V4), at 25"764; 8. R. Laconi (F, Yamaha), at 28"571; 9. J. Kocinski (USA, Honda V4), at 41"358; 10. K. Roberts Junior (USA, Modenas KR3), at 41"373; 11. N. Aoki (J, Suzuki), at 48"310; 12. R. Waldmann (D, Modenas KR3), at 50"942; 13. J. Van den Goorbergh (NL, Honda V2), at 1'10"545; 14. M. Wait (USA, Honda V2), at 1'14"721; 15. S. Smart (GB, Honda V2), at 1'14"779. 16 classified.
Fastest lap: A. Barros (BR, Honda V4), 1'46"810 (159.322 km/h). New record. Old: M. Doohan (AUS, Honda V4, 1'46"861/1997).

### 4th October - Australian GP - Phillip Island

Pole position: M. Doohan (AUS, Honda V4), 1'33"162 (171.881 km/h).

1. M. Doohan (AUS, Honda V4), 27 laps in 42'42"511 (168.719 km/h); 2. S. Crafar (NZ, Yamaha), at 0"818; 3. A. Crivillé (E, Honda V4), at 2"684; 4. A. Barros (BR, Honda V4), at

2"727; 5. N. Abé (J, Yamaha), at 9"060; 6. N. Aoki (J, Suzuki), at 12"961; 7. R. Laconi (F, Yamaha), at 13"056; 8. M. Biaggi (I, Honda V4), at 14"111; 9. T. Okada (J, Honda V4), at 36"458; 10. K. Roberts Junior (USA, Modenas KR3), at 43"354; 11. J. Van den Goorbergh (NL, Honda V2), at 1'00"551; 12. J. Kocinski (USA, Honda V4), at 1'05"755; 13. M. Wait (USA, Honda V2), at 1'07"659; 14. M. Willis (AUS, Suzuki), at 1'10"720; 15. S. Smart (GB, Honda V2), at 1'30"432. 16 classified.
Fastest lap: S. Crafar (NZ, Yamaha), 1'33"868 (170.588 km/h). New record. Old: M. Doohan (AUS, Honda V4, 1'34"113/1997).

### 25th October - Argentinian GP - Buenos Aires

Pole position: M. Doohan (AUS, Honda V4), 1'44"193 (150.298 km/h).

1. M. Doohan (AUS, Honda V4), 27 laps in 47'07"332 (149.547 km/h); 2. T. Okada (J, Honda V4), at 4"762; 3. A. Barros (BR, Honda V4), at 5"590; 4. N. Abé (J, Yamaha), at 27"685; 5. M. Biaggi (I, Honda V4), at 30"254; 6. R. Laconi (F, Yamaha), at 30"441; 7. J.-M. Bayle (F, Yamaha), at 30"647; 8. C. Checa (E, Honda V4), at 30"944; 9. S. Gibernau (E, Honda V2), at 32"808; 10. J. Kocinski (USA, Honda V4), at 41"714; 11. K. Roberts Junior (USA, Modenas KR3), at 46"746; 12. N. Aoki (J, Suzuki), at 48"264; 13. S. Crafar (NZ, Yamaha), at 1'02"063; 14. J. Van den Goorbergh (NL, Honda V2), at 1'03"255; 15. R. Waldmann (D, Modenas KR3), at 1'06"271. 21 classified.
Fastest lap: T. Okada (J, Honda V4), 1'44"122 (150.400 km/h). New record. Old: D. Beattie (AUS, Suzuki, 1'44"654/1995).

## The 1999 Calender

| 18 April | Malaysia | Sepang* |
| 25 April | Japan | Motegi |
| 9 May | Spain | Jerez de la Frontera* |
| 23 May | France | Le Castellet |
| 6 June | Italy | Mugello |
| 20 June | Catalunya | Catalunya |
| 26 June | Netherlands | Assen* |
| 4 July | Great Britain | Donington* |
| 18 July | Germany | Sachsenring |
| 8 August | To be announced | |
| 22 August | Czecg Republic | Brno |
| 5 September | San Marino | To be announced |
| 19 September | Valencia | Valencia* |
| 3 October | Australia | Phillip Island* |
| 10 October | South Africa | Welkom* |
| 24 October | Rio | Jacarepagua* |
| 31 October | Argentina | Buenos Aires |

(*): Circuit to be homologated, either for the first time or a renewal.
Dependent on the homologation of the Estoril circuit by the FIM, the Portuguese GP is the first reserve in case of any cancellation, at the date planned for a reserve, or any other appropriate date.
Concerning the homologation of the circuits, the Council of Directors of the FIM has taken the following decision: the circuits have to be homologated by the 31st December of the previous year. However, exceptions can be granted up to three months before the date of the event in specific cases, depending on what type of work is needed.

## Final classification

| 1. Michael Doohan | Australia | Honda | 260 |
| 2. Massimiliano Biaggi | Italy | Honda | 208 |
| 3. Alex Crivillé | Spain | Honda | 198 |
| 4. Carlos Checa | Spain | Honda | 139 |
| 5. Alexandre Barros | Brasil | Honda | 138 |
| 6. Norifumi Abé | Japan | Yamaha | 128 |
| 7. Simon Crafar | New Zealand | Yamaha | 119 |
| 8. Tadayuki Okada | Japan | Honda | 106 |
| 9. Nobuatsu Aoki | Japan | Suzuki | 101 |
| 10. Régis Laconi | France | Yamaha | 86 |

11. S. Gibernau (E, Honda), 72; 12. J. Kocinski (USA, Honda), 64; 13. K. Roberts Junior (USA, Modenas), 59; 14. R. Waldmann (D, Modenas), 46; 15. J. Van den Goorbergh (NL, Honda), 40; 16. J.-M. Bayle (F, Yamaha), 28; 17. G. McCoy (AUS, Honda), 23; 18. K. Nanba (J, Yamaha), 22; 19. M. Wait (USA, Honda), 17; 20. N. Haga (J, Yamaha), 16; 21. S. Smart (GB, Honda), 14; 22. Y. Kagayama (J, Suzuki), 10; 23. L. Cadalora (I, Yamaha), 10; 24. B. Garcia (F, Honda), 10; 25. N. Fujiwara (J, Yamaha), 9; 26. E. Suter (CH, MuZ-Swissauto), 7; 27. G. Lavilla (E, Honda), 5; 28. D. Romboni (I, MuZ-Swissauto), 4; 29. J. McGuiness (GB, Honda), 4; 30. S. Gimbert (F, Honda), 4; 31. F. Cristobal (E, Honda), 4; 32. J.-B. Borja (E, Honda), 3; 33. M. Willis (AUS, Suzuki), 2; 34. F. Carpani (I, Honda), 1. 34 classified.

*Side-car statistics*

### 17th May - Salzburgring - Austria
Pole position: S. Webster/D. James (GB, LCR-Honda R4), 1'25"001 (180.209 km/h).
1. S. Webster/D. James (GB, LCR-Honda R4), 22 laps in 31'49"285 (176.503 km/h); 2. M. Schlosser/D. Hauser (CH, LCR-BRM Swissauto), at 8"684; 3. M. Bösiger/J. Egli (CH, LCR-Honda R4), at 8"823(*); 4. P. Güdel/C. Güdel (CH, LCR-BRM Swissauto), at 9"074; 5. K. Klaffenböck/A. Hänni (A/CH, LCR-ADM R4), at 19"696; 6. S. Abbott/J. Biggs (GB, Windle-ADM R4), at 42"964; 7. K. Caspersen/J. Olsen (DK, LCR-ADM R4), at 1'31"235; 8. B. Gray/S. Pointer (GB, LCR-ADM R4), one lap down; 9. S. Soutar/D. Kellett (AUS, LCR-ADM R4); 10. W. Galbiati/G. Sala (I, LCR-Suzuki); 11. D. Van de Velde/A. Kolloch (B/D, LCR-Suzuki); 12. R. Koster/J. Klaffenböck (CH/A, LCR-ADM R4), two laps down; 13. P. Steenbergen/R. Steenbergen (NL, LCR-ADM R4), three laps down. 13 classified. Fastest lap: M. Bösiger/J. Egli (CH, LCR-Honda R4), 1'24"942 (180.334 km/h). New Record (new track).

### 27th June - Assen - Holland
Pole position: S. Webster/D. James (GB, LCR-Honda R4), 2'08"030 (170.088 km/h).
1. S. Webster/D. James (GB, LCR-Honda R4), 17 laps in 37'41"023 (163.730 km/h); 2. K. Klaffenböck/A. Hänni (A/CH, LCR-ADM R4), at 21"532; 3. M. Bösiger/J. Egli (CH, LCR-Honda R4), at 29"914(*); 4. B. Janssen/F.-G. Van Kessel (NL, LCR-BRM Swissauto), at 1'27"070; 5. S. Soutar/D. Kellett (AUS, LCR-ADM R4), at 2'10"217; 6. K. Caspersen/J. Olsen (DK, LCR-ADM R4), one lap down; 7. M. Schlosser/D. Hauser (CH, LCR-BRM Swissauto); 8. K. Liechti/D. Locher (CH, LCR-BRM Swissauto); 9. B. Fleury/J. Fleury (NZ, LCR-TFR R4); 10. B. Gray/P. Hill (GB, LCR-ADM R4); 11.

I. Guy/G. Partridge (GB, LCR-BRM Swissauto), two laps down. 11 classified. Fastest lap: S. Webster/D. James (GB, LCR-Honda R4), 2'08"196 (169.868 km/h). Record: S. Webster/D. James (GB, LCR-Honda R4, 2'07"799/1997),

### 5th July - Donington Park - Great Britain
Pole position: S. Webster/D. James (GB, LCR-Honda R4), 1'36"598 (149.928 km/h).
1. S. Webster/D. James (GB, LCR-Honda R4), 25 laps in 41'32"724 (145.250 km/h); 2. P. Güdel/C. Güdel (CH, LCR-BRM Swissauto), at 8"991; 3. M. Bösiger/J. Egli (CH, LCR-Honda R4), at 13"708(*); 4. K. Klaffenböck/A. Hänni (A/CH, LCR-ADM R4), at 19"933; 5. M. Schlosser/D. Hauser (CH, LCR-BRM Swissauto), at 25"598; 6. B. Gray/S. Pointer (GB, LCR-ADM R4), one lap down; 7. K. Caspersen/J. Olsen (DK, LCR-ADM R4); 8. S. Muldoon/C. Gusman (GB, LCR-ADM R4); 9. R. Koster/N. Long (CH/GB, LCR-ADM R4); 10. M. Whittington/P. Woodhead (GB, LCR-Yamaha); 11. K. Liechti/D. Locher (CH, LCR-BRM Swissauto); 12. I. Ashley/A. Hetherington (USA/GB, LCR-ADM R4), two laps down; 13. P. Steenbergen/R. Steenbergen (NL, LCR-ADM R4). 13 classified. Fastest lap: S. Webster/D. James (GB, LCR-Honda R4), 1'37"623 (148.354 km/h). Record: S. Abbott/J. Biggs (GB, Windle-ADM, 1'36"489/1996).

### 12th July - Most - Czech Republic
Pole position: S. Webster/D. James (GB, LCR-Honda R4), 1'30"562 (164.891 km/h).
1. S. Muldoon/C. Gusman (GB, LCR-ADM R4), 24 laps in 46'24"318 (128.717 km/h); 2. M. Schlosser/D. Hauser (CH, LCR-BRM Swissauto), at 20"634; 3. S. Abbott/J. Biggs (GB, Windle-ADM R4), at 44"826; 4. M. Neumann/C. Parzer (D/A, LCR-ADM R4), at 50"536; 5. P. Güdel/C. Güdel (CH, LCR-BRM Swissauto), at 51"879; 6. B. Janssen/F.-G. Van Kessel (NL, LCR-BRM Swissauto), at 54"636; 7. B. Gray/P. Hill (GB, LCR-ADM R4), at 1'06"403; 8. S. Webster/D. James (GB, LCR-Honda R4), at 1'06"794; 9. B. Fleury/J. Fleury (NZ, LCR-TFR R4), at 1'42"176; 10. S. Soutar/D. Kellett (AUS, LCR-ADM R4), one lap down; 11. K. Caspersen/J. Olsen (DK, LCR-ADM R4); 12. M. Bösiger/J. Egli (CH, LCR-Honda R4)(*); 13. P. Steenbergn/R. Steenbergen (NL, LCR-ADM R4), two laps down. 13 classified. Fastest lap: M. Schlosser/D. Hauser (CH, LCR-BRM Swissauto), 1'52"268 (133.011 km/h). Record: S. Webster/D. James (GB, LCR-Honda R4, 1'31"209/1997).

### 9th August - Oschersleben - Germany
Pole position: S. Webster/D. James (GB, LCR-Honda R4), 1'30"733 (145.495 km/h).
1. S. Webster/D. James (GB, LCR-Honda R4), 25 laps in 39'11"586 (140.344 km/h); 2. S. Abbott/J. Biggs (GB, Windle-ADM R4), at 6"236; 3. K. Klaffenböck/A. Hänni (A/CH, LCR-ADM R4), at 7"657; 4. M. Bösiger/J. Egli (CH, LCR-Honda R4), at 10"608(*); 5. P. Güdel/C. Güdel (CH, LCR-BRM Swissauto), at 42"202; 6. M. Schlosser/D. Hauser (CH, LCR-BRM Swissauto), at 46"301; 7. B. Janssen/F.-G. Van Kessel (NL, LCR-BRM Swissauto), at 56"812; 8. S. Soutar/D. Kellett (AUS, LCR-ADM R4), at 1'18"810; 9. J. Steinhausen/F. Schmidt (D, LCR-Suzuki), at 1'29"917; 10. B. Gallros/P. Berglund (S, LCR-ADM), one lap down; 11. K. Liechti/D. Locher (CH, LCR-BRM Swissauto); 12. R. Body/A. Peach (GB, LCR-BRM Swissauto); 13. D. Van de Velde/A. Kolloch (B/D, LCR-Suzuki); 14. C. Streubel/A. Krieg (D, LCR-Yamaha); 15. R. Koster/T. Gries (CH/D, LCR-ADM), two laps down. 16 classified. Fastest lap: S. Webster/D. James (GB, LCR-Honda R4), 1'32"168 (143.230 km/h). New Record (new circuit).

### Final classification
| | | |
|---|---|---|
| 1. Steve Webster/David James | | 124 |
| 2. Klaus Klaffenböck/Adolf Hänni | | 90 |
| 3. Markus Schlosser/Daniel Hauser | | 87 |
| 4. Paul Güdel/Charly Güdel | | 80 |
| 5. Steve Abbott/Jamie Biggs | | 47 |

6. S. Muldoon/C. Gusman, 45; 7. S. Soutar/D. Kellett, 44; 8. K. Caspersen/J. Olsen, 42; 9. B. Janssen/F.-G. Van Kessel, 36; 10. B. Gray/S. Pointer/P. Hill, 36; 11. K. Liechti/D. Locher, 31; 12. B. Fleury/J. Fleury, 22; 13. J. Steinhausen/F. Schmidt, 17; 14. R. Koster/J. Klaffenböck/R. Long/T. Gries, 15; 15. P. Steenbergen/R. Steenbergen, 15; 16. M. Neumann/C. Parzer, 13; 17. D. Van de Velde/A. Kolloch, 10; 18. I. Guy/G. Partridge, 10; 19. I. Ashley/A. Hetherington/P. Fund, 10; 20. W. Galbiati/G. Sala, M. Whittington/P. Woodhead and B. Gallros/P. Berglund, 7; 23. R. Body/A. Peach, 5; 24. C. Streubel/A. Krieg and E. Bertschi/A. Huber, 3. 25 classified.

**27th September - Rijeka - Croatia**
Pole position: M. Bösiger/J. Egli (CH, LCR-Honda R4), 1'30"874 (*)
1. K. Klaffenböck/A. Hänni (A/CH, LCR-ADM R4), 17 laps in 29'34"442 (143.122 km/h); 2. P. Güdel/C. Güdel (CH, LCR-BRM Swissauto), at 0"654; 3. S. Webster/D. James (GB, LCR-Honda R4), at 9"590; 4. M. Bösiger/J. Egli (CH, LCR-Honda R4), at 18"865(*); 5. M. Schlosser/D. Hauser (CH, LCR-BRM Swissauto), at 22"605; 6. S. Muldoon/C. Gusman (GB, LCR-ADM R4), at 27"582; 7. K. Liechti/D. Locher (CH, LCR-BRM Swissauto), at 1'19"547; 8. J. Steinhausen/F. Schmidt (D, LCR-Suzuki), at 1'28"673; 9. S. Soutar/D. Kellett (AUS, LCR-ADM R4), at 1'32"288; 10. B. Fleury/J. Fleury (NZ, LCR-TFR R4), one lap down; 11. K. Caspersen/J. Olsen (DK, LCR-ADM R4); 12. I. Ashley/P. Found (USA/GB, LCR-ADM R4); 13. I. Guy/G. Partridge (GB, LCR-BRM Swissauto); 14. E. Bertschi/A. Huber (CH, LCR-Suzuki); 15. P. Steenbergen/R. Steenbergen (NL, LCR-ADM R4). 16 classified. Fastest lap: P. Güdel/C. Güdel (CH, LCR-BRM Swissauto), 1'41"866 (147.299 km/h). Record: S. Webster/D. James (GB, LCR-Honda R4, 1'37"351/1997).

(*): M. Bösiger/J. Egli, uses a new outfit in which the rider is seated and does not score any world cup points.

**19th April - Vallelunga - Italy**

1. M. Whittington/P. Woodhead (GB, LCR-Yamaha); 2. P. Hanquet/R. Dury (B, LCR-Suzuki); 3. C. Stirrat/S. English (GB, Windle-ADM); 4. T. Rope/R. Lawrence (GB, Windle-Suzuki); 5. L. Kuipers/K. Kruip (NL, KMS-Yamaha); 6. P. Steenbergen/R. Steenbergen (NL, LCR-Honda); 7. P. Croft/S. Parnell (GB, LCR-Yamaha); 8. H. Talens/H. Kappert (NL, LCR-Yamaha); 9. R. Hughes/S. Smith (GB, LCR-Krauser); 10. S. Dagnino/F. Dagnino (ITA, LCR-Suzuki); 11. E. Olcese/A. Zanellato (ITA, Donaska-Suzuki). 11 classified.

**12th July - Rijeka - Croatia**
1. J. Steinhausen/F. Schmidt (D, LCR-Suzuki); 2. M. Whittington/P. Woodhead (GB, LCR-Yamaha); 3. T. Rope/R. Lawrence (GB, Windle-Suzuki); 4. C. Stirrat/S. English (GB, Windle-ADM); 5. S. Hall/N. Wood (GB, LCR-Suzuki); 6. E. Olcese/F. Caloni (I, Donaska-Suzuki); 7. C. Baert/T. Ruiter (B(NL, LCR-Honda ADM). 7 classified.

**26th July - Croft - Great Britain**
1. J. Steinhausen/F. Schmidt (D, LCR-Suzuki); 2. D. Hendry/N. Miller (GB, Suzuki); 3. J.-N. Minguet/S. Voilque (F, LCR-Suzuki); 4. T. Baker/L. Aubrey (GB, LCR-Krauser); 5. T. Rope/R. Lawrence (GB, Windle-Suzuki); 6. C. Stirrat/S. English (GB, Windle-ADM); 7. A. Hodge/J. McLean (GB, Krauser); 8. S. Hall/N. Wood (GB, LCR-Suzuki); 9. L. Kuipers/K. Kruip (NL, KMS-Yamaha); 10. C. Woodward/S. Woodward (GB, Windle-Krauser); 11. H. Talens/H. Kappert (NL, LCR-Yamaha); 12. P. Croft/S. Parnell (GB, LCR-Yamaha); 13. A. Percy/E. Kiff (GB, LCR-Yamaha); 14. R. Hughes/S. Smith (GB, LCR-Krauser); 15. C. Baert/T. Ruiter (B/NL, LCR-Honda ADM).

**16th August - Schleiz - Germany**
1. J. Steinhausen/F. Schmidt (D, LCR-Suzuki); 2. D. Van de Velde/A. Kolloch (B/D, LCR-Suzuki); 3. J. Skene/N. Miller (GB, Suzuki); 4. J.-N. Minguet/S. Voilque (F, LCR-Suzuki); 5. T. Baker/R. Long (GB, LCR-Krauser); 6. M. Van Gils/T. Van Gils (NL, LCR-Suzuki); 7. S. Hall/N. Wood (GB, LCR-Suzuki); 8. U. Schneider/A. Kölsch (D, Honda); 9. C. Baert/T. Ruiter (B/NL, LCR); 10. S. Kiser/M. Sanapo (CH, Kawasaki); 11. E. Hug/S. Kubli (CH, Suzuki); 12. T. Hansen/O. Pedersen (DK, LCR-Yamaha); 13. H. Talens/H. Kappert (NL, LCR-ADM). 13 classified.

**6th September - Assen - Holland**
1. J.-N. Minguet/S. Voilque (F, LCR-Suzuki); 2. M. Van Gils/T. Van Gils (NL, LCR-Suzuki); 3. L. Kuipers/K. Kruip (NL, KMS-Yamaha); 4. P. Steenbergen/R. Steenbergen (NL, LCR-Honda); 5. C. Baert/T. Ruiter (B/NL, LCR-Honda ADM); 6. R. Geleijnse/B. Bosman (NL, LCR-Suzuki); 7. J.-C. Voilque/M. Voilque (F, LCR-Suzuki); 8. H. Talens/H. Kappert (NL, LCR-Yamaha). 8 classified.

**Final classification**

| | |
|---|---|
| 1. Jörg Steinhausen/Frank Schmidt | 75 |
| 2. Jean-Noël Minguet/Stéphane Voilque | 54 |
| 3. Martin Whittington/Paul Woodhead | 45 |
| 4. Tim Rope/Rick Lawrence | 40 |
| 5. Clive Stirrat/Steve English | 39 |

6. L. Kuipers/K. Kruip, 34; 7. M. Van Gils/T. Van Gils, 30; 8. S. Hall/N. Wood, 28; 9. C. Baert/T. Ruiter, 28; 10. T. Baker/L. Aubrey/R. Long, 24; 11. H. Talens/H. Kappert, 24; 12. P. Steenbergen/R. Steenbergen, 23; 13. P. Hanquet/R. Dury, D. Hendry/N. Miller and D. Van de Velde/A. Kolloch, 20; 16. J. Skene/N. Miller, 16; 17. E. Olcese/A. Zanellato/F. Caloni, 15; 18. P. Croft/S. Parnell, 13; 19. R. Geleijnse/B. Bosman, 10; 20. A. Hodge/J. McLean and J.-C. Voilque/M. Voilque, 9; 22. R. Hughes/S. Smith, 9; 23. U. Schneider/A. Kölsch, 8; 24. S. Dagnino/F. Dagnino, C. Woodard/S. Woodard and S. Kiser/M. Sanapo, 6; 27. E. Hug/S. Kubli, 5; 28. T. Hansen/O. Pedersen, 4; 29. A. Percy/E. Kiff, 3. 29 classified.

*Superbike*

### 22nd March - Australia - Phillip Island
Pole position (superpole): T. Corser (AUS, Ducati), 1'34"971 (168.683 km/h). Best time in qualifying: P. Goddard (AUS, Suzuki), 1'34"251 (169.971 km/h).
Race I: 1. Carl Fogarty (GB, Ducati), 22 laps in 35'38"433 (164.812 km/h); 2. T. Corser (AUS, Ducati), at 1''040; 3. N. Haga (J, Yamaha), at 3''131; 4. P. Chili (I, Ducati), at 9''929; 5. A. Yanagawa (J, Kawasaki), at 15''271; 6. M. Willis (AUS, Suzuki), at 24''840; 7. C. Edwards (USA, Honda), at 28''494; 8. N. Hodgson (GB, Kawasaki), at 30''350; 9. A. Slight (NZ, Honda), at 30''961; 10. S. Russell (USA, Yamaha), at 37''120; 11. G. Lavilla (E, Ducati), at 38''115; 12. P. Bontempi (I, Kawasaki), at 41''307; 13. L. Pedercini (I, Ducati), at 51''070; 14. M. Campbell (AUS, Ducati), at 53''346; 15. I. Jerman (SK, Kawasaki), at 53''601. 26 classified. Fastest lap: C. Fogarty (GB, Ducati), 1'35"772 (167.272 km/h).
Race II: 1. N. Haga (J, Yamaha), 22 laps in 35'35"822 (165.013 km/h); 2. A. Slight (NZ, Honda), at 0''071; 3. C. Fogarty (GB, Ducati), at 6''655; 4. P. Goddard (AUS, Suzuki), at 8''505; 5. A. Yanagawa (J, Kawasaki), at 8''520; 6. T. Corser (AUS, Ducati), at 16''297; 7. C. Edwards (USA, Honda), at 20''846; 8. S. Russell (USA, Yamaha), at 20''911; 9. M. Willis (AUS, Suzuki), at 32''676; 10. S. Martin (AUS, Ducati), at 34''278; 11. G. Lavilla (E, Ducati), at 43''210; 12. J. Whitham (GB, Suzuki), at 43''230; 13. S. Giles (AUS, Honda), at 43''886; 14. C. Connell (AUS, Ducati), at 50''891; 15. A. Gramigni (I, Ducati), at 58''236. 24 classified. Fastest lap: A. Slight (NZ, Honda), 1'35"700 (167.398 km/h).

### 13th April - Great Britain - Donington
Pole position: T. Corser (AUS, Ducati), 1'33.707 (154.554 km/h).
Race I: 1. N. Haga (J, Yamaha), 25 laps in 39'41"163 (152.055 km/h); 2. T. Corser (AUS, Ducati), at 4''030; 3. P. Chili (I, Ducati), at 10''158; 4. A. Slight (NZ, Honda), at 10''509; 5. A. Yanagawa (J, Kawasaki), at 15''809; 6. C. Edwards (USA, Honda), at 17''845; 7. C. Fogarty (GB, Ducati), at 21''616; 8. J. Whitham (GB, Suzuki), at 24''944; 9. P. Goddard (AUS, Suzuki), at 25''207; 10. S. Hislop (GB, Yamaha), at 25''400; 11. C. Walker (GB, Kawasaki), at 36''346; 12. N. Hodgson (GB, Kawasaki), at 45''330; 13. S. Russell (USA, Yamaha), at 45''696; 14. P. Bontempi (I, Kawasaki), at 45''832; 15. J. Haydon (GB, Suzuki), at 52''390. 23 classified. Fastest lap: N. Haga (J, Yamaha), 1'34"560 (153.159 km/h).
Race II: 1. N. Haga (J, Yamaha), 25 laps in 39'35"544 (152.416 km/h); 2. T. Corser (AUS, Ducati), at 1''524; 3. C. Fogarty (GB, Ducati), at 8''214; 4. A. Slight (NZ, Honda), at 15''025; 5. P. Chili (I, Ducati), at 18''758; 6. N. MacKenzie (GB, Yamaha), at 19''253; 7. C. Edwards (USA, Honda), at 19''304; 8. J. Whitham (GB, Suzuki), at 25''956; 9. S. Hislop (GB, Yamaha), at 32''259; 10. P. Goddard (AUS,

### 10th May - Italy - Monza
Pole position (superpole): A. Slight (NZ, Honda), 1'46"651 (194.766 km/h). Best time in qualifying: A. Slight (NZ, Honda), 1'47"163 (193.835 km/h).
Race I: 1. C. Edwards (USA, Honda), 18 laps in 32'24"648 (192.269 km/h); 2. A. Slight (NZ, Honda), at 0''083; 3. T. Corser (AUS, Ducati), at 5''634; 4. N. Hodgson (GB, Kawasaki), at 6''096; 5. P. Chili (I, Ducati), at 6''147; 6. C. Fogarty (GB, Ducati), at 6''237; 7. P. Goddard (AUS, Suzuki), at 20''281; 8. J. Whitham (GB, Suzuki), at 24''424; 9. N. Haga (J, Yamaha), at 29''318; 10. G. Lavilla (E, Ducati), at 29''538; 11. A. Meklau (A, Ducati), at 29''651; 12. A. Gramigni (I, Ducati), at 40''880; 13. I. Jerman (SK, Kawasaki), at 1'03''283; 14. L. Pedercini (I, Ducati), at 1'12''562; 15. E. Korpiaho (SF, Kawasaki), at 1'15''038. 20 classified. Fastest lap: A. Slight (NZ, Honda), 1'46"856 (194.392 km/h).
Race II: 1. C. Edwards (USA, Honda), 18 laps in 32'29"458 (191.795 km/h); 2. C. Fogarty (GB, Ducati), at 2''697; 3. P. Chili (I, Ducati), at 4''295; 4. T. Corser (AUS, Ducati), at 10''641; 5. J. Whitham (GB, Suzuki), at 18''439; 6. A. Yanagawa (J, Kawasaki), at 18''464; 7. N. Hodgson (GB, Kawasaki), at 25''502; 8. P. Goddard (AUS, Suzuki), at 25''610; 9. A. Meklau (A, Ducati), at 28''125; 10. N. Haga (J, Yamaha), at 28''134; 11. P. Bontempi (I, Kawasaki), at 36''917; 12. I. Jerman (SK, Kawasaki), at 53''692; 13. A. Gramigni (I, Ducati), at 53''864; 14. L. Pedercini (I, Ducati), at 1'12''800; 15. E. Korpiaho (SF, Kawasaki), at 1'13''704. 21 classified. Fastest lap: A. Slight (NZ, Honda), 1'46"866 (194.374 km/h).

### 24th May - Spain - Albacete
Pole position (superpole): N. Haga (J, Yamaha), 1'32''322 (137.999 km/h) (*). Best time in qualifying: G. Lavilla (E, Ducati), 1'31''631 (139.040 km/h).
Race I: 1. P. Chili (I, Ducati), 20 laps in 34'32''554 (122.944 km/h); 2. T. Corser (AUS, Ducati), at 1''316; 3. G. Lavilla (E, Ducati), at 3''809; 4. A. Slight (NZ, Honda), at 10''650; 5. C. Edwards (USA, Honda), at 11''978; 6. S. Russell (USA, Yamaha), at 12''112; 7. N. Hodgson (GB, Kawasaki), at 12''894; 8. A. Gramigni (I, Ducati), at 36''202; 9. C. Fogarty (GB, Ducati), at 46''785; 10. N. Haga (J, Yamaha), at 51''169; 11. J. Whitham (GB, Suzuki), at 52''889; 12. P. Bontempi (I, Kawasaki), at 53''550; 13. A. Yanagawa (J, Kawasaki), at 53''658; 14. P. Goddard (AUS, Suzuki), at 54''959; 15. E. Korpiaho (SF, Kawasaki), at 1'05''985. 20 classified. Fastest lap: P. Chili (I, Ducati), 1'41''284 (125.788 km/h).
Race II: 1. C. Fogarty (GB, Ducati), 20 laps in 31'09''535 (136.295 km/h); 2. A. Slight (NZ, Honda), at 6''032; 3. T. Corser (AUS, Ducati), at 8''807; 4. N. Haga (J, Yamaha), at 15''357; 5. P. Chili (I, Ducati), at 16''162; 6. P. Bontempi (I, Kawasaki), at 20''656; 7. A. Yanagawa (J, Kawasaki), at 20''744; 8. P. Goddard (AUS, Suzuki), at 29''677; 9. S. Russell (USA, Yamaha), at 30''991; 10. J. Whitham (GB, Suzuki), at 1'00''057; 11. J.-M. Delétang (F, Yamaha), at 1'00''728; 12. I. Jerman (SK, Kawasaki), at 1'07''780; 13. F. Protat (F, Ducati), at 1'15''505; 14. N. Hodgson (GB, Kawasaki), at 1'21''942; 15. J. Mrkyvka (CZ, Honda), at 1'37''421. 16 classified. Fastest lap: A. Slight (NZ, Honda), 1'32''845 (137.222 km/h).

Suzuki), at 33''457; 11. S. Russell (USA, Yamaha), at 42''292; 12. C. Walker (GB, Kawasaki), at 44''433; 13. P. Bontempi (I, Kawasaki), at 48''476; 14. J. Haydon (GB, Suzuki), at 51''432; 15. T. Rymer (GB, Suzuki), at 1'02''060. 23 classified. Fastest lap: N. Haga (J, Yamaha), 1'33''880 (154.269 km/h).

### 7th June - Germany - Nürburgring
Pole position (superpole): T. Corser (AUS, Ducati), 1'40"484 (163.225 km/h). Best time in qualifying: A. Slight (NZ, Honda), 1'39"519 (164.808 km/h).
Race I: 1. A. Slight (NZ, Honda), 21 laps in 40'31''963 (141.628 km/h); 2. C. Edwards (USA, Honda), at 6''608; 3. P. Chili (I, Ducati), at 12''436; 4. A. Yanagawa (J, Kawasaki), at 16''677; 5. N. Haga (J, Yamaha), at 44''204; 6. P. Goddard (AUS, Suzuki), at 44''485; 7. T. Corser (AUS, Ducati), at 44''745; 8. P. Bontempi (I, Kawasaki), at 56''233; 9. J. Whitham (GB, Suzuki), at 59''296; 10. A. Gramigni (I, Ducati), at 59''519; 11. S. Russell (USA, Yamaha), at 1'20''123; 12. L. Pedercini (I, Ducati), at 1'30''446; 13. C. Fogarty (GB, Ducati), at 1'40''282; 14. I. Jerman (SK, Kawasaki), at one lap; 15. R. Xaus (E, Suzuki). 22 classified. Fastest lap: A. Slight (NZ, Honda), 1'53''516 (144.487 km/h).
Race II: 1. P. Chili (I, Ducati), 21 laps in 40'48''961 (140.645 km/h); 2. C. Edwards (USA, Honda), at 11''117; 3. T. Corser (AUS, Ducati), at 11''925; 4. A. Slight (NZ, Honda), at 34''889; 5. A. Yanagawa (J, Kawasaki), at 37''330; 6. G. Lavilla (E, Ducati), at 55''872; 7. N. Haga (J, Yamaha), at 1'04''479; 8. P. Goddard (AUS, Suzuki), at 1'14''487; 9. P. Bontempi (I, Kawasaki), at 1'21''927; 10. J. Whitham (GB, Suzuki), at 1'23''325; 11. N. Hodgson (GB, Kawasaki), at 1'23''810; 12. U. Mark (D, Suzuki), at 1'40''250; 13. C. Fogarty (GB, Ducati), at 1'49''074; 14. L. Pedercini (I, Ducati), at one lap; 15. I. Jerman (SK, Kawasaki). 23 classified. Fastest lap: P. Chili (I, Ducati), 1'54''508 (143.235 km/h).

### 21st June - San Marino - Misano
Pole position (superpole): T. Corser (AUS, Ducati), 1'33"729 (155.938 km/h). Best time in qualifying: T. Corser (AUS, Ducati), 1'33''793 (155.832 km/h).
Race I: 1. A. Slight (NZ, Honda), 25 laps in 39'54''406 (152.606 km/h); 2. T. Corser (AUS, Ducati), at 0''720; 3. C. Edwards (USA, Honda), at 2''304; 4. C. Fogarty (GB, Ducati), at 5''068; 5. A. Yanagawa (J, Kawasaki), at 10''273; 6. J. Whitham (GB, Suzuki), at 27''881; 7. N. Hodgson (GB, Kawasaki), at 31''647; 8. S. Russell (USA, Yamaha), at 40''899; 9. A. Meklau (A, Ducati), at 1'03''420; 10. U. Mark (D, Suzuki), at 1'05''941; 11. A. Gramigni (I, Ducati), at 1'09''029; 12. L. Pedercini (I, Ducati), at 1'18''771; 13. P. Blora (I, Ducati), at 1'22''198; 14. A. Stroud (NZ, Kawasaki), at 1'22''227; 15. I. Jerman (SK, Kawasaki), at 1'22''578. 22 classified. Fastest lap: A. Slight (NZ, Honda), 1'34''665 (154.397 km/h).
Race II: 1. A. Slight (NZ, Honda), 25 laps in 39'49''893 (152.894 km/h); 2. T. Corser (AUS, Ducati), at 1''058; 3. C. Fogarty (GB, Ducati), at 3''269; 4. C. Edwards (USA, Honda), at 13''450; 5. A. Yanagawa (J, Kawasaki), at 13''547; 6. S. Russell (USA, Yamaha), at 18''889; 7. G. Lavilla (E, Ducati), at 38''590; 8. N. Hodgson (GB, Kawasaki), at 38''701; 9. A. Meklau (A, Ducati), at 40''104; 10. I. Jerman (SK, Kawasaki), at 1'05''947; 11. P. Bontempi (I, Kawasaki), at 1'07''477; 12. A. Gramigni (I, Ducati), at 1'07''945; 13. U. Mark (D, Suzuki), at 1'09''703; 14. L. Pedercini (I, Ducati), at 1'21''669; 15. A. Stroud (NZ, Kawasaki), at 1'39''780. 19 classified. Fastest lap: A. Slight (NZ, Honda), 1'34''719 (154.309 km/h).

### 5th July - South Africa - Kyalami
Pole position (superpole): P. Chili (I, Ducati), 1'43''803 (147.776 km/h). Best time in qualifying: T. Corser (AUS, Ducati), 1'43''845 (147.716 km/h).
Race I: 1. P. Chili (I, Ducati), 25 laps in 43'45''405 (146.069 km/h); 2. C. Fogarty (GB, Ducati), at 1''301; 3. G. Lavilla (E, Ducati), at 8''294; 4. J. Whitham (GB, Suzuki), at 8''721; 5. P. Goddard (AUS, Suzuki), at 9''140; 6. A.

Yanagawa (J, Kawasaki), at 10"673; 7. N. Haga (J, Yamaha), at 10"688; 8. A. Slight (NZ, Honda), at 16"802; 9. C. Edwards (USA, Honda), at 17"082; 10. S. Russell (USA, Yamaha), at 37"723; 11. A. Gramigni (I, Ducati), at 1'06"067; 12. P. Bontempi (I, Kawasaki), at 1'12"741; 13. I. Jerman (SK, Kawasaki), at 1'24"722; 14. A. Stroud (NZ, Kawasaki), at one lap; 15. F. Protat (F, Ducati). 17 classified. Fastest lap: P. Chili (I, Ducati), 1'43"970 (147.538 km/h).
Race II: 1. P. Chili (I, Ducati), 25 laps in 43'45"115 (146.085 km/h); 2. C. Fogarty (GB, Ducati), at 0"230; 3. N. Haga (J, Yamaha), at 0"410; 4. C. Edwards (USA, Honda), at 1"285; 5. A. Yanagawa (J, Kawasaki), at 1"337; 6. P. Goddard (AUS, Suzuki), at 9"805; 7. T. Corser (AUS, Ducati), at 18"151; 8. A. Slight (NZ, Honda), at 31"715; 9. S. Russell (USA, Yamaha), at 37"409; 10. P. Bontempi (I, Kawasaki), at 49"942; 11. I. Jerman (SK, Kawasaki), at 56"962; 12. A. Stroud (NZ, Kawasaki), at 1'01"154; 13. L. Pedercini (I, Ducati), at 1'02"722; 14. A. Gramigni (I, Ducati), at 1'16"367; 15. F. Protat (F, Ducati), at one lap. 16 classified. Fastest lap: A. Yanagawa (J, Kawasaki), 1'44"151 (147.282 km/h).

**12th July - United States - Laguna Seca**
Pole position (superpole): T. Corser (AUS, Ducati), 1'26"325 (150.547 km/h). Best time in qualifying: D. Chandler (USA, Kawasaki), 1'26"367 (150.474 km/h).
Race I: 1. T. Corser (AUS, Ducati), 12 laps in 17'35"408 (147.765 km/h) (*); 2. A. Yanagawa (J, Kawasaki), at 7"646; 3. D. Chandler (USA, Kawasaki), at 7"656; 4. B. Bostrom (USA, Honda), at 10"388; 5. C. Fogarty (GB, Ducati), at 10"451; 6. J. Whitham (GB, Suzuki), at 10"750; 7. P. Chili (I, Ducati), at 11"232; 8. A. Slight (NZ, Honda), at 12"871; 9. N. Hodgson (GB, Kawasaki), at 14"018; 10. J. Hacking (USA, Yamaha), at 14"224; 11. C. Edwards (USA, Honda), at 15"725; 12. A. Yates (USA, Suzuki), at 16"144; 13. G. Lavilla (E, Ducati), at 22"928; 14. P. Goddard (AUS, Suzuki), at 24"272; 15. S. Russell (USA, Yamaha), at 27"531. 23 classified. Fastest lap: T. Corser (AUS, Ducati), 1'27"149 (149.123 km/h).
Race II: 1. N. Haga (J, Yamaha), 28 laps in 41'07"668 (147.462 km/h); 2. T. Corser (AUS, Ducati), at 0"488; 3. B. Bostrom (USA, Honda), at 4"715; 4. P. Chili (I, Ducati), at 4"725; 5. J. Whitham (GB, Suzuki), at 5"733; 6. N. Hodgson (GB, Kawasaki), at 16"842; 7. J. Hacking (USA, Yamaha), at 22"273; 8. P. Goddard (AUS, Suzuki), at 28"479; 9. A. Gramigni (I, Ducati), at 29"018; 10. C. Edwards (USA, Honda), at 43"357; 11. I. Jerman (SK, Kawasaki), at 59"827; 12. L. Pedercini (I, Ducati), at 1'14"092; 13. R. Orlando (USA, Kawasaki), at one lap. 13 classified. Fastest lap: N. Haga (J, Yamaha), 1'27"340 (148.797 km/h).

**2nd August - Europe - Brands Hatch**
Pole position (superpole):T. Corser (AUS, Ducati), 1'34"999 (158.591 km/h) (*). Best time in qualifying: C. Edwards (USA, Honda), 1'25"775 (175.645 km/h).
Race I: 1. C. Edwards (USA, Honda), 25 laps in 36'16"391 (173.062 km/h); 2. A. Slight (NZ, Honda), at 0"103; 3. S. Russell (USA, Yamaha), at 10"761; 4. C. Fogarty (GB, Ducati), at 12"322; 5. J. Whitham (GB, Suzuki), at 17"245; 6. N. MacKenzie (GB, Yamaha), at 20"577; 7. T. Corser (AUS, Ducati), at 23"526; 8. S. Hislop (GB, Yamaha), at 25"196; 9. P. Chili (I, Ducati), at 29"704; 10. P. Goddard (AUS, Suzuki), at 31"166; 11. S. Emmett (GB, Ducati), at 31"359; 12. N. Haga (J, Yamaha), at 41"056; 13. T. Bayliss (AUS, Ducati), at 59"363; 14. M. Llewellyn (GB, Ducati), at 1'06"585; 15. A. Gramigni (I, Ducati), at 1'22"439. 21 classified. Fastest lap:

A. Slight (NZ, Honda), 1'26"245 (174.688 km/h).
Race II: 1. T. Corser (AUS, Ducati), 25 laps in 36'07"237 (173.793 km/h); 2. C. Fogarty (GB, Ducati), at 3"240; 3. J. Whitham (GB, Suzuki), at 4"227; 4. C. Edwards (USA, Honda), at 5"366; 5. A. Slight (NZ, Honda), at 5"551; 6. P. Chili (I, Ducati), at 19"192; 7. N. Haga (J, Yamaha), at 19"876; 8. S. Russell (USA, Yamaha), at 20"030; 9. N. Hodgson (GB, Kawasaki), at 20"308; 10. N. MacKenzie (GB, Yamaha), at 20"467; 11. S. Hislop (GB, Yamaha), at 29"315; 12. J. Haydon (GB, Suzuki), at 30"128; 13. P. Goddard (AUS, Suzuki), at 30"345; 14. J. Reynolds (GB, Ducati), at 40"866; 15. T. Bayliss (AUS, Ducati), at 52"379. 21 classified. Fastest lap: J. Whitham (GB, Suzuki), 1'26"164 (174.852 km/h).

**30th August - Austria - A1-Ring**
Pole position (superpole): A. Slight (NZ, Honda), 1'30"340 (172.069 km/h). Best time in qualifying: A. Slight (NZ, Honda), 1'30"476 (171.811 km/h).
Race I: 1. A. Slight (NZ, Honda), 25 laps in 38'03"873 (170.158 km/h); 2. P. Chili (I, Ducati), at 1"155; 3. C. Fogarty (GB, Ducati), at 1"321; 4. A. Yanagawa (J, Kawasaki), at 7"771; 5. J. Whitham (GB, Suzuki), at 9"262; 6. T. Corser (AUS, Ducati), at 15"465; 7. C. Edwards (USA, Honda), at 19"287; 8. N. Hodgson (GB, Kawasaki), at 19"684; 9. N. Haga (J, Yamaha), at 23"902; 10. P. Goddard (AUS, Suzuki), at 35"152; 11. G. Lavilla (E, Ducati), at 36"285; 12. S. Russell (USA, Yamaha), at 36"358; 13. A. Gramigni (I, Ducati), at 1'10"238; 14. A. Meklau (A, Ducati), at 1'16"925; 15. I. Jerman (SK, Kawasaki), at 1'20"589. 26 classified. Fastest lap: P. Chili (I, Ducati), 1'30"447 (171.866 km/h).
Race II: 1. A. Slight (NZ, Honda), 25 laps in 38'03"213 (170.208 km/h); 2. C. Fogarty (GB, Ducati), at 0"181; 3. P. Chili (I, Ducati), at 1"972; 4. A. Yanagawa (J, Kawasaki), at 6"014; 5. T. Corser (AUS, Ducati), at 6"281; 6. J. Whitham (GB, Suzuki), at 19"436; 7. G. Lavilla (E, Ducati), at 19"881; 8. P. Goddard (AUS, Suzuki), at 19"934; 9. C. Edwards (USA, Honda), at 23"665; 10. N. Hodgson (GB, Kawasaki), at 24"238; 11. S. Russell (USA, Yamaha), at 38"571; 12. N. Haga (J, Yamaha), at 46"417; 13. A. Meklau (A, Ducati), at 56"090; 14. A. Gramigni (I, Ducati), at 58"383; 15. I. Jerman (SK, Kawasaki), at 1'18"266. 21 classified. Fastest lap: T. Corser (AUS, Ducati), 1'30"276 (172.91 km/h).

**6th September - Netherlands - Assen**
Pole position (superpole): P. Chili (I, Ducati), 2'09"983 (167.532 km/h) (*). Best time in qualifying: A. Slight (NZ, Honda), 2'03"708 (176.030 km/h).
(*): superpole declared wet.
Race I: 1. P. Chili (I, Ducati), 16 laps in 33'28"451 (173.478 km/h); 2. C. Fogarty (GB, Ducati), at 0"158; 3. T. Corser (AUS, Ducati), at 3"948; 4. A. Slight (NZ, Honda), at 19"009; 5. C. Edwards (USA, Honda), at 19"898; 6. P. Goddard (AUS, Suzuki), at 22"025; 7. A. Yanagawa (J, Kawasaki), at 22"091; 8. N. Haga (J, Yamaha), at 38"844; 9. S. Russell (USA, Yamaha), at

38"964; 10. N. Hodgson (GB, Kawasaki), at 44"653; 11. A. Gramigni (I, Ducati), at 58"171; 12. I. Jerman (SK, Kawasaki), at 1'07"225; 13. M. Innamorati (I, Kawasaki), at 1'17"891; 14. E. Korpiaho (SF, Kawasaki), at 1'23"563; 15. A. Stroud (NZ, Kawasaki), at 1'44"960. 17 classified. Fastest lap: P. Chili (I, Ducati), 2'04"526 (174.874 km/h).
Race II: 1. C. Fogarty (GB, Ducati), 16 laps in 33'30"118 (173.334 km/h); 2. A. Slight (NZ, Honda), at 5"278; 3. T. Corser (AUS, Ducati), at 5"425; 4. C. Edwards (USA, Honda), at 12"755; 5. J. Whitham (GB, Suzuki), at 12"818; 6. A. Yanagawa (J, Kawasaki), at 12"924; 7. P. Goddard (AUS, Suzuki), at 13"037; 8. N. Haga (J, Yamaha), at 35"852; 9. N. Hodgson (GB, Kawasaki), at 48"400; 10. I. Jerman (SK, Kawasaki), at 48"813; 11. M. Innamorati (I, Kawasaki), at 1'20"702; 12. E. Korpiaho (SF, Kawasaki), at 1'28"560; 13. A. Stroud (NZ, Kawasaki), at 1'28"815; 14. H. Platacis (D, Kawasaki), at one lap. 14 classified. Fastest lap: C. Fogarty (GB, Ducati), 2'04"554 (174.835 km/h).

**4th October - Japan - Sugo**
Pole position (superpole): T. Corser (AUS, Ducati), 1'30"160 (149.214 km/h). Best time in qualifying: N. Haga (J, Yamaha), 1'30"036 (149.420 km/h).
Race I: 1. K. Kitagawa (J, Suzuki), 25 laps in 38'03"718 (147.272 km/h); 2. A. Ryo (J, Suzuki), at 0"307; 3. C. Fogarty (GB, Ducati), at 1"073; 4. A. Yanagawa (J, Kawasaki), at 1"684; 5. S. Russell (USA, Yamaha), at 11"905; 6. N. Hodgson (GB, Kawasaki), at 13"333; 7. A. Slight (NZ, Honda), at 14"742; 8. S. Itoh (J, Honda), at 14"972; 9. W. Yoshikawa (J, Yamaha), at 15"327; 10. P. Goddard (AUS, Suzuki), at 15"555; 11. J. Whitham (GB, Suzuki), at 15"711; 12. P. Chili (I, Ducati), at 26"329; 13. C. Edwards (USA, Honda), at 30"160; 14. S. Takeishi (J, Kawasaki), at 31"598; 15. Y. Takeda (J, Honda), at 31"640. 21 classified. Fastest lap: A. Ryo (J, Suzuki), 1'30"133 (149.292 km/h).
Race II: 1. N. Haga (J, Yamaha), 25 laps in 38'00"953 (147.451 km/h); 2. A. Yanagawa (J, Kawasaki), at 1"382; 3. A. Ryo (J, Suzuki), at 1"566; 4. C. Fogarty (GB, Ducati), at 7"859; 5. K. Kitagawa (J, Suzuki), at 10"749; 6. A. Slight (NZ, Honda), at 11"885; 7. W. Yoshikawa (J, Yamaha), at 12"127; 8. K. Haga (J, Yamaha), at 21"419; 9. J. Whitham (GB, Suzuki), at 24"193; 10. P. Goddard (AUS, Suzuki), at 24"211; 11. S. Takeishi (J, Kawasaki), at 25"301; 12. S. Russell (USA, Yamaha), at 26"028; 13. C. Edwards (USA, Honda), at 33"970; 14. Y. Takeda (J, Honda), at 34"191; 15. G. Lavilla (E, Ducati), at 53"723. 18 classified. Fastest lap: N. Haga (J, Yamaha), 1'30"028 (149.433 km/h).

## Final classification

| | | | |
|---|---|---|---|
| 1. Carl Fogarty | Great Britain | Ducati | 351.5 |
| 2. Aaron Slight | New Zealand | Honda | 347 |
| 3. Troy Corser | Australia | Ducati | 328.5 |
| 4. Pierfrancesco Chili | Italy | Ducati | 293.5 |
| 5. Colin Edwards | United States | Honda | 279.5 |
| 6. Noriyuki Haga | Japan | Yamaha | 258 |
| 7. Akira Yanagawa | Japan | Kawasaki | 210 |
| 8. Jamie Whitham | Great Britain | Suzuki | 173 |
| 9. Peter Goddard | Australia | Suzuki | 155 |
| 10. Scott Russell | United States | Yamaha | 130.5 |

11. N. Hodgson (GB, Kawasaki), 124.5; 12. G. Lavilla (E, Ducati), 83.5; 13. P. Bontempi (I, Kawasaki), 58; 14. A. Gramigni (I, Ducati), 56; 15. I. Jerman (SK, Kawasaki), 47; 16. K. Kitagawa (J, Suzuki), 36; 17. A. Ryo (J, Suzuki), 36; 18. A. Meklau (A, Ducati), 31; 19. N. MacKenzie (GB, Yamaha), 26; 20. S. Hislop (GB, Yamaha), 26. 53 classified.

*Supersport*

### 13th April - Great Britain - Donington Park

Pole position: P. Casoli (I, Ducati), 1'38"286 (147.353 km/h).

1. P. Casoli (I, Ducati), 23 laps in 38'01"766 (145.985 km/h); 2. Y. Briguet (CH, Ducati), at 0"287; 3. M. Meregalli (I, Yamaha), at 13"135; 4. V. Guareschi (I, Yamaha), at 14"319; 5. P. Riba Cabana (E, Ducati), at 14"962; 6. F. Pirovano (I, Suzuki), at 15"120; 7. W. Zeelenberg (NL, Yamaha), at 28"782; 8. S. Chambon (F, Suzuki), at 37"278; 9. H. Whitby (GB, Honda), at 42"472; 10. B. Garcia (F, Ducati), at 46"130; 11. G. Bussei (I, Suzuki), at 46"641; 12. R. Teneggi (I, Ducati), at 48"710; 13. T. Körner (D, Kawasaki), at 52"651; 14. J. Teuchert (D, Yamaha), at 52"711; 15. M. Innamorati (I, Kawasaki), at 59"137. 23 classified. Fastest lap: Y. Briguet (CH, Ducati), 1'38"296 (147.338 km/h).

### 10th May - Italy - Monza

Pole position: C. Migliorati (I, Ducati), 1'53"235 (183.441 km/h).

1. F. Pirovano (I, Suzuki), 16 laps in 30'33"406 (181.276 km/h); 2. C. Migliorati (I, Ducati), at 0"524; 3. V. Guareschi (I, Yamaha), at 0"610; 4. M. Meregalli (I, Yamaha), at 0"674; 5. W. Zeelenberg (NL, Yamaha), at 1"037; 6. P. Casoli (I, Ducati), at 12"439; 7. P. Riba Cabana (E, Ducati), at 23"195; 8. J.-E. Gomez (F, Suzuki), at 27"422; 9. G. Fiorillo (I, Suzuki), at 27"779; 10. J.-P. Ruggia (F, Bimota), at 28"861; 11. C. Mariottini (I, Bimota), at 38"156; 12. H. Steinbauer (D, Kawasaki), at 38"347; 13. F. Monaco (I, Ducati), at 38"884; 14. C. Cogan (F, Yamaha), at 38"957; 15. R. Ulm (A, Yamaha), at 45"004. 19 classified. Fastest lap: F. Pirovano (I, Suzuki), 1'53"508 (183.000 km/h).

### 24th May - Spain - Albacete

Pole position: F. Pirovano (I, Suzuki), 1'34"841 (134.334 km/h).

1. F. Pirovano (I, Suzuki), 20 laps in 34'39"845 (122.513 km/h); 2. S. Chambon (F, Suzuki), at 28"338; 3. P. Riba Cabana (E, Ducati), at 33"675; 4. M. Meregalli (I, Yamaha), at 42"878; 5. W. Zeelenberg (NL, Yamaha), at 46"321; 6. V. Guareschi (I, Yamaha), at 46"832; 7. G. Fiorillo (I, Suzuki), at 46"854; 8. P. Casoli (I, Ducati), at 47"522; 9. S. Foti (I, Bimota), at 48"178; 10. F. Riquelme (E, Ducati),

at 48"188; 11. C. Cogan (F, Yamaha), at 48"318; 12. R. Ulm (A, Yamaha), at 54"896; 13. M. Garcia (F, Ducati), at 1'07"924; 14. C. Mariottini (I, Bimota), at 1'11"404; 15. W. Tortoroglio (I, Suzuki), at 1'16"173. 24 classified. Fastest lap: F. Pirovano (I, Suzuki), 1'41"029 (126.106 km/h).

### 7th June - Germany - Nürburgring

Pole position: V. Guareschi (I, Yamaha), 1'45"274 (155.799 km/h).

1. S. Charpentier (F, Honda), 18 laps in 36'23"471 (135.211 km/h); 2. P. Riba Cabana (E, Ducati), at 1"556; 3. V. Guareschi (I, Yamaha), at 2"760; 4. R. Ulm (A, Yamaha), at 3"737; 5. J. Teuchert (D, Yamaha), at 3"840; 6. W. Zeelenberg (NL, Yamaha), at 13"136; 7. M. Lucchiari (I, Ducati), at 18"292; 8. M. Risitano (I, Kawasaki), at 22"938; 9. G. Bussei (I, Suzuki), at 26"955; 10. S. Chambon (F, Suzuki), at 28"020; 11. C. Kellner (D, Suzuki), at 28"410; 12. T. Körner (D, Kawasaki), at 28"551; 13. H. Kaufmann (D, Yamaha), at 31"930; 14. C. Mariottini (I, Bimota), at 53"520; 15. C. Migliorati (I, Ducati), at 1'11"739. 22 classified. Fastest lap: P. Riba Cabana (E, Ducati), 1'58"303 (138.640 km/h).

### 21st June - San Marino - Misano

Pole position: V. Guareschi (I, Yamaha), 1'37"609 (149.740 km/h).

1. F. Pirovano (I, Suzuki), 23 laps in 38'10"227 (146.784 km/h); 2. M. Meregalli (I, Yamaha), at 2"328; 3. C. Migliorati (I, Ducati), at 10"274; 4. S. Chambon (F, Suzuki), at 11"567; 5. P. Riba Cabana (E, Ducati), at 19"850; 6. M. Risitano (I, Kawasaki), at 30"275; 7. F. Monaco (I, Ducati), at 32"274; 8. A. Conti (I, Suzuki), at 32"913; 9. M. Gallina (I, Ducati), at 38"516; 10. J. Teuchert (D, Yamaha), at 41"122; 11. K. Muggeridge (AUS, Honda), at 41"716; 12. G. Bussei (I, Suzuki), at 42"335; 13. G. Fiorillo (I, Suzuki), at 44"785; 14. V. Iannuzzo (I, Yamaha), at 44"921; 15. C. Kellner (D, Suzuki), at 46"033. 20 classified. Fastest lap: V. Guareschi (I, Yamaha), 1'38"094 (148.999 km/h).

### 5th July - South Africa - Kyalami

Pole position: P. Riba-Cabana (E, Ducati), 1'48"049 (141.968 km/h).

1. S. Chambon (F, Suzuki), 23 laps in 42'11"652 (139.360 km/h); 2. V. Guareschi (I, Yamaha), at 0"744; 3. F. Pirovano (I, Suzuki), at 4"018; 4. P. Casoli (I, Ducati), at 5"462; 5. B. MacLeod (AfS, Suzuki), at 5"775; 6. C. Migliorati (I, Ducati), at 17"012; 7. R. Teneggi (I, Ducati), at 23"667; 8. R. Wood (AfS, Honda), at 26"050; 9. G. Bussei (I, Suzuki), at 28"075; 10. J. Toseland (GB, Honda), at 28"107; 11. M. Meregalli (I, Yamaha), at 28"328; 12. M. Lucchiari (I, Ducati), at 30"657; 13. W. Zeelenberg (NL, Yamaha), at 32"878; 14. M. Risitano (I, Kawasaki), at 33"110; 15. W. Tortoroglio (I,

Suzuki), at 33"764. 21 classified. Fastest lap: C. Migliorati (I, Ducati), 1'48"646 (141.188 km/h).

### 12th July - United States - Laguna Seca

Pole position: S. Chambon (F, Suzuki), 1'30"691 (143.299 km/h).

1. P. Casoli (I, Ducati), 25 laps in 38'21"547 (141.166 km/h); 2. S. Chambon (F, Suzuki), at 0"364; 3. J. Pridmore (USA, Suzuki), at 2"252; 4. V. Guareschi (I, Yamaha), at 3"870; 5. C. Migliorati (I, Ducati), at 8"160; 6. M. Lucchiari (I, Ducati), at 23"452; 7. W. Zeelenberg (NL, Yamaha), at 34"164; 8. R. Ulm (A, Yamaha), at 48"431; 9. W. Daemen (B, Kawasaki), at 1'01"895; 10. G. Bussei (I, Suzuki), at 1'03"196; 11. S. Nebel (D, Kawasaki), at 1'09"171; 12. J. Rodriguez (E, Yamaha), at 1'09"532; 13. A. Aerts (B, Yamaha), at 1'30"366; 14. E. Schnackenberg (USA, Suzuki), at 1'39"980; 15. J. Jacobi (USA, Yamaha), at one lap. 17 classified. Fastest lap: P. Riba Cabana (E, Ducati), 1'30"742 (143.219 km/h).

### 2nd August - Europe - Brands-Hatch

Pole position: P. Casoli (I, Ducati), 1'29"805 (167.763 km/h).

1. F. Pirovano (I, Suzuki), 22 laps in 33'25"952 (165.234 km/h); 2. V. Guareschi (I, Yamaha), at 0"127; 3. Y. Briguet (CH, Ducati), at 0"273; 4. C. Migliorati (I, Ducati), at 0"998; 5. P. Riba Cabana (E, Ducati), at 11"909; 6. M. Lucchiari (I, Ducati), at 20"071; 7. S. Chambon (F, Suzuki), at 21"427; 8. J. Toseland (GB, Honda), at 21"476; 9. W. Tortoroglio (I, Suzuki), at 21"850; 10. A. Conti (I, Suzuki), at 23"220; 11. G. Bussei (I, Suzuki), at 26"366; 12. P. Borley (GB, Honda), at 26"568; 13. R. Ulm (A, Yamaha), at 28"499; 14. S. Charpentier (F, Honda), at 28"568; 15. P. Casoli (I, Ducati), at 29"697. 25 classified. Fastest lap: S. Chambon (F, Suzuki), 1'30"238 (166.958 km/h).

### 30th August - Austria - A1-Ring

Pole position: P. Riba Cabana (E, Ducati), 1'35"746 (162.354 km/h).

1. F. Pirovano (I, Suzuki), 23 laps in 37'11"081 (160.250 km/h); 2. S. Chambon (F, Suzuki), at 0"163; 3. V. Guareschi (I, Yamaha), at 6"185; 4. M. Meregalli (I, Yamaha), at 8"866; 5. W. Zeelenberg (NL, Yamaha), at 10"225; 6. P. Casoli (I, Ducati), at 18"475; 7. M. Lucchiari (I, Ducati), at 20"240; 8. C. Kellner (D, Suzuki), at 24"667; 9. G. Bussei (I, Suzuki), at 24"775; 10. R. Ulm (A, Yamaha), at 25"453; 11. W. Tortoroglio (I, Suzuki), at 28"142; 12. J. Toseland (GB, Honda), at 38"102; 13. T. Körner (D, Kawasaki), at 38"611; 14. A. Conti (I, Suzuki), at 38"693; 15. R. Teneggi (I, Ducati), at 39"490. 23 classified. Fastest lap: C. Migliorati (I, Ducati), 1'35"853 (162.173 km/h).

### 6th September - Netherlands - Assen

Pole position: V. Guareschi (I, Yamaha), 2'10"706 (166.605 km/h).

1. V. Guareschi (I, Yamaha), 16 laps in 35'35"382 (163.166 km/h); 2. F. Pirovano (I, Suzuki), at 0"925; 3. S. Chambon (F, Suzuki), at 1"771; 4. C. Migliorati (I, Ducati), at 9"377; 5. M. Pajic (NL, Kawasaki), at 22"595; 6. M. Meregalli (I, Yamaha), at 25"447; 7. C. Mariottini (I, Kawasaki), at 27"226; 8. R. Ulm (A, Yamaha), at 27"799; 9. T. Hartelman (NL, Honda), at 28"872; 10. R. Teneggi (I, Ducati), at 34"347; 11. G. Bussei (I, Suzuki), at 34"914; 12. G. Fiorillo (I, Suzuki), at 35"219; 13. K. McCarthy (AUS, Honda), at 46"445; 14. J. Hanson (S, Honda), at 48"321; 15. J. Rodriguez (E, Yamaha), at 53"361. 22 classified. Fastest lap: F. Pirovano (I, Suzuki), 2'12"035 (164.928 km/h).

## Final classification

| | | |
|---|---|---|
| 1. Fabrizio Pirovano (I) | Suzuki | 171 |
| 2. Vittoriano Guareschi (I) | Yamaha | 149 |
| 3. Stéphane Chambon (F) | Suzuki | 137 |
| 4. Paolo Casoli (I) | Ducati | 92 |
| 5. Massimo Meregalli (I) | Yamaha | 90 |
| 6. Cristiano Migliorati (I) | Ducati | 84 |
| 7. Pere Riba Cabana (E) | Ducati | 78 |
| 8. Wilco Zeelenberg (NL) | Yamaha | 64 |
| 9. Giovanni Bussei (I) | Suzuki | 46 |
| 10. Robert Ulm (A) | Yamaha | 43 |

11. M. Lucchiari (I, Ducati), 42; 12. Y. Briguet (CH, Ducati), 36; 13. S. Charpentier (F, Honda), 27; 14. G. Fiorillo (I, Suzuki), 23; 15. M. Risitano (I, Kawasaki), 20; 16. R. Teneggi (I, Ducati), 20; 17. J. Teuchert (D, Yamaha), 19; 18. C. Mariottini (I, Bimota/Kawasaki), 18; 19. J. Toseland (GB, Honda), 18; 20. J. Pridmore (USA, Suzuki), 16; 21. A. Conti (I, Suzuki), 16; 22. C. Kellner (D, Suzuki), 14; 23. W. Tortoroglio (I, Suzuki), 14; 24. F. Monaco (I, Ducati), 12; 25. M. Pajic (NL, Kawasaki), 11; 26. B. MacLeod (AfS, Suzuki), 11; 27. T. Körner (D, Kawasaki), 10; 28. R. Wood (AfS, Honda), 8; 29. J.-E. Gomez (F, Suzuki), 8; 30. T. Hartelmann (NL, Honda), 7; 31. W. Daemen (B, Kawasaki), 7; 32. M. Gallina (I, Ducati), 7; 33. S. Foti (I, Bimota), 7; 34. H. Whitby (GB, Honda), 7; 35. C. Cogan (F, Yamaha), 7; 36. F. J. Riquelme (E, Ducati), 6; 37. J.-P. Ruggia (F, Bimota), 6; 38. B. Garcia (F, Ducati), 6; 39. S. Nebel (D, Kawasaki), 5; 40. K. Muggeridge (AUS, Honda), 5; 41. J. Rodriguez (E, Yamaha), 5; 42. P. Borley (GB, Honda), 4; 43. H. Steinbauer (D, Kawasaki), 4; 44. K. McCarthy (AUS, Honda), 3; 45. A. Aerts (B, Yamaha), 3; 46. H. Kaufmann (D, Yamaha), 3; 47. M. Garcia (F, Ducati), 3; 48. J. Hanson (S, Honda), 2; 49. E. Schnackenberg (USA, Suzuki), 2; 50. V. Iannuzzo (I, Yamaha), 2; 51. J. Jacobi (USA, Yamaha), 1; 52. M. Innamorati (I, Kawasaki), 1. 52 classified.

*Supermono*

The champion: Katja Poensgen. Born: 23rd September 1976, in Heppenheim. First race: 1993. Race record: takes part of the ADAC Junior Cup in 1994 (3rd place in Hockenheim); 1st of the ADAC Junior Cup and champion of Italy in 1995 (Suzuki); 10th of the German 125cc championship in 1996 (Yamaha); 63rd of European supersport championship en 1997 (Suzuki); 1st of the Supermono Cup (BMR-Suzuki), 24th of the German supersport championship and 29th of the German Pro Superbike championship (Suzuki) in 1998.

### 13th April - Donington - Great Britain
1. C. Ramsey (GB, Ducati 572), 15 laps in 26'21"106 (137.399 km/h); 2. J. Barton (GB, Ducati 572), at 23"482; 3. S. Richardson (GB, MHD 640), at 1'24"022; 4. P. Goldstein (GB, KTM 612), at 1'29"215; 5. A. Stringer (GB, Harris Yamaha 686), at 1'48"194; 6. G. Cotterell (GB, Norton 680), at 1'52"787; 7. R. Cutts (GB, Ducati 550), at one lap; 8. M. Lawes (GB, Nico Bakker 740); 9. P. Harrison (GB, Rotax); 10. R. Sheperd (GB, Sheperd 795); 11. C. Chitty (GB, Tigcraft); 12. K. Langridge (GB, Sidrat BMW 670); 13. P. Street (GB, Harris 640); 14. L. Barry (GB, Slipsteam Yamaha); 15. M. Fischer (GB, BMW F650), at two laps. 15 classified. Fastest lap: C. Ramsey (GB, Ducati 572), 1'44"287 (138.874 km/h).

### 10th May - Monza - Italy
1. K. Poensgen (D, BMR-Suzuki 741), 11 laps in 22'34"014 (168.752 km/h); 2. J. Barton (GB, Ducati 572), at 5"853; 3. S. Ruth (GB, Tigcraft 725), at 16"645; 4. F. Reisky (D, OV-20 762), at 29"145; 5. G. Cotterell (GB, Norton 680), at 1'13"219; 6. R. Shepherd (GB, Shepherd 795), at 1'13"279; 7. A. Stringer (GB, Harris Yamaha), at 1'13"411. 7 classified. Fastest lap: K. Poensgen (D, BMR-Suzuki 741), 2'00"754 (172.019 km/h).

### 24th May - Albacete - Spain
1. K. Poensgen (D, BMR-Suzuki 741), 15 laps in 25'09"324 (126.617 km/h); 2. S. Ruth (GB, Tigcraft 725), at 0"547; 3. S. Marlow (GB, Norton 690), at 5"193; 4. E. Burgess (GB, MuZ-Slipstream), at 12"160; 5. J. Barton (GB, Ducati 572), at 43"946; 6. A. Stringer (GB, Harris Yamaha), at 1'02"899; 7. F. Reisky (D, OV-20 762), at 1'04"520; 8. P. Goldstein (GB, KTM 612), at 1'08"190; 9. E. Cairo (I, Rapp), at 1'09"856; 10. R. Shepherd (GB, Shepherd 795), at 1'24"132; 11. G. Cotterell (GB, Norton 680), at one lap; 12. N. Manning (GB, Tigcraft-BMR); 13. L. Barry (GB, Slipstream Yamaha). 13 classified. Fastest lap: K. Poensgen (D, BMR-Suzuki 741), 1'39"355 (128.281 km/h).

### 7th June - Nürburgring - Germany
1. K. Poensgen (D, BMR-Suzuki 741), 12 laps in 25'50"379 (126.949 km/h); 2. M. Kehrmann (D, Pami), at 14"599; 3. F. Reisky (D, OV-20 762), at 20"126; 4. G. Metzler (D, BMZ Suzuki), at 51"396; 5. P. Goldstein (GB, KTM 612), at 1'23"862; 6. G. Cotterell (GB, Norton 680), at 1'48"921; 7. R. Cutts (GB, Ducati 550), at 1'58"239; 8. M. Lawes (GB, Nico Bakker 740), at 2'18"297; 9. R. Muller (A, AWS Rotax), at one lap; 10. A. Wolff (D, Ducati); 11. M. Fischer (D, BMW F650), at three laps. 11 classified. Fastest lap: F. Reisky (D, OV-20 762), 2'04"907 (131.310 km/h).

### 21st June - Misano - Italy
1. K. Poensgen (D, BMR-Suzuki 741), 15 laps in 25'55"737 (140.924 km/h); 2. S. Ruth (GB, Tigcraft 725), at 0"514; 3. J. Barton (GB, Ducati 572), at 27"689; 4. R. Shepherd (GB, Shepherd 795), at 35"303; 5. F. Reisky (D, OV-20 762), at 40"179; 6. F. Chinaglia (I, Honda), at 53"224; 7. N. Manning (GB, Tigcraft-BMR), at 1'08"978; 8. P. Goldstein (GB, KTM 612), at 1'09"969; 9. G. Cotterell (GB, Norton 680), at 1'10"356; 10. A. Stringer (GB, Harris Yamaha), at 1'11"403; 11. L. Barry (GB, Slipstream Yamaha), at one lap. 11 classified. Fastest lap: K. Poensgen (D, BMR-Suzuki 741), 1'42"268 (142.918 km/h).

### 2nd August - Brands Hatch - Great Britain
1. E. Burgess (GB, MuZ-Slipstream 760), 15 laps in 23'38"874 (159.274 km/h); 2. K. Poensgen (D, BMR-Suzuki 741), at 2"937; 3. S. Marlow (GB, Norton 690), at 3"165; 4. D. Morris (GB, BMW F650), at 21"845; 5. D. Walker (GB, Tigcraft 686), at 55"287; 6. P. Goldstein (GB, KTM 612), at 1'03"145; 7. N. Manning (GB, Tigcraft BMW 650), at 1'09"361; 8. A. Stringer (GB, Harris Yamaha 686), at 1'09"688; 9. G. Cotterell (GB, Norton 720), at 1'10"334; 10. M. Garbin (I, Yamaha), at 1'17"488; 11. S. Richardson (GB, MHD Rotax 640), at 1'17"830; 12. R. Cutts (GB, Ducati 550), at 1'18"142; 13. M. Lawes (GB, Nico Bakker 740), at 1'26"285; 14. E. Hurst (GB, Tigcraft BMW 680), at 1'40"004; 15. S. Shaw (GB, Yamaha 690), at 1'40"347. 26 classified. Fastest lap: K. Poensgen (D, BMR-Suzuki 741), 1'33"295 (161.487 km/h).

### 30th August - A1-Ring - Austria
1. E. Burgess (GB, MuZ-Slipstream 760), 17 laps in 29'08"594 (151.128 km/h); 2. S. Marlow (GB, Norton 690), at 14"113; 3. S. Ruth (GB, Tigcraft 725), at 17"187; 4. N. Manning (GB, Tigcraft BMW 650), at 1'11"560; 5. G. Cotterell (GB, Norton 720), at 1'22"977; 6. G. Metzler (D, BMZ Suzuki), at 1'27"128; 7. R. Cutts (GB, Ducati 550), at 1'30"976; 8. L. Barry (GB, Spondon 760), at one lap; 9. J. Schluckebier (D, JPS Supermono); 10. M. Fischer (D, BMW F650), at two laps. 10 classified. Fastest lap: K. Poensgen (D, BMR-Suzuki 741), 1'41"067 (153.806 km/h).

### 6th September - Assen - Netherlands
1. E. Burgess (GB, MuZ-Slipstream 760), 12 laps in 27'57"090 (155.816 km/h); 2. S. Marlow (GB, Norton 690), at 0"254; 3. J. Barton (GB, Ducati 572), at 12"795; 4. D. Morris (GB, BMW F650), at 24"572; 5. L. Van Dijk (NL, Alpha-Impex), at 43"812; 6. H. Smees (NL, Yamaha 660), at 1'03"765; 7. R. Cutts (GB, Ducati 550), at 1'03"992; 8. E. Hurst (GB, Tigcraft BMW 680), at 1'27"798; 9. M. Lawes (GB, Nico Bakker 740), at 1'37"060; 10. E. Lammers (NL, Rotax), at 1'55"501; 11. G. Cotterell (GB, Norton 720), at 2'11"185; 12. L. Barry (GB, Spondon 760), at 2'23"912; 13. W. Reinbergen (NL, PGR Yamaha), at one lap; 14. K. Dijk (NL, MuZ). 14 classified. Fastest lap: S. Marlow (GB, Norton 690), 2'17"537 (158.331 km/h).

## Final classification

| | | |
|---|---|---|
| 1. Katja Poensgen (D) | BMR-Suzuki 741 | 120 |
| 2. Ellott Burges (GB) | MuZ-Slipstream 760 | 88 |
| 3. John Barton (GB) | Ducati 572 | 83 |
| 4. Steve Marlow (GB) | Norton 690 | 72 |
| Steve Ruth (GB) | Tigcraft 725 | 72 |

6. G. Cotterell (GB, Norton 720), 66; 7. P. Goldstein (GB, KTM 612), 50; 8. F. Reisky (D, OV-20 762), 49; 9. A. Stringer (GB, Harris Yamaha 686), 44; 10. R. Cutts (GB, Ducati 550), 40; 11. N. Manning-Morton (GB, Tigcraft BMW 650) and R. Shepherd (GB, Shepherd 795), 35; 13. D. Morris (GB, BMW F650) and M. Lawes (GB, Nico Bakker 740), 26; 15. C. Ramsey (GB, Ducati 572), 25; 16. G. Metzler (D, BMZ Suzuki), 23; 17. L. Barry (GB, Spondon 760), 22; 18. S. Richardson (GB, MHD Rotax 640), 21; 19. M. Kehrmann (D, Pami), 20; 20. M. Fischer (D, BMW F650), 12; 21. D. Walker (GB, Tigcraft 686) and L. Van Dijk (NL, Alpha-Impex), 11; 23. F. Chinaglia (I, Honda), H. Smees (NL, Yamaha 660) and E. Hurst (GB, Tigcraft BMW 680), 10: 26. P. Harrison (GB, Rotax), E. Cairo (I, Rapp), R. Muller (A, AWS Rotax) and J. Schluckebier (D, JPS Supermono), 7; 30. A. Wolff (D, Ducati), M. Garbin (I, Yamaha) and E. Lammers (NL, Rotax), 6; 33. C. Chitty (GB, Tigcraft), 5; 34. K. Langrdge (GB, Sidrat BMW 670), 4; 35. P. Street (GB, Harris 640) and W. Reinbergen (NL, Yamaha), 3; 37. K. Dijk (NL, MuZ), 2; 38. S. Shaw (GB, Yamaha 690). 38 classified.

*Endurance*

**18th-19th April - 24 Hours of Le Mans - France**
Pole position: S. Charpentier/B. Stey/N. Dussauge (F, Honda), 2'04"086 (128.669 km/h).
1. B. Sebileau/T. Paillot/I. Jerman (F/F/SLO, Kawasaki), 747 laps in 24 h. 00'48"687 (137.962 km/h); 2. P. Bontempi/G. Lavilla/J. D'Orgeix (I/E/F, Kawasaki), at 1 lap; 3. J.-M. Delétang/C. Lindholm/J.-P. Jeandat (F/S/F, Yamaha), at 9 laps; 4. C. Lavieille/D. Polen/M. Lucchiari (F/USA/I, Honda), at 10 laps; 5. S. Coutelle/P. Dobé/A. Van Den Bossche (F, Suzuki), at 21 laps; 6. C. Guyot/A. Lussiana/S. Scarnato (F, Kawasaki), at 28 laps; 7. T. Pereira/M. Graziano/F. Texeira (P/F/P, Suzuki), at 31 laps; 8. J.-E. Gomez/T. Rymer/B. Morrison (F/GB/GB, Suzuki), at 36 laps; 9. S. Charpentier/B. Stey/N. Dussauge (F, Honda), at 43 laps; 10. M. Robert/C. Loustalet/C. Charles-Artigues (F, Kawasaki), at 51 laps; 11. S. Gabrieli/A. Bronec/J.-P. Schneider (F, Yamaha), at 52 laps; 12. S. Neff/F. Herfort/D. Morillon (F, Kawasaki), at 58 laps; 13. P. Carrara/T. Pochon/C. Desmaris (F, Suzuki), at 59 laps; 14. B. Destoop/J. Guérin/F. Boutin (F, Honda), at 60 laps; 15. G. Jolivet/D. Cherrueau/F. Subais (F, Suzuki), at 64 laps. 34 classified.

**11th-12th July - 24 Hours of Spa-Francorchamps - Belgium**
Pole position: C. Lavieille/D. Polen/W. Costes (F/USA/F, Honda), 2'32"600 (164.383 km/h).
1. C. Lavieille/D. Polen/W. Costes (F/USA/F, Honda), 481 laps en 24 h. 02'42"244 (139.389 km/h); 2. B. Sebileau/I. MacPherson/J. D'Orgeix (F/GB/F, Kawasaki), at 3 laps; 3. T. Pereira/M. Graziano/F. Teixeira (P/F/P, Suzuki), at 15 laps; 4. B. Sampson/T. Rees/W. Nowland (GB, Suzuki), at 17 laps; 5. V. Eisen/B. Cuzin/T. Capela (F, Kawasaki), at 20 laps; 6. M. Fissette/D. Jadoul/A. Kempener (B, Suzuki), at 21 laps; 7. C. Künzi/M. Rieder/H. Graf (CH, Kawasaki), at 24 laps; 8. E. L'Herbette/J.-P. Leblanc/J.-L. Buffard (F, Kawasaki), at 27 laps; 9. P. Linden/R. Nicotte/E. Mizera (S/F/F, Honda), at 28 laps; 10. C. Laurent/E. Lentaigne/F. Girardot (F, Honda), at 29 laps; 11. F. Coing-Belley/C. Di Marino/A. Bronec (F, Yamaha), at 32 laps; 12. S. Strauch/T. Röthig/R. Altzschner (D, Suzuki), at 34 laps; 13. W. Van Achter/J. Van Zweeden/H. Verboven (B/NL/B, Suzuki), at 35 laps; 14. M. Granie/P. Lagamme/A. Servais (F/B/B, Kawasaki), at 36 laps; 15. B. Destoop/J.-F. Le Glatin/J. Guérin (F, Honda), at 36 laps. 44 classified.

**12th-13rd September - Bol d'Or in Castellet - France**
Pole position: B. Sebileau/I. Jerman/I. MacPherson (F/SLO/GB, Kawasaki), 1'58"349 (177.340 km/h).
1. P. Goddard/T. Rymer/B. Morrison (AUS/GB/GB, Suzuki), 666 laps en 24 h. 00'33"583 (161.720 km/h); 2. B. Bonhuil/E. Mahé/A. Van den Bossche (F, Suzuki), at 3 laps; 3. C. Lavieille/D. Polen/W. Costes (F/USA/F, Honda), at 7 laps; 4. J.-P. Jeandat/M. Lucchiari/P. Riba Cabana (F/I/E, Honda), at 12 laps; 5. S. Gabrieli/P. Thomas/D. Crassous (F, Yamaha), at 24 laps; 6. E. L'Herbette/J.-P. Leblanc/J.-L. Buffard (F, Kawasaki), at 40 laps; 7. B. Sampson/W. Nowland/T. Rees (GB/AUS/NZ, Suzuki), at 42 laps; 8. D. Ulmann/C. Haquin/E. Maubon (F, Kawasaki), at 45 laps; 9. F. Ciciliani/Y. Legaudu/L. Holon (F, Kawasaki), at 48 laps; 10. E. Lentaigne/F. Girardot/C. Laurent (F, Honda), at 51 laps; 11. E. Resmond/M. Martin/M. Perez (F, Suzuki); 12. C. Charles-Artigues/C. Loustalet/M. Robert (F, Kawasaki), at 53 laps; 13. R. Treffort/P. Bondu/Y. Parrage (F, Honda); 14. B. Destoop/J. Guérin/J.-F. Leglatin (F, Honda), at 54 laps. 39 classified.

### The 1999 Calender

| | |
|---|---|
| 10th-11th April | Le Mans 24 hours/France |
| 3rd May | Donington/Great Britain (*) |
| 10th-11th July | 24 Hours of Liege at Spa-Francorchamps/Belgium |
| 25th July | 8 Hours at Suzuki/Japan |
| 15th August | Oschersleben/Germany (*) |
| 18th-19th September | Bol d'Or or Castellet/France |

(*): TBA

### Final classification

| | | | |
|---|---|---|---|
| 1. Christian Lavieille (F) | Honda | | 108 |
| 1. Doug Polen (USA) | Honda | | 108 |
| 3. Bertrand Sebileau (F) | Kawasaki | | 90 |
| 4. William Costes (F) | Honda | | 82 |
| 5. Jéhan D'Orgeix (F) | Kawasaki | | 80 |

6. T. Rymer and B. Morrison (GB, Suzuki), 66; 8. A. Van den Bossche (F, Suzuki), 62; 9. J.-P. Jeandat (F, Yamaha/Honda), 58; 10. M. Lucchiari (I, Honda), 52; 11. P. Goddard (AUS, Suzuki), 50; 12. I. Jerman and Thierry Paillot (SLO/F, Kawasaki), 50; 14. F. Teixeira, M. Graziano and T. Pereira (P/F/P, Suzuki), 50; 17. B. Sampson, T. Rees and W. Nowland (GB, Suzuki), 44; 20. B. Bonhuil and E. Mahé (F, Suzuki), 40; 22. I. MacPherson (GB, Kawasaki), 40; 23. P. Bontempi and G. Lavilla (I/E, Kawasaki), 40; 25. J.-P. Leblanc, J.-L. Buffard and E. L'Herbette (F, Kawasaki), 36; 28. J.-M. Delétang and C. Lindholm (F/S, Yamaha), 32; 30. S. Gabrieli (F, Yamaha), 32; 31. M. Fissette and D. Jadoul (B, Suzuki), 30; 33. P. Riba Cabana (E, Honda), 26; 34. M. Robert, C. Loustalet and C. Charles-Artigues (F, Kawasaki), 26; 37. T. Ukawa and S. Itoh (J, Honda), 25; 39. D. Thomas and D. Crassous (AUS/F, Yamaha), 22; 41. T. Capela, B. Cuzin and V. Eisen (F, Kawasaki), 22; 44. S. Coutelle and P. Dobé (F, Suzuki), 22; 46. P. Linden, R. Nicotte and E. Mizera (S/F/F, Honda), 22; 49. W. Van Achter and J. Van Zweeden (B/NL, Suzuki), 22; 51. A. Bronec (F, Yamaha), 22; 52. A. Barros and S. Gibernau (BRA/E, Honda), 20; 54. A. Kempener (B, Suzuki), 20; 55. S. Scarnato, C. Guyot and A. Lussiana (F, Kawasaki), 20; 58. M. Rieder, H. Graf and C. Künzi (CH, Kawasaki), 18; 61. O. Ulmann, C. Haquin and E. Maubon (F, Kawasaki), 16; 64. C. Edwards and T. Okada (USA/J, Honda), 16; 66. J.-E. Gomez (F, Suzuki), 16; 67. F. Coing-Belley and C. Di Marino (F, Yamaha), 16; 69. B. Stey, S. Charpentier and N. Dussauge (F, Honda), 14; 72. T. Serizawa and S. Takeishi (J, Kawasaki), 13; 74. W. Daemen (B, Suzuki), 12; 75. H.-R. Portmann and W. Graf (CH, Kawasaki), 12; 77. D. Buckmaster and M. Craggill (AUS, Kawasaki), 11; 79. D. Spriet (B, Suzuki), 10; 80. S. Crafar and N. Haga (NZ/J, Yamaha), 10; 82. H. Verboven (B, Suzuki), 10; 83. J.-P. Schneider (F, Yamaha), 10; 84. H. Izutsu and N. Hodgson (J/GB, Kawasaki), 9; 86. J.-F. Braut, S. Neff and K. Nashimoto (F/F/J, Honda), 8; 89. S. Russell and N. Fujiwara (USA/J, Yamaha), 8; 91. K. Gasser, R. Breitenstein and K. Bühlmann (CH, Yamaha), 8; 94. H. Aoki and M. Kamada (J, Honda), 7; 96. P. Knutti (CH, Kawasaki), 6; 97. M. Tamada and S. Nakatani (J, Honda), 6; 99. B. Müller (CH, Kawasaki), 6; 100. P. Donischal, A. Paulus and F. Forêt (F, Yamaha), 6; 103. A. Ryo and K. Kitagawa (J, Suzuki), 5; 105. L. Tauber, F. Tauziède and P. Portas (F, Ducati), 4; 108. O. Nishijima and T. Yamamoto (J, Kawasaki), 4; 110. F. Müller, S. Waldmeier and O. Falcon (F, Honda), 4; 113. S. Aubry (F, Yamaha), 4; 114. T. Kaneyasu and Y. Sugai (J, Honda), 3; 116. M. Saito and T. Fukami (J, Yamaha), 2; 118. K. Schmidt, R. Seefeldt and M. Josch (D, Yamaha), 2; 121. F. Popot, D. Amani Jouan and C. Mesdagh (F, Kawasaki), 2; 124. T. Yamaguchi and H. Maruyama (J, Honda), 1.

**26th July - 8 Hours of Suzuka - Japan**
Pole position: S. Itoh/T. Ukawa (J, Honda), 2'12"317.
1. S. Itoh/T. Ukawa (J, Honda), 212 laps en 8 h. 01'54"740 (154.780 km/h); 2. S. Gibernau/A. Barros (E/BR, Honda), at 43"238; 3. C. Edwards/T. Okada (USA/J, Honda), at 2'09"009; 4. S. Takeishi/T. Serizwa (J, Kawasaki), at un lap; 5. M. Craggill/D. Buckmaster (AUS, Kawasaki), at 2 laps; 6. N. Haga/S. Crafar (J/NZ, Yamaha); 7. N. Hodgson/H. Izutsu (GB/J, Kawasaki), at 3 laps; 8. S. Russell/N. Fujiwara (USA/J, Yamaha); 9. H. Aoki/M. Kamada (J, Honda); 10. M. Tamada/S. Nakatomi (J, Honda), at 5 laps; 11. K. Kitagawa/A. Ryo (J, Suzuki), at 6 laps; 12. O. Nishijima/T. Yamamoto (J, Kawasaki), at 8 laps; 13. T. Kaneyasu/Y. Sugai (J, Honda), at 10 laps; 14. M. Saito/T. Fukami (J, Yamaha); 15. J. Van den Goorbergh/J. Maeda (NL/J, Honda), at 12 laps. 41 classified.

Massimiliano Sabbatani, Alexander Hofmann.
▽

### 125 cc

The champion: Massimiliano Sabbatani/Italy. Races record: 47th of the European 125cc championship in 1997 (Aprilia); 125cc European champion and 125cc Italian vice-champion in 1998 (Honda).

**19th April - Albacete - Spain**
1. A. Molina (E, Honda), 22 laps in 35'56"305 (129.986 km/h); 2. K. Nöhles (D, Honda), at 0"422; 3. Al. Nieto (E, Aprilia), at 1"571; 4. R. De Puniet (F, Honda), at 1"752; 5. S. Zocchi (I, Aprilia), at 12"250; 6. A. Zappa (I, Honda), at 14"375; 7. D. Tocca (I, Aprilia), at 17"043; 8. D. Mico (E, Aprilia), at 24"257; 9. A. Romagnoli (I, Honda), at 24"284; 10. C. Pistoni (I, Honda), at 27"611; 11. A. Brannetti (I, Honda), at 27"723; 12. G. Talmacsi (H, Honda), at 27"918; 13. M. Sabbatani (I, Honda), at 28"042; 14. R. Chiarello (I, Aprilia), at 28"055; 15. M. Borciani (I, Honda), at 28"892. Fastest lap: K. Nöhles (D, Honda), 1'36"662 (131.803 km/h).

**17th May - Salzburgring - Austria**
1. R. Chiarello (I, Aprilia), 17 laps in 26'31"400 (163.633 km/h); 2. R. Stolz (D, Honda), at 0"087; 3. K. Nöhles (D, Honda), at 0"321; 4. M. Sabbatini (I, Honda), at 0"404; 5. M. Borciani (I, Honda), at 0"672; 6. G. Caffiero (I, Honda), at 0"852; 7. M. Petrini (I, Aprilia), at 2"956; 8. A. Brannetti (I, Honda), at 9"870; 9. C. Pistoni (I, Honda), at 10"089; 10. P. Mellauner (I, Honda), at 10"304; 11. A. Molina (E, Honda), at 10"702; 12. G. Talmacsi (H, Honda), at 13"055; 13. D. Heidolf (D, Honda), at 17"401; 14. C. Gemmel (D, Honda), at 17"693; 15. D. Reissmann (D, Honda), at 17"802. Fastest lap: K. Nöhles (D, Honda), 1'32"083 (166.349 km/h).

**24th May - Donington Park - Great Britain**
1. F. Cerroni (I, Aprilia), 23 laps in 29'24"538 (147.810 km/h); 2. R. Stolz (D, Honda), at 0"450; 3. G. Caffiero (I, Honda), at 9"415; 4. S. Zocchi (I, Aprilia), at 11"074; 5. A. Molina (E, Honda), at 11"410; 6. R. Chiarello (I, Aprilia), at 11"748; 7. A. Brannetti (I, Honda), at 12"294; 8. M. Borciani (I, Honda), at 12"667; 9. A. Romagnoli (I, Honda), at 12"677; 10. M. Petrini (I, Aprilia), at 12"870; 11. M. Sabbatani (I, Honda), at 27"641; 12. D. Heidolf (D, Honda), at 27"721; 13. R. Romboli (I, Honda), at 28"053; 14. C. Pistoni (I, Honda), at 33"261; 15. D. Mateer (GB, Honda), at 33"777. Fastest lap: A. Molina (E, Honda), 1'15"991 (149.220 km/h).

**21st June - Carole - France**
1. M. Poggiali (I, Honda), 35 laps in 38'01"731 (113.480 km/h); 2. M. Sabbatani (I, Honda), at 1"433; 3. K. Nöhles (D, Honda), at 1"644; 4. A. Zappa (I, Aprilia), at 10"156; 5. S. Zocchi (I, Aprilia), at 13"088; 6. M. Borciani (I, Honda), at 15"936; 7. A. Brannetti (I, Honda), at 20"429; 8. R. De Puniet (F, Honda), at 20"759; 9. G. Caffiero (I, Honda), at 28"470; 10. R. Harms (DK, Honda), at 42"392; 11. D. Tocca (I, Aprilia), at 53"235; 12. C. Pistoni (I, Honda), at 53"591; 13. C. Gemmel (D, Honda), at 1'03"022; 14. R. Romboli (I, Honda), at 1'04"906; 15. R. Chiarello (I, Aprilia), at one lap. Fastest lap: M. Sabbatani (I, Honda), 1'04"241 (115.160 km/h).

**12th July - Most - Czech Republic**
1. M. Poggiali (I, Honda), 20 laps in 34'03"046 (146.182 km/h); 2. R. Stolz (D, Honda), at 7"582; 3. M. Borciani (I, Honda), at 14"792; 4. C. Cipriani (I, Aprilia), at 17"508; 5. D. Reissmann (D, Honda), at 26"078; 6. M. Stief (D, Yamaha), at 30"207; 7. K. Nöhles (D, Honda), at 31"805; 8. A. Brannetti (I, Honda), at 34"447; 9. M. Sabbatani (I, Honda), at 34"712; 10. R. Chiarello (I, Aprilia), at 45"402; 11. A. Romagnoli (I, Honda), at 45"549; 12. G. Caffiero (I, Honda), at 46"238; 13. R. De Puniet (F, Honda), at 46"332; 14. R. Harms (DK, Honda), at 1'33"597; 15. P. Mellauner (I, Honda), at 1'40"861. Fastest lap: K. Nöhles (D, Honda), 1'37"777 (152.724 km/h).

**23rd August - Misano - Italy**
1. S. Sanna (I, Aprilia), 22 laps in 30'15"567 (152.156 km/h); 2. K. Nöhles (D, Honda), at 2"069; 3. M. Poggiali (I, Honda), at 2"275; 4. A. Brannetti (I, Honda), at 4"777; 5. A. Zappa (I, Honda), at 4"952; 6. M. Sabbatani (I, Honda), at 5"141; 7. M. Borciani (I, Honda), at 17"593; 8. R. Chiarello (I, Aprilia), at 19"372; 9. C. Cipriani (I, Honda), at 19"573; 10. M. Petrini (I, Aprilia), at 20"037; 11. A. Romagnoli (I, Honda), at 26"050; 12. G. Caffiero (I, Honda), at 26"510; 13. M. Tresoldi (CH, Honda), at 27"706; 14. D. Heidolf (D, Honda), at 46"217; 15. B. Stern (SL, Suzuki), at 48"027. Fastest lap: K. Nöhles (D, Honda), 1'21"156 (154.724 km/h).

**27th September - Rijeka - Croatia**
1. R. De Puniet (F, Honda), 16 laps in 27'53"215 (143.48 km/h); 2. M. Sabbatani (I, Honda), at 0"106; 3. S. Sanna (I, Aprilia), at 0"446; 4. M. Poggiali (I, Honda), at 5"765; 5. B. Absmeier (D, Aprilia), at 16"781; 6. R. Stolz (D, Honda), at 19"325; 7. A. Brannetti (I, Honda), at 19"612; 8. D. Reissmann (D, Honda), at 20"450; 9. A. Zappa (I, Aprilia), at 20"492; 10. C. Cipriani (I, Aprilia), at 22"355; 11. M. Stief (D, Yamaha), at 23"775; 12. K. Nöhles (D, Honda), at 34"248; 13. M. Petrini (I, Aprilia), at 34"461; 14. R. Chiarello (I, Aprilia), at 34"541; 15. G. Talmacsi (H, Aprilia), at 38"445. Fastest lap: R. De Puniet (F, Honda), 1'41"592 (147.696 km/h).

**18th October - Braga - Portugal**
1. M. Sabbatani (I, Honda), 24 laps in 32'39"488 (133.162 km/h); 2. R. Stolz (D, Honda), at 7"263; 3. A. Zappa (I, Honda), at 8"401; 4. A. Brannetti (I, Honda), at 8"995; 5. M. Stief (D, Yamaha), at 9"060; 6. R. Chiarello (I, Aprilia), at 10"600; 7. D. Tocca (I, Aprilia), at 32"123; 8. M. Tresoldi (CH, Honda), at 32"320; 9. J. Petit (F, Honda), at 47"252; 10. J. Leite (P, Honda), at 1'12"854; 11. D. Nacher (E, Honda), at one lap; 12. E. Ekki (H, Honda); 13. D. Marti (E, Honda). 13 classified. Fastest lap: K. Nöhles (D, Honda), 1'20"369 (135.276 km/h).

**1st November - Cartagena - Spain**
1. K. Nöhles (D, Honda), 21 laps in 35'25"811 (123.759 km/h); 2. A. Brannetti (I, Honda), at 9"040; 3. M. Sabbatani (I, Honda), at 9"666; 4. J. Sarda (E, Honda), at 12"899; 5. R. Stolz (D, Honda), at 19"460; 6. C. Pistoni (I, Honda), at 21"703; 7. R. Chiarello (I, Aprilia), at 23"166; 8. C. Cipriani (I, Aprilia), at 23"519; 9. D. Heidolf (D, Honda), at 39"246; 10. J. Petit (F, Honda), at 40"445; 11. A. Araujo (E, Honda); 12. M. Tresoldi (CH, Honda); 13. A. Zappa (I, Honda); 14. R. de Puniet (F, Honda); 15. D. Tocca (I, Aprilia). Fastest lap: K. Nöhles (D, Honda), 1'39"656 (125.712 km/h).

**Final classification**

| | | | |
|---|---|---|---|
| 1. Massimiliano Sabbatani | | | |
| | Italy | Honda | 119 |
| 2. Klaus Nöhles | | | |
| | Germany | Honda | 110 |
| 3. Reinhard Stolz | | | |
| | Germany | Honda | 101 |

4. A. Brannetti (I, Honda), 94; 5. M. Poggiali (I, Honda), 79; 6. R. Chiarello (I, Aprilia), 73; 7. A. Zappa (I, Honda), 60; 8. M. Borciani (I, Honda), 55; 9. R. de Puniet (F, Honda), 51; 10. S. Sanna (I, Aprilia), 41; 11. A. Molina Fuentes (E, Honda), 41; 12. G. Caffiero (I, Honda), 41; 13. S. Zocchi (I, Aprilia), 35; 14. C. Cipriani (I, Aprilia), 34; 15. C. Pistoni (I, Honda), 29; 16. M. Stief (D, Yamaha), 26; 17. F. Cerroni (I, Aprilia), 25; 18. D. Tocca (I, Aprilia), 24; 19. M. Petrini (I, Aprilia), 24; 20. A. Romagnoli (I, Honda), 24; 21. D. Reissmann (D, Honda), 20; 22. A. Gonzalez Nieto (E, Aprilia), 16; 23. D. Heidolf (D, Honda), 16; 24. M. Tresoldi (CH, Honda), 15; 25. J. Sarda (E, Honda) 13; 26. J. Petit (F, Honda), 13; 27. B. Absmeier (D, Aprilia), 11; 28. G. Talmacsi (H, Honda), 9; 29. D. Mico (E, Aprilia), 8; 30. R. Harms (DK, Honda), 8; 31. P. Mellauner (I, Honda), 7; 32. J. Leite (P, Honda), 6; 33. A.-D. Nacher (E, Honda) and A. Araujo (E, Honda), 5; 35. C. Gemmel (D, Honda), 5; 36. R. Romboli (I, Honda), 5; 37. E. Emri (H, Honda), 4; 38. D. Marti (E, Honda), 3; 39. B. Stern (SK, Aprilia) and D. Mateer (IRL, Honda), 1. 40 classified.

### 250 cc

The champion: Alexander Hofmann-Hammad. Born on 25th May 1980, at Mindel. First race: 1984. First GP: German GP 1998 (250). Races record: 80cc motocross champion in Germany in 1992 (Yamaha); 80cc motocross champion in Germany in 1993 (Yamaha); 125cc motocross champion ADAC Junior in 1994 (Yamaha); 48th of the European 125cc championship in 1996; 28th of the 125 cc world championship, 41st of the 125cc European championship and 125cc vice-champion in Germany in 1997 (Yamaha); 29th of the 250cc world championship, 250cc European champion and 250cc champion in Germany in 1998 (Honda).

**19th April - Albacete - Spain**
1. I. Clementi (I, Yamaha), 25 laps in 39'31"452 (134.310 km/h); 2. E. Gavira (E, Honda), at 4"368; 3. A. Hofmann (D, Honda), at 4"808; 4. J. Allemand (F, Honda), at 22"240; 5. F. Cotti (I, Honda), at 23"458; 6. M. Ober (D, Honda), at 25"545; 7. I. Bonilla (E, Honda), at 36"267; 8. M. Bolwerk (NL, Honda), at 36"361; 9. M. Lagrive (F, Honda), at 53"567; 10. V. Castka (SK, NER-Honda), at 53"597; 11. V. Philippe (F, Honda), at 53"968; 12. J. Janssen (NL, Honda), at 56"340; 13. G. Parolari (CH, Aprilia), at 59"491; 14. L.-O. Bulto (E, Honda), at 1'05"030; 15. R. Markink (NL, Honda), at 1'05"170. Fastest lap: I. Clementi (I, Yamaha), 1'33"685 (135.992 km/h).

**17th May - Salzburgring - Austria**
1. A. Hofmann (D, Honda), 19 laps in 32'34"463 (148.911 km/h); 2. A. Coates (GB, Honda), at 6"249; 3. M. Bolwerk (NL, Honda), at 10"619; 4. G. Parolari (CH, Aprilia), at 18"467; 5. M. Witzeneder (A, Honda), at 20"056; 6. M. Baldinger (D, Honda), at 26"221; 7. M. Neukirchen (D, Aprilia), at 27"975; 8. M. Lagrive (F, Honda), at 44"143; 9. F. Cotti (I, Honda), at 1'04"630; 10. D. Giugovaz (I, Aprilia), at 1'05"618; 11. U. Bolterauer (A, Honda), at 1'05"852; 12. A. Schmidt (D, Honda), at 1'29"398; 13. V. Castka (SK, NER-Honda), at 1'40"072; 14. J. Allemand (F, Honda), at one lap; 15. D. Brockmann (D, Honda). Fastest lap: A. Hofmann (D, Honda), 1'40"067 (153.077 km/h).

**24th May - Donington Park - Great Britain**
1. D. Giugovaz (I, Aprilia), 24 laps in 29'14"490 (155.120 km/h); 2. A. Hofmann (D, Honda), at 0"089; 3. J. Allemand (F, Honda), at 21"320; 4. W. Coulter (GB, Honda), at 21"563; 5. F. Cotti (I, Honda), at 24"071; 6. M. Lagrive (F, Honda), at 26"015; 7. V. Castka (SK, NER-Honda), at 28"948; 8. M. Bolwerk (NL, Honda), at 36"961; 9. S. Yuzi (MAL, Honda), at 47"921; 10. A. Schmidt (D, Honda), at 52"429; 11. D. Johnson (GB, Honda), at 52"836; 12. S. Edwards (GB, Honda), at 53"094; 13. D. Bosch (E, Aprilia), at 1'01"774; 14. J. Janssen (NL, Honda), at 1'02"298; 15. H. Danninger (A, Honda), at 1'15"227. Fastest lap: D. Giugovaz (I, Aprilia), 1'11"880 (157.76 km/h).

**21st June - Carole - France**
1. F. Cotti (I, Honda), 37 laps in 39'10"286 (116.465 km/h); 2. A. Hofmann (D, Honda), at 0"079; 3. I. Clementi (I, Yamaha), at 0"802; 4. J. Allemand (F, Honda), at 5"096; 5. I. Antonelli (I, Aprilia), at 5"259; 6. M. Baldinger (D, Honda), at 6"719; 7. V. Philippe (F, Honda), at 16"249; 8. D. Giugovaz (I, Aprilia), at 21"796; 9. J. Janssen (NL, Honda), at 30"225; 10. D. Ribalta Bosch (E, Aprilia), at 34"266; 11. S. Harms (DK, Honda), at 45"344; 12. V. Catska (SK, NER-Honda), at 45"521; 13. M. Bolwerk (NL, Honda), at 45"987; 14. S. Yuzi (MAL, Honda), at 54"031; 15. G. Parolari (CH, Aprilia), at one lap. Fastest lap: I. Clementi (I, Yamaha), 1'02"669 (118.049 km/h).

**12th July - Most - Czech Republic**
1. A. Hofmann (D, Honda), 22 laps in 34'18"617 (159.584 km/h); 2. D. Giugovaz (I, Aprilia), at 0"278; 3. T. Kaya (J, TSR-Honda), at 6"799; 4. J. Allemand (F, Honda), at 21"533; 5. F. Cotti (I, Honda), at 25"845; 6. M. Ober (D, Honda), at 32"030; 7. J. Jansen (NL, Honda), at 32"293; 8. M. Bolwerk (NL, Honda), at 35"508; 9. G. Parolari (CH, Aprilia), at 42"577; 10. M. Baldinger (D, Honda), at 48"464; 11. V. Castka (SK, NER-Honda), at 49"282; 12. T. Lackner (D, Aprilia), at 1'12"349; 13. S. Harms (DK, Honda), at 1'13"606; 14. R. Rous (CZ, Yamaha), at 1'30"056; 15. R. Ek (S, Yamaha), at one lap. Fastest lap: D. Giugovaz (I, Aprilia), 1'32"658 (161.161 km/h).

**23rd August - Misano - Italy**
1. I. Antonelli (I, Aprilia), 24 laps in 32'11"057 (156.061 km/h); 2. D. Giugovaz (I, Aprilia), at 5"333; 3. M. Ober (D, Honda), at 13"148; 4. V. Phillipe (F, Honda), at 13"575; 5. J. Janssen (NL, Honda), at 24"231; 6. M.-H. Kuan (MAL, Honda), at 27"309; 7. R. Markink (NL, Honda), at 45"700; 8. C. Caliumi (I Honda), at 54"070; 9. G. Rizmayer (H, Honda), at 58"338; 10. D. Brockmann (D, Honda), at 58"936; 11. H. Danninger (A, Honda), at 59"658; 12. V. Mirogiannis (GR, Yamaha), at 1'06"557; 13. J. Lis Ortega (E, Yamaha),

at one lap; 14. W. Dieltjens (B, Honda); 15. C. König (B, Honda), at two laps. Fastest lap: I. Antonelli (I, Aprilia), 1'19"099 (158.747 km/h).

**27th September - Rijeka - Croatia**

1. J. Allemand (F, Honda), 20 laps in 33'27"037 (149.521 km/h); 2. M. Ober (D, Honda), at 0"114; 3. A. Hofmann (D, Honda), at 0"116; 4. M. Bolwerk (NL, Honda), at 15"671; 5. D. Giugovaz (I, Aprilia), at 32"053; 6. V. Phillipe (F, Honda), at 33"877; 7. I. Clementi (I, Yamaha), at 47"781; 8. M. Baldinger (D, Honda), at 50"459; 9. F. Cotti (I, Honda), at 1'04"775; 10. V. Castka (SK, NER-Honda), at 1'25"693; 11. D. Brockmann (D, Honda), at 1'26"811; 12. J. Janssen (NL, Honda), at 1'26"813; 13. G. Parolari (CH, Aprilia), at 1'26"815; 14. J. Lis Ortega (E, Yamaha), at 1'37"340; 15. H. Danninger (A, Honda), at one lap. Fastest lap: J. Allemand (F, Honda), 1'38"645 (152.109 km/h).

**18th October - Braga - Portugal**

1. J. Allemand (F, Honda), 26 laps 34'20"551 (137.183 km/h); 2. D. Giugovaz (I, Aprilia), at 6"142; 3. A. Hofmann (D, Honda), at 26"339; 4. V. Philippe (F, Honda), at 29"704; 5. F. Cotti (I, Honda), at 30"569; 6. I. Clementi (I, Yamaha), at 37"536; 7. S. Yuzi (MAL, NER-Honda), at 44"206; 8. V. Castka (SK, NER-Honda), at 44"962; 9. M. Baldinger (D, Honda), at 44"985; 10. J. Janssen (NL, Honda), at 45"776: 11. G. Rizmayer (H, Honda), at 45"871; 12. G. Parolari (CH, Aprilia), at 55"925; 13. A. Coates (GB, Honda), at 58"236; 14. D. Brockmann (D, Honda), at 1'12"854; 15. M. Bolwerk (NL, Honda), at 1'22"770. Fastest lap: J. Allemand (F, Honda), 1'18"087 (139.231 km/h).

**1st November - Cartagena - Spain**

1. J. Allemand (F, Honda), 23 laps in 38'06"153 (126.039 km/h); 2. F. Cotti (I, Honda), at 6"585; 3. M. Ober (D, Honda), at 6"618; 4. A. Coates (GB, Honda), at 8"780; 5. I. Clementi (I, Yamaha), at 8"868; 6. M. Baldinger (D, Honda), at 19"280; 7. V. Phillipe (F, Honda), at 29"891; 8. D. Ribalta (E, Aprilia), at 31"162; 9. D. Giugovaz (I, Aprilia), at 33"239; 10. V. Castka (SK, Honda), at 33"446; 11. Y. Sharol (MAL, Honda); 12. I. Silva (E, Honda); 13. S. Di Stefano (I, Honda); 14. D. Guardiola (E, Honda); 15. G. Parolari (CH, Aprilia). Fastest lap: J. Allemand (F, Honda), 1'38"076 (127.738 km/h).

**Final classification**

| | | | |
|---|---|---|---|
| 1. Alexander Hofmann | Germany | Honda | 138 |
| 2. Julien Allemand | France | Honda | 132 |
| 3. Diego Giugovaz | Italy | Aprilia | 117 |

4. F. Cotti (I, Honda), 103; 5. M. Ober (D, Honda), 72; 6. I. Clementi (I, Yamaha), 71; 7. V. Phillipe (F, Honda), 59; 8. M. Bolwerk (NL, Honda), 57; 9. M. Baldinger (D, Honda), 51; 10. V. Castka (SK, Honda), 47; 11. J. Janssen (NL, Honda), 43; 12. I. Antonelli (I, Aprilia), 36; 13. A. Coates (GB, Honda), 36; 14. G. Parolari (CH, Aprilia), 13; 15. M. Lagrive (F, Honda), 25; 16. Y. Sharol (MAL, Honda), 23; 17. E. Gavira (E, Honda), 20; 18. D. Ribalata Bosch (E, Aprilia), 17; 19. T. Kayo (J, TSR-Honda), 16; 20. D. Brockmann (D, Honda), 14; 21. W. Coulter (GB, Honda), 13; 22. G. Ritzmayer (H, Honda), 12; 23. M. Witzeneder (A, Honda), 11; 24. K. Meng Heng (MAL, Honda), 10; 25. R. Markink (NL, Honda), 10; 26. A. Schmidt (D, Honda), 10; 27. M. Neukrichen (D, Aprilia), 9; 28. I. Bonilla (E, Honda), 9; 29. C. Caliumi (I, Honda), 8; 30. S. Harms (DK, Honda), 8; 31. H. Danninger (A, Honda), 7; 32. D. Johnson (D, Honda) and U. Bolterauer (A, Honda), 5; 34. J. Lis Ortega (E, Yamaha), 5; 35. I. Silva (E, Honda), V. Mirosiannis (GR, Yamaha), T. Lackner (D, Aprilia) and S. Edwards (GB, Honda), 4; 39. S. Di Stefano (I, Honda), 3; 40. W. Dieltjens (B, Honda), R. Rous (CZ, Yamaha), L.-O. Bulto (E, Honda) and D. Guardiola (E, Honda), 2; 44. C. König (B, Honda) and R. Ek (S, Yamaha), 1. 45 classified.

**Supersport**

The champion: Jan Hansson/Sweden. Races record: 29th of the 250cc European championship and 28th of the 250cc "open" Sapnish championship in 1995 (Honda); 28th of the 250cc European championship in 1996 (Honda); 49th of the supersport European championship in 1997 (Honda); supersport European champion in 1998 (Honda).

**8th March - Le Mans - France**

1. J. Hanson (S, Honda), 21 laps in 45'09"988 (123,722 km/h); 2. T. Hartelman (NL, Honda), at 2"740; 3. O. Fernandez-Alventosa (E, Honda), at 5"905; 4. G. Giabbani (F, Kawasaki), at 5"956; 5. D. Tomas-Perez (E, Honda), at 48"067; 6. B. Stey (F, Honda), at 50"654; 7. D. Checa-Carrera (E, Honda), at 51"972; 8. A. Schaden (D, Suzuki), at 51"907; 9. S. Le Grelle (B, Suzuki), at 58"198; 10. H. Saiger (A, Yamaha), at 1'31"842; 11. M. Johansson (S, Honda), at one lap; 12. M. Balaz (CZ, Ducati); 13. R. Bocek (CZ, Honda); 14. D.-S. Sundby (N, Suzuki); 15. M. Wegscheider (D, Suzuki), at two laps. Fastest lap: G. Giabbani (F, Kawasaki), 2'05"555 (127,163 km/h).

**19th April - Albacete - Spain**

1. O. Fernandez Albentosa (E, Honda), 26 laps in 42'46"495 (129.067 km/h); 2. D. Tomas Perez (E, Honda), at 9"285; 3. G. Giabbani (F, Kawasaki), at 18"644; 4. D. Checa Carrera (E, Honda), at 21"958; 5. T. Hartelman (NL, Honda), at 22"069; 6. J.-M. Vasquez (E, Honda), at 24"513; 7. L. Dickinson (GB, Honda), at 25"297; 8. J. Nilsson (S, Honda), at 28"093; 9. T. Saeby (N, Honda), at 30"378; 10. R. Bocek (CZ, Honda), at 33"120; 11. M. Johansson (S, Honda), at 36"244; 12. S. Le Grelle (B, Suzuki), at 44"374; 13. D.-S. Sundby (N, Suzuki), at 46"296; 14. W. Sören (DK, Yamaha), at 47"464; 15. M. Van Deelen (NL, Honda), at 48"330. Fastest lap: O. Fernandez Albentosa (E, Honda), 1'37"421 (130.777 km/h).

**17th May - Salzburgring - Austria**

1. H. Kaufmann (D, Yamaha), 22 laps in 37'03"639 (151.551 km/h); 2. M. Schulten (D, Suzuki), at 2"617; 3. D. Tomas Perez (E, Honda), at 15"015; 4. C. Kellner (D, Suzuki), at 17"867; 5. D.-S. Sundby (N, Suzuki), at 20"748; 6. J. Teuchert (D, Yamaha), at 20"995; 7. H. Steinbauer (D, Kawasaki), at 23"561; 8. A. Luger (A, Suzuki), at 29"018; 9. T. Hartelmann (NL, Honda), at 49"391; 10. M. Salas (E, Honda), at 54"183; 11. H. Röckl (D, Yamaha), at 58"049; 12. M. Kratzer (D, Ducati), at 1'04"683; 13. J. Ilmberger (D, Ducati), at 1'16"446; 14. S. Le Grelle (B, Suzuki), at 1'17"482; 15. E. Wilding (A, Honda), at 1'19"927. Fastest lap: H. Kaufmann (D, Yamaha), 1'37"167 (157.646 km/h).

**24th May - Donington Park - Great Britain**

1. D. Thomas (GB, Suzuki), 29 laps in 36'17"064 (151.050 km/h); 2. P. Borley (GB, Honda), at 0"814; 3. L. Dickinson (GB, Honda), at 10"293; 4. K. Harris (GB, Honda), at 22"156; 5. D. Tomas Perez (E, Honda), at 22"793; 6. P. Breslin (GB, Honda), at 22"923; 7. M. Burr (GB, Honda), at 24"463; 8. J.-M. Vazquez (E, Honda), at 24"815; 9. D. Heal (GB, Honda), at 25"021; 10. D. Wood (GB, Honda), at 34"017; 11. D. Checa Carrera (E, Honda), at 37"713; 12. M. Johansson (S, Honda), at 37"774; 13. M. Horner (GB, Kawasaki), at 37"884; 14. T. Hartelmann (NL, Honda), at 39"093; 15. S. Le Grelle (B, Honda), at 39"412. Fastest lap: P. Borley (GB, Honda), 1'14"236 (152.750 km/h).

**12th July - Most - Czech Republic**

1. M. Schulten (D, Suzuki), 24 laps in 38'33"879 (154.886 km/h); 2. J. Oelschlager (D, Honda), at 22"446; 3. M. Johansson (S, Honda), at 29"603; 4. J. Hansson (S, Honda), at 30"335; 5. D. Tomas Perez (E, Honda), at 38"591; 6. R. Penzkofer (D, Yamaha), at 38"606; 7. A. Luger (CZ, Suzuki), at 38"882; 8. H. Röckl (D, Yamaha), at 49"196; 9. M. Kratzer (SK, Ducati), at 49"419; 10. D.-S. Sundby (N, Suzuki), at 57"326; 11. D. Messori (I, Suzuki), at 57"336; 12. E. Buchner (D, Suzuki), at 1'14"944; 13. T. Fritsche (CZ, Kawasaki), at 1'16"972; 14. M. Balaz (CZ, Ducati), at 1'29"972; 15. R. Livi (I, Ducati), at one lap. Fastest lap: M. Schulten (D, Suzuki), 1'35"162 (156.919 km/h).

**23rd August - Misano - Italy**

1. G. Fiorillo (I, Suzuki), 28 laps in 38'27"855 (152.345 km/h) ; 2. L. Pasini (I, Ducati), at 13"033; 3. L. Conforti (I, Kawasaki), at 14"822; 4. J.-F. Cortinovis (F, Honda), at 15"134; 5. S. Le Grelle (B, Suzuki), at 15"571; 6. D. Checa Carrera (E, Honda), at 21"709; 7. F. Brugnera (I, Suzuki), at 22"769; 8. G. Tarizzo (I, Suzuki), at 32"982; 9. J. Hansson (S, Honda), at 35"196; 10. D.-S. Sundby (N, Suzuki), at 41"786; 11. G. Villa (I, Ducati), at 52"524; 12. A. Corradini (I, Honda), at 53"529; 13. D. Tomas Perez (E, Honda), at 58"203; 14. R. Ruozi (I, Ducati), at 1'00"653; 15. L. Mauri (I, Suzuki), at 1'01"022. Fastest lap: G. Fiorillo (I, Suzuki), 1'21"459 (154.148 km/h).

**27th September - Rijeka - Croatia**

1. F. Furlan (I, Ducati), 16 laps in 27'06"809 (147.575 km/h); 2. L. Conforti (I, Kawasaki), at 4"559; 3. M. Schulten (D, Suzuki), at 5"477; 4. J. Hanson (S, Honda), at 45"248; 5. G. Giabbani (F, Kawasaki), at 47"655; 6. W. Ukusic (H, Kawasaki), at 53"022; 7. J. Ilmberger (SK, Ducati), at 56"449; 8. S. Le Grelle (B, Suzuki), at 56"754; 9. G. Tarizzio (I, Suzuki), at 58"682; 10. R. Marcolongo (I), at 59"537; 11. V. Zivec (SK, Kawasaki), at 1'01"473; 12. M. Johansson (S, Honda), at 1'03"121; 13. F. Brugnara (I, Suzuki), at 1'05"350; 14. M. Kratzer (SK, Ducati), at 1'07"933; 15. D. Checa Carrera (E, Honda), at 1'10"797. Fastest lap: F. Furlan (I, Ducati), 1'39"855 (150.265 km/h).

**18th October - Braga - Portugal**

1. C. Kellner (D, Suzuki), 30 laps in 40'52"702 (132.980 km/h); 2. J. Hanson (S, Honda), at 8"613; 3. D. Tomas Perez (E, Honda), at 27"510; 4. R. Reigoto (P, Kawasaki), at 27"735; 5. F. Teixeira (P, Suzuki), at 36"750; 6. M. Johansson (S, Honda), at 36"918; 7. A. Machado (BR, Ducati), at 43"322; 8. G. Tarrizio (I, Suzuki), at 43"344; 9. M. Sanchini (I, Ducati), at 44"296; 10. D.-S. Sundby (N, Suzuki), at 44"820; 11. D. Messori (I, Suzuki), at 46"739; 12. F. Riquelme (E, Ducati), at 1'00"441; 13. K. Poensgen (D, Suzuki), at 1'01"587; 14. J.-M. Vazquez (E, Honda), at 1'01"956: 15. J.-M. Rosales (E, Honda), at 1'09"825. Fastest lap: M. Schulten (D, Suzuki), 1'20"832 (134.501 km/h).

**1st November - Cartagena - Spain**

1. M. Schulten (D, Suzuki), 24 laps in 40'36"479 (123.404 km/h); 2. M. Manzano (I, Honda), at 6"075; 3. D. Checa Carrera (E, Honda), at 6"278; 4. C. Kellner (D, Suzuki), at 6"727; 5. J. Hansson (S, Honda), at 23"935; 6. A. Escobar (E, Honda), at 24"501; 7. M. Sanchini (I, Ducati), at 28"295; 8. J.-M. Vasquez (E, Honda), at 30"106; 9. E. Ullastres (E, Yamaha), at 33"645; 10. M. Johansson (S, Honda), at 47"124; 11. F. Teixeira (P, Suzuki); 12. J. Lindström (S, Suzuki); 13. K. Poensgen (D, Suzuki); 14. J.-M. Martinez (E, Honda); 15. M. Wegscheider (D, Suzuki), at one lap. Fastest lap: D. Checa Carrera (E, Honda), 1'40"346 (124.346 km/h).

**Final classification**

| | | | |
|---|---|---|---|
| 1. Jan Hansson | Sweden | Honda | 99 |
| 2. Michael Schulten | Germany | Suzuki | 86 |
| 3. David Tomas Perez | Spain | Honda | 78 |

4. D. Checa Carrera (E, Honda), 56; 5. C. Kellner (D, Suzuki), 51; 6. M. Johansson (S, Honda), 51; 7. O. Fernandez Albentosa (E, Honda), 41; 8. T. Hartelman (NL, Honda), 41; 9. L. Conforti (I, Kawasaki), 40; 10. G. Giabbani (F, Kawasaki), 40; 11. S. Le Grelle (B, Suzuki), 36; 12. D.-S. Sundby (N, Suzuki), 35; 13. J.-M. Martin Vasquez (E, Honda), 29; 14. F. Furlan (I, Ducati), L. Pasini (I, Ducati), D. Thomas (GB, Suzuki) and H. Kaufmann (D, Yamaha), 25; 18. L. Dickinson (GB, Honda), 25; 19. G. Tarizzo (I, Suzuki), 24; 20. J. Ölschläger (D, Honda), P. Borley (GB, Honda) and M. Manzano (I, Honda), 20; 23. A. Luger (CZ, Suzuki), 17; 24. J.-F. Cortinovis (F, Honda), 16; 25. F. Teixeira (P, Suzuki), 16; 26. M. Sanchini (I, Ducati), 16; 27. R. Reigoto (P, Kawasaki) and K. Harris (GB, Honda), 13; 29. F. Brugnara (I, Suzuki), 13; 30. H. Röckl (D), 13; 31. M. Kratzer (SK, Ducati), 13; 32. J. Ilmberger (SK, Ducati), 12; 33. P. Breslin (GB, Honda), 11; 34. W. Ukusic (H, Kawasaki), R. Penzkofer (D, Yamaha), M. Burr (GB, Honda), J. Teuchert (D, Yamaha), B. Stey (F, Honda) and A. Escobar (E, Honda), 10; 40. D. Messori (I, Suzuki), 10; 41. A. Machado (P, Ducati) and H. Steinbauer (D, Kawasaki), 9; 43. R. Bocek (CZ, Honda), 9; 44. D. Heal (GB, Honda) and A. Schaden (D, Suzuki), 8; 46. D. Wood (GB, Honda), T. Saeby (N, Honda) and E. Ullastres (E, Yamaha), 7; 49. R. Marcolongo (I), G. Villa (I, Ducati), M. Tey Salas (E, Honda) and H. Saiger (A, Yamaha), 6; 53. M. Balaz (SK, Ducati), 6; 54. K. Poensgen (D, Suzuki), 6; 55. V. Zivec (SK, Kawasaki) and A. Corradini (I, Honda), 5; 57. F. Riquelme (E, Ducati), E. Buchner (D, Suzuki), M. Horner (GB, Kawasaki) and J. Lindström (S, Suzuki), 4; 61. R. Ruozi (I, Ducati) and T. Fritzsche (CZ, Kawasaki), 3; 63. L. Mauri (I, Suzuki), H. Soren (DK, Yamaha) and J.-M. Martinez (E, Honda), 2; 66. M. Wegscheider (I, Suzuki), 2; 67. J.-M. Rosales (E, Honda), P. Bentivogli (I, Suzuki), R. Livi (I, Ducati), E. Wilding (A, Honda) and M. Van Deelen (NL, Honda), 1. 71 classified.

Europe

*Jan Hansson.*
▽

# Germany

## 125 cc

**The champion:** Reinhard Stolz. Born on 22nd January 1976, in Bernau. First race: 1993. **Races record:** 2nd of the ADAC Junior Cup in 1995; 28th of the 125cc European championship and 6th of the 125cc German championship in 1996 (Honda); 39th of the 125cc European championship and 7th of the 125cc German championship in 1997 (Yamaha); 3rd of the 125cc European championship and 125cc champion in Germany in 1998 (Honda).

**26th April - Zweibrücken:** 1. O. Perschke (Yamaha); 2. M. Stief (Yamaha); 3. C. Gemmel (Honda); 4. R. Bachmann (CH, Honda); 5. R. Schmidt (Honda); 6. J. Lutzenberger (Honda); 7. M. Oertel (Honda); 8. D. Reissmann (Honda); 9. A. Kariger (Yamaha); 10. R. Stolz (Honda); 11. D. Heidolf (Honda); 12. F. Koch (Honda); 13. T. Schwabbauer (Honda); 14. P. Ebner (Honda); 15. C. Treutlein (Aprilia).
**3rd May - Hockenheim:** 1. R. Stolz (Honda); 2. M. Stief (Yamaha); 3. K. Nöhles (Honda); 4. B. Absmeier (Aprilia); 5. O. Perschke (Yamaha); 6. D. Heidolf (Honda); 7. D. Reissmann (Honda); 8. C. Gemmel (Honda); 9. J. Lutzenberger (Honda); 10. R. Harms (DK, Honda); 11. M. Geissler (Honda); 12. M. Oertel (Honda); 13. J. Smrz (CZ, Honda); 14. R. Knöfler (Yamaha); 15. B. Jerzenbeck (Yamaha).
**1st June - Salzburgring - Austria:** 1. D. Heidolf (Honda); 2. K. Nöhles (Honda); 3. B. Absmeier (Aprilia); 4. M. Stief (Honda); 5. C. Gemmel (Honda); 6. J. Lutzenberger (Honda); 7. A. Eble (Aprilia); 8. A. Kariger (Yamaha); 9. O. Perschke (Yamaha); 10. P. Hafenegger (Honda); 11. M. Hattinger (A, Honda); 12. J. Schmidt (Honda); 13. R. Schmidt (Honda); 14. B. Jerzenbeck (Yamaha); 15. M. Oertel (Honda).
**14th June - Oschersleben:** 1. R. Stolz (Honda); 2. R. Harms (DK, Honda); 3. B. Absmeier (Aprilia); 4. D. Heidolf (Honda); 5. O. Perschke (Yamaha); 6. R. Schmidt (Honda); 7. R. Bachmann (CH, Honda); 8. K. Nöhles (Honda); 9. J. Lutzenberger (Honda); 10. C. Gemmel (Honda); 11. M. Oertel (Honda); 12. A. Kariger (Yamaha); 13. J. Schmidt (Honda); 14. C. Treutlein (Aprilia); 15. A. Eble (Honda).
**28th June - Lechfeld:** 1. B. Absmeier (Aprilia); 2. K. Nöhles (Honda); 3. R. Stolz (Honda); 4. D. Heidolf (Honda); 5. M. Stief (Yamaha); 6. C. Gemmel (Honda); 7. A. Kariger (Yamaha); 8. B. Jerzenbeck (Yamaha); 9. O. Perschke (Yamaha); 10. R. Bachmann (CH, Honda); 11. R. Schmidt (Honda); 12. M. Oertel (Honda); 13. J. Smrz (CZ, Honda); 14. C. Treutlein (Aprilia); 15. R. Knöfler (Yamaha).
**5th July - Most - Czech Republic:** 1. R. Stolz (Honda); 2. K. Nöhles (Honda); 3. M. Stief (Yamaha); 4. D. Reissmann (Honda); 5. B. Absmeier (Aprilia); 6. A. Molina (E, Honda); 7. D. Heidolf (Honda); 8. R. Bachmann (CH, Honda); 9. C. Gemmel (Honda); 10. C. Treutlein (Aprilia); 11. J. Schmidt (Honda); 12. B. Jerzenbeck (Yamaha); 13. P. Hafenegger (Honda); 14. A. Kariger (Yamaha); 15. R. Schmidt (Honda).
**26th July - Brno - Czech Republic:** 1. J. Hules (CZ, Honda); 2. K. Nöhles (Honda); 3. R. Stolz (Honda); 4. B. Absmeier (Aprilia); 5. D. Reissmann (Honda); 6. D. Heidolf (Honda); 7. O. Perschke (Yamaha); 8. R. Bachmann (CH, Honda); 9. C. Gemmel (Honda); 10. B. Jerzenbeck (Yamaha); 11. J. Smrz (CZ, Honda); 12. J. Lutzenberger (Honda); 13. A. Kariger (Honda); 14. J. Schmidt (Honda); 15. R. Schmidt (Honda).
**2nd August - Nürburgring:** 1. D. Reissmann (Honda); 2. R. Stolz (Honda); 3. B. Absmeier (Aprilia); 4. O. Perschke (Yamaha); 5. M. Stief (Yamaha); 6. D. Heidolf (Honda); 7. R. Bachmann (CH, Honda); 8. J. Lutzenberger (Honda); 9. J. Smrz (CZ, Honda); 10. C. Treutlein (Aprilia); 11. R. Harms (DK, Honda); 12. R. Schmidt (Honda); 13. J. Schmidt (Honda); 14. A. Götti (CH, Honda); 15. A. Eble (Honda).
**16th August - Schleizer Dreieck:** 1. K. Nöhles (Honda); 2. D. Reissmann (Honda); 3. B. Absmeier (Aprilia); 4. R. Stolz (Honda); 5. D. Heidolf (Honda); 6. O. Perschke (Yamaha); 7. A. Kariger (Yamaha); 8. B. Jerzenbeck (Yamaha); 9. C. Gemmel (Honda); 10. R. Knöfler (Yamaha); 11. P. Hafenegger (Honda); 12. R. Schmidt (Honda); 13. F. Koch (Honda); 14. C. Treutlein (Aprilia); 15. J. Schmidt (Honda).
**6th September - Hockenheim:** 1. D. Reissmann (Honda); 2. B. Absmeier (Aprilia); 3. D. Heidolf (Honda); 4. R. Stolz (Honda); 5. J. Lutzenberger (Honda); 6. M. Stief (Yamaha); 7. R. Knöfler (Yamaha); 8. B. Jerzenbeck (Yamaha); 9. R. Schmidt (Honda); 10. J. Smrz (CZ, Honda); 11. P. Hafenegger (Honda); 12. C. Gemmel (Honda); 13. A. Kariger (Yamaha); 14. K. Nöhles (Honda); 15. C. Treutlein (Aprilia).

### Final classification

| | | |
|---|---|---|
| 1. Reinhard Stolz | Honda | 163 |
| 2. Bernhard Absmeier | Aprilia | 149 |
| 3. Klaus Nöhles | Honda | 136 |
| 4. Dirk Heidolf | Honda | 124 |
| 5. Dirk Reissmann | Honda | 113 |

6. M. Stief (Yamaha), 101; 7. O. Perschke (Yamaha), 94; 8. C. Gemmel (Honda), 78; 9. J. Lutzenberger (Honda), 58; 10. R. Bachmann (CH, Honda), 55; 11. R. Schmidt (Honda), 49; 12. A. Kariger (Yamaha), 47; 13. B. Jerzenbeck (Yamaha), 41; 14. R. Harms (DK, Honda), 31; 15. J. Smrz (CZ, Honda), 27; 16. M. Oertel (Honda), 26; 17. C. Treutlein (Aprilia), 22; 18. J. Schmidt (Honda), 22; 19. P. Hafenegger (Honda), 21; 20. R. Knöfler (Yamaha), 19; 21. A. Eble (Honda), 13; 22. F. Koch (Honda), 8; 23. T. Schwabbauer (Honda), 3. 23 classified.

## 250 cc

**The champion:** Alexander Hofmann-Hammad. Born on 25th May 1980, in Mindel. First race: 1984. First GP: German GP 1998 (250). **Races record:** 80cc motocross champion in Germany in 1992 (Yamaha); 80cc motocross champion in Germany in 1993 (Yamaha); 125cc motocross ADAC Junior champion in 1994 (Yamaha); 48th of the 125cc European championship in 1996; 28th of the 125cc world championship, 41th of the 125cc European championship and 125cc vice-champion in Germany in 1997 (Yamaha); 29th of the 250cc world championship, 250cc European champion and 250cc champion in Germany in 1998 (Honda).

**26th April - Zweibrücken:** 1. A. Hofmann (Honda); 2 . A. Matikainen (SF, Honda); 3. A. Göbel (Honda); 4. M. Baldinger (Honda); 5. M. Neukirchen (Aprilia); 6. U. Bolterauer (A, Honda); 7. M. Ranacher (Honda); 8. D. Brockmann (Honda); 9. D. Petzold (Honda); 10. T. Lackner (Aprilia); 11. M. Guigas (Yamaha); 12. S.-E. Harms (DK, Honda). 12 classified.
**3rd May - Hockenheim:** 1. A. Hofmann (Honda); 2. M. Baldinger (Honda); 3. M. Ober (Honda); 4. M. Neukirchen (Aprilia); 5. G. Parolari (CH, Aprilia); 6. A. Schmidt (Honda); 7. A. Matikainen (SF, Honda); 8. T. Lackner (Aprilia); 9. D. Brockmann (Honda); 10. A. Göbel (Honda); 11. S.-E. Harms (DK, Honda); 12. N. Rank (Honda); 13. F. Fiedler (Honda); 14. R. Heierli (CH, Honda); 15. M. Ranacher (Honda).
**1st June - Salzburgring - Austria:** 1. A. Hofmann (Honda); 2. M. Ober (Honda); 3. M. Neukirchen (Aprilia); 4. M. Baldinger (Honda); 5. H. Danninger (A, Honda); 6. A. Schmidt (Honda); 7. M. Witzeneder (A, Honda); 8. D. Brockmann (Honda); 9. J. Mairhofer (A, Aprilia); 10. H. Sommer (A, Honda); 11. M. Ranacher (Honda); 12. D. Petzold (Honda); 13. N. Rank (Honda); 14. F. Fiedler (Honda); 15. B. Herrmann (Honda).
**14th June - Oschersleben:** 1. A. Hofmann (Honda); 2. M. Neukirchen (Aprilia); 3. M. Baldinger (Honda); 4. S. Harms (DK, Honda); 5. M. Ranacher (Honda); 6. D. Brockmann (Honda); 7. N. Rank (Honda); 8. F. Fiedler (Honda); 9. B. Stasa (CZ, Aprilia); 10. M. Berger (Honda); 11. B. Van Deik (NL, Honda); 12. R. Rasmussen (DK, Honda); 13. T. Rothe (Honda); 14. W. Igel (Honda); 15. A. Grosse (Honda).
**28th June - Lechfeld:** 1. A. Hofmann (Honda); 2. M. Baldinger (Honda); 3. M. Neukirchen (Aprilia); 4. M. Ober (Honda); 5. M. Ranacher (Honda); 6. F. Fiedler (Honda); 7. B. Stasa (CZ, Aprilia); 8. N. Rank (Honda); 9. D. Brockmann (Honda); 10. A. Göbel (Honda); 11. M. Berger (Honda); 12. A. Grosse (Honda); 13. R. Göbel (Aprilia). 13 classified.
**5th July - Most - Czech Republic:** 1. A. Hofmann (Honda); 2. M. Ober (Honda); 3. M. Ranacher (Honda); 4. M. Baldinger (Honda); 5. G. Rizmayer (H, Honda); 6. S. Harms (DK, Honda); 7. B. Stasa (CZ, Aprilia); 8. R. Rous (CZ, Yamaha); 9. N. Rank (Honda); 10. D. Brockmann (Honda); 11. T. Lucas (Aprilia); 12. A. Göbel (Honda); 13. L. Langer (Yamaha); 14. U. Bolterauer (A, Honda); 15. P. Polansky (Honda).
**26th July - Brno - Czech Republic:** 1. A. Hofmann (Honda); 2. M. Ober (Honda); 3. M. Baldinger (Honda); 4. G. Rizmayer (H, Honda); 5. A. Schmidt (Honda); 6. D. Brockmann (Honda); 7. B. Stasa (CZ, Aprilia); 8. U. Bolterauer (A, Honda); 9. A. Göbel (Honda); 10. M. Klass (Yamaha); 11. N. Rank (Honda); 12. M. Berger (Honda); 13. R. Göbel (Aprilia).
**2nd August - Nürburgring:** 1. A. Hofmann (Honda); 2. M. Ober (Honda); 3. M. Baldinger (Honda); 4. S.-E. Harms (DK, Honda); 5. D. Brockmann (Honda); 6. A. Schmidt (Honda); 7. B. Stasa (CZ, Aprilia); 8. N. Rank (Honda); 9. F. Fiedler (Honda); 10. R. Heierli (CH, Honda); 11. M. Ranacher (Aprilia); 12. T. Rothe (Honda); 13. U. Bolterauer (A, Honda); 14. L. Berlage (B, Honda); 15. C. Koenig (B, Honda).
**16th August - Schleizer Dreieck:** 1. A. Hofmann (Honda); 2. M. Ober (Honda); 3. M. Baldinger (Honda); 4. M. Ranacher (Honda); 5. N. Rank (Honda); 6. N. Richardson (GB, Honda); 7. B. Stasa (CZ, Aprilia); 8. A. Schmidt (Honda); 9. T. Lucas (Aprilia); 10. U. Bolterauer (A, Honda); 11. F. Fiedler (Honda); 12. T. Rothe (Honda); 13. D. Brockmann (Honda); 14. D. Petzold (Honda); 15. A. Göbel (Honda).
**6th September - Hockenheim:** 1. A. Hofmann (Honda); 2. M. Ober (Honda); 3. M. Baldinger (Honda); 4. D. Brockmann (Honda); 5. A. Witsch (Honda); 6. B. Herrmann (Honda); 7. A. Schmidt (Honda); 8. F. Fiedler (Honda); 9. S.-E. Harms (DK, Honda); 10. M. Klass (Yamaha); 11. B. Stasa (CZ, Honda); 12. R. Heierli (CH, Honda); 13. T. Rothe (Honda); 14. D. Petzold (Honda); 15. M. Berger (Honda).

### Final classification

| | | |
|---|---|---|
| 1. Alexander Hofmann-Hammad | Honda | 250 |
| 2. Mike Baldinger | Honda | 162 |
| 3. Markus Ober | Honda | 149 |
| 4. Dirk Brockmann | Honda | 91 |
| 5. Marcel Ranacher | Aprilia | 79 |

6. M. Neukirchen (Aprilia), 78; 7. A. Schmidt (Honda), 64; 8. N. Rank (Honda), 63; 9. B. Stasa (CZ, Aprilia), 62; 10. A. Göbel (Honda), 58; 11. S.-E. Harms (DK, Honda), 58; 12. F. Fiedler (Honda), 51; 13. U. Bolterauer (A, Honda), 39; 14. D. Petzold (Honda), 28; 15. M. Berger (Honda), 28; 16. T. Rothe (Honda), 26; 17. M. Klass (Yamaha), 21; 18. R. Göbel (Aprilia), 18; 19. T. Lackner (Aprilia), 16; 20. G. Parolari (CH, Aprilia), 11; 21. T. Lucas (Aprilia), 8; 22. W. Igel (Honda), 5; 23. T. Rummer (Aprilia), 2. 23 classified.

## Supersport

**The champion:** Jörg Teuchert. Born on 27th February 1970, in Lauf. First race: 1986 (enduro). **Races record:** 80cc endurance champion in Germany in 1987; 125cc endurance champion in Germany in 1989; 6th of the 125cc endurance German championship in 1990; 5th of the 125cc endurance German championship in 1991; 7th of the rally German championship in 1993; 2nd of the German Yamaha Cup in 1994; 8th of the supersport German championship in 1995; 19th of the supersport European championship and 5th of the supersport German championship in 1996 (Yamaha); 24th of the supersport world championship and supersport champion in Germany in 1997 (Yamaha); 17th of the supersport world championship and supersport champion in Germany in 1998 (Yamaha).

**26th April - Zweibrücken:** 1. T. Körner (Kawasaki); 2. M. Schulten (Suzuki); 3. A. Friedrich (Suzuki); 4. A. Schaden (Suzuki); 5. J. Ölschläger (Honda); 6. S. Scheschowitsch (Suzuki); 7. H. Röckl (Yamaha); 8. R. Jänisch (Suzuki); 9. G. Lindner (Kawasaki); 10. R. Stelzer (Suzuki); 3. T. Hoemke (Suzuki); 14. E. Buchner (Suzuki); 15. T. Kuttruf (Yamaha).
**3rd May - Hockenheim:** 1. T. Körner (Kawasaki); 2. C. Kellner (Suzuki); 3. H. Steinbauer (Kawasaki); 4. M. Schulten (Suzuki); 5. J. Teuchert (Yamaha); 6. R. Jänisch (Suzuki); 7. S. Scheschowitsch (Suzuki); 8. V. Bähr (Kawasaki); 9. S. Nebel (Kawasaki); 10. D. Heydt (Kawasaki); 11. G. Lindner (Kawasaki); 12. J. Ölschläger (Honda); 13. T. Klink (Ducati); 14. R. Penzkofer (Yamaha); 15. M. Barth (Suzuki).
**1st June - Salzburgring - Austria:** 1. H. Steinbauer (Kawasaki); 2. H. Kaufmann (Yamaha); 3. J. Teuchert (Yamaha); 4. C. Kellner (Suzuki); 5. M. Barth (Suzuki); 6. T. Körner (Kawasaki); 7. T. Hinterreiter (A, Kawasaki); 8. J. Ölschläger (Honda); 9. M. Schulten (Suzuki); 10. V. Bähr (Kawasaki); 11. R. Penzkofer (Yamaha); 12. P. Koller (Suzuki); 13. A. Luger (Suzuki); 14. A. Schaden (Suzuki); 15. K.

Reinhard Stolz, Alexander Hofmann.
▽

Poensgen (Suzuki).

**14th June - Oschersleben:** 1. J. Teuchert (Yamaha); 2. T. Körner (Kawasaki); 3. C. Kellner (Suzuki); 4. M. Schulten (Suzuki); 5. H. Steinbauer (Kawasaki); 6. R. Jänisch (Suzuki); 7. T. Klink (Ducati); 8. D. Heydt (Kawasaki); 9. A. Friedrich (Suzuki); 10. J. Ölschläger (Honda); 11. R. Strack (Yamaha); 12. M. Barth (Suzuki); 13. R. Penzkofer (Yamaha); 14. T. Hoemke (Suzuki); 6. M. Barth (Suzuki); 5. A. Friedrich (Ducati); 6. M. Schulten (Suzuki); 7. H. Kaufmann (Yamaha); 8. P. Koller (Suzuki); 9. S. Scheschowitsch (Suzuki); 10. D. Heydt (Kawasaki); 11. J. Ölschläger (Honda); 12. H. Steinbauer (Kawasaki); 13. G. Lindner (Suzuki); 14. R. Penzkofer (Yamaha); 15. T. Klink (Ducati).

**5th July - Most - Czech Republic:** 1. M. Schulten (Suzuki); 2. J. Teuchert (Yamaha); 3. C. Kellner (Suzuki); 4. M. Barth (Suzuki); 5. P. Koller (Suzuki); 6. H. Kaufmann (Yamaha); 7. J. Ölschläger (Honda); 8. H. Steinbauer (Kawasaki); 9. S. Scheschowitsch (Suzuki); 10. D. Heydt (Kawasaki); 11. T. Klink (Ducati); 12. A. Luger (Suzuki); 13. J. Hanson (Honda); 14. R. Penzkofer (Yamaha); 15. A. Schaden (Suzuki).

**26th July - Brno - Czech Republic:** 1. H. Steinbauer (Kawasaki); 2. J. Teuchert (Yamaha); 3. T. Körner (Kawasaki); 4. C. Kellner (Suzuki); 5. S. Scheschowitsch (Suzuki); 6. J. Ölschläger (Honda); 7. M. Schulten (Suzuki); 8. P. Koller (Suzuki); 9. M. Barth (Suzuki); 10. G. Lindner (Yamaha); 11. R. Penzkofer (Yamaha); 12. K. Poensgen (Suzuki); 13. T. Klink (Ducati); 14. T. Fritsche (Kawasaki); 15. S. Sebrich (Suzuki).

**2nd August - Nürburgring:** 1. T. Körner (Kawasaki); 2. J. Teuchert (Yamaha); 3. C. Kellner (Suzuki); 4. H. Steinbauer (Kawasaki); 5. M. Barth (Suzuki); 6. P. Koller (Suzuki); 7. D. Heydt (Kawasaki); 9. A. Heiler (Yamaha); 10. G. Lindner (Suzuki); 11. S. Sebrich (Suzuki); 12. T. Kuttruf (Yamaha); 13. V. Bähr (Kawasaki); 14. E. Buchner (Suzuki); 15. J. Boesfeld (NL, Yamaha).

**16th August - Schleizer Dreieck:** 1. M. Schulten (Suzuki); 2. M. Barth (Suzuki); 3. J. Teuchert (Yamaha); 4. J. Ölschläger (Honda); 5. P. Koller (Suzuki); 6. T. Körner (Kawasaki); 7. C. Kellner (Suzuki); 8. G. Lindner (Suzuki); 9. H. Steinbauer (Kawasaki); 10. R. Penzkofer (Yamaha); 11. T. Heiler (Yamaha); 12. A. Friedrich (Ducati); 13. T. Hartelmann (NL, Honda); 14. E. Buchner (Suzuki); 15. K. Poensgen (Suzuki).

**6th September - Hockenheim:** 1. J. Teuchert (Yamaha); 2. C. Kellner (Suzuki); 3. T. Körner (Kawasaki); 4. S. Scheschowitsch (Suzuki); 5. M. Schulten (Suzuki); 6. M. Barth (Suzuki); 7. A. Friedrich (Ducati); 8. A. Heiler (Yamaha); 9. V. Bähr (Kawasaki); 10. G. Lindner (Suzuki); 11. R. Penzkofer (Yamaha); 12. J. Ölschläger (Honda); 13. E. Buchner (Suzuki); 14. D. Heydt (Kawasaki); 15. T. Kuttruf (Yamaha).

**Final classification**

| | | |
|---|---|---|
| 1. Jörg Teuchert | Yamaha | 178 |
| 2. Thomas Körner | Kawasaki | 163 |
| 3. Michael Schulten | Suzuki | 137 |
| 4. Christian Kellner | Suzuki | 127 |
| 5. Harald Steinbauer | Kawasaki | 116 |

6. M. Barth (Suzuki), 92; 7. J. Ölschläger (Honda), 81; 8. S. Scheschowitsch (Suzuki), 57; 9. P. Koller (Suzuki), 53; 10. A. Friedrich (Suzuki), 48; 11. D. Heydt (Kawasaki), 43; 12. G. Lindner (Kawasaki/Suzuki), 43; 13. H. Kaufmann (Yamaha), 40; 14. R. Penzkofer (Yamaha), 35; 15. R. Jänisch (Suzuki), 29; 16. V. Bähr (Kawasaki), 25; 17. T. Klink (Ducati), 23; 18. A. Heiler (Yamaha), 20; 19. A. Schaden (Suzuki), 18; 20. E. Buchner (Suzuki), 14; 21. H. Röckl (Yamaha), 10; 22. S. Sebrich (Suzuki), 8; 23. A. Luger (Suzuki), 8; 24. K. Poensgen (Suzuki), 8; 25. R. Strack (Yamaha), 6; 26. R. Stelzer (Suzuki), 6; 27. T. Kuttruff (Yamaha), 6; 28. T. Hoemke (Suzuki), 6. 28 classified.

**Superbike**

**The champion:** Andreas Meklau. Born on 7th June 1967, in Bruck/Mur (Austria). First race: 1989. First GP: Australian GP, 1993 (500). **Races record:** superbike champion in Austria in 1990; superbike champion in Austria in 1991; 37th of the superbike world championship and superbike champion in Austria in 1992 (Ducati); 35th of the 50cc world championship (ROC Yamaha), 15th of the superbike European championship and 9th of the superbike European championship in 1993 (Ducati); 6th of the superbike world championship in 1994 (Ducati); 13th of the superbike world championshipin 1995 (Ducati); 18th of the superbike world championship and 4th of the Pro Superbike German championship in 1996 (Ducati); 18th the superbike world championship and 3rd of the Superbike German championship in 1997 (Ducati); 18th of the superbike world championship and superbike champion in Germany in 1998 (Ducati).

**26th April - Zweibrücken:** Race I: 1. C. Lindholm (S, Yamaha); 2. J. Schmid (Kawasaki); 3. R. Kellenberger (CH, Honda); 4. K. McCarthy (AUS, Suzuki); 5. J. Berner (SF, Kawasaki); 6. A. Meklau (A, Ducati); 7. H. Hadrawa (Ducati); 8. W. Dimperl (Ducati); 9. F. Heidger (Kawasaki); 10. L. Kraus (Kawasaki); 11. N. Manz (Suzuki); 12. P. Leuthard (CH, Kawasaki); 13. H. Fath (Ducati); 14. H. Kitsch (Kawasaki); 15. F. Franz (Kawasaki). Race II: 1. J. Schmid (Kawasaki); 2. K. McCarthy (AUS, Suzuki); 3. R. Kellenberger (CH, Honda); 4. C. Lindholm (S, Yamaha); 5. A. Meklau (A, Ducati); 6. J. Ekerold (AfS, Kawasaki); 7. S. Truninger (CH, Yamaha); 8. S. Vitzthum (A, Ducati); 9. R. Hüber (Kawasaki); 10. J. Berner (SF, Kawasaki); 11. P. Leuthard (CH, Kawasaki); 12. H. Kitsch (Kawasaki); 13. H. Skora (Suzuki); 14. F. Heidger (Kawasaki); 15. C. Schneider (Kawasaki).

**3rd May - Hockenheim:** Race I: 1. C. Lindholm (S, Yamaha); 2. J. Schmid (Kawasaki); 3. U. Mark (Suzuki); 4. A. Meklau (A, Ducati); 5. R. Kellenberger (CH, Honda); 6. J. Ekerold (AfS, Kawasaki); 7. R. Xaus (E, Suzuki); 8. J. Berner (SF, Kawasaki); 9. H. Kitsch (Kawasaki); 10. P. Leuthard (CH, Kawasaki); 11. F. Heidger (Kawasaki); 12. D. Guderian (Kawasaki); 13. R. Hüber (Kawasaki); 14. C. Schneider (Kawasaki); 15. N. Manz (Suzuki). Race II: 1. J. Schmid (Kawasaki); 2. C. Lindholm (S, Yamaha); 3. A. Meklau (A, Ducati); 4. U. Mark (Suzuki); 5. R. Kellenberger (CH, Honda); 6. R. Xaus (E, Suzuki); 7. M. Rudroff (Ducati); 8. J. Berner (SF, Kawasaki); 9. F. Heidger (Kawasaki); 10. H. Kitsch (Kawasaki); 11. R. Hüber (Kawasaki); 12. J. Ekerold (AfS, Kawasaki); 13. N. Manz (Suzuki); 14. D. Guderian (Kawasaki); 15. P. Leuthard (CH, Kawasaki).

**31st May - Salzburgring - Austria:** Race I: 1. A. Meklau (A, Ducati); 2. C. Lindholm (S, Yamaha); 3. U. Mark (Suzuki); 4. R. Kellenberger (CH, Honda); 5. J. Ekerold (AfS, Kawasaki); 6. M. Rudroff (Ducati); 7. R. Hüber (Kawasaki); 8. R. Xaus (E, Suzuki); 9. J. Berner (SF, Kawasaki); 10. W. Dimperl (Ducati); 11. J. Wolfsteiner (A, Kawasaki); 12. H. Skora (Suzuki); 13. S. Vitzthum (A, Ducati); 14. C. Häusle (A, Ducati); 15. A. Folger (Kawasaki). Race II: 1. A. Meklau (A, Ducati); 2. C. Lindholm (S, Yamaha); 3. U. Mark (Suzuki); 4. R. Kellenberger (CH, Honda); 5. J. Ekerold (AfS, Kawasaki); 6. R. Xaus (E, Suzuki); 7. M. Rudroff (Ducati); 8. R. Hüber (Kawasaki); 9. S. Vitzthum (A, Ducati); 10. F. Heidger (Kawasaki); 11. J. Wolfsteiner (A, Kawasaki); 12. D. Guderian (Kawasaki); 13. J. Berner (SF, Kawasaki); 14. C. Schneider (Kawasaki); 15. A. Folger (Kawasaki).

**14th June - Oschersleben:** Race I: 1. J. Schmid (Kawasaki); 2. A. Meklau (A, Ducati); 3. U. Mark (Suzuki); 4. R. Xaus (E, Suzuki); 5. R. Kellenberger (CH, Honda); 6. J. Ekerold (AfS, Kawasaki); 7. H. Kitsch (Kawasaki); 8. J. Berner (SF, Kawasaki); 9. F. Heidger (Kawasaki); 10. M. Ober (Suzuki); 11. C. Schneider (Kawasaki); 12. S. Truninger (CH, Yamaha); 13. H. Skora (Suzuki); 14. S. Vitzthum (A, Ducati); 15. D. Guderian (Kawasaki). Race II: 1. J. Schmid (Kawasaki); 2. A. Meklau (A, Ducati); 3. U. Mark (Suzuki); 4. R. Kellenberger (CH, Honda); 5. J. Ekerold (AfS, Kawasaki); 6. R. Xaus (E, Suzuki); 7. R. Hüber (Kawasaki); 8. M. Ober (Suzuki); 9. H. Kitsch (Kawasaki); 10. S. Truninger (CH, Yamaha); 11. C. Schneider (Kawasaki); 12. J. Berner (SF, Kawasaki); 13. D. Guderian (Kawasaki); 14. S. Vitzthum (A, Ducati); 15. H. Skora (Suzuki).

**5th July - Most - Czech Republic:** Race I: 1. A. Meklau (A, Ducati); 2. J. Schmid (Kawasaki); 3. R. Kellenberger (CH, Honda); 4. C. Lindholm (S, Yamaha); 5. U. Mark (Suzuki); 6. J. Ekerold (AfS, Kawasaki); 7. M. Rudroff (Ducati); 8. J. Berner (SF, Kawasaki); 9. R. Hüber (Kawasaki); 10. H. Kitsch (Kawasaki); 11. M. Ober (Suzuki); 12. P. Leuthard (CH, Kawasaki); 13. S. Vitzthum (A, Ducati); 14. C. Schneider (Kawasaki); 15. J. Wolfsteiner (Kawasaki). Race II: 1. A. Meklau (A, Ducati); 2. C. Lindholm (S, Yamaha); 3. R. Kellenberger (CH, Honda); 4. U. Mark (Suzuki); 5. J. Schmid (Kawasaki); 6. R. Xaus (E, Suzuki); 7. M. Rudroff (Ducati); 8. R. Hüber (Kawasaki); 9. J. Ekerold (AfS, Kawasaki); 10. H. Kitsch (Kawasaki); 11. J. Berner (SF, Kawasaki); 12. M. Ober (Suzuki); 13. S. Vitzthum (A, Ducati); 14. B. Camlek (Yamaha); 15. D. Guderian (Kawasaki).

**12th July - Pannonia-Ring - Hungary**

Race I: 1. J. Schmid (Kawasaki); 2. R. Xaus (E, Suzuki); 3. A. Meklau (A, Ducati); 4. R. Kellenberger (CH, Honda); 5. U. Mark (Suzuki); 6. C. Kellner (Suzuki); 7. C. Lindholm (S, Yamaha); 8. S. Vitzthum (A, Ducati); 9. H. Kitsch (Kawasaki); 10. C. Zaiser (Honda); 11. J. Berner (SF, Kawasaki); 12. M. Rudroff (Ducati); 13. J. Ekerold (AfS, Kawasaki); 14. V. Krumme (Kawasaki); 15. M. Barth (Suzuki). Race II: 1. A. Meklau (A, Ducati); 2. U. Mark (Suzuki); 3. J. Ekerold (AfS, Kawasaki); 4. M. Rudroff (Ducati); 5. R. Hüber (Kawasaki); 6. C. Lindholm (S, Yamaha); 7. S. Vitzthum (A, Ducati); 8. H. Kitsch (Kawasaki); 9. J. Vegh (H, Yamaha); 10. J. Berner (SF, Kawasaki); 11. H. Skora (Suzuki); 12. P. Leuthard (CH, Kawasaki); 13. S. Truninger (CH, Yamaha); 14. R. Xaus (E, Suzuki); 15. H. Platacis (Kawasaki).

**2nd August - Nürburgring**

Race I: 1. A. Meklau (A, Ducati); 2. J. Schmid (Kawasaki); 3. C. Lindholm (S, Yamaha); 4. U. Mark (Suzuki); 5. J. Ekerold (AfS, Kawasaki); 6. R. Hüber (Kawasaki); 7. A. Hofmann (CH, Honda); 8. J. Berner (SF, Kawasaki); 9. M. Rudroff (Ducati); 10. H. Kitsch (Kawasaki); 11. P. Linden (S, Ducati); 12. M. Kellenberger (CH, Honda); 13. S. Vitzthum (A, Ducati); 14. P. Leuthard (CH, Kawasaki); 15. S. Truninger (CH, Yamaha). Race II: 1. J. Schmid (Kawasaki); 2. U. Mark (Suzuki); 3. C. Lindholm (S, Yamaha); 4. J. Ekerold (AfS, Kawasaki); 5. R. Xaus (E, Suzuki); 6. R. Kellenberger (CH, Honda); 7. A. Meklau (A, Ducati); 8. M. Rudroff (Ducati); 9. P. Linden (S, Ducati); 10. R. Hüber (Kawasaki); 11. A. Hofmann (CH, Honda); 12. W. Dimperl (Ducati); 13. M. Kellenberger (CH, Honda); 14. J. Berner (SF, Kawasaki); 15. P. Leuthard (CH, Kawasaki).

**6th September - Hockenheim**

Race I: 1. J. Schmid (Kawasaki); 2. C. Lindholm (S, Yamaha); 3. C. Kellner (Suzuki); 4. A. Meklau (A, Ducati); 5. M. Rudroff (Ducati); 6. H. Kitsch (Kawasaki); 7. P. Linden (S, Ducati); 8. F. Heidger (Kawasaki); 9. C. Monsch (CH, Honda); 10. J. Schmidt (Suzuki); 11. R. Kellenberger (CH, Honda); 12. A. Hofmann (CH, Ducati); 13. V. Krumme (Kawasaki); 14. P. Leuthard (CH, Kawasaki); 15. C. Schneider (Kawasaki). Race II: 1. C. Lindholm (S, Yamaha); 2. J. Schmid (Kawasaki); 3. U. Mark (Suzuki); 4. A. Meklau (A, Ducati); 5. R. Xaus (E, Suzuki); 6. A. Hofmann (CH, Ducati); 7. C. Kellner (Suzuki); 8. J. Ekerold (AfS, Kawasaki); 9. M. Rudroff (Ducati); 10. H. Kitsch (Kawasaki); 11. C. Ehrenberger (Suzuki); 12. P. Leuthard (CH, Kawasaki); 13. M. Edwards (Kawasaki); 14. J. Schmidt (Suzuki); 15. W. Dimperl (Ducati).

**Final classification**

| | | |
|---|---|---|
| 1. Andreas Meklau (A) | Ducati | 294 |
| 2. Jochen Schmid | Kawasaki | 286 |
| 3. Christer Lindholm (S) | Yamaha | 253 |
| 4. Udo Mark | Suzuki | 197 |
| 5. Roger Kellenberger (CH) | Honda | 167 |

6. J. Ekerold (AfS, Kawasaki, 144); 7. R. Xaus (E, Suzuki, 114); 8. M. Rudroff (Ducati, 103); 9. J. Berner (SF, Kawasaki), 96; 10. H. Kitsch (Kawasaki, 90); 11. R. Hüber (Kawasaki, 84); 12. S. Vitzthum (A, Ducati, 56); 13. F. Heidger (Kawasaki, 53); 14. P. Leuthard (CH, Kawasaki, 50); 15. K. McCarthy (AUS, Suzuki), 33; 16. C. Schneider (Kawasaki, 30); 17. S. Truninger (CH, Yamaha, 29); 18. W. Dimperl (Ducati, 24); 19. H. Skora (Suzuki, 24); 20. D. Guderian (Kawasaki, 22); 21. J. Schmidt (Suzuki, 15); 22. N. Manz (Suzuki, 15); 23. J. Wolfsteiner (A, Kawasaki, 12); 24. H. Hadrawa (Ducati, 9); 25. J. Vegh (H, Yamaha, 8); 26. L. Kraus (Kawasaki, 8); 27. A. John (Kawasaki, 5); 28. B. Camlek (Yamaha, 4); 29. K. Poensgen (Suzuki, 3); 30. H. Fath (Ducati, 3); 31. C. Häusle (A, Ducati, 3); 32. M. Bordihn (Kawasaki, 2); 33. F. Franz (Kawasaki, 2); 34. M. Mendel (Yamaha, 1); 35. H. Platacis (Kawasaki, 1). 35 classified.

## Germany

*Jörg Teuchert, Andreas Meklau.*

▽

*France*

## 125 cc

The champion: Randy de Puniet. Born on 14th February 1981, in Andrésy. First GP: French GP, 1998 (125). Races record: winner of the Typhoon Cup in 1995; 4th of the Promosport 125 French Cup and 4th of the Cagiva Mito French Cup in 1996; 42nd of the 125cc European championship, 125cc French vice-champion, 125cc French "national" champion (Honda) and winner of the Cagiva Mito Cup in 1997; 9th of the 125cc European championship and 125cc French champion in 1998 (Honda).

### 8th March - Le Mans
1. R. de Puniet (Honda); 2. F. Terrier (Honda); 3. J. Petit (Honda); 4. S. Duterne (Honda); 5. J. Leleu (Honda); 6. M. Lougassi (Honda); 7. G. Fouet (Honda); 8. L. Frémy (Honda); 9. E. Defortescu (Honda); 10. V. Laconi (Honda); 11. H. Louiset (Honda); 12. E. Palacios (Yamaha); 13. D. Martin (Yamaha); 14. J. Servaes (Honda); 15. L. Guignat (Honda).

### 29th March - Magny-Cours
1. N. Dussauge (Honda); 2. R. de Puniet (Honda); 3. F. Terrier (Honda); 4. J. Petit (Honda); 5. S. Duterne (Honda); 6. G. Lefort (Honda); 7. H. Louiset (Honda); 8. G. Fouet (Honda); 9. J. Leleu (Honda); 10. E. Defortescu (Honda); 11. J.-M. Louis (Aprilia); 12. O. Jouret (Honda); 13. J. Grégoire (Honda); 14. D. Krzyzanowski (Honda); 15. N. Doublet (Honda).

### 5th April - Albi
1. N. Dussauge (Honda); 2. R. de Puniet (Honda); 3. D. Krzyzanowski (Honda); 4. M. Lougassi (Honda); 5. S. Duterne (Honda); 6. J.-M. Louis (Aprilia); 7. G. Fouet (Honda); 8. N. Doublet (Honda); 9. J. Leleu (Honda); 10. V. Laconi (Honda); 11. L. Larregain (Yamaha); 12. J. Grégoire (Honda); 13. J. Servaes (Honda); 14. F. Martinez (Honda); 15. H. Louiset (Honda).

### 3rd May - Carole
1. R. De Puniet (Honda); 2. N. Dussauge (Honda); 3. F. Terrier (Honda); 4. J.-M. Louis (Aprilia); 5. S. Duterne (Honda); 6. G. Lefort (Honda); 7. J. Servaes (Honda); 8. H. Louiset (Honda); 9. E. Dubray (Honda); 10. N. Papouin (Honda); 11. V. Laconi (Honda); 12. J. Grégoire (Honda); 13. L. Frémy (Honda); 14. Y. Horrenberger (Honda); 15. N. Doublet (Honda).

### 17th May - Nogaro
1. F. Terrier (Honda); 2. J. Petit (Honda); 3. M. Lougassi (Honda); 4. S. Duterne (Honda); 5. G. Fouet (Honda); 6. G. Lefort (Honda); 7. D. Krzyzanowski (Honda); 8. E. Dubray (Honda); 9. J. Servaes (Honda); 10. J. Grégoire (Honda); 11. L. Larregain (Yamaha); 12. N. Papouin (Honda); 13. N. Doublet (Honda); 14. E. Palacios (Yamaha); 15. O. Jouret (Honda).

### 24th May - Le Vigeant
1. J. Petit (Honda); 2. S. Duterne (Honda); 3. G. Lefort (Honda); 4. M. Lougassi (Honda); 5. F. Terrier (Honda); 6. J. Servaes (Honda); 7. G. Fouet (Honda); 8. H. Louiset (Honda); 9. J.-M. Louis (Aprilia); 10. D. Krzyzanowski (Honda); 11. N. Papouin (Honda); 12. J. Leleu (Honda); 13. L. Guignat (Honda); 14. V. Laconi (Honda); 15. L. Frémy (Honda).

### 14th June - Lédenon
1. R. de Puniet (Honda); 2. J.-M. Louis (Aprilia); 3. S. Duterne (Honda); 4. M. Lougassi (Honda); 5. J. Petit (Honda); 6. F. Terrier (Honda); 7. D. Krzyzanowski (Honda); 8. H. Louiset (Honda); 9. G. Fouet (Honda); 10. N. Papouin (Honda); 11. G. Lefort (Honda); 12. L. Frémy (Honda); 13. F. Martinez; 14. J. Grégoire (Honda); 15. L. Guignat (Honda).

### 5th July - Le Castellet
1. R. de Puniet (Honda); 2. G. Lefort (Honda); 3. F. Terrier (Honda); 4. D. Krzyzanowski (Honda); 5. M. Lougassi (Honda); 6. G. Fouet (Honda); 7. S. Duterne (Honda); 8. J. Servaes (Honda); 9. O. Jouret (Honda); 10. J. Leleu (Honda); 11. J. Grégoire (Honda); 12. N. Doublet (Honda); 13. J.-M. Louis (Aprilia); 14. L. Frémy (Honda); 15. E. Dubray (Honda).

### 4th October - Carole
1. E. Dubray (Honda); 2. H. Louiset (Honda); 3. J.-M. Louis (Aprilia): 4. D. Krzyzanowski (Honda); 5. J. Petit (Honda); 6. G. Fouet (Honda); 7. N. Doublet (Honda); 8. E. Palacios (Yamaha); 9. O. Jouret (Honda); 10. J. Servaes (Honda); 11. R. de Puniet (Honda); 12. J. Leleu (Honda); 13. S. Duterne (Honda); 14. E. Defortescu (Brothers); 15. Villain (Yamaha).

### Final classification
1. Randy de Puniet Honda 145
2. Frédéric Terrier Honda 114
3. Jimmy Petit Honda 96
4. S. Duterne (Honda), 95; 5. M. Lougassi (Honda), 76; 6. J.-M. Louis (Aprilia), 74; 7. G. Lefort (Honda), 71; 8. N. Dussauge (Honda), 70; 9. D. Krzyzanowski (Honda), 68; 10. G. Fouet (Honda), 66.

## 250 cc

The champion: Vincent Philippe. Born on 11th January 1978, in Trépot. First race: 1992. First GP: French GP, 1997 (125). Races record: 12th of the French Yamaha Cup in 1993; 8th of the French Yamaha Cup in 1994; 16th of the 125cc French championship, 9th of the 125cc French "national" championship and mountain French champion in 1996; 7th of the 125cc French championship, 3rd of the 125cc French "national" championship and mountain French champion in 1997; 7th of the 250cc European championship and 125cc French champion in 1998 (Honda).

### 8th March - Le Mans
1. R. Sègues (Honda); 2. M. Lagrive (Honda); 3. F. Poulle (Honda); 4. F. Sohier (Honda); 5. J. Allemand (Honda); 6. E. Maizeret (Honda); 7. H. Mora (Aprilia); 8. Y. de Grandidier (Honda); 9. R. Peron (Honda); 10. A. Paulus (Yamaha); 11. D. Tarozzi (Aprilia); 12. D. Testa (Aprilia); 13. C. Vacherie (Honda); 14. D. Raphanaud (Yamaha); 15. L. De Lalande (Honda).

### 29th March - Magny-Cours
1. J. Allemand (Honda); 2. M. Lagrive (Honda); 3. F. Sohier (Honda); 4. F. Poulle (Honda); 5. T. Falcone (Aprilia); 6. O. Stableau (Honda); 7. E. Maizeret (Honda); 8. D. Raphanaud (Yamaha); 9. R. Peron (Honda); 10. A. Paulus (Yamaha).

### 5th April - Albi
1. V. Philippe (Honda); 2. M. Lagrive (Honda); 3. F. Poulle (Honda); 4. J. Allemand (Honda); 5. F. Sohier (Honda); 6. E. Maizeret (Honda); 7. D. Testa (Aprilia). 7 classified.

### 3rd May - Carole
1. J. Allemand (Honda); 2. V. Philippe (Honda); 3. H. Mora (Aprilia); 4. M. Lagrive (Honda); 5. F. Poulle (Honda); 6. F. Sohier (Honda); 7. O. Stableau (Honda); 8. E. Maizeret (Honda); 9. D. Raphanaud (Yamaha); 10. S. Pont (Honda); 11. A. Paulus (Yamaha); 12. C. Vacherie (Honda); 13. J.-P. Dambrine (Honda). 13 classified.

### 17th May - Nogaro
1. V. Philippe (Honda); 2. F. Poulle (Honda); 3. Y. de Grandidier (Honda); 4. O. Stableau (Honda); 5. E. Maizeret (Honda); 6. S. Pont (Honda); 7. D. Tarozzi (Aprilia); 8. H. Mora (Aprilia). 8 classified.

### 24th May - Le Vigeant
1. V. Philippe (Honda); 2. F. Poulle (Honda); 3. H. Mora (Aprilia); 4. Y. de Grandidier (Honda); 5. F. Sohier (Honda); 6. A. Paulus (Yamaha); 7. J.-M. Resh (Yamaha); 8. D. Tarozzi (Aprilia); 9. C. Vacherie (Honda); 10. M. Sonzini (Yamaha); 11. L. De Lalande (Honda). 11 classified.

### 14th June - Lédenon
1. J. Allemand (Honda); 2. V. Philippe (Honda); 3. F. Poulle (Honda); 4. M. Lagrive (Honda); 5. Y. de Grandidier (Honda); 6. F. Sohier (Honda); 7. L.-L. Maisto; 8. S. Pont (Honda); 9. O. Stableau (Honda); 10. A. Paulus (Yamaha); 11. J.-M. Resh (Yamaha); 12. N. Boyer; 13. C. Vacherie (Honda).

### 5th July - Le Castellet
1. R. de Puniet (Honda); 2. V. Philippe (Honda); 3. F. Sohier (Honda); 4. Y. de Grandidier (Honda); 5. F. Poulle (Honda); 6. O. Stableau (Honda); 7. E. Maizeret (Honda); 8. A. Paulus (Yamaha); 9. D. Bugnon. 9 classified.

### 4th October - Carole
1. J. Allemand (Honda); 2. V. Philippe (Honda); 3. F. Sohier (Honda); 4. A. Paulus (Yamaha); 5. D. Raphanaud (Yamaha); 6. E. Maizeret (Honda); 7. Y. de Grandidier (Honda); 8. Metro (Aprilia); 9. C. Vacherie (Honda); 10. Eruam (Aprilia); 11. Raffeau; 12. Congard (Aprilia).

### Final classification
1. Vincent Philippe Honda 155
2. Julien Allemand Honda 124
3. Franck Poulle Honda 112
4. F. Sohier (Honda), 93; 5. M. Lagrive (Honda), 86; 6. Y. de Grandidier (Honda), 79; 7. E. Maizeret (Honda), 67; 8. A. Paulus (Yamaha) 54; 9. H. Mora (Aprilia), 49; 10. O. Stableau (Honda), 49.

## Supersport

The champion: Jehan D'Orgeix. Born on 30th April 1963. First GP: Spanish GP, 1993 (500). Races record: 15th of the endurance world championship in 1991 (Kawasaki); 21st of the superbike world championship in 1992 (Kawasaki); 16th of the IRTA ranking 500 in 1993 (Yamaha); 26th of the endurance world championship in 1994 (Suzuki); 5th of the endurance world championship, 6th of the supersport European championship and supersport France champion in 1995 (Kawasaki); 19th of the endurance world championship and 4th of the supersport French championship in 1996 (Kawasaki); 8th of the endurance world championship, supersport French champion and 19th of the superbike French championship in 1997 (Kawasaki); 5th of the endurance world championship and supersport French champion in 1998 (Kawasaki).

### 8th March - Le Mans
1. B. Sebileau (Kawasaki); 2. D. Muscat (Ducati); 3. J.-F. Cortinovis (Honda); 4. C. Cogan (Yamaha); 5. J. D'Orgeix (Kawasaki); 6. J.-Y. Mounier (Kawasaki); 7. J. Nogueira (Suzuki); 8. E. Mahé (Suzuki); 9. F. Forêt (Ducati); 10. J.-E. Gomez (Suzuki); 11. L. Brian (Honda); 12. P. Dobé (Suzuki); 13. S. Aubry (Kawasaki); 14. L. Holon (Kawasaki); 15. G. Giabbani (Kawasaki).

### 29th March - Magny-Cours
1. P. Dobé (Suzuki); 2. J. D'Orgeix (Kawasaki); 3. D. Muscat (Ducati); 4. E. Mahé (Suzuki); 5. B. Sebileau (Kawasaki); 6. S. Scarnato (Kawasaki); 7. S. Charpentier (Honda); 8. L. Holon (Kawasaki); 9. A. Van den Bossche (Suzuki); 10. J.-F. Cortinovis (Honda); 11. B. Stey (Honda); 12. G. Giabbani (Kawasaki); 13. J.-Y. Mounier (Kawasaki); 14. J. Nogueira (Suzuki); 15. S. Aubry (Kawasaki).

### 5th April - Albi
1. D. Muscat (Ducati); 2. J. D'Orgeix (Kawasaki); 3. J.-F. Cortinovis (Honda); 4. J.-Y. Mounier (Kawasaki); 5. G. Giabbani (Kawasaki); 6. L. Holon (Kawasaki); 7. B. Stey (Honda); 8. P. Perin (Suzuki); 9. P. Dobé (Suzuki); 10. F. Rousseau (Kawasaki); 11. J. Guérin (Honda); 12. L. Béguelin (Honda); 13. O. Louis (Suzuki). 13 classified.

### 3rd May - Carole
1. S. Charpentier (Honda); 2. J.-E. Gomez (Suzuki); 3. T. Paillot (Kawasaki); 4. L. Holon (Kawasaki); 5. J. D'Orgeix (Kawasaki); 6. B. Sebileau (Kawasaki); 7. J.-Y. Mounier (Kawasaki); 8. S. Scarnato (Kawasaki); 9. G. Giabbani (Kawasaki); 10. J.-F. Cortinovis (Honda); 11. E. Mahé (Yamaha); 12. J. Nogueira (Suzuki); 13. B. Stey (Honda); 14. J. Guérin (Honda); 15. S. Aubry (Kawasaki).

### 17th May - Nogaro
1. J. D'Orgeix (Kawasaki); 2. S. Scarnato (Kawasaki); 3. E. Mahé (Suzuki); 4. J.-E. Gomez (Suzuki); 5. J.-F. Cortinovis (Honda); 6. B. Sebileau (Kawasaki); 7. L. Holon (Kawasaki); 8.

*Randy De Puniet, Vincent Philippe.*
▽

J.-Y. Mounier (Kawasaki); 9. J. Nogueira (Suzuki); 10. B. Stey (Honda); 11. F. Rousseau (Kawasaki); 12. P. Perin (Suzuki); 13. J. Guérin (Honda); 14. O. Four (Suzuki); 15. S. Aubry (Kawasaki).

**24th May - Le Vigeant**
1. J. D'Orgeix (Kawasaki); 2. S. Scarnato (Kawasaki); 3. B. Sebileau (Kawasaki); 4. L. Holon (Kawasaki); 5. J.-E. Gomez (Suzuki); 6. J.-F. Cortinovis (Honda); 7. B. Stey (Honda); 8. E. Mahé (Suzuki); 9. J. Nogueira (Suzuki); 10. T. Paillot (Kawasaki); 11. P. Perin (Suzuki); 12. F. Miguet (Kawasaki); 13. P. Picaut (Honda); 14. P. Plateaux (Suzuki); 15. M. Levrel (Kawasaki).

**14th June - Lédenon**
1. S. Scarnato (Kawasaki); 2. J. D'Orgeix (Kawasaki); 3. L. Holon (Kawasaki); 4. J.-F. Cortinovis (Honda); 5. B. Sebileau (Kawasaki); 6. E. Mahé (Yamaha); 7. J.-Y. Mounier (Kawasaki); 8. J.-E. Gomez (Suzuki); 9. B. Stey (Honda); 10. T. Paillot (Kawasaki); 11. G. Giabbani (Kawasaki); 12. D. Muscat (Ducati); 13. P. Perrin (Suzuki); 14. F. Rousseau (Kawasaki); 15. S. Aubry (Kawasaki).

**5th July - Le Castellet**
1. B. Sebileau (Kawasaki); 2. S. Scarnato (Kawasaki); 3. J. D'Orgeix (Kawasaki); 4. T. Paillot (Kawasaki); 5. L. Holon (Kawasaki); 6. J.-E. Gomez (Suzuki); 7. J.-Y. Mounier (Kawasaki); 8. D. Muscat (Ducati); 9. G. Giabbani (Kawasaki); 10. B. Stey (Honda); 11. P. Perrin (Suzuki); 12. J.-F. Cortinovis (Honda); 13. F. Rousseau (Kawasaki); 14. S. Aubry (Kawasaki); 15. C. Fernandez (Suzuki).

**4th October - Carole**
1. D. Muscat (Ducati); 2. S. Charpentier (Honda); 3. J. D'Orgeix (Kawasaki); 4. J.-Y. Mounier (Kawasaki); 5. J.-F. Cortinovis (Honda); 6. G. Muteau (Ducati); 7. T. Paillot (Kawasaki); 8. B. Sebileau (Kawasaki); 9. S. Scarnato (Kawasaki); 10. Destoop; 11. P. Perrin (Suzuki); 12. B. Stey (Honda); 13. Gallis (Kawasaki); 14. Munsch (Ducati); 15. Veghini (Laverda).

**Final classification**
1. Jehan D'Orgeix     Kawasaki    142
2. Sébastien Scarnato   Kawasaki    110
3. Bertrand Sebileau    Kawasaki    108
4. D. Muscat (Ducati), 98; 5. J.-F. Cortinovis (Honda), 6. L. Holon (Kawasaki), 80; 7. J.-E. Gomez (Suzuki), 68; 8. J.-Y. Mounier (Kawasaki), 62; 9. E. Mahé (Suzuki), 60; 10. S. Charpentier (Honda), 54.

## Superbike-Stockbike

The champion: Christophe Guyot. Races record: 91st of the superbike worldchampionship in 1991 (Honda); 64th of the superbike European championship in 1993 (Kawasaki); 14th of the endurance world championship in 1994 (Honda); 17th of the endurance world championship and 6th of the superbike French championship in 1995 (Honda); 42nd of the endurance world championship in 1996 (Honda); 15th of the endurance world championship and 20th of the superbike French championship in 1997 (Honda); 55th of the endurance world championship and superbike French champion in 1998 (Kawasaki).

**8th March - Le Mans**
1. B. Sebileau (Kawasaki SBK); 2. A. Bousseau (Suzuki SBK); 3. T. Rogier (Yamaha STB); 4. S. Waldmeier (Yamaha STB); 5. C. Guyot (Kawasaki SBK); 6. B. Bonhuil (Kawasaki STB); 7. J.-M. Delétang (Yamaha SBK); 8. B. Cazade (Yamaha STB); 9. J.-P. Guinand (Kawasaki STB); 10. F. Moreira (Kawasaki STB); 11. V. Bocquet (Yamaha STB); 12. M. Robert; 13. C. Haquin (Kawasaki STB); 14. C. Nogueira (Suzuki SBK); 15. F. Ciciliani (Ducati SBK).

**29th March - Magny-Cours**
1. B. Sebileau (Kawasaki SBK); 2. C. Guyot (Kawasaki SBK); 3. F. Protat (Honda SBK); 4. D. Crassous (Yamaha STB); 5. T. Rogier (Yamaha STB); 6. E. Mizera (Yamaha STB); 7. J.-F. Braut (Yamaha STB); 8. D. Marzloff (Kawasaki SBK); 9.

B. Cazade (Yamaha STB); 10. J.-P. Guinand (Kawasaki STB); 11. F. Ciciliani (Ducati SBK); 12. B. Bonhuil (Kawasaki STB); 13. F. Forêt (Yamaha STB); 14. J. Foray (Yamaha STB); 15. V. Bocquet (Yamaha STB).

**5th April - Albi**
1. C. Guyot (Kawasaki SBK); 2. J.-P. Guinand (Kawasaki STB); 3. T. Rogier (Yamaha STB); 4. J.-F. Braut (Yamaha STB); 5. C. Mouzin (Yamaha STB); 6. B. Bonhuil (Kawasaki STB); 7. S. Neff (Yamaha STB); 8. J. Foray (Yamaha STB); 9. B. Cazade (Yamaha STB); 10. V. Bocquet (Yamaha STB); 11. E. Mizera (Yamaha STB); 12. C. Nogueira (Suzuki SBK); 13. P. Thomas (Honda SBK); 14. F. Protat (Honda SBK); 15. C. Loustalet (Kawasaki STB).

**3rd May - Carole**
1. B. Sebileau (Kawasaki SBK); 2. C. Guyot (Kawasaki SBK); 3. B. Cazade (Yamaha STB); 4. J.-F. Braut (Yamaha STB); 5. T. Rogier (Yamaha STB); 6. S. Neff (Yamaha STB); 7. D. Marzloff (Kawasaki SBK); 8. G. Muteau (Kawasaki STB); 9. F. Protat (Honda SBK); 10. R. Di Foggia (Ducati SBK); 11. F. Ciciliani (Ducati SBK); 12. J.-P. Guinand (Kawasaki STB); 13. V. Bocquet (Yamaha STB); 14. J. Foray (Yamaha STB); 15. F. Moreira (Kawasaki STB).

**17th May - Nogaro**
1. F. Protat (Ducati SBK); 2. C. Guyot (Kawasaki SBK); 3. B. Cazade (Yamaha STB); 4. S. Neff (Yamaha STB); 5. T. Rogier (Yamaha STB); 6. F. Forêt (Yamaha STB); 7. D. Crassous (Yamaha STB); 8. C. Loustalet (Kawasaki STB); 9. J.-P. Guinand (Kawasaki STB); 10. B. Bonhuil (Kawasaki STB); 11. J.-F. Braut (Yamaha STB); 12. V. Bocquet (Yamaha STB); 13. E. Mizera (Yamaha STB); 14. R. Di Foggia (Ducati SBK); 15. P. Thomas (Honda SBK).

**24th May - Le Vigeant**
1. B. Sebileau (Kawasaki SBK); 2. C. Guyot (Kawasaki SBK); 3. F. Forêt (Yamaha STB); 4. J.-F. Braut (Yamaha STB); 5. B. Cazade (Yamaha STB); 6. E. Mizera (Yamaha STB); 7. C. Mouzin (Yamaha STB); 8. D. Marzloff (Kawasaki SBK); 9. T. Rogier (Yamaha STB); 10. F. Boutin (Yamaha STB); 11. C. Herriberry (Yamaha STB); 12. V. Bocquet (Yamaha STB); 13. J. Foray (Yamaha STB); 14. B. Bonhuil (Kawasaki STB); 15. C. Di Marino (Yamaha SBK).

**14th June - Lédenon**
1. B. Sebileau (Kawasaki SBK); 2. J.-F. Braut (Yamaha STB); 3. F. Protat (Ducati SBK); 4. C. Guyot (Kawasaki SBK); 5. F. Forêt (Yamaha STB); 6. T. Rogier (Yamaha STB); 7. B. Cazade (Yamaha STB); 8. S. Neff (Yamaha STB); 9. J. Foray (Yamaha STB); 10. P. Donischal; 11. V. Bocquet (Yamaha STB); 12. D. Marzloff (Kawasaki SBK); 13. F. Boutin (Yamaha STB); 14. C. Herriberry (Yamaha STB); 15. C. Rebuttini.

**5th July - Le Castellet**
1. J.-M. Delétang (Yamaha SBK); 2. D. Crassous (Yamaha STB); 3. T. Rogier (Yamaha STB); 4. F. Forêt (Yamaha STB); 5. S. Scarnato (Kawasaki SBK); 6. E. Mizera (Yamaha STB); 7. B. Cazade (Yamaha STB); 8. D. Marzloff (Kawasaki SBK); 9. S. Neff (Yamaha STB); 10. M. Garcia (Yamaha STB); 11. B. Colaisseau (Yamaha SBK); 12. J.-F. Le Glatin; 13. J.-P. Guinand (Kawasaki STB); 14. C. Herriberry (Yamaha STB); 15. J. Foray (Yamaha STB).

**4th October - Carole**
1. F. Forêt (Yamaha STB); 2. B. Sebileau (Kawasaki SBK); 3. C. Guyot (Kawasaki SBK); 4. J.-F. Braut (Yamaha STB); 5. B. Cazade (Yamaha STB); 6. R. Di Foggia (Ducati SBK); 7. F. Boutin (Yamaha STB); 8. Ulmann (Kawasaki); 9. V. Bocquet (Yamaha STB); 10. T. Rogier (Yamaha STB); 11. D. Marzloff (Kawasaki SBK); 12. E. Mizera (Yamaha STB); 13. B. Bonhuil (Kawasaki STB); 14. J.-P. Guinand (Kawasaki STB); 15. Agogue (Yamaha).

**Final classification**
1. Christophe Guyot    Kawasaki    134
2. Bertrand Sebileau   Kawasaki    132,5
3. Jean-François Braut   Yamaha     86

4. T. Rogier (Yamaha), 83; 5. B. Cazade (Yamaha), 79; 6. F. Forêt (Yamaha), 78; 7. F. Protat (Ducati), 66; 8. S. Neff (Yamaha), 47; 9. J.-P. Guinand (Kawasaki), 46; 10. D. Crassous (Yamaha), 42.

## Side-cars

The champions: Minguet/Voilque.

**8th March - Le Mans**
1. Minguet/Voilque (LCR-AED); 2. Tuauden/Gougaud (LCR-AED); 3. Hansen/Soares (LCR-Suzuki); 4. Kestler/P. Gelot (LCR-Suzuki); 5. Michon/Sicard (LCR-Suzuki); 6. Ferrand/Lopez; 7. Joron/Virey (LCR-Suzuki); 8. B. Morio/Ph. Morio; 9. Delannoy/Renoud Grappin (LCR-Yamaha); 10. Gauthier/Gruel (LCR); 11. Le Vennec/Le Crenn; 12.Martin/Brunet; 13. Gauthier/Walle (LCR); 14. D. Babin/S. Babin; 15. R. Peugeot/V. Peugeot.

**29th March - Magny-Cours**
1. Minguet/Voilque (LCR-AED); 2. Tuauden/Gougaud (LCR-AED); 3. Hansen/Soares (LCR-Suzuki); 4. Kestler/Thomassier (LCR-Suzuki); 5. Michon/Sicard (LCR-Suzuki); 6. Joron/Virey (LCR-Suzuki); 7. Le Bail/Lecawez (LCR); 8. Thomas/Artmann (LCR-Yamaha); 9. Voilque/Voilque (LCR-Suzuki); 10. Niogret/Bourgeois (LCR).

**5th April - Albi**
1. Tuauden/Gougaud (LCR-AED); 2. Minguet/Voilque (LCR-AED); 3. Kestler/Thomassier (LCR-Suzuki); 4. Voilque/Voilque (LCR-Suzuki); 5. Gautier/Walle (LCR); 6. Delannoy/Renoud-Grappin (LCR-Yamaha); 7. Mercier/Gelot (LCR-Suzuki). 7 classified.

**3rd May - Carole**
1. Minguet/Voilque (LCR-AED); 2. Hansen/Soares (LCR-Suzuki); 3. Kestler/Thomassier (LCR-Suzuki); 4. Le Bail/Gouger (LCR); 5. Joron/Virey (LCR-Suzuki); 6. Niogret/Lavalette (LCR); 7. Pelet/Delpeyroux (Pascut-Honda); 8. Pellegrin/Dupouy (LCR-ADM); 9. Martin/Brunet (LCR-Suzuki).

**17th May - Nogaro**
1. Minguet/Voilque (LCR-AED); 2. Hansen/Soares (LCR-Suzuki); 3. Tuauden/Gougaud (LCR-AED); 4. Kestler/Thomassier (LCR-Suzuki); 5. Pelet/Delpeyroux (Pascut-Honda); 6. Le Bail/Aubert (LCR); 7. Delannoy/Renoud-Grappin (LCR-Yamaha); 8. Mercier/Gelot (LCR-Suzuki); 9. Gautier/Walle (LCR-Suzuki); 10. Dureau/Roux (Seymaz).

**24th May - Le Vigeant**
1. Minguet/Voilque (LCR-AED); 2. Hansen/Soares (LCR-Suzuki); 3. Tuauden/Gougaud (LCR-AED); 4. Kestler/Thomassier (LCR-Suzuki); 5. Pelet/Delpeyroux (Pascut-Honda); 6. Delannoy/Renoud-Grappin (LCR-Yamaha); 7. Niogret/Lavalette (LCR); 8. Le Bail/Aubert (LCR-Suzuki); 9. Voilque/Voilque (LCR-Suzuki); 10. Martin/Brunet (LCR-Suzuki).

**5th July - Le Castellet**
1. Minguet/Voilque (LCR-AED); 2. Pelet/Delpeyroux (Pascut-Honda); 3. Joron/ Viret; 4. Kestler/Thomassier (LCR-Suzuki); 5. Delannoy/Renoud-Grappin (LCR-Yamaha); 6. Pellegrin/Benloucif; 7. Niogret/Lavalette (LCR); 8. Lacroix/Michel; 9. Voilque/Voilque (LCR-Suzuki); 10. Martin/Brunet (LCR-Suzuki); 11. Gautier/Vannier (LCR-Suzuki).

**4th October - Carole**
1. Hansen/Soares (LCR-Suzuki); 2. Minguet/Voilque (LCR-AED); 3. Gautier/Vannier (LCR-Suzuki); 4. Jacques/Barbe (Windle-Yamaha); 5. Kestler/Thomassier (LCR-Suzuki).

**Final classification**
1. Minguet/Voilque, 175; 2. Hansen/Soares, 137; 3. Tuaden/Gougaud, 113; 4. Kestler/Thomassier, 97; 5. Pelet/Delpeyroux, 69.

*Jehan D'Orgeix, Christophe Guyot*
▽

*France*

## 125 cc

The champion: Chris Palmer. Premier GP: British GP, 1996 (125). Races record: 37th of the 125cc European championship in 1995 (Honda); British champion 125 in 1998 (Honda).

**29th March - Brands Hatch**
1. R. Appleyard (Honda); 2. C. Palmer (Honda); 3. P. Owens (Honda); 4. G. Morris (Honda); 5. L. Jackson (Honda); 6. L. Haslam (Honda); 7. P. Notman (Honda); 8. I. Lougher (Honda); 9. P. Jennings (Yamaha); 10. S. Patrickson (Honda).

**26th April - Oulton Park**
1. I. Lougher (Honda); 2. A. Green (Honda); 3. P. Notman (Honda); 4. P. Owens (Honda); 5. C. Palmer (Honda); 6. S. Patrickson (Honda); 7. P. Robinson (Honda); 8. G. Morris (Honda); 9. T. Tunstall (Honda); 10. D. Mateer (Honda).

**3rd May - Thruxton**
1. C. Palmer (Honda); 2. P. Owens (Honda); 3. L. Haslam (Honda); 4. I. Lougher (Honda); 5. D. Mateer (Honda); 6. A. Green (Honda); 7. L. Jackson (Honda); 8. G. Morris (Honda); 9. S. Patrickson (Honda); 10. T. Tunstall (Honda).

**10th May - Snetterton**
1. P. Owens (Honda); 2. S. Patrickson (Honda); 3. D. Cahill (Honda); 4. L. Jackson (Honda); 5. D. Mateer (Honda); 6. R. Appleyard (Honda); 7. P. Robinson (Honda); 8. M. Frost (Honda); 9. C. Gray (Honda); 10. D. Gawley (Honda).

**21st June - Donington**
1. R. Appleyard (Honda); 2. A. Green (Honda); 3. P. Jennings (Honda); 4. C. Palmer (Honda); 5. G. Morris (Honda); 6. M. Ford-Dunn (Honda); 7. I. Lougher (Honda); 8. A. Notman (Honda); 9. S. Patrickson (Honda); 10. L. Jackson (Honda).

**19th July - Oulton Park**
1. C. Palmer (Honda); 2. A. Notman (Honda); 3. A. Green (Honda); 4. I. Lougher (Honda); 5. G. Morris (Honda); 6. T. Tunstall (Honda); 7. S. Patrickson (Honda); 8. D. Mateer (Honda); 9. R. Appleyard (Honda); 10. D. Barton (Honda).

**9th August - Knockhill**
1. L. Haslam (Honda); 2. R. Appleyard (Honda); 3. A. Green (Honda); 4. D. Gawley (Honda); 5. S. Patrickson (Honda); 6. C. Palmer (Honda); 7. A. Notman (Honda); 8. L. Jackson (Honda); 9. C. Gray (Honda); 10. R. Haslam (Honda).

**16th August - Mallory Park**
1. I. Lougher (Honda); 2. P. Jennings (Honda); 3. A. Notman (Honda); 4. S. Patrickson (Honda); 5. L. Jackson (Honda); 6. G. Gray (Honda); 7. C. Palmer (Honda); 8. T. Tunstall (Honda); 9. D. Gawley (Honda); 10. R. Appleyard (Honda).

**31st August - Cadwell Park**
1. L. Jackson (Honda); 2. D. Barton (Honda); 3. I. Lougher (Honda); 4. A. Green (Honda); 5. C. Palmer (Honda); 6. L. Haslam (Honda); 7. R. Appleyard (Honda); 8. M. Ford-Dunn (Honda); 9. J. Goodall (Honda); 10. D. Gawley (Honda).

**6th September - Silverstone**
1. P. Jennings (Honda); 2. I. Lougher (Honda); 3. A. Green (Honda); 4. R. Appleyard (Honda); 5. C. Palmer (Honda); 6. D. Barton (Honda); 7. K. Tibble (Honda); 8. L. Haslam (Honda); 9. D. Gawley (Honda); 10. S. Patrickson (Honda).

**20th September - Brands Hatch**
1. D. Barton (Honda); 2. P. Jennings (Honda); 3. C. Palmer (Honda); 4. R. Appleyard (Honda); 5. L. Haslam (Honda); 6. S. Patrickson (Honda); 7. L. Jackson (Honda); 8. P. Robinson (Honda); 9. A. Notman (Honda); 10. D. Gawley (Honda).

**27th September - Donington**
1. I. Lougher (Honda); 2. D. Barton (Honda); 3. D. Gawley (Honda); 4. A. Green (Honda); 5. R. Haslam (Honda); 6. L. Haslam (Honda); 7. M. Ford-Dunn (Honda); 8. C. Palmer (Honda); 9. K. Tibble (Honda); 10. L. Jackson (Honda).

**Final classification**
| | | |
|---|---|---|
| 1. Chris Palmer | Honda | 159 |
| 2. Ian Lougher | Honda | 157 |
| 3. Robin Appleyard | Honda | 128 |

4. A. Green (Honda), 124; 5. S. Patrickson (Honda), 103; 6. L. Jackson (Honda), 100; 7. L. Haslam (Honda), 99; 8. P. Jennings (Honda), 94; 9. D. Barton (Honda), 85; 10. P. Owens (Honda), 74.

## 250 cc

The champion: Woolsey Coulter. Born on 2nd February 1964, in Irland. First GP: British GP, 1997 (250). Races record: 23rd of the 250cc European championship in 1988 (Honda); 45th of the TT Formula One world championship (Honda) and 16th of the 250cc European championship (Aprilia) in 1989; 11th of the 250cc European championship in 1991 (Yamaha); 27th of the 250cc European championship in 1992 (Yamaha); 3rd of the 250cc Great Britain championship in 1996 (Honda); 34th of the 250cc world championship, 21st of the 250cc European championship and 250cc British champion in 1998 (Honda).

**29th March - Brands Hatch**
1. P. Jones (Aprilia); 2. C. Ramsay (Honda); 3. A. Patterson (Honda); 4. J. Davies (Honda); 5. S. Turner (Honda); 6. J. McGuiness (Honda); 7. S. Sawford (Honda); 8. A. Coates (Honda); 9. E. McManus (Honda); 10. T. Levy (Honda).

**26th April - Oulton Park**
1. W. Coulter (Honda); 2. G. May (Aprilia); 3. J. McGuiness (Honda); 4. J. Davis (Honda); 5. A. Coates (Honda); 6. S. Turner (Honda); 7. S. Norval (Honda); 8. A. Patterson (Honda); 9. J. Creith (Honda); 10. S. Sawford (Honda).

**3rd May - Thruxton**
1. W. Coulter (Honda); 2. J. Davis (Honda); 3. S. Norval (Honda); 4. C. Ramsay (Honda); 5. J. McGuiness (Honda); 6. S. Sawford (Honda); 7. M. Ruddock (Honda); 8. T. Levy (Honda); 9. R. Frear (Honda); 10. G. Lee (Yamaha).

**10th May - Snetterton**
1. S. Norval (Honda); 2. E. McManus (Yamaha); 3. S. Edwards (Honda); 4. R. Frear (Honda); 5. G. Haslam (Honda); 6. M. Ruddock (Honda); 7. T. Levy (Honda); 8. A. Clarke (Honda); 9. L. Lee (Yamaha); 10. S. Summerfield (Honda).

**21st June - Donington**
1. S. Norval (Honda); 2. T. Kayo (J, Honda); 3. J. McGuiness (Honda); 4. G. May (Aprilia); 5. C. Ramsay (Honda); 6. T. Levy (Honda); 7. A. Clarke (Honda); 8. S. Sawford (Honda); 9. H. Hincks (Honda); 10. R. Frear (Honda).

**4th July - Donington**
1. W. Coulter (Honda); 2. T. Kayo (J, Honda); 3. S. Turner (Honda); 4. J. McGuiness (Honda); 5. C. Ramsay (Honda); 6. S. Norval (Honda); 7. G. Haslam (Honda); 8. H. Hincks (Honda); 9. T. Levy (Honda); 10. J. Davis (Honda).

**5th July - Donington**
1. C. Ramsay (Honda); 2. W. Coulter (Honda); 3. S. Turner (Honda); 4. S. Norval (Honda); 5. H. Hincks (Honda); 6. J. Davis (Honda); 7. A. Clarke (Honda); 8. A. Coates (Honda); 9. J. Creith (Honda); 10. T. Levy (Honda).

**19th July - Oulton Park**
1. W. Coulter (Honda); 2. C. Ramsay (Honda); 3. J. Davis (Honda); 4. H. Hincks (Honda); 5. D. Johnson (Honda); 6. M. Ruddock (Honda); 7. A. Clarke (Honda); 8. A. Hutchinson (Honda); 9. P. Jones (Aprilia); 10. S. Edwards (Honda).

**9th August - Knockhill**
1. J. Davis (Honda); 2. S. Turner (Honda); 3. C. Ramsay (Honda); 4. S. Norval (Honda); 5. J. McGuiness (Honda); 6. M. Ruddock (Honda); 7. A. Coates (Honda); 8. S. Edwards (Honda); 9. D. Johnson (Honda); 10. P. Stead (Honda).

**16th August - Mallory Park**
1. W. Coulter (Honda); 2. J. McGuiness (Honda); 3. S. Norval (Honda); 4. D. Johnson (Honda); 5. A. Coates (Honda); 6. G. May (Aprilia); 7. F. Frear (Honda); 8. S. Sawford (Honda); 9. S. Turner (Honda); 10. G. Haslam (Honda).

**31st August - Cadwell Park**
1. W. Coulter (Honda); 2. J. Davis (Honda); 3. C. Ramsay (Honda); 4. S. Norval (Honda); 5. G. May (Aprilia); 6. R. Frear (Honda); 7. S. Thompson (Honda); 8. M. Ruddock (Honda); 9. S. Sawford (Honda); 10. P. Dedman (Honda).

**6th September - Silverstone**
1. S. Norval (Honda); 2. W. Coulter (Honda); 3. J. McGuiness (Honda); 4. S. Turner (Honda); 5. A. Coates (Honda); 6. M. Bolwerk (NL, Honda); 7. S. Edwards (Honda); 8. R. Frear (Honda); 9. G. Lee (Yamaha); 10. M. Ruddock (Honda).

**20th September - Brands Hatch**
1. J. McGuiness (Honda); 2. W. Coulter (Honda); 3. S. Turner (Honda); 4. A. Coates (Honda); 5. G. Lee (Yamaha); 6. C. Ramsay (Honda); 7. G. May (Aprilia); 8. S. Sawford (Honda); 9. P. Stead (Honda); 10. M. Ruddock (Honda).

**27th September - Donington**
1. G. May (Aprilia); 2. C. Ramsay (Honda); 3. S. Norval (Honda); 4. S. Turner (Honda); 5. A. Coates (Honda); 6. J. McGuiness (Honda); 7. M. Ruddock (Honda); 8. P. Stead (Honda); 9. G. Lee (Yamaha); 10. R. Frear (Honda).

**Final classification**
| | | |
|---|---|---|
| 1. Woolsey Coulter | Honda | 210 |
| 2. Shane Norval | Honda | 183 |
| 3. Callum Ramsay | Honda | 174 |

4. J. McGuiness (Honda), 150; 5. J. Davis (Honda), 139; 6. S. Turner (Honda), 126; 7. G. May (Aprilia), 97; 8. A. Coates (Honda), 82; 9. M. Ruddock (Honda); 10. S. Sawford (Honda).

## Supersport

The champion: John Crawford. Races record: 42nd of the Thunderbike Trophy in 1995 (Honda); supersport British champion in 1998 (Suzuki).

**29th March - Brands Hatch**
1. J. Crawford (Suzuki); 2. P. Brown (Honda); 3. S. Plater (Honda); 4. H. Whitby (Honda); 5. A. Pallot (Honda); 6. D. Thomas (Suzuki); 7. P. Jennings (Honda); 8. S. Wickens (Yamaha); 9. D. Rathbone (Honda); 10. I. Bennett (Kawasaki).

**26th April - Oulton Park**
1. M. Llewellyn (Honda); 2. G. Richards (Honda); 3. P. McCallen (Honda); 4. P. Borley (Honda); 5. A. Tinsley (Honda); 6. S. Plater (Honda); 7. J. Chapman (Honda); 8. D. Rathbone (Honda); 9. S. Byrne (Yamaha); 10. J. Crawford (Suzuki).

**3rd May - Thruxton**
1. S. Plater (Honda); 2. G. Richards (Honda); 3. P. Brown (Honda); 4. P. Borley (Honda); 5. D. Thomas (Suzuki); 6. S. Byrne (Yamaha); 7. S. Wickens (Yamaha); 8. S. Smith (Honda); 9. R. Frost (Honda); 10. D. Deaumont (Honda).

**10th May - Snetterton**
1. S. Byrne (Yamaha); 2. J. Crawford (Suzuki); 3. S. Wickens (Yamaha); 4. P. Brown (Honda); 5. D. Thomas (Suzuki); 6. P. Borley (Honda); 7. P. Breslin (Honda); 8. L. Dickinson (Honda); 9. A. Pallot (Honda); 10. M. Burr (Honda).

**21st June - Donington**
1. J. Crawford (Suzuki); 2. P. Brown (Honda); 3. P. Borley (Honda); 4. P. Breslin (Honda); 5. S. Byrne (Yamaha); 6. S. Plater (Honda); 7. D. Thomas (Suzuki); 8. P. Jennings (Honda); 9. K. Harris (Honda); 10. M. Burr (Honda).

**19th July - Oulton Park**
1. S. Plater (Honda); 2. K. Harris (Honda); 3. H. Whitby (Honda); 4. A. Pallot (Honda); 5. D. Rathbone (Honda); 6. J. Crawford (Suzuki); 7. L. Dickinson (Honda); 8. P. Brown (Honda); 9. P. Borley (Honda); 10. J. Chapman (Honda).

**9th August - Knockhill**
1. J. Moodie (Honda); 2. J. Crawford (Suzuki); 3. S. Plater (Honda); 4. P. Breslin (Honda); 5. P. Borley (Honda); 6. P. Brown (Honda); 7. H. Whitby (Honda); 8. M. Burr (Honda); 9. D. Rathbone (Honda); 10. S. Wickens (Yamaha).

**16th August - Mallory Park**
1. S. Plater (Honda); 2. D. Thomas (Suzuki); 3. J. Crawford (Suzuki); 4. K. Muggeridge (AUS, Honda); 5. P. Borley (Honda); 6. G. Richards

*Woolsey Coulter.*

(Honda); 7. P. Brown (Honda); 8. R. Frost (Honda); 9. K. Harris (Honda); 10. C. Burns (Honda).

### 31st August - Cadwell Park
1. P. Brown (Honda); 2. S. Plater (Honda); 3. J. Moodie (Honda); 4. H. Whitby (Honda); 5. W. Nowland (Suzuki); 6. K. Harris (Honda); 7. P. Borley (Honda); 8. D. Rathbone (Honda); 9. G. Richards (Honda); 10. P. Jennings (Honda).

### 6th September - Silverstone
1. J. Crawford (Suzuki); 2. S. Plater (Honda); 3. J. Moodie (Honda); 4. P. Brown (Honda); 5. W. Nowland (Suzuki); 6. K. Muggeridge (AUS, Honda); 7. K. Harris (Honda); 8. G. Richards (Honda); 9. M. Burr (Suzuki); 10. A. Tinsley (Honda).

### 20th September - Brands Hatch
1. J. Crawford (Suzuki); 2. W. Nowland (Suzuki); 3. G. Richards (Honda); 4. K. Muggeridge (AUS, Honda); 5. S. Byrne (Honda); 6. A. Pallot (Honda); 7. P. Borley (Honda); 8. L. Dickinson (Honda); 9. S. Wickens (Yamaha); 10. P. Jennings (Honda).

### 27th September - Donington
1. S. Plater (Honda); 2. J. Crawford (Suzuki); 3. K. McCarthy (NZ, Honda); 4. G. Richards (Honda); 5. W. Nowland (Suzuki); 6. P. Borley (Honda); 7. K. Muggeridge (AUS, Honda); 8. P. Young (Honda); 9. H. Whitby (Honda); 10. S. Wickens (Yamaha).

### Final classification
1. John Crawford     Suzuki     192(*)
2. Steve Plater     Honda     192
3. Paul Brown     Honda     134
4. P. Borley (Honda), 109; 5. G. Richards (Honda), 99; 6. S. Byrne (Yamaha), 67; 7. S. Wickens (Yamaha), 65; 8. H. Whitby (Honda), 62; 9. D. Thomas (Suzuki), 62; 10. D. Harris (Honda), 58.

### Superbike

The champion: Niall MacKenzie. Born on 19th July 1961, in Stirling/Great Britain. First race: 1981. First GP: British GP, 1984 (250). Races record: Cumbria Club champion in 1981; 250cc and 350cc Autralian champion, 500 Production Scottish champion in 1982; winner of the World Cup Yamaha Pro-Am in 1983; 28th of the European championship 250 and British champion 350 in 1984 (Armstrong); 28th of the 250cc world championship, 250 and 350 cc British champion in 1985 (Armstrong); 21st of the 250cc world championship, 250cc British champion (Armstrong) and 11th of the 500cc world championship in 1986 (Suzuki); 5th of the 500cc world championship in 1987 (Honda); 6th of the 500cc world championship and 13th of the world championshipTT Formula One in 1988 (Honda); 7th of the 500cc world championship in 1989 (Yamaha); 33rd of the 250cc world championship(Yamaha), 4th of the 500cc world championship (Suzuki) and 33th of the superbike world championship (Yamaha) in 1990; 17th of the 500cc world championship (Yamaha) and 23rd of the superbike world championship (Honda) in 1991; 11th of the 500cc world championship in 1992 (Yamaha); 9th of the 500cc world championship (ROC Yamaha), 34th of the superbike world championship and 36th of the European championship superbike (Ducati) in 1993; 10th of the 500cc world championship (ROC Yamaha) and 102nd of the endurance world championship (Suzuki) in 1994; 18th of the 250cc world championship(Aprilia) in 1995; 34th of the superbike world championship and superbike British champion in 1996 (Yamaha); 29th of the superbike world championship in 1997 (Yamaha); 19th of the superbike world championship and superbike British champion in 1998 (Yamaha).

### 29th March - Brands Hatch
Course I: 1. C. Walker (Kawasaki); 2. S. Emmett (Ducati); 3. J. Haydon (Suzuki); 4. T. Bayliss (AUS, Ducati); 5. T. Rymer (Suzuki); 6. N. MacKenzie (Yamaha); 7. S. Hislop (Yamaha); 8. I. MacPherson (Kawasaki); 9. J. Reynolds (Ducati); 10. M. Rutter (Honda). Course II: 1. N. MacKenzie (Yamaha); 2. S. Hislop (Yamaha); 3. C. Walker (Kawasaki); 4. S. Emmett (Ducati); 5. T. Bayliss (AUS, Ducati); 6. T. Rymer (Suzuki); 7. I. MacPherson (Kawasaki); 8. J. Haydon (Suzuki); 9. M. Rutter (Honda); 10. J. Reynolds (Ducati).

### 26th April - Oulton Park
Course I: 1. M. Rutter (Honda); 2. T. Rymer (Suzuki); 3. C. Walker (Kawasaki); 4. N. MacKenzie (Yamaha); 5. J. Haydon (Suzuki); 6. I. Simpson (Honda); 7. T. Bayliss (AUS, Ducati); 8. M. Llewellyn (Ducati); 9. S. Hislop (Yamaha); 10. I. MacPherson (Kawasaki). Course II: 1. S. Hislop (Yamaha); 2. N. MacKenzie (Yamaha); 3. C. Walker (Kawasaki); 4. J. Haydon (Suzuki); 5. T. Bayliss (AUS, Ducati); 6. I. Simpson (Honda); 7. R. Stringer (Kawasaki); 8. J. Robinson (Ducati); 9. P. Giles (Kawasaki); 10. B. Sampson (Kawasaki).

### 3rd May - Thruxton
Course 1: 1. N. MacKenzie (Yamaha); 2. T. Rymer (Suzuki); 3. S. Hislop (Yamaha); 4. J. Haydon (Suzuki); 5. C. Walker (Kawasaki); 6. M. Rutter (Honda); 7. R. Stringer (Kawasaki); 8. T. Bayliss (Australie, Ducati); 9. I. Simpson (Honda); 10. P. Giles (Kawasaki). Course II: 1. N. MacKenzie (Yamaha); 2. S. Hislop (Yamaha); 3. I. MacPherson (Kawasaki); 4. T. Rymer (Suzuki); 5. J. Haydon (Suzuki); 6. I. Simpson (Honda); 7. R. Stringer (Kawasaki); 8. P. Giles (Kawasaki); 9. J. Reynolds (Ducati); 10. P. Graves (Ducati).

### 10th May - Snetterton
Course I: 1. S. Hislop (Yamaha); 2. N. MacKenzie (Yamaha); 3. C. Walker (Kawasaki); 4. J. Haydon (Suzuki); 5. T. Bayliss (AUS, Ducati); 6. T. Rymer (Suzuki); 7. M. Llewellyn (Ducati); 8. J. Reynolds (Ducati); 9. I. Simpson (Honda); 10. M. Rutter (Honda). Course II: 1. T. Rymer (Suzuki); 2. C. Walker (Kawasaki); 3. S. Hislop (Yamaha); 4. N. MacKenzie (Yamaha); 5. T. Bayliss (AUS, Ducati); 6. M. Llewellyn (Ducati); 7. M. Rutter (Honda); 8. J. Reynolds (Kawasaki); 9. I. MacPherson (Kawasaki); 10. P. Graves (Ducati).

### 21st June - Donington
Course I: 1. S. Hislop (Yamaha); 2. J. Haydon (Suzuki); 3. C. Walker (Kawasaki); 4. T. Bayliss (AUS, Ducati); 5. T. Rymer (Suzuki); 6. I. MacPherson (Kawasaki); 7. S. Emmett (Ducati); 8. J. Reynolds (Ducati); 9. I. Simpson (Honda); 10. J. Robinson (Ducati). Course II: 1. N. MacKenzie (Yamaha); 2. S. Hislop (Yamaha); 3. J. Haydon (Suzuki); 4. C. Walker (Kawasaki); 5. T. Rymer (Suzuki); 6. J. Reynolds (Ducati); 7. M. Rutter (Honda); 8. I. MacPherson (Kawasaki); 9. I. Simpson (Honda); 10. S. Emmett (Ducati).

### 19th July - Oulton Park
Course I: 1. T. Bayliss (AUS, Ducati); 2. N. MacKenzie (Yamaha); 3. S. Hislop (Yamaha); 4. J. Reynolds (Ducati); 5. T. Rymer (Suzuki); 6. J. Haydon (Suzuki); 7. S. Emmett (Ducati); 8. P. Graves (Ducati); 9. P. Giles (Kawasaki); 10. D. Heal (Honda). Course II: 1. S. Emmett (Ducati); 2. N. MacKenzie (Yamaha); 3. S. Hislop (Yamaha); 4. J. Haydon (Suzuki); 5. J. Reynolds (Ducati); 6. I. MacPherson (Kawasaki); 7. C. Walker (Kawasaki); 8. M. Llewellyn (Ducati); 9. B. Sampson (Kawasaki); 10. T. Rymer (Suzuki).

### 9th August - Knockhill
Course I: 1. N. MacKenzie (Yamaha); 2. C. Walker (Kawasaki); 3. J. Reynolds (Ducati); 4. M. Llewellyn (Ducati); 5. T. Bayliss (AUS, Ducati); 6. S. Emmett (Ducati); 7. T. Rymer (Suzuki); 8. P. Giles (Kawasaki); 9. M. Vincent (Kawasaki); 10. B. Sampson (Kawasaki). Course II: 1. N. MacKenzie (Yamaha); 2. S. Hislop (Yamaha); 3. T. Bayliss (AUS, Ducati); 4. C. Walker (Kawasaki); 5. M. Rutter (Honda); 6. T. Rymer (Suzuki); 7. M. Llewellyn (Ducati); 8. J. Haydon (Suzuki); 9. J. Reynolds (Ducati); 10. S. Emmett (Ducati).

### 16th August - Mallory Park
Course I: 1. M. Llewellyn (Ducati); 2. J. Reynolds (Ducati); 3. M. Rutter (Honda); 4. T. Rymer (Suzuki); 5. S. Emmett (Ducati); 6. S. Hislop (Yamaha); 7. N. MacKenzie (Yamaha); 8. M. Vincent (Kawasaki); 9. P. Giles (Kawasaki); 10. J. Haydon (Suzuki). Course II: 1. C. Walker (Kawasaki); 2. N. MacKenzie (Yamaha); 3. M. Rutter (Honda); 4. T. Rymer (Suzuki); 5. J. Reynolds (Ducati); 6. M. Llewellyn (Ducati); 7. S. Hislop (Yamaha); 8. S. Emmett (Ducati); 9. R. Stringer (Kawasaki); 10. P. Giles (Kawasaki).

### 31st August - Cadwell Park
Course I: 1. C. Walker (Kawasaki); 2. M. Rutter (Honda); 3. T. Bayliss (AUS, Ducati); 4. I. MacPherson (Kawasaki); 5. M. Llewellyn (Ducati); 6. J. Reynolds (Ducati); 7. N. MacKenzie (Yamaha); 8. T. Rymer (Suzuki); 9. M. Vincent (Kawasaki); 10. P. Giles (Kawasaki). Course II: 1. C. Walker (Kawasaki); 2. J. Reynolds (Ducati); 3. I. MacPherson (Kawasaki); 4. M. Llewellyn (Ducati); 5. N. MacKenzie (Yamaha); 6. T. Rymer (Suzuki); 7. S. Emmett (Ducati); 8. M. Vincent (Kawasaki); 9. C. Hipwell (Suzuki); 10. N. Nottingham (Yamaha).

### 6th September - Silverstone
Course I: 1. J. Haydon (Suzuki); 2. N. MacKenzie (Yamaha); 3. M. Rutter (Honda); 4. J. Reynolds (Ducati); 5. S. Emmett (Ducati); 6. I. Simpson (Honda); 7. M. Vincent (Kawasaki); 8. P. Giles (Kawasaki); 9. T. Bayliss (AUS, Ducati); 10. P. Graves (Ducati). Course II: 1. T. Bayliss (AUS, Ducati); 2. C. Walker (Kawasaki); 3. M. Rutter (Honda); 4. J. Reynolds (Ducati); 5. J. Haydon (Suzuki); 6. N. MacKenzie (Yamaha); 7. I. MacPherson (Kawasaki); 8. T. Rymer (Suzuki); 9. M. Llewellyn (Ducati); 10. I. Simpson (Honda).

### 20th September - Brands Hatch
Course I: 1. S. Hislop (Yamaha); 2. J. Reynolds (Ducati); 3. C. Walker (Kawasaki); 4. N. MacKenzie (Yamaha); 5. M. Llewellyn (Ducati); 6. M. Rutter (Honda); 7. I. MacPherson (Kawasaki); 8. S. Emmett (Ducati); 9. T. Rymer (Suzuki); 10. I. Simpson (Honda). Course II: 1. J. Reynolds (Ducati); 2. C. Walker (Kawasaki); 3. N. MacKenzie (Yamaha); 4. I. MacPherson (Kawasaki); 5. S. Hislop (Yamaha); 6. S. Emmett (Ducati); 7. I. Simpson (Honda); 8. M. Rutter (Honda); 9. M. Llewellyn (Ducati); 10. J. Haydon (Suzuki).

### 27th September - Donington
Course I: 1. C. Walker (Kawasaki); 2. M. Rutter (Honda); 3. I. MacPherson (Kawasaki); 4. N. MacKenzie (Yamaha); 5. J. Haydon (Suzuki); 6. T. Bayliss (AUS, Ducati); 7. M. Llewellyn (Ducati); 8. I. Simpson (Honda); 9. S. Emmett (Ducati); 10. J. Reynolds (Ducati). Course II: 1. M. Rutter (Honda); 2. M. Llewellyn (Ducati); 3. T. Rymer (Suzuki); 4. J. Haydon (Suzuki); 5. C. Walker (Kawasaki); 6. D. Wood (Kawasaki); 7. J. Reynolds (Ducati); 8. P. Giles (Kawasaki); 9. C. Hipwell (Suzuki); 10. N. Nottingham (Yamaha).

### Final classification
1. Niall MacKenzie     Yamaha     387
2. Chris Walker     Kawasaki     360
3. Steve Hislop     Yamaha     295
4. J. Reynolds (Ducati), 252; 5. T. Rymer (Suzuki), 242; 6. M. Rutter (Honda), 235; 7. J. Haydon (Suzuki), 228; 8. T. Bayliss (AUS, Ducati), 201; 9. S. Emmett (Ducati) et M. Llewellyn (Ducati), 170.

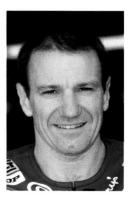

Niall MacKenzie.
▽

Manuel
Poggiali.

## 125 cc

The champion: Manuel Poggiali. Born on 14th February 1983, à San Marino. First race: 1994. First GP: Imola GP, 1998 (125). Races record: 5th of the minimotos Junior B Italian championship in 1994; 2nd of the minimotos Italian championship in 1995; minimotos Italian champion in 1997; 5th of the 125cc European championship, 125cc GPItalian champion and winner of the 125cc Italian Honda Trophy in 1998 (Honda).

### 5th April - Magione
1. S. Zocchi (Aprilia); 2. M. Poggiali (Honda); 3. M. Sabbatani (Honda); 4. W. De Angelis (Honda); 5. A. Brannetti (Honda); 6. G. Caffiero (Honda); 7. R. Chiarello (Aprilia); 8. A. Cadalora (Honda); 9. M. Borciani (Honda); 10. A. Romagnoli (Aprilia); 11. A. Iommi (Honda); 12. D. Tocca (Aprilia); 13. R. Romboli (Honda); 14. A. Zappa (Honda); 15. C. Cipriani (Aprilia).

### 10th May - Binetto
1. M. Poggiali (Honda); 2. A. Iommi (Honda); 3. S. Zocchi (Aprilia); 4. R. Romboli (Honda); 5. M. Petrini (Aprilia); 6. R. Chiarello (Aprilia); 7. P. Mellauner (Honda); 8. M. Sabbatani (Honda); 9. F. Benelli (Honda); 10. F. Pambianco (Honda); 11. D. Tocca (Aprilia); 12. W. De Angelis (Honda); 13. A. Melone (Honda); 14. S. Aliscioni (Aprilia); 15. S. Zerbo (Aprilia).

### 19th July - Imola
1. M. Poggiali (Honda); 2. S: Sanna (Aprilia); 3. M. Sabbatani (Honda); 4. M. Borciani (Honda); 5. A. Zappa (Honda); 6. G. Caffiero (Honda); 7. R. Chiarello (Aprilia); 8. C. Cipriani (Aprilia); 9. W. De Angelis (Honda); 10. C. Pistoni (Honda); 11. L. Ancona (Sandroni); 12. D. Tocca (Aprilia); 13. M. Petrini (Aprilia); 14. F. Ricci (Honda); 15. A. Berta (Honda).

### 26th July - Varano
1. M. Sabbatani (Honda); 2. A. Zappa (Honda); 3. R. Chiarello (Aprilia); 4. A. Brannetti (Honda); 5. C. Pistoni (Honda); 6. M. Poggiali (Honda); 7. A. Romagnoli (Honda); 8. M. Petrini (Aprilia); 9. C. Cipriani (Aprilia); 10. W. De Angelis (Honda); 11. R. Romboli (Honda); 12. C. Magnani (Aprilia); 13. J. Donelli (Honda); 14. A. Masoni (Honda); 15. A. De Angelis (Honda).

### 11th October - Misano
1. S. Sanna (Aprilia); 2. C. Cipriani (Aprilia); 3. A. Zappa (Honda); 4. M. Sabbatani (Honda); 5. R. Chiarello (Aprilia); 6. M. Petrini (Aprilia); 7. R. Romboli (Honda); 8. S. Zocchi (Aprilia); 9. C. Pistoni (Honda); 10. W. De Angelis (Honda); 11. A. De Angelis (Honda); 12. C. Magnani (Honda); 13. F.-A. Gentili (Honda); 14. A. Narduzzi (Honda); 15. E. Leardini (Honda).

### Final classification
1. Manuel Poggiali Honda 80
2. Massimiliano Sabbatani
Honda 70
3. Stefano Zocchi Aprilia 49
4. A. Zappa (Honda), 49; 5. R. Chiarello (Aprilia), 46; 6. S. Sanna (Aprilia), 45; 7. C. Cipriani (Aprilia), 36; 8. W. De Angelis (Honda), 32; 9. M. Petrini (Aprilia), 32; 10. R. Romboli (Honda), 30. 34 classified.

Diego
Giugovaz.

## 250 cc

The champion: Diego Giugovaz. Born on 11th October 1972, in Milan. First GP: Imola GP, 1998 (250). Races record: 40th of the 125cc European championship in 1996 (Aprilia); 125cc Sport-Production Italian champion in 1997 (Aprilia); 31st of the 250cc world championship, 3rd of the 250cc European championship and 250cc Italian champion in 1998 (Aprilia).

### 5th April - Magione
1. D. Giugovaz (Aprilia); 2. I. Antonelli (Aprilia); 3. I. Clementi (Yamaha); 4. M. Sanchini (Aprilia); 5. M. Mariotti (Aprilia); 6. C. Caliumi (Honda); 7. M. Mambelli (Honda); 8. G. Sartoni (Honda); 9. S. Di Stefano (Honda); 10. M. Ragni (Honda); 11. M. Morselli (Honda); 12. T. Isola (Yamaha). 12 classified.

### 10th May - Binetto
1. D. Giugovaz (Aprilia); 2. I. Antonelli (Aprilia); 3. F. Cotti (Honda); 4. M. Sanchini (Aprilia); 5. C. Caliumi (Honda); 6. M. Ragni (Yamaha); 7. G. Sartoni (Honda); 8. P. Maccariello (Honda); 9. M. De Matteo (Aprilia); 10. G. Lucchetti (Aprilia); 11. M. Morselli (Honda); 12. O. Vitali (Honda). 12 classified.

### 19th July - Imola
1. I. Antonelli (Aprilia); 2. D. Giugovaz (Aprilia); 3. F. Cotti (Honda); 4. M. De Matteo (Aprilia); 5. C. Caliumi (Honda); 6. P. Maccariello (Honda); 7. M. Mambelli (Honda); 8. M. Sanchini (Aprilia); 9. F. Sandroni (Aprilia); 10. M. Morselli (Honda). 10 classified.

### 26th July - Varano
1. D. Giugovaz (Aprilia); 2. I. Antonelli (Aprilia); 3. F. Cotti (Honda); 4. C. Caliumi (Honda); 5. F. Sandroni (Aprilia); 6. P. Maccariello (Honda); 7. M. Mariotti (Aprilia); 8. M. Morselli (Honda); 9. T. Isola (Yamaha); 10. D. Porto (Yamaha); 11. O. Vitali (Honda). 11 classified.

### 11th October - Misano
1. F. Cotti (Honda); 2. I. Clementi (Yamaha); 3. M. De Matteo (Aprilia); 4. F. Sandroni (Aprilia); 5. G. Sartoni (Honda); 6. S. Di Stefano (Honda); 7. M. Morselli (Honda); 8. F. Bergonzoni (Honda); 9. A. Boccia (Aprilia). 9 classified.

### Final classification
1. Diego Giugovaz Aprilia 95
2. Igor Antonelli Aprilia 85
3. Filippo Cotti Honda 73
4. C. Caliumi (Honda), 45; 5. I. Clementi (Yamaha), 36; 6. M. De Matteo (Aprilia), 36; 7. M. Sanchini (Aprilia), 34; 8. F. Sandroni (Aprilia), 31; 9. G. Sartoni (Honda), 28; 10. P. Maccariello (Honda), 28. 21 classified.

## Supersport

The champion: Angelo Conti. Born on 9th September 1964, à Dongo/Como. Races record: 34th of the Thunderbike Trophy and 21st of the supersport European championship in 1995 (Yamaha); 18e of the supersport European championship in 1996 (Kawasaki); supersport European champion and 10th of the supersport

*Angelo Conti.*

Italian championship in 1997 (Ducati); 21st of the supersport world cup and supersport Italian champion in 1998 (Suzuki).

## 29th March - Misano
1. Y. Briguet (CH, Ducati) (*); 2. F. Pirovano (Suzuki); 3. S. Chambon (F, Suzuki) (*); 4. M. Gallina (Ducati); 5. P. Riba Cabana (SPA, Ducati) (*); 6. L. Pasini (Ducati); 7. M. Colombo (Ducati); 8. F. Monaco (Ducati); 9. G. Fiorillo (Suzuki); 10. A. Conti (Suzuki); 11. M. Degiovanni (Honda); 12. C. Mariottini (Bimota); 13. A. Calasso (Honda); 14. R. Ruozi (Ducati); 15. V. Tortoroglio (Suzuki).

## 3rd May - Misano
1. C. Migliorati (Ducati); 2. M. Lucchiari (Ducati); 3. A. Mazzali (Ducati); 4. A. Calasso (Honda); 5. S. Foti (Bimota); 6. F. Monaco (Ducati); 7. V. Iannuzzo (Yamaha); 8. A. Conti (Suzuki); 9. M. Gallina (Ducati); 10. R. Ruozi (Ducati); 11. F. Brugnara (Suzuki); 12. M. Brugnera (Kawasaki); 13. R. Panichi (Honda); 14. L. pedersoli (Yamaha); 15. G. Maran (Kawasaki).

## 31st May - Vallelunga
1. L. Pasini (Ducati); 2. M. Gallina (Ducati); 3. M. Colombo (Ducati); 4. A. Conti (Suzuki); 5. V. Iannuzzo (Yamaha); 6. F. Monaco (Ducati); 7. A. Mazzali (Ducati); 8. N. Russo (Honda); 9. L. Pedersoli (Yamaha); 10. B. Bergamelli (Suzuki); 11. L. Pini (Suzuki); 12. F. Celebrano (Honda); 13. V. De Marco (Suzuki); 14. R. Ruozi (Ducati); 15. M. Agazzi (Ducati).

## 28th June - Misano
1. A. Conti (Suzuki); 2. F. Monaco (Ducati); 3. V. Iannuzzo (Yamaha); 4. M. Colombo (Ducati); 5. C. Mariottini (Bimota); 6. A. Corradini (Honda); 7. I. Bellezza (Ducati); 8. F. Brugnera (Kawasaki); 9. G. Maran (Kawasaki); 10. S. Suzzi (Ducati); 11. F. Crimini (Suzuki); 12. R. Fabbroni (Suzuki); 13. G. Pertile (Kawasaki); 14. C. Carotti

(Bimota). 14 classified.

## 20th September - Mugello
Cancelled.

## Final classification
1. Angelo Conti     Suzuki    55
2. Francesco Monaco   Ducati    51
3. Michele Gallina     Ducati    47
4. M. Colombo (Ducati), 42; 5. L. Pasini (Ducati), 41; 6. V. Iannuzzo (Yamaha), 36; 7. C. Migliorati (Ducati), 25; 8. F. Pirovano (Suzuki), 25; 9. A. Mazzali (Ducati), 25; 10. M. Lucchiari (Ducati), 20. 36 classified.

## Superbike

The champion: Paolo Blora. Born on 12th October 1970, in Pavia. Races record: 16th of the superbike European championship in 1990 (Yamaha); 10th of the superbike European championship in 1991 (Ducati); 46th of the supersport European championship in 1993 (Honda); superbike Italian champion in 1998 (Ducati).

*Paolo Blora.*

## 29th March - Misano
1. G. Cantalupo (Ducati); 2. P. Blora (Ducati); 3. I. Arnoldi (Ducati); 4. M. Accornero (Suzuki); 5. M. Dall'Aglio (Yamaha); 6. L. Pittaluga (Yamaha); 7. P. Malvini (Ducati); 8. F. Biasion (Kawasaki); 9. D. Marchetti (Ducati); 10. F. Pojer (Ducati); 11. L. pezzoni (Suzuki); 12. F. Campagnari (Kawasaki); 13. G. Destro (Kawasaki); 14. A. Carpinelli (Ducati); 15. S. Giudici (Ducati).

## 3rd May - Misano
1. G. Cantalupo (Ducati); 2. P. Blora (Ducati); 3. M. Dall'Aglio (Yamaha); 4. M. Accornero (Suzuki); 5. F. Pojer (Ducati); 6. ? Valtolini (Yamaha); 7. F. Biasion (Kawasaki); 8. D. Marchetti (Ducati); 9. P. Malvini (Ducati); 10. G. Destro (Kawasaki); 11. E. Chiapello (Kawasaki); 12. M.-A. Gerbaudo

(Ducati); 13. R. Leonetti (Yamaha); 14. S. Giudici (Ducati); 15. A. Carpinelli (Ducati).

## 31st May - Vallelunga
1. G. Cantalupo (Ducati); 2. P. Blora (Ducati); 3. M. Dall'Aglio (Yamaha); 4. I. Arnoldi (Ducati); 5. M. Accornero (Suzuki); 6. M. Boccelli (Ducati); 7. G. Valtulini (Yamaha); 8. F. Pojer (Ducati); 9. E. Chiapello (Kawasaki); 10. L. Pezzoni (Suzuki); 11. M.-A. Gerbaudo (Ducati); 12. R. Bosio (Ducati); 13. D. Marchetti (Ducati); 14. G. Salvatore (Suzuki); 15. D. Tognon (Honda).

## 28th June - Misano
1. P. Blora (Ducati); 2. M. Dall'Aglio (Yamaha); 3. E. Bastianini (Ducati); 4. M. Accornero (Suzuki); 5. F. Pojer (Ducati); 6. D. Marchetti (Ducati); 7. G. Valtulini (Yamaha); 8. L. Pezzoni (Suzuki); 9. M. Boccelli (Ducati); 10. M. Pastore (Kawasaki); 11. F. Campagnari (Kawasaki); 12. P. Bosetti (Ducati); 13. M.-A. Gerbaudo (Ducati); 14. M. Giorgi (Suzuki); 15. P. Fabi (Suzuki).

## 20th September - Mugello
Cancelled.

## Final classification
1. Paolo Blora     Ducati    85
2. Giorgio Cantalupo   Ducati    75
3. Marco Dall'Aglio   Yamaha    63
4. M. Accornero (Suzuki), 50; 5. F. Pojer (Ducati), 36; 6. I. Arnoldi (Ducati), 29; 7. G. Valtulini (Yamaha), 28; 8. D. Marchetti (Ducati), 28; 9. L. Pezzoni (Suzuki), 19; 10. M. Boccelli (Ducati), 17. 28 classified.

## Switzerland

### Promo Cup 125

**12th April - Lédenon - France**
Race I: 1. F. Michaillat (Cagiva); 2. X. Hofer (Cagiva); 3. L. Seiler (Cagiva); 4. S. Cadamagnani (Cagiva). 4 classified. Race II: 1. F. Michaillat (Cagiva); 2. X. Hofer (Cagiva); 3. L. Seiler (Cagiva); 4. S. Cadamagnani (Cagiva). 4 classified.

**28th June - Boécourt-La Caquerelle**
Race I: 1. A. Mastel (Suzuki). 1 classé. Race II: 1. A. Mastel (Suzuki). 1 classé.

**12th July - Châtel - Les Paccots**
1. F. Michaillat (Cagiva); 2. L. Seiler (Cagiva); 3. A. Mastel (Suzuki). 3 classified.

**4th October - Lignières**
Race I: 1. L. Seiler (Cagiva); 2. X. Hofer (Cagiva); 3. F. Michaillat (Cagiva). 3 classified. Race II: 1. X. Hofer (Cagiva); 2. L. Seiler (Cagiva); 3. F. Michaillat (Cagiva); 4. A. Mastel (Suzuki). 4 classified.

### Final classification
1. François Michaillat  Cagiva  94.5
2. Lionel Seiler  Cagiva  89
3. Amos Mastel  Suzuki  79
4. X. Hofer (Cagiva), 75; 5. S. Cadamagnani (Cagiva), 19.5. 5 classified.

### Supersport

**12th April - Lédenon - France**
Race I: 1. R. Knecht (Suzuki); 2. A. Hofer (Honda); 3. M. Bachmann (Ducati); 4. A. Schwegler (Honda); 5. T. Meier (Kawasaki); 6. M. Kessler (Ducati); 7. P. Krummenacher (Honda); 8. R. Strack (Yamaha); 9. R. Stamm (Kawasaki); 10. D. Duss (Ducati); 11. M. Schmid (Kawasaki); 12. J. Broder (Ducati); 13. D. Von Känel (Ducati). 13 classified. Race II: 1. A. Schwegler (Honda); 2. D. Duss (Ducati); 3. R. Strack (Yamaha); 4. R. Knecht (Suzuki); 5. R. Stamm (Kawasaki); 6. P. Krummenacher (Honda); 7. T. Meier (Kawasaki); 8. A. Hofer (Honda); 9. M. Kessler (Ducati); 10. M. Weibel (Ducati); 11. M. Schmid (Kawasaki); 12. J. Naranjo (Ducati); 13. D. Von Känel (Ducati); 14. J. Broder (Ducati). 14 classified.

**24th May - Oschersleben - Germany**
Race I: 1. R. Knecht (Suzuki); 2. A. Schwegler (Honda); 3. A. Hofer (Honda); 4. A. Hauser (Honda); 5. T. Meier (Kawasaki); 6. P. Krummenacher (Honda); 7. M. Bachmann (Ducati); 8. M. Kessler (Ducati); 9. J. Broder (Ducati); 10. J. Lang (Yamaha); 11. M. Weibel (Ducati); 12. R. Van der Lek (Yamaha); 13. M. Schmid (Kawasaki); 14. M. Port (Yamaha); 15. D. Von Känel (Ducati). Race II: 1. R. Knecht (Suzuki); 2. A. Schwegler (Honda); 3. D. Duss (Ducati); 4. A. Hauser (Honda); 5. T. Meier (Kawasaki); 6. A. Hofer (Honda); 7. J. Lang (Yamaha); 8. J. Broder (Ducati); 9. M. Kessler (Ducati); 10. M. Weibel (Ducati); 11. M. Schmid (Kawasaki); 12. M. Port (Yamaha); 13. D. Von Känel (Ducati). 13 classified.

**28th June - Boécourt-La Caquerelle**
Race I: 1. J.-L. Papaux (Kawasaki); 2. R. Knecht (Suzuki); 3. A. Schwegler (Honda); 4. A. Hauser (Honda); 5. D. Duss (Ducati); 6. T. Meier (Kawasaki); 7. R. Stamm (Kawasaki); 8. J. Broder (Ducati); 9. M. Bachmann (Ducati); 10. D. Von Känel (Ducati). 10 classified. Race II: 1. J.-L. Papaux (Kawasaki); 2. R. Knecht (Suzuki); 3. A. Schwegler (Honda); 4. A. Hauser (Honda); 5. D. Duss (Ducati); 6. T. Meier (Kawasaki); 7. R. Stamm (Kawasaki); 8. C.-A. Jaggi (Ducati); 9. M. Bachmann (Ducati); 10. J. Broder (Ducati); 11. D. Von Känel (Ducati). 11 classified.

**12th July - Châtel - Les Paccots**
1. J.-L. Papaux (Kawasaki); 2. A. Schwegler (Honda); 3. A. Hauser (Honda); 4. R. Knecht (Suzuki); 5. D. Duss (Ducati); 6. P. Krummenacher (Honda); 7. R. Stamm (Kawasaki); 8. F. Bischof (A, Honda); 9. T. Meier (Kawasaki); 10. J. Broder (Ducati); 11. D. Von Känel (Ducati). 11 classified.

**19th july - Magny-Cours - France**
Race I: 1. R. Knecht (Suzuki); 2. A. Schwegler (Honda); 3. A. Hofer (Honda); 4. A. Hauser (Honda); 5. R. Stamm (Kawasaki); 6. T. Meier (Kawasaki); 7. M. Bachmann (Ducati); 8. J. Broder (Ducati); 9. M. Kessler (Ducati); 10. M. Schmid (Kawasaki). 10 classified. Race II: 1. R. Knecht (Suzuki); 2. A. Hofer (Honda); 3. A. Hauser (Honda); 4. T. Meier (Kawasaki); 5. R. Stamm (Kawasaki); 6. M. Bachmann (Ducati); 7. J. Broder (Ducati); 8. M. Schmid (Kawasaki); 9. D. Duss (Ducati); 10. D. Von Känel (Ducati). 10 classified.

**13th September - Pannonia Ring**
Race I: 1. R. Knecht (Suzuki); 2. A. Schwegler (Honda); 3. A. Hauser (Honda); 4. M. Schmid (Kawasaki); 5. T. Meier (Kawasaki); 6. A. Hofer (Honda); 7. M. Kessler (Ducati); 8. R. Van der Lek (Yamaha); 9. M. Bachmann (Ducati). 9 classified. Race II: 1. R. Knecht (Suzuki); 2. A. Schwegler (Honda); 3. A. Hofer (Honda); 4. A. Hauser (Honda); 5. D. Duss (Ducati); 6. M. Schmid (Kawasaki); 7. M. Kessler (Ducati); 8. M. Bachmann (Ducati). 8 classified.

### Final classification
1. Rolf Knecht  Suzuki  195
2. Adrian Schwegler  Honda  161
3. Andi Hofer  Honda  116
4. A. Hauser (Honda), 113; 5. D. Duss (Ducati), 92; 6. T. Meier (Kawasaki), 87; 7. J.-L. Papaux (Kawasaki), 75; 8. M. Bachmann (Ducati), 73; 9. R. Stamm (Kawasaki), 66; 10. J. Broder (Ducati), 59. 22 classified.
Mountain FMS Cup: 1. Jean-Luc Papaux (Kawasaki), 75; 2. Rolf Knecht (Suzuki), 53; 3. Adrian Schwegler (Honda), 52.

### Monobike

**12th April - Lédenon - France**
Race I: 1. H. Weinmann (Yamaha); 2. T. Kausch (Honda); 3. T. Müller (Honda); 4. R. Hauser (Honda); 5. A. Joliat (Yamaha); 6. C. Biesele (MuZ); 7. M. Knechtli (KTM); 8. T. Klötzli (KTM); 9. H. Scherly (Kawasaki); 10. G. Casillo (Husqvarna). 10 classified. Race II: 1. T. Kausch (Honda); 2. U. Fischer (Honda); 3. R. Hauser (Honda); 4. T. Müller (Honda); 5. A. Joliat (Yamaha); 6. C. Biesele (MuZ); 7. T. Klötzli (KTM); 8. G. Casillo (Husqvarna). 8 classified.

**14th June - Colmar-Berg - Luxembourg**
1. F. Egli (MuZ); 2. T. Klötzli (KTM); 3. T. Müller (Honda); 4. C. Biesele (MuZ); 5. R. Hauser (Honda). 5 classified.

**28th June - Boécourt-La Caquerelle**
Race I: 1. T. Kausch (Honda); 2. N. Dähler (Kawasaki); 3. P. Kaufmann (Husqvarna); 4. U. Fischer (Honda); 5. R. Knechtli (KTM); 6. H. Weinmann (Yamaha); 7. F. Egli (MuZ); 8. E. Haag (Yamaha); 9. A. Joliat (Yamaha); 10. T. Klötzli (KTM); 11. R. Hauser (Honda); 12. G. Casillo (Husqvarana); 13. T. Müller (Honda); 14. A. Christen (Kawasaki). 14 classified. Race II: 1. N. Dähler (Kawasaki); 2. T. Kausch (Honda); 3. P. Kaufmann (Husqvarna); 4. U. Fischer (Honda); 5. A. Joliat (Yamaha); 6. R. Knechtli (KTM); 7. F. Egli (MuZ); 8. E. Haag (Yamaha); 9. H. Weinmann (Yamaha); 10. G. Casillo (Husqvarna); 11. T. Müller (Honda); 12. T. Klötzli (KTM); 13. R. Hauser (Honda); 14. A. Christen (Kawasaki). 14 classified.

**12th July - Châtel - Les Paccots**
1. N. Dähler (Kawasaki); 2. T. Kausch (Honda); 3. P. Kaufmann (Husqvarna); 4. A. Joliat (Yamaha); 5. U. Fischer (Honda); 6. E. Haag (Yamaha); 7. H. Weinmann (Yamaha); 8. T. Müller (Honda); 9. T. Klötzli (KTM); 10. L. Krummenacher (Honda); 7. R. Stamm (Kawasaki); 8. F. Bischof (A, Honda); 9. T. Meier (Kawasaki); 10. J. Broder (Ducati); 11. D. Von Känel (Ducati). 11 classified.

**6th September - Dijon - France**
Race I: 1. N. Dähler (Kawasaki); 2. F. Egli (MuZ); 3. T. Kausch (Honda); 4. T. Müller (Honda); 5. P. Kaufmann (Husqvarna); 6. A. Joliat (Yamaha); 7. A. Hofmaenner (MuZ). 7 classified. Race II: 1. T. Kausch (Honda); 2. P. Kaufmann (Husqvarna); 3. U. Fischer (Honda); 4. T. Müller (Honda); 5. F. Egli (MuZ); 6. A. Joliat (Yamaha). 6 classified.

### Final classification
1. Niklaus Dähler  Kawasaki  95
2. Peter Kaufmann  Husqvarna  79
3. Fritz Egli  MuZ  74
4. U. Fischer (Honda), 73; 5. T. Müller (Honda), 71; 6. A. Joliat (Yamaha), 62; 7. T. Klötzli (KTM), 50; 8. R. Hauser (Honda), 41.5; 9. H.-P. Weinmann (Yamaha), 38.5; 10. C. Biesele (MuZ), 28. 18 classified.
Mountain FMS Cup: 1. Niklaus Dähler (Kawasaki), 70; 2. Peter Kaufmann (Husqvarna), 48; 3. Urs Fischer (Honda), 37.

### Side-cars

**25th March - Le Castellet - France**
1. P. Güdel/C. Güdel (LCR-BRM Swissauto); 2. S. Webster/D. James (GB, LCR-Honda); 3. M. Bösiger/J. Egli (LCR-Honda) ; 4. K. Liechti/D. Locher (LCR-BRM Swissauto); 5. M. Häberli/J. Sauter (Suzuki); 6. E. Hug/S. Kubli (Lüthi-Suzuki). 6 classified.

**10th May - Most - Czech Republic**
Race I: 1. M. Bösiger/J. Egli (LCR-Honda) ; 2. M. Häberli/J. Sauter (Suzuki); 3. E. Bertschi/U. Wäfler (LCR-Suzuki); 4. Schneider/Rodler (D, LCR-Honda); 5. S. Kiser/M. Sanapo (Kawasaki); 6. R. Kutschke/L. Kutschke (D, LCR-Honda); 7. C. Steiner/J. Koloska (LCR-Suzuki); 8. M. Mooser/A. Schrag (Moto Guzzi); 9. U. Kutschke/T. Kutschke (D, LCR-Honda). 9 classified. Race II: 1. M. Bösiger/J. Egli (LCR-Honda) ; 2. E. Bertschi/U. Wäfler (LCR-Suzuki); 3. S. Kiser/M. Sanapo (Kawasaki); 4. Schneider/Rodler (D, LCR-Honda); 5. R. Kutschke/L. Kutschke (D, LCR-Honda); 6. C. Steiner/J. Koloska (LCR-Suzuki); 7. M. Mooser/A. Schrag (Moto Guzzi); 8. U. Kutschke/T. Kutschke (D, LCR-Honda). 8 classified.

**28th June - Boécourt-La Caquerelle**
Race I: 1. E. Bertschi/U. Wäfler (LCR-Suzuki); 2. M. Häberli/J. Sauter (Suzuki); 3. S. Kiser/M. Sanapo (Kawasaki); 4. E. Hug/S. Kubli (Lüthi-Suzuki); 5. C. Steiner/J. Koloska (LCR-Suzuki); 6. M. Mooser/A. Schrag (Moto Guzzi). 6 classified. Race II: 1. E. Bertschi/U. Wäfler (LCR-Suzuki); 2. M. Häberli/J. Sauter (Suzuki); 3. S. Kiser/M. Sanapo (Kawasaki); 4. E. Hug/S. Kubli (Lüthi-Suzuki); 5. C. Steiner/J. Koloska (LCR-Suzuki); 6. M. Mooser/A. Schrag (Moto Guzzi). 6 classified.

**12th July - Châtel - Les Paccots**
1. E. Bertschi/U. Wäfler (LCR-Suzuki); 2. M. Häberli/J. Sauter (Suzuki); 3. E. Hug/S. Kubli (Lüthi-Suzuki); 4. S. Kiser/M. Sanapo (Kawasaki); 5. C. Steiner/J. Koloska (LCR-Suzuki); 6. M. Mooser/A. Schrag (Moto Guzzi). 6 classified.

**4th October - Lignières**
Race 1: 1. M. Häberli/J. Sauter (Suzuki); 2. E. Bertschi/U. Wäfler (LCR-Suzuki); 3. E. Hug/S. Kubli (Lüthi-Suzuki); 4. C. Steiner/J. Koloska (LCR-Suzuki); 5. M. Mooser/A. Schrag (Moto Guzzi). 5 classified. Race II: 1. E. Bertschi/U. Wäfler (LCR-Suzuki); 2. E. Hug/S. Kubli (Lüthi-Suzuki); 3. C. Steiner/J. Koloska (LCR-Suzuki); 4. M. Mooser/A. Schrag (Moto Guzzi); 5. K. Liechti/D. Locher (LCR-BRM). 5 classified.

### Final classification
1. Bertschi/Wäfler  165
2. Häberli/Sauter  123
3. Hug/Kubli  89

*Bertschi/Wäfler, François Michaillat, Rolf Knecht.*
▽

4. Steiner/Koloska, 83; 5. Kiser/Sanapo, 78; 6. Mooser/Schrag, 73; 7. Schneider/Rodler, 32; 8. Liechti/Locher, 27; 9. Güdel/Güdel, 25; 10. Kutschke/Kutschke, 24. 12 classified.
Mountain FMS Cup: 1. Bertschi/Wäfler, 75; 2. Häberli/Sauter, 60; 3. Kiser/Sanapo, 45.

## Supermotard

### Prestige category

#### 24th May - Lignières
Race I: 1. G. Salvador (F, KTM); 2. S. Widmer (Folan); 3. D. Müller (Yamaha); 4. B. Gautschi (KTM); 5. E. Maillard (HVA); 6. R. Oehri (Yamaha); 7. M. Burgherr (KTM); 8. T. Rosenblatt (F, RST); 9. W. Schudel (Honda); 10. G. Schäfer (HVA); 11. P. Singele (HVA); 12. O. Monnier (Monnier XR); 13. R. Baumgartner (Yamaha); 14. R. Aebi (Aebi Rotax); 15. H. Freidig (Husaberg). 21 classified. Race II: 1. G. Salvador (F, KTM); 2. D. Müller (Yamaha); 3. B. Gautschi (KTM); 4. K. Kinigardner (A, KTM); 5. S. Widmer (Folan); 6. S. Zachmann (Suzuki); 7. M. Götz (KTM); 8. R. Oehri (Yamaha); 9. T. Rosenblatt (F, RST); 10. F. Chopineaux (F, RST); 11. M. Burgherr (KTM); 12. P. Singele (HVA); 13. W. Schudel (Honda); 14. G. Schäfer (HVA); 15. H. Freidig (Husaberg). 22 classified.

#### 7th June - Frutigen
Race I: 1. D. Müller (Yamaha); 2. G. Salvador (F, KTM); 3. B. Gautschi (KTM); 4. E. Jaquet (B, HVA); 5. M. Burgherr (KTM); 6. E. Hostettler (MuZ); 7. F. Chopineaux (F, RST); 8. R. Baumgartner (Yamaha); 9. E. Maillard (HVA); 10. T. Rosenblatt (F, RST); 11. G. Schäfer (HVA); 12. R. Oehri (Yamaha); 13. M. Kiok (D, Honda); 14. P. Fischer (RST); 15. M. Götz (KTM). 23 classified. Race II: 1. G. Salvador (F, KTM); 2. D. Müller (Yamaha); 3. B. Gautschi (KTM); 4. M. Götz (KTM); 5. E. Maillard (HVA); 6. R. Baumgartner (Yamaha); 7. E. Jaquet (B, HVA); 8. M. Burgherr (KTM); 9. F. Chopineaux (F, RST); 10. R. Oehri (Yamaha); 11. G. Schäfer (HVA); 12. R. Bosonnet (HVA); 13. M. Kiok (D, Honda); 14. M. Alpsteg (Yamaha); 15. E. Hostettler (MuZ). 23 classified.

#### 5th July - Eschenbach
Race I: 1. D. Müller (Yamaha); 2. G. Salvador (F, KTM); 3. J. Künzel (D, Husqvarna); 4. B. Gautschi (KTM); 5. S. Zachmann (Suzuki); 6. S. Widmer (Folan); 7. F. Chopineaux (F, RST); 8. M. Götz (KTM); 9. M. Burgherr (KTM); 10. T. Rosenblatt (F, RST); 11. W. Gruhler (D, Honda); 12. P. Singele (Husqvarna); 13. K. Marti (Yamaha); 14. P. Möri (Yamaha); 15. M. Alpsteg (Yamaha). Race II: 1. D. Müller (Yamaha); 2. J. Künzel (D, Husqvarna); 3. B. Gautschi (KTM); 4. F. Chopineaux (F, RST); 5. W. Gruhler (D, Honda); 6. M. Götz (KTM); 7. M. Burgherr (KTM); 8. T. Rosenblatt (F, RST); 9. P. Singele (Husqvarna); 10. S. Widmer (Folan); 11. R. Baumgartner (Yamaha); 12. P. Möri (Yamaha); 13. M. Alpsteg (Yamaha); 14. E. Maillard (HVA); 15. K. Marti (Yamaha).

#### 13th September - Lignières
Race I: 1. G. Salvador (F, KTM); 2. D. Müller (Yamaha); 3. B. Gautschi (KTM); 4. S. Zachmann (Suzuki); 5. M. Götz (KTM); 6. E. Maillard (Husky); 7. P. Singele (HVA); 8. P. Möri (Yamaha); 9. R. Walther (Yamaha); 10. T. Rosenblatt (F, RST); 11. O. Girard (F, Kramit); 12. T. Godel (F, RST); 13. G. Schäfer (HVA); 14. M. Burgherr (KTM); 15. R. Bantli (Yamaha). 23 classified. Race II: 1. B. Gautschi (KTM); 2. G. Salvador (F, KTM); 3. S. Zachmann (Suzuki); 4. M. Götz (KTM); 5. D. Müller (Yamaha); 6. O. Girard (F, Kramit); 7. P. Singele (HVA); 8. S. Widmer (Folan); 9. R. Walther (Yamaha); 10. T. Rosenblatt (F, RST); 11. R. Baumgartner (Yamaha); 12. G. Schäfer (HVA); 13. O. Monnier (Monnier Honda);

14. P. Möri (Yamaha); 15. E. Hostettler (MuZ). 23 classified.

#### 4th October - Thoune
Race I: 1. B. Gautschi (KTM Duke); 2. S. Zachmann (Suzuki); 3. J. Künzel (D, Husqvarna); 4. S. Duchen (F, RST); 5. T. Rosenblatt (F, RST-Kawasaki); 6. M. Götz (KTM); 7. D. Müller (Yamaha); 8. S. Widmer (Vertemati); 9. E. Maillard (Husqvarna); 10. R. Oehri (Yamaha); 11. T. Godel (F, RST); 12. P. Möri (Yamaha); 13. P. Singele (Husqvarna); 14. H. Freidig (Husaberg); 15. E. Hostettler (MuZ). 23 classified. Race II: 1. S. Duchen (F, RST); 2. S. Widmer (Vertemati); 3. B. Gautschi (KTM Duke); 4. J. Künzel (D, Husqvarna); 5. S. Zachmann (Suzuki); 6. M. Götz (KTM); 7. D. Müller (Yamaha); 8. R. Baumgartner (Yamaha); 9. C. Fawer (Monnier XR); 10. M. Burgherr (KTM); 11. T. Rosenblatt (F, RST-Kawasaki); 12. E. Hostettler (MuZ); 13. E. Maillard (Husqvarna); 14. T. Godel (F, RST); 15. P. Möri (Yamaha). 22 classified.

#### 11th October - Frauenfeld
Race I: 1. J. Künzel (D, Husqvarna); 2. B. Gautschi (KTM Duke); 3. S. Zachmann (Suzuki); 4. M. Götz (KTM); 5. D. Müller (Yamaha); 6. S. Duchen (F, RST); 7. M. Burgherr (KTM); 8. P. Singele (Husqvarna); 9. R. Chételat (Monnier XR); 10. T. Rosenblatt (F, RST-Kawasaki); 11. R. Walther (Yamaha); 12. R. Bantli (Yamaha); 13. P. Möri (Yamaha); 14. W. Schudel (Honda); 15. R. Baumgartner (Yamaha). 24 classified. Race II: 1. J. Künzel (D, Husqvarna); 2. B. Gautschi (KTM Duke); 3. M. Götz (KTM); 4. S. Zachmann (Suzuki); 5. D. Müller (Yamaha); 6. S. Duchen (F, RST); 7. T. Rosenblatt (F, RST-Kawasaki); 8. W. Schudel (Honda); 9. R. Walther (Yamaha); 10. M. Burgherr (KTM); 11. P. Singele (Husqvarna); 12. R. Oehri (Yamaha); 13. P. Möri (Yamaha); 14. M. Messerli (Yamaha); 15. M. Alpsteg (Yamaha). 23 classified.

#### Final classification
1. Beat Gautschi    KTM Duke    190
2. Daniel Müller    Yamaha    177
3. Gilles Salvador (F)    KTM Duke    131
4. M. Götz (KTM), 113; 5. S. Zachmann (Suzuki), 105; 6. J. Künzel (D, Husqvarna), 100; 7. T. Rosenblatt (F, RST), 78; 8. S. Widmer (Folan), 77; 9. M. Burgherr (KTM), 72; 10. P. Singele (HVA), 54. 37 classified.

## Old motorcycles

### Solo
#### 28th June - Boécourt-La Caquerelle
Race I: 1. H. Schnider (Honda); 2. U. Bachmann (Triumph); 3. J. Kaufmann (Honda); 4. U. Kaufmann (Honda); 5. R. Larice (Ducati); 6. J.-F. Ischer (Laverda); 7. R. Röthig (Kawasaki); 8. W. Dolder (Kawasaki); 9. P. Aregger (Ducati) 10. M. Senn (Ducati); 11. C. Schwendimann (Moto Morini); 12. W. Jaberg (Motosacoche); 13. K. Dengler (Gilera); 14. W. Spinnler (Ducati); 15. E. Heiz (Matchless). 46 classified. Race II: 1. I. Spicher (BSA); 2. J. Rutz (Rudge); 3. J.-F. Ischer (Ducati); 4. T. Müller (Scott); 5. A. Rümmel (Norton); 6. R. Larice (Ducati); 7. H. Schnider (Honda); 8. R. Pfister (AJS); 9. B. Baggenstos (Suzuki); 10. C. Graf (Norton Manx); 11. R. Hage (BSA); 12. R. Siegfried (Sunbeam); 13. W. Kleiner (Triumph); 14. H. Brönnimann (Aermacchi); 15. R. Portmann (Harley-Davidson). 43 classified.

#### 12th July - Châtel-Saint-Denis - Les Paccots
1. R. Pfister (AJS); 2. R. Röthig (Kawasaki); 3. A. Sommer (Yamaha); 4. H. Brönnimann (Aermacchi); 5. W. Spinnler (Ducati); 6. R. von Ballmoos (Benelli); 7. U. Bachmann (Triumph); 8. R. Hage (BSA); 9. T. Zürcher (Triumph); 10. U. Kaufmann (Honda); 11. J. Kaufmann (Moto Guzzi); 12. R. Brönnimann (Triton); 13. J.-F. Ischer (Laverda); 14. K.

Blattmann (Harley-Davidson); 15. C. Charrière (Norton).

#### 4th October - Lignières
Race I: 1. R. Hage (BSA); 2. R. Pfister (AJS); 3. J. Rutz (Rudge); 4. B. Jud (Rudge); 5. E. Schönbächler (AJS); 6. C. Schwendimann (Moto Morini); 7. F. Glauser (Aermacchi); 8. A. Zollinger (Bultaco); 9. P. Agner (Ducati); 10. M. Müller (Ducati); 11. H. Schär (Norton); 12. M. Baggenstos (Suzuki); 13. T. Wyss (Norton); 14. W. Kausch (Velocette); 15. T. Zürcher (Triumph). Race II: 1. B. Jud (Rudge); 2. J. Rutz (Rudge); 3. C. Schwendimann (Moto Morini); 4. K. Kunz (Ducati); 5. U. Kaufmann (Egli-Honda); 6. R. Portmann (Harley-Davidson); 7. T. Zürcher (Triumph); 8. H. Schnider (Honda); 9. R. Von Ballmoos (Benelli); 10. M. Müller (Ducati); 11. M. Senn (Ducati); 12. T. Müller (Scott); 13. A. Zollinger (Bultaco); 14. W. Dolder (Kawasaki); 15. R. Pfister (AJS).

#### Final classification
1. Jakob Rutz    Rudge    56
2. Reto Pfister    AJS    54
3. Heinz Schnider    Honda    42
4. B. Jud (Rudge), 38; 5. R. Hage (BSA), 38; 6. C. Schwendimann (Moto Morini), 31; 7. U. Kaufmann (Egli-Honda), 30; 8. U. Bachmann (Triumph) et R. Röthig (Kawasaki), 29; 10. J.-F. Ischer (Laverda), 29. 44 classified.

## Side-cars

#### 28th June - Boécourt-La Caquerelle
Race I: 1. Fankhauser/Fankhauser (Suzuki); 2. Flück/Fankhauser (Suzuki), 3. Lemp/Lemp (Norton); 4. Blaser/Kunz (Ariel); 5. Müller/Landoff (BMW); 6. Kulmer/Anderegg (BMW); 7. Ruckstuhl/Dinten (BSA Hornet); 8. Sonnay/Sauteur (Suzuki); 9. Fässler/Fässler (BMW). 9 classified. Race II: 1. Ruckstuhl/Eppre (BMW); 2. Lemp/Lemp (Norton); 3. Müller/Landoff (BMW); 4. Kulmer/Anderegg (BMW); 5. Flück/Fankhauser (Suzuki); 6. Ruckstuhl/Dinten (BSA Hornet); 7. Fässler/Fässler (BMW); 8. Fankhauser/Fankhauser (Suzuki); 9. Brändle/Fritz (Douglas). 9 classified.

#### 12th July - Châtel-Saint-Denis - Les Paccots
1. Sonnay/Sauteur (Suzuki); 2. Blaser/Kunz (Ariel); 3. Fässler/Fässler (BMW); 4. Ruckstuhl/Dinten (BSA Hornet); 5. Fankhauser/Fankhauser (Suzuki); 6. Lemp/Lemp (Norton); 7. Müller/Landolt (BMW); 8. Kulmer/Anderegg (BMW); 9. Ruckstuhl/Epprecht (BMW). 9 classified.

#### 4th October - Lignières
Race I: 1. Müller/Landolt (BMW); 2. Fankhauser/Fankhauser (Suzuki); 3. Kulmer/Anderegg (BMW); 4. Flück/Zünd (Suzuki); 5. Stamm/Müller (Suzuki); 6. Ruckstuhl/Epprecht (BMW); 7. Ruckstuhl/Dinten (BMW); 8. Fässler/Fässler (BMW); 9. Blaser/Kunz (Ariel); 10. Lemp/Lemp (Norton). 10 classified. Race II: 1. Fässler/Fässler (BMW); 2. Ruckstuhl/Dinten (BMW); 3. Ruckstuhl/Epprecht (BMW); 4. Flück/Zünd (Suzuki); 5. Blaser/Kunz (Ariel); 6. Lemp/Lemp (Norton); 7. Müller/Landolt (BMW); 8. Stamm/Müller (Suzuki); 9. Fankhauser/Fankhauser (Suzuki); 10. Kulmer/Anderegg (BMW). 10 classified.

#### Final classification
1. Fankhauser/Fankhauser    64
2. Müller/Landolt    61
3. Fässler/Fässler    58
4. Ruckstuhl/Epprecht, 58; 5. Flück/Zünd, 57; 6. Lemp/Lemp, 56; 7. Ruckstuhl/Dinten, 52; 8. Blaser/Kunz, 51; 9. Kulmer/Anderegg, 47; 10. Sonnay/Sauteur, 33. 12 classified.

*Niklaus Dähler, Jakob Rutz, Fankhauser/ Fankhauser.*
▽

*Japan*

## 125 cc

The champion: Hideyuki Nakajo. Born on 6th September 1968, in Nara Prefecture. First race: 1988. First GP: Japanese GP, 1992 (125). Races record: 2nd of the 125cc Japanese "national" championship in 1990 (Honda); 8th of the 125cc Japanese championship in 1991 (Honda); 3rd of the 125cc Japanese championship in 1992 (Honda); 28th of the 125cc world championship and 125cc Japanese vice-champion in 1993 (Honda); 11th of the 125cc world championship in 1994; 9th of the 125cc world championship in 1995 (Honda); 125cc Japanese vice-champion in 1996 (Honda); 22th of the 125cc world championship in 1997 (Honda); 125cc Japanese champion in 1998 (Honda).

### 12th April - Motegi
1. H. Nakajo (Honda); 2. K. Takao (Honda); 3. K. Kubo (Yamaha); 4. M. Yamada (Honda); 5. T. Ide (Honda); 6. T. Yamamoto (Honda); 7. K. Uezu (Yamaha); 8. H. Matsunaga (Honda); 9. S. Ueki (Honda); 10. K. Takada (Honda).

### 26th April - Sugo
1. M. Nakamura (Honda); 2. H. Nakajo (Honda); 3. T. Kato (Honda); 4. R. Yokoe (Yamaha); 5. K. Uezu (Yamaha); 6. M. Yamada (Honda); 7. S. Ito (Honda); 8. K. Nagata (Honda); 9. T. Furuhashi (Honda); 10. J. Inageda (Honda).

### 17th May - Tsukuba
1. M. Nakamura (Honda); 2. H. Nakajo (Honda); 3. K. Kubo (Yamaha); 4. M. Yamada (Honda); 5. H. Yoda (Honda);

6. J. Inageda (Honda); 7. S. Sugaya (Honda); 8. Y. Sasajima (Honda); 9. M. Sakai (Honda); 10. S. Ito (Honda).

### 31st May - Suzuka
1. H. Nakajo (Honda); 2. S. Sugaya (Honda); 3. Y. Fujioka (Honda); 4. H. Kikuchi (Honda); 5. T. Kato (Honda); 6. N. Osaki (Yamaha); 7. D. Sakai (Honda); 8. T. Ide (Honda); 9. J. Inageda (Honda); 10. J. Okada (Honda).

### 9th August - Mine
1. H. Kikuchi (Honda); 2. J. Okada (Honda); 3. M. Nakamura (Honda); 4. N. Osaki (Yamaha); 5. T. Yamamoto (Honda); 6. J. Inageda (Honda); 7. R. Kiyonari (Honda); 8. K. Kubo (Yamaha); 9. S. Sugaya (Honda); 10. K. Amano (Honda).

### 6th September - Suzuka
1. N. Osaki (Yamaha); 2. J. Inageda (Honda); 3. T. Yamamoto (Honda); 4. K. Amano (Honda); 5. H. Yoda (Honda); 6. K. Uezu (Yamaha); 7. K. Hayahara (Yamaha); 8. Y. Fujioka (Honda); 9. Y. Imai (Honda); 10. M. Ono (Honda).

### 20th September - Tsukuba
1. J. Inageda (Honda); 2. K. Uezu (Yamaha); 3. J. Okada (Honda); 4. T. Yamamoto (Honda); 5. D. Sakai (Honda); 6. R. Yokoe (Yamaha); 7. N. Ohsaki (Yamaha); 8. M. Ono (Honda); 9. Y. Konno (Honda); 10. S. Sugaya (Honda).

### 18th October - Ti
1. H. Nakajo (Honda); 2. D. Sakai (Honda); 3. K. Uezu (Yamaha); 4. K. Kubo (Yamaha); 5. N. Ohsaki (Yamaha); 6. M. Nakamura (Honda); 7. T. Kato (Honda); 8. H. Kikuchi (Honda); 9. K. Hayahara (Yamaha); 10. R. Yokoe (Yamaha).

## 250 cc

The champion: Shinya Nakano. Born on 10th October 1977, in Chiba Prefecture. First race: 1982. First GP: Japanese GP, 1998 (250). Races record: pocket bike regional Eastern Kanto champion in 1985; 3rd of the Kanto 125cc SP regional championship and 6th of the Kanto 250cc SP regional championship in 1994; 12th of the 125cc Japanese championship in 1995; 6th of the 125cc Japanese championship in 1996; 5th of the 250cc Japanese championship in 1997; 19th of the 250cc world championship and

250cc Japanese champion in 1998 (Yamaha).

### 12th April - Motegi
1. S. Nakano (Yamaha); 2. D. Kato (Honda); 3. N. Matsudo (Yamaha); 4. M. Tamada (Honda); 5. C. Kameya (Suzuki); 6. S. Harada (Yamaha); 7. R. Sawada (Honda); 8. Y. Kagayama (Suzuki); 9. T. Yamaguchi (Honda); 10. H. Noda (Honda).

### 26th April - Sugo
1. S. Nakano (Yamaha); 2. Y. Kagayama (Suzuki); 3. R. Sawada (Honda); 4. C. Kameya (Suzuki); 5. D. Kato (Honda); 6. S. Harada (Yamaha); 7. T. Yamaguchi (Honda); 8. M. Tamada (Honda); 9. T. Onodera (Yamaha); 10. H. Noda (Honda).

### 17th May - Tsukuba
1. S. Nakano (Yamaha); 2. N. Matsudo (Yamaha); 3. C. Kameya (Suzuki); 4. M. Tamada (Honda); 5. T. Yamaguchi (Honda); 6. T. Kayo (TSR-Honda); 7. T. Sekiguchi (Yamaha); 8. K. Eguchi (Yamaha); 9. S. Nakatomi (Honda); 10. H. Noda (Honda).

### 31st May - Suzuka
1. S. Nakano (Yamaha); 2. D. Kato (Honda); 3. N. Matsudo (Yamaha); 4. C. Kameya (Suzuki); 5. M. Tamada (Honda); 6. H. Noda (Honda); 7. S. Harada (Yamaha); 8. T. Sekiguchi (Yamaha); 9. T. Yamaguchi (Honda); 10. S. Nakatomi (Honda).

### 9th August - Mine
1. S. Nakano (Yamaha); 2. C. Kameya (Suzuki); 3. N. Matsudo (Yamaha); 4. T. Kayou (TSR-Honda); 5. T. Yamaguchi (Honda); 6. H. Noda (Honda); 7. S. Nakatomi (Honda); 8.

*1.Hideyuki Nakajoh,*
*2.Shinya Nakano.*

T. Sekiguchi (Yamaha); 9. Y. Yamashita (Yamaha); 10. K. Eguchi (Yamaha).

### 6th September - Suzuka
1. M. Tamada (Honda); 2. H. Noda (TSR-Honda); 3. T. Yamaguchi (Honda); 4. S. Nakano (Yamaha); 5. S. Harada (Yamaha); 6. T. Sekiguchi (Yamaha); 7. T. Kayou (TSR-Honda); 8. K. Eguchi (Yamaha); 9. T. Nagaoka (Yamaha); 10. N. Tamura (Yamaha).

### 20th September - Tsukuba
1. S. Nakano (Yamaha); 2. C. Kameya (Suzuki); 3. D. Kato (Honda); 4. N. Matsudo (Yamaha); 5. T. Yamaguchi (Honda); 6. T. Kayou (TSR-Honda); 7. T. Sekiguchi (Yamaha); 8. S. Nakatomi (Honda); 9. S. Oikawa (Yamaha); 10. K. Eguchi (Yamaha).

### 18th October - Ti
1. S. Nakano (Yamaha); 2. N. Matsudo (Yamaha); 3. C. Kameya (Suzuki); 4. M. Tamada (Honda); 5. S. Harada (Yamaha); 6. T. Yamaguchi (Honda); 7. T. Kayou (Honda); 8. S. Nakatomi (Honda); 9. H. Noda (TS-Honda); 10. Y. Kagayama (Suzuki).

### Superbike

The champion: Shinichi Itoh. Born on 7th December 1966, in Miyagi Prefecture. First race: 1984. First GP: Japanese GP, 1988 (500). Races record: Formula Three Japanese champion in 1985; 16th of the 250cc Japanese "national" championship in 1986 (Honda); 5th of the 250cc Japanese championship in 1987 (Honda); 73rd of the endurance world championship and 500cc vice-Japanese champion in 1988 (Honda); 32nd of the 500cc world championship and 6th of the 500cc Japanese championship in 1989 (Honda); 36th of the 500cc world championship and Japanese champion 500 in 1990 (Honda); 101st of the endurance world championship and 3rd of the 500cc Japanese championship in 1991 (Honda); 16th of the 500cc world championship and 8th of the 500cc Japanese championship in 1992 (Honda); 7th of the 500cc world championship in 1993 (Honda); 7th of the 500cc world championship and 60th of the endurance world championship in 1994 (Honda); 5th of the 500cc world championship and 45th of the endurance world championship in 1995 (Honda); 12th of the 500cc world championship and 116th of the endurance world championship in 1996 (Honda); 35th of

the endurance world championship in 1997 (Honda); Japanese champion superbike in 1998 (Honda).

### 12th April - Motegi
1. W. Yoshikawa (Yamaha); 2. K. Kitagawa (Suzuki); 3. H. Izutsu (Kawasaki); 4. K. Haga (Yamaha); 5. T. Hamaguchi (Suzuki); 6. T. Sowa (Honda); 7. A. Watanabe (Suzuki); 8. I. Asai (Ducati); 9. M. Kamada (Honda); 10. T. Arakaki (Honda).

### 26th April - Sugo
1. A. Ryo (Suzuki); 2. S. Itoh (Honda); 3. S. Takeishi (Kawasaki); 4. K. Kitagawa (Suzuki); 5. T. Serizawa (Kawasaki); 6. T. Sowa (Honda); 7. K. Haga (Yamaha); 8. T. Hamaguchi (Suzuki); 9. G. Kamada (Honda); 10. I. Asai (Ducati).

### 17th May - Tsukuba
1. S. Itoh (Honda); 2. T. Serizawa (Kawasaki); 3. S. Takeishi (Kawasaki); 4. W. Yoshikawa (Yamaha); 5. K. Kitagawa (Suzuki); 6. A. Ryo (Suzuki); 7. T. Hamaguchi (Suzuki); 8. K. Haga (Yamaha); 9. T. Sowa (Honda); 10. I. Asai (Ducati).

### 31st May - Suzuka
1. S. Itoh (Honda); 2. K. Kitagawa (Suzuki); 3. W. Yoshikawa (Yamaha); 4. K. Haga (Yamaha); 5. A. Ryo (Suzuki); 6. S. Takeishi (Kawasaki); 7. N. Haga (Yamaha); 8. H. Izutsu (Kawasaki); 9. Y. Takeda (Honda); 10. O. Nishijima (Kawasaki).

### 9th August - Mine
1. S. Itoh (Honda); 2. S. Takeishi (Kawasaki); 3. K. Kitagawa (Suzuki); 4. Y. Takeda (Honda); 5. T. Serizawa (Kawasaki); 6. T. Sowa (Honda); 7. T. Hamaguchi (Suzuki); 8. A. Watanabe (Suzuki); 9. G. Kamada (Honda); 10. T. Yamamoto (Kawasaki).

### 6th September - Suzuka
1. S. Takeishi (Kawasaki); 2. Y. Takeda (Honda); 3. T. Sowa (Honda); 4. K. Kitagawa (Suzuki); 5. A. Ryo (Suzuki); 6. T. Hamaguchi (Suzuki); 7. A. Watanabe (Suzuki); 8. T. Arakaki (Honda); 9. H. Izutsu (Kawasaki); 10. S. Imai (Kawasaki).

### 20th September - Tsukuba
1. S. Itoh (Honda); 2. A. Ryo (Suzuki); 3. Y. Takeda (Honda); 4. W. Yoshikawa (Yamaha); 5. A. Watanabe (Suzuki); 6. K. Haga (Yamaha); 7. H. Izutsu (Kawasaki); 8. T. Hamaguchi (Suzuki); 9. T. Serizawa (Kawasaki); 10. G. Kamada (Honda).

### 18th October - Ti
1. S. Itoh (Honda); 2. A. Ryo (Suzuki); 3. W. Yoshikawa (Yamaha); 4. H. Izutsu (Kawasaki); 5. K. Kitagawa (Suzuki); 6. S. Takeishi (Kawasaki); 7. K. Haga (Yamaha); 8. T. Serizawa (Kawasaki); 9. Y. Takeda (Honda); 10. O. Nishijima (Kawasaki).

◁
*3. Shinichi Itoh.*

## United States

### 250 cc

**15th February - Phoenix**
1. C. Sorensen (Yamaha); 2. R. Sands (Yamaha); 3. T. Mori (J, Honda); 4. R. Renfrow (Honda); 5. M. Foster (Yamaha); 6. J. Cubbage (Yamaha); 7. A. Salaverria (Aprilia); 8. B. Keith (Honda); 9. R. Fee (CAN, Honda); 10. K. Roberts (Honda).

**6th March - Daytona Beach**
1. T. Mori (J, Honda); 2. R. Sands (Yamaha); 3. C. Sorensen (Yamaha); 4. R. Renfrow (Honda); 5. R. Fee (CAN, Honda); 6. K. Roberts (Honda); 7. G. Terranova (Yamaha); 8. K. Kunitsugu (Honda); 9. A. Law (Honda); 10. L. Lavado (VEN, Yamaha).

**19 April - Laguna Seca**
1. R. Sands (Yamaha); 2. K. Roberts (Honda); 3. M. Foster (Yamaha); 4. T. Mori (J, Honda); 5. B. Keith (Honda); 6. M. Montoyo (Honda); 7. R. Fee (CAN, Honda); 8. J. Cubbage (Yamaha); 9. G. Terranova (Yamaha); 10. J. Vos (Honda).

**26 April - Willow Springs**
1. R. Sands (Yamaha); 2. C. Sorensen (Yamaha); 3. G. Terranova (Yamaha); 4. K. Roberts (Honda); 5. T. Mori (J, Honda); 6. M. Montoya (Yamaha); 7. R. Renfrow (Honda); 8. A. Salaverria (Aprilia); 9. B. Keith (Honda); 10. J. Vos (Honda).

**3rd May - Sonoma**
1. C. Sorensen (Yamaha); 2. A. Salverria (Aprilia); 3. K. Roberts (Honda); 4. R. Sands (Yamaha); 5. G. Terranova (Yamaha); 6. R. Renfrow (Honda); 7. R. Fee (CAN, Honda); 8. T. Mori (J, Honda); 9. M. Montaya (Yamaha); 10. B. Keith (Honda).

**31st May - Road Atlanta**
1. R. Sands (Yamaha); 2. T. Mori (J, Honda); 3. K. Roberts (Honda); 4. G. Terranova (Yamaha); 5. C. Sorenson (Yamaha); 6. M. Foster (Yamaha); 7. A. Salaverria (Aprilia); 8. B. Keith (Honda); 9. L. Acree (Honda); 10. G. Esser (Honda).

**14th June - Road America**
1. R. Sands (Yamaha); 2. C. Sorensen (Yamaha); 3. K. Roberts (Honda); 4. B. Keith (Honda); 5. R. Renfrow (Honda); 6. M. Foster (Yamaha); 7. J. Vos (Honda); 8. G. Esser (Honda); 9. G. Terranova (Yamaha); 10. P. Melneciuc (Honda).

**21st June - Loudon**
1. R. Sands (Yamaha); 2. K. Roberts (Honda); 3. R. Renfrow (Honda); 4. J. Randolph (Honda); 5. M. Miller (Yamaha); 6. J. Vos (Honda); 7. J. Wood (Yamaha); 8. C. Sorensen (Yamaha); 9. B. Keith (Honda); 10. C. Healy (Yamaha).

**19th July - Mid Ohio**
1. K. Roberts (Honda); 2. C. Sorensen (Yamaha); 3. R. Sands (Yamaha); 4. M. Foster (Yamaha); 5. R. Renfrow (Honda); 6. B. Keith (Honda); 7. G. Esser (Honda); 8. B. Gibson (Honda); 9. L. Acree (Honda); 10. L. Cortes (Honda).

**2nd August - Brainerd**
1. C. Sorensen (Yamaha); 2. R. Renfrow (Honda); 3. R. Sands (Yamaha); 4. M. Foster (Yamaha); 5. K. Roberts (Honda); 6. G. Esser (Honda); 7. G. Terranova (Yamaha); 8. B. Keith (Honda); 9. J. Vos (Honda); 10. B. Gibson (Honda).

**6th September - Fountain**
1. K. Roberts (Honda); 2. C. Sorensen (Yamaha); 3. R. Sands (Yamaha); 4. R. Renfrow (Honda); 5. M. Foster (Yamaha); 6. G. Terranova (Yamaha); 7. J. Vos (Honda); 8. R. Landers (Honda); 9. G. Esser (Honda); 10. P. Melneciuc (Honda).

**4th October - Las Vegas**
1. K. Roberts (Honda); 2. R. Sands (Yamaha); 3. T. Mori (J, Honda); 4. C. Sorensen (Yamaha); 5. J. Cubbage (Yamaha); 6. G. Esser (Honda); 7. G. Terranova (Yamaha); 8. C. Ulrich (Yamaha); 9. J. Vos (Honda); 10. E. Sorbo (Yamaha).

### Final classification
1. Roland Sands    Yamaha    394
2. Kurtis Roberts    Honda    358
3. Chuck Sorensen    Yamaha    347
4. R. Renfrow (Honda), 263; 5. G. Terranova (Yamaha), 241; 6. G. Esser (Honda), 235; 7. J. Vos (Honda), 224; 8. T. Mori (J, Honda), 219; 9. M. Foster (Yamaha) et B. Keith (Honda), 212.

### Supersport 600
The champion: Steve Crevier. Born on 18th June 1965, in Montréal/Québec. Races record: 20th of the superbike US championship in 1987; 8th of the 250cc US championship and 56th of the 250cc US championship in 1988; 29th of the superbike world championship (Yamaha), 90th of the endurance FIM Cup (Honda) and 17th of the 250cc US championship in 1989; 19th of the superbike US championship in 1990; 27th of the superbike world championship, 19th of the superbike US championship, 13th of the 600cc supersport US championship and 18th of the 750cc supersport US championship in 1991 (Kawasaki); 14th of the superbike US championship, 600cc supersport US vicechampion and 12th of the 750cc supersport US championship in 1992; 24th of the superbike US championship, 4th of the 600cc supersport US championship and 95th of the 750cc supersport US championship in 1993; 6th of the superbike US championship and 3rd of the 600cc supersport US championship in 1994; 47th of the superbike world championship, 8th of the superbike US championship and 7th of the 600cc supersport US championship in 1995 (Kawasaki); 10th of the superbike US championship and 8th of the 600cc supersport US championship in 1996; 39th of the superbike world championship, 4th of the superbike US championship and 4th of the 600cc supersport US championship in 1997 (Honda); 600cc supersport champion US in 1998 (Suzuki).

**15th February - Phoenix**
1. D. Chandler (Kawasaki); 2. A. Yates (Suzuki); 3. J. Pridmore (Suzuki); 4. S. Crevier (CAN, Suzuki); 5. N. Hayden (Suzuki); 6. M. Duhamel (CAN, Honda); 7. S. Rapp (Suzuki); 8. B. Bostrom (Honda); 9. E. Bostrom (Honda); 10. R. Alexander Junior (Suzuki).

**8 mars - Daytona Beach**
1. D. Chandler (Kawasaki); 2. E. Bostrom (Honda); 3. M. Duhamel (CAN, Honda); 4. S. Crevier (CAN, Suzuki); 5. N. Hayden (Suzuki); 6. B. Bostrom (Honda); 7. J. Pridmore (Suzuki); 8. L. Pegram (Suzuki); 9. T. Hayden (Kawasaki); 10. S. Rapp (Suzuki).

**19 April - Laguna Seca**
1. D. Chandler (Kawasaki); 2. M. Duhamel (CAN, Honda); 3. N. Hayden (Suzuki); 4. B. Bostrom (Honda); 5. E. Bostrom (Honda); 6. S. Crevier (CAN, Suzuki); 7. T. Mori (J, Honda); 8. S. Rapp (Suzuki); 9. T. Hayden (Kawasaki); 10. K. Roberts (Honda).

**26 April - Willow Springs**
1. N. Hayden (Suzuki); 2. M. Duhamel (CAN, Honda); 3. S. Crevier (CAN, Suzuki); 4. B. Bostrom (Honda); 5. J. Pridmore (Suzuki); 6. D. Chandler (Kawasaki); 7. R. Alexander (Suzuki); 8. T. Hayden (Kawasaki); 9. K. Roberts (Honda); 10. L. Pegram (Suzuki).

**3rd May - Sonoma**
1. M. Duhamel (CAN, Honda); 2. S. Crevier (CAN, Suzuki); 3. E. Bostrom (Honda); 4. J. Pridmore (Suzuki); 5. S. Rapp (Suzuki); 6. R. Alexander Junior (Suzuki); 7. T. Mori (Honda); 8. B. Bostrom (Honda); 9. C. Carr (Kawasaki); 10. K. Roberts (Honda).

**31st May - Road Atlanta**
1. B. Bostrom (Honda); 2. S. Crevier (CAN, Suzuki); 3. E. Bostrom (Honda); 4. A. Yates (Suzuki); 5. J. Pridmore (Suzuki); 6. T. Hayden (Kawasaki); 7. K. Roberts (Honda); 8. S. Rapp (Suzuki); 9. E. Wood (Kawasaki); 10. L. Pegram (Suzuki).

**14th June - Road America**
1. D. Chandler (Kawasaki); 2. A. Yates (Suzuki); 3. M. Duhamel (CAN, Honda); 4. S. Crevier (CAN, Suzuki); 5. B. Bostrom (Honda); 6. N. Hayden (Suzuki); 7. E. Bostrom (Honda); 8. T. Hayden (Kawasaki); 9. T. Harrington (Kawasaki); 10. T. Mori (J, Honda).

**21st June - Loudon**
1. D. Chandler (Kawasaki); 2. A. Yates (Suzuki); 3. B. Bostrom (Honda); 4. S. Crevier (CAN, Suzuki); 5. E. Bostrom (Honda); 6. N. Hayden (Suzuki); 7. J. Pridmore (Suzuki); 8. R. Alexander (Suzuki); 9. E. Wood (Kawasaki); 10. S. Rapp (Suzuki).

**11th July - Laguna Seca**
1. D. Chandler (Kawasaki); 2. E. Bostrom

*Steve Crevier (4).*
▽

(Honda); 3. N. Hayden (Suzuki); 4. S. Crevier (Suzuki); 5. B. Bostrom (Honda); 6. J. Pridmore (Suzuki); 7. T. Hayden (Kawasaki); 8. K. Roberts (Honda); 9. L. Pegram (Suzuki); 10. N. Wait (Kawasaki).

### 19th July - Mid Ohio
1. S. Crevier (CAN, Suzuki); 2. T. Hayden (Kawasaki); 3. D. Chandler (Kawasaki); 4. J. Pridmore (Suzuki); 5. E. Bostrom (Honda); 6. L. Pegram (Suzuki); 7. B. Bostrom (Honda); 8. S. Rapp (Suzuki); 9. J. Hanshaw (Suzuki); 10. J. Gill (Kawasaki).

### 2nd August - Brainerd
1. A. Yates (Suzuki); 2. E. Bostrom (Honda); 3. S. Crevier (CAN, Suzuki); 4. J. Pridmore (Suzuki); 5. N. Hayden (Suzuki); 6. B. Bostrom (Honda); 7. D. Chandler (Kawasaki); 8. T. Hayden (Kawasaki); 9. N. Wait (Kawasaki); 10. S. Rapp (Suzuki).

### 6th September - Fountain
1. L. Pegram (Suzuki); 2. E. Bostrom (Honda); 3. T. Hayden (Kawasaki); 4. D. Chandler (Kawasaki); 5. N. Hayden (Suzuki); 6. S. Crevier (CAN, Suzuki); 7. J. Pridmore (Suzuki); 8. A. Yates (Suzuki); 9. T. Harrington (Kawasaki); 10. K. Roberts (Honda).

### 4th October - Las Vegas
1. A. Yates (Suzuki); 2. N. Hayden (Suzuki); 3. L. Pegram (Suzuki); 4. E. Bostrom (Honda); 5. D. Chandler (Kawasaki); 6. J. Pridmore (Suzuki); 7. S. Rapp (Suzuki); 8. S. Crevier (CAN, Suzuki); 9. R. Alexander (Suzuki); 10. T. Mori (Honda).

### Final classification
1. Steve Crevier    Suzuki    366
2. Doug Chandler    Kawasaki    353
3. Eric Bostrom    Honda    337
4. N. Hayden (Suzuki), 314; 5. B. Bostrom (Honda), 307; 6. J. Pridmore (Suzuki), 284; 7. T. Hayden (Kawasaki), 277; 8. L. Pegram (Suzuki), 275; 9. S. Rapp (Suzuki), 273; 10. A. Yates (Suzuki), 233.

### Superbike
The champion: Ben Bostrom. Born on 7th May 1974, in Redding/California. First race: 1982. Races record: AMA Rookie of the year and 6th of the US National 600 Dirt Track championship in 1992; 82nd of the US Super Twins championship in 1993; 9th of the US 883 Dirt Track championship, 14th of the US 600 National Dirt Track championship and 20th of the US Super Twins championship in 1994; 7th of the US Super Twins championship, 20th of the 600cc supersport US championship and 38th of the 750cc supersport US championship in 1995; 4th of the 600cc supersport US championship, 22nd of the 750cc supersport US championship and US Super Twins vice-champion in 1996; 750cc supersport US vice-champion, 12th of the 600cc supersport US championship and 16th of the superbike US championship in 1997;

22nd of the superbike world championship and champion US superbike in 1998 (Honda).

### 15th February - Phoenix
1. A. Gobert (AUS, Ducati); 2. M. Mladin (AUS, Suzuki); 3. A. Yates (Suzuki); 4. D. Chandler (Kawasaki); 5. J. Hacking (Yamaha); 6. M. Duhamel (CAN, Honda); 7. T. Stevens (Ducati); 8. S. Crevier (CAN, Suzuki); 9. B. Bostrom (Honda); 10. J. Pridmore (Suzuki).

### 8th March - Daytona Beach
1. S. Russell (Yamaha); 2. D. Chandler (Kawasaki); 3. J. Hacking (Yamaha); 4. M. Mladin (AUS, Suzuki); 5. B. Bostrom (Honda); 6. A. Yates (Suzuki); 7. T. Kipp (Ducati); 8. A. Gobert (AUS, Ducati); 9. T. Stevens (Ducati); 10. L. Pegram (Suzuki).

### 19th April - Laguna Seca
1. M. Duhamel (CAN, Honda); 2. D. Chandler (Kawasaki); 3. M. Mladin (AUS, Suzuki); 4. B. Bostrom (Honda); 5. S. Crevier (CAN, Suzuki); 6. R. Oliver (Yamaha); 7. T. Kipp (Ducati); 8. P. Picotte (CAN, Harley-Davidson); 9. M. Hale (Ducati); 10. L. Pegram (Suzuki).

### 26th April - Willow Springs
1. M. Duhamel (CAN, Honda); 2. A. Gobert (AUS, Ducati); 3. M. Mladin (AUS, Suzuki); 4. B. Bostrom (Honda); 5. D. Chandler (Kawasaki); 6. P. Picotte (CAN, Harley-Davidson); 7. S. Rapp (Ducati); 8. S. Crevier (CAN, Suzuki); 9. R. Oliver (Yamaha); 10. C. Adams (Suzuki).

### 3rd May - Sonoma
1. M. Duhamel (CAN, Honda); 2. D. Chandler (Kawasaki); 3. M. Mladin (AUS, Suzuki); 4. B. Bostrom (Honda); 5. S. Crevier (CAN, Suzuki); 6. T. Kipp (Ducati); 7. P. Picotte (CAN, Harley-Davidson); 8. S. Rapp (Suzuki); 9. T. Wilson Junior (Harley-Davidson); 10. R. Oliver (Yamaha).

### 30th May - Road Atlanta
1. M. Duhamel (CAN, Honda); 2. A. Gobert (AUS, Ducati); 3. B. Bostrom (Honda); 4. R. Oliver (Yamaha); 5. D. Chandler (Kawasaki); 6. M. Mladin (AUS, Suzuki); 7. J. Hacking (Yamaha); 8. T. Kipp (Ducati); 9. A. Yates (Suzuki); 10. T. Stevens (Ducati).

### 31st May - Road Atlanta
1. A. Gobert (AUS, Ducati); 2. M. Duhamel (CAN, Honda); 3. B. Bostrom (Honda); 4. D. Chandler (Kawasaki); 5. J. Hacking (Yamaha); 6. A. Yates (Suzuki); 7. T. Kipp (Ducati); 8. T. Stevens (Ducati); 9. R. Oliver (Yamaha); 10. M. Mladin (AUS, Suzuki).

### 14th June - Road America
1. A. Gobert (AUS, Ducati); 2. M. Duhamel (CAN, Honda); 3. B. Bostrom (Honda); 4. A. Yates (Suzuki); 5. D. Chandler (Kawasaki); 6. J. Hacking (Yamaha); 7. T. Kipp (Ducati); 8. R. Oliver (Yamaha); 9. S. Crevier (CAN, Suzuki); 10. T. Wilson Junior (Harley-Davidson).

### 21st June - Loudon
1. A. Yates (Suzuki); 2. J. Hacking (Yamaha); 3. A. Gobert (AUS, Ducati); 4. S. Crevier (CAN, Suzuki); 5. T. Stevens (Ducati); 6. T. Hayden (Kawasaki); 7. B. Bostrom (Honda); 8. R. Oliver (Yamaha); 9. D. Chandler (Kawasaki); 10. L. Pegram (Suzuki).

### 19th July - Mid Ohio
1. A. Yates (Suzuki); 2. J. Hacking (Yamaha); 3. T. Kipp (Ducati); 4. B. Bostrom (Honda); 5. E: Bostrom (Honda); 6. R. Oliver (Yamaha); 7. M. Mladin (AUS, Suzuki); 8. D. Chandler (Kawasaki); 9. T. Hayden (Kawasaki); 10. J. James (Harley-Davidson).

### 2nd August - Brainerd
1. E. Bostrom (Honda); 2. M. Mladin (Suzuki); 3. B. Bostrom (Honda); 4. J. Pridmore (Ducati); 5. T. Stevens (Ducati); 6. R. Oliver (Yamaha); 7. D. Chandler (Kawasaki); 8. A. Yates (Suzuki); 9. S. Crevier (CAN, Suzuki); 10. J. Szoke (Ducati).

### 6th September - Foutain
1. E. Bostrom (Honda); 2. M. Mladin (AUS, Suzuki); 3. J. Pridmore (Ducati); 4. P. Picotte (CAN, Harley-Davidson); 5. B. Bostrom (Honda); 6. D. Chandler (Kawasaki); 7. R. Oliver (Yamaha); 8. A. Yates (Suzuki); 9. S. Crevier (CAN, Suzuki); 10. L. Pegram (Suzuki).

### 4th October - Las Vegas
1. M. Mladin (AUS, Suzuki); 2. B. Bostrom (Honda); 3. E. Bostrom (Honda); 4. P. Picotte (CAN, Harley-Davidson); 5. T. Stevens (Ducati); 6. S. Crevier (CAN, Suzuki); 7. R. Oliver (Yamaha); 8. M. Smith (Harley-Davidson); 9. T. Hayden (Kawasaki); 10. T. Kipp (Ducati).

### Final classification
1. Ben Bostrom    Honda    355
2. Doug Chandler    Kawasaki    274
3. Matthew Mladin    Suzuki    330
4. R. Oliver (Yamaha), 285; 5. A. Yates (Suzuki), 266; 6. T. Kipp (Ducati), 256; 7. S. Crevier (CAN, Suzuki), 255; 8. J. Hacking (Yamaha), 251; 9. A. Gobert (AUS, Ducati), 249; 10. Mi. Duhamel (CAN, Honda), 236.

### The 1999 Calender

|  |  |
| --- | --- |
| 7th March | Daytona International Speedway |
| 21st March | Phoenix |
| 18th April | Willow Springs |
| 25th April | Sears Point |
| 2nd May | Laguna Seca |
| 6th June | Road Atlanta |
| 13th June | Road America |
| 20th June | Loudon |
| 11th July | Laguna Seca (supersport only) |
| 18th July | Lexington |
| 1st August | Brainerd |
| 29th August | Fountain |
| 3rd October | Las Vegas |

*Ben Bostrom*
▽

Achevé d'imprimer
sur les presses de l'Imprimerie Sézanne à Bron (69) - France
le 13 novembre 1998